Nicomachean Ethics

Aristotle

Nicomachean Ethics

translated, with introduction,
notes, and glossary, by

Terence Irwin

Hackett Publishing Company

INDIANAPOLIS / CAMBRIDGE

Aristotle: 384-322 B.C.

Copyright © 1985 by Terence Irwin
All Rights Reserved
Designed by Mark E. Van Halsema
Cover design by Richard L. Listenberger
Printed in the United States of America

03 02 01 00 99 98   11 12 13 14 15 16

For further information address the publisher
  Hackett Publishing Company, Inc.
  P.O. Box 44937
  Indianapolis, Indiana 46244-0937

Library of Congress Cataloging in Publication Data

Aristotle.
  Nicomachean ethics.

  Bibliography: p.
  Includes index.
  1. Ethics. I. Irwin, Terence. II. Title.
B430.A5179   1985   171'.3   84-15772
ISBN 0-915145-65-0
ISBN 0-915145-66-9 (pbk.)

The paper used in this publication meets the minimum requirements of American National Standard for Information Sciences—Permanence of Paper for Printed Library Materials, ANSI Z39.48-1984.

∞

Contents

Nicomachean Ethics

Contents

Preface

This translation attempts to make Aristotle's terse and concentrated Greek fairly intelligible to those who read him in English. I have, for example, divided Aristotle's longer and more complex sentences, and tried to make explicit the points that he conveys by hints or allusions. However, I have wanted to avoid making Aristotle appear to say more than he actually says, and therefore have distinguished elucidations and supplements from the actual rendering of the Greek words (see Introduction, sec. 'This Edition'). I hope the translation is clear and explicit enough to show how Aristotle's argument proceeds, in general and in detail, and at the same time literal enough to show what grounds the text offers for different lines of interpretation. At each stage I have benefited from the work of previous translators, and above all from the admirably scholarly and fluent version by Sir David Ross. The notes and glossary are meant to make the translation more intelligible, sometimes by defending particular interpretations, sometimes by indicating the inadequacy of an English term for capturing the Greek completely. At the same time, since there is no full and recent English commentary on the *Nicomachean Ethics*, I have thought it useful to include some exegetical notes. These are not a commentary, but provide some information that may be helpful to readers who are beginning the study of the *Ethics*, and are often puzzled (as they should be) about the exact drift of the argument in particular passages. In the notes and glossary I do not cite secondary works, but I often rely on them, especially on the commentaries by Gauthier and Jolif and by Stewart (see "Further Reading" for details).

The publisher's readers were Daniel Devereux, Richard Kraut, Anthony Long, Alexander Nehamas and Donald Zeyl. I don't know what I owe to each individually, but I know that together they have made many useful suggestions about improvements to the translation; in particular, their criticisms have helped to make the final draft more like natural English than the earlier drafts were. The reader who has devoted most time and effort to the improvement of the translation, and who has improved it most, is John Cooper; I am deeply grateful to him for his remarkable generosity and helpfulness. He examined part of an early draft, and the whole penultimate draft; his careful criticisms and skillful suggestions have caused many improvements in both accuracy and style. If the translation has any merits, many of them will be due to him; in fairness to him, however, I should point out that I have sometimes, and always with hesitation and reluctance, failed to follow his advice. In this project, as in many others, I owe most to Gail Fine. Apart from giving help and support in many more important ways, she read more than one draft of the translation, criticized it vigorously, and encouraged me to improve it. Susan Sauvé read the proofs with vigilance and goodwill. The staff of Hackett Publishing Company have been invariably courteous, patient and helpful; they originally suggested the project, and have guided and supported it at every stage.

Aristotle's *Ethics* is not just for philosophers, or for philosophers of a particular school. I was fortunate enough to be introduced to the *Ethics* by three very different philosophers with complementary interests in it: G. J. Warnock, J. L. Ackrill and M. F. Burnyeat. I would be pleased if this edition suggested to new readers some of the many fruitful lines of approach to this work, and even helped them to see why study of the *Ethics* is one of the greatest pleasures philosophy has to offer.

Many errors and imperfections must still be present in this published version. If readers will send me suggestions for improvement, I will be most grateful.

T. H. Irwin
Cornell University
Ithaca, New York
October, 1984

Introduction

Why Read the Ethics*?*

Aristotle's ethical works matter to the student of moral behaviour. Aristotle provides the closest and most detailed analysis of Greek attitudes and aspirations, modified and criticized from his own point of view. Traditional Greek ideals of the best life (i 5); the canon of virtues that made someone an acceptable and admirable member of society (iii–v); the problems and conflicts of social life (viii 13–ix 3) – all these are examined by a dispassionate and careful observer.

For the historian of moral theory Aristotle's ethics is important as a primary source of mediaeval, and hence of modern, ethical thought. The *Ethics* provide the framework of Aquinas' account of the moral virtues; they have been read and cited as an influence by modern theorists – in the nineteenth century by Henry Sidgwick, in the twentieth by John Rawls, among many others.

But what has Aristotle to offer the contemporary reader interested in moral problems and in reflective thinking about them? The concrete detail that makes him interesting to the historian of Greece may seem to remove him from our concerns and interests. We do not readily value all the Aristotelian virtues; we will not be immediately inclined to find the magnanimous person (iv 3) as admirable as Aristotle finds him. And if Aristotle has been influential in moral theory, has his contribution been absorbed and superseded?

First of all, the contemporary student can learn from Aristotle's treatment of some problems of contemporary interest. His account of voluntary action and conditions for responsibility (iii 1,5); of purposive action and practical inference (iii 2-3, vii 3); of the nature and variety of pleasure (vii 11-14, x 1-5) — these have been justly admired for their stimulus to further thought on these issues.

However, Aristotle is important to the contemporary philosopher most of all because he does not share exactly our immediate concerns in moral theory. He does not ask the questions we would find it natural to ask about ethics — the contents of the *Ethics* look rather different from the contents of modern works on ethics. But when we take the trouble to understand Aristotle's questions, we can see that they are worth asking.

Aristotle's Life and Works

Aristotle was born in Stagira in Macedon, in 384, and hence was never a citizen of Athens, where he spent most of his life. He was a member of Plato's Academy from 367 to Plato's death in 347, when he left Athens, first for the eastern Aegean islands, and then for Macedon. Here he was a tutor of Alexander, the son of Philip the king of Macedon. He returned to Athens in 334 and founded his own school in the Lyceum. In 323 Alexander died, and Aristotle — apparently because of anti-Macedonian feeling in Athens — left for Chalcis, where he died in 322.

Aristotle was a Macedonian, and associated with the rising Macedonian dynasty that eventually founded an empire ruling over the previously independent city-states of Greece, and then over much of western Asia. Historians like to see here the transition from the age of the city-states to the age of empire, first the Macedonian and then (after 146) the Roman. It is surprising to some that this transition leaves no mark in Aristotle's ethical and political works. Aristotle still thinks of a Greek city as the natural and desirable form of community, and of the virtues of the citizen of such a city as the virtues needed for the best life. Probably we should not be surprised. Aristotle and his contemporaries did not know that the Macedonian empire would last and would be replaced by the Roman; and the rise of Macedon probably made little difference to the character of Greek social life or to individual and collective attitudes.

One major intellectual interest of Aristotle's is empirical inquiry and theory in biology—this is the subject of about a quarter of the extant Aristotelian corpus. Aristotle's biological works reflect his emphasis on detailed observation and comparison of circumstances, structure and behaviour of different animals. We may see some of the same interests in his classification and description of the virtues and the corresponding types of people.

A further major influence on Aristotle is Plato. Aristotle takes over Plato's interest in dialectic, logic, metaphysics and ethics. He is a keen critic of Plato (i 6); and Plato's concerns lead Aristotle to quite un-Platonic conclusions. In ethics Aristotle agrees rather closely with Plato's main aims and lines of argument.

It is easy, but seriously misleading, to present the 'empirical' and the 'Platonic' aspects of Aristotle as two sides of a conflict, or at least a tension, in his thought. In fact they are very closely connected. Aristotle examines nature, and interprets the empirical evidence, in the light of his own theoretical conceptions, especially his conceptions of form, matter (see CAUSE in Glossary) and END (see Glossary). The clearest statements of his programme, especially relevant to the study of human nature in the *Ethics*, are *Phys.* ii and *PA* i, 1.

Aristotle's works can be divided into groups:
(1) Logic and dialectic have no specific subject-matter, but are relevant in principle to all areas of inquiry. They examine

the proper forms of argument for different purposes—dialectic, syllogistic and demonstrative (see INFERENCE, SCIENCE); *Categories, De Interpretatione, Analytics, Topics* (together usually called the *Organon*) are in this group.

(2) Philosophy of NATURE considers the principles required for understanding MOVEMENT and change in general, especially for living organisms with SOULS. *Physics, De Caelo, De Generatione et Corruptione, De Anima, Parva Naturalia, De Partibus Animalium, De Generatione Animalium, De Motu Animalium* are in this group.

(3) First philosophy considers being in general, both unchanging (theology) and changing (hence the principles also used in natural philosophy). The *Metaphysics* addresses these matters.

(4) Practical science considers ACTION (in the narrow sense), and hence includes the *Ethics* and *Politics*.

(5) Productive science is concerned with PRODUCTION, including the *Rhetoric* and *Poetics*.

It is easy to see that some of the same questions about the same things might belong to more than one area of inquiry, and that (4) and (5) introduce an apparently different principle of division from (1)–(3). See ETHICS, SCIENCE; cf. *Met.* 982b11, 993b20, vi 1; *PA* 640a1.

Aristotle does not obtrude the rest of his philosophy into ethical questions (see note to 1155b1). But the reader who has read *Phys.* ii, *PA* i 1, *DA* ii 1–4, and *Met.* ix 1–8, will understand the arguments better in e.g. i 7, ii 5, vii 3, ix 9, x 4–8. Aristotle's account of dialectic is presupposed in his method in ETHICS. See also ACTIVITY, CAPACITY, CAUSE, FUNCTION, HUMAN BEING, SCIENCE, SOUL.

Background

Aristotle faces questions partly set by 'the many and the wise' (see ETHICS # 4), both common views and more or less systematic reflection on them. Some of his sources may be briefly indicated (see 'Aristotle's Literary References').

A traditional conception of HAPPINESS and the GOOD person finds the ideal life in a Homeric hero, displaying strength and BRAVERY in battle, leadership in political life and receiving HONOUR as his reward. However, this life is dangerous; success is precarious, liable to the sort of reversal of fortune presented in, e.g., Sophocles' *Ajax*.

At the same time Greek moralists want to encourage JUSTICE and concern for others as a virtue that is no less FINE and admirable than bravery and strength. This may require restraint on the single-minded pursuit of success and honour. It seems to require sacrifice of my own interests for the sake of other people's. When appeals to divine rewards and punishments seemed unconvincing, moralists looked for some reason to persuade someone concerned with his own happiness to be just.

Dangers and difficulties in traditional ideals provoked different reactions:

(1) 'Avoid the dangerous ambitions of the hero; live a quiet, unambitious and secure life, and then happiness won't be so easily lost.' (See Herodotus, iii 39–42, v 92.)

(2) 'Avoid the dangers of justice. The rules of justice are nothing but conventional norms imposed by the LAWS and expectations of society. They are irrelevant to human NATURE, which is best satisfied by the satisfaction of our immediate desires.' (See Plato, *Gorg.* 482c–492c.)

(3) 'Avoid the dangers of bravery and justice and turn to higher things, to the life of pure thought and study, away from the vicissitudes of the world.' (See Plato, *Rep.* 493b–e, *Tht.* 172d–177b.)

Aristotle wants to answer the criticism of the traditional virtues that makes them irrelevant to a rational person's conception of his happiness. He does not retain the traditional views unmodified; but bravery, restraint of appetites, concern for honour and other-regarding aims are all defended as parts of happiness. Their relation is clearest in the account of magnanimity (iv 3) and friendship (esp. ix 8–9). Here Aristotle's aim is very similar to Plato's in the *Republic*.

Misunderstandings of Aristotle

Objection: When Aristotle makes my happiness my ultimate end, he is accepting psychological hedonism. But he is wrong. I can value lots of things for their own sake apart from my pleasure or contentment.

Reply: Aristotle's conception of HAPPINESS does not identify happiness with pleasure.

Objection: When Aristotle requires me to aim at my own happiness above all, he endorses an immoral and objectionable version of egoism. Surely I can, and justifiably do, value, e.g., the welfare of other people for its own sake, not simply as a means to my happiness. Doesn't Aristotle make genuine altruism impossible?

Reply: The objection rests on a mistake about the relation between happiness and other intrinsic goods. (See notes to 1097b3 and to 1170b5.)

Objection: Aristotle claims that virtue of character requires a MEAN or intermediate state, moderation that avoids extremes. But sometimes extremes are good and moderation bad. Sometimes, for instance, it is good to be extremely angry, not just moderately angry, and sometimes it is good to give away a lot of money, not just a moderate amount.

Reply: The doctrine of the mean does not advise this sort of moderation. See note to 1106a26.

Objection: Aristotle leaves no place for distinctively moral reasoning. The only practical function of reason that he allows is deliberation about means to ends. The only reasoning he allows is quasi-technical calculation about how to get what we want. He allows no reasoning about whether the ends we are pursuing are the morally right ones.

Reply: Aristotle's conception of decision and of 'things

promoting ends' does not imply this sort of restriction. (See DECISION # 2, notes to 1111b27, 1112b11.)

Objection: By making the judgements of the intelligent person the ultimate standard of the morally virtuous action Aristotle commits himself to a conservative view of morality. To know what the virtuous action is we must ask an intelligent person. But how do we recognize one except by relying on the conventional judgements of our society?

Reply: The intelligent person need not accept all of conventional morality. Since he deliberates about the components of happiness (see INTELLIGENCE # 1), he may well form a conception of the good and of the virtues that differs from the conventional conception. To the extent that we can do some of the right deliberation ourselves, we can see that the intelligent person is right if he disagrees with conventional judgements.

Objection: The virtues Aristotle describes are perhaps suitable for a Greek gentleman wanting to act according to his station in life. But they are irrelevant to us when we live in different conditions and most of us do not think so highly of these aristocratic values.

Reply: The types of actions belonging to each virtue are, not surprisingly, suitable primarily for the social and historical conditions familiar to Aristotle. But it does not follow that the STATES and attitudes corresponding to the different virtues are historically limited in the same way. (See e.g. notes to 1115a30, 1123a34.)

Questions About Aristotle

While some natural objections to Aristotle's theory have been found to rest on misunderstandings that can be dispelled by closer study, some related objections and questions are not to be dismissed so easily. Often Aristotle's own argument is brief, inexplicit and incomplete on some important issues.

Introduction

Is happiness a reasonable first principle for ethics? Happiness is supposed to be the ultimate end which any rational agent has good reason to refer to when he decides how to live, what sort of person to be, what states of character to acquire. But can any conception of an ultimate end provide the right sort of guidance here? Should we perhaps decide what to do on moral grounds, without reference to some further end?

How informative is Aristotle's own conception of happiness? He argues that happiness is ACTIVITY according to virtue. How then do we tell what states are virtues? If we are not simply to follow conventional judgements, we must apparently turn again to happiness – but what sort of answer will we find here?

How does the intelligent person know what promotes happiness? This question raises again our previous question about the informativeness of Aristotle's conception of happiness. The reader can best answer this question by asking how each of the particular virtues could be shown to promote happiness as Aristotle conceives it. (Cf. notes to 1123a34, 1125b26, 1128a4.) Aristotle answers the question most fully in his defence of friendship, ix 9.

Does Aristotle show that we have reason to be moral? One task of the *Ethics* is to support Plato's claim in the *Republic* that we are better off being just, concerned with the interests of others, than being unjust. Aristotle does not face this question explicitly in Book v, on justice. He comes nearest to an answer in his account of friendship.

How much practical guidance does Aristotle really offer? Despite his emphasis on the practical function of ETHICS, 1103b26, he does not offer many specific moral rules. He discusses e.g. few of the questions that have divided utilitarians from non-utilitarians in modern ethics (but cf. note to 1127a4). Here we should remember:
(i) Aristotle is more concerned with identifying the right

states of character than with specifying the range of actions associated with them.

(ii) He thinks detailed ethical instructions require reference to social and political conditions; and these are discussed in the *Politics*.

The Structure of the Ethics

The work translated here and often called 'Aristotle's *Ethics*' is the *Nicomachean Ethics* (*Ethica Nicomachea*, or *EN*), one of three detailed treatises on ethics in the Aristotelian corpus; the others are the *Eudemian Ethics* and the *Magna Moralia*. (Nicomachus and Eudemus may have been the original editors of the works named after them, after Aristotle's death, or he may have dedicated the works to them.) The *MM* is generally agreed not to have been written by Aristotle. It may still contain genuine Aristotelian doctrine identical to the doctrine of neither the *EN* nor the *EE*. The *EE* is by Aristotle, and is generally (but not universally) supposed to predate the *EN*. All three works cover many of the same topics in interestingly different ways, and comparative study is often rewarding. A special puzzle is raised by the three books common to the *EN* and the *EE* (see note to 1129a3).

Probably the *EN* we have was not intended for publication in exactly its present form. Like most of the Aristotelian corpus, it is probably Aristotle's lecture notes, perhaps edited after his death. This origin would explain why the argument is often compressed (e.g. in i 6)—perhaps intended for oral elaboration—and why the order of topics within a book is not always easy to follow. The order is in any case fairly loose—Aristotle takes up topics as they naturally lead into each other, and then resumes his main topic. (Cf. 1095b14, 1097b15.)

The present division into books is due to Aristotle's early editors. It partly reflects the requirements of ancient book-production. The book divisions correspond to natural breaks at the end of Books i, v, vi, vii, and ix, but not at the end of ii, iii, iv, or viii. Other natural breaks are at the end of iii 5, vii 10, x 5 and x 8. Divisions into chapters are due to modern editors; I have followed the more common capitulation found in modern editions.

This Edition

Readers will understand the translation better if they consult the notes and glossary. The glossary discusses some of Aristotle's most important terms, and indicates where a particular English rendering may be inexact or misleading; see, e.g., the entries HAPPINESS, VIRTUE and INTELLIGENCE. I have tried not to use too many English terms to render a single Greek term, or the same English term to render different and important Greek terms.

The italicized headings in the translation are all insertions, not part of Aristotle's text. The numbering is meant to suggest the structure of the argument. In more complicated passages the headings are fuller and more frequent, and therefore embody more controversial assumptions about the right interpretation of a particular passage. Reference letters and numbers inserted into the translation itself (e.g., in i 2, vii 3, vii 11) are aids to the reader with no direct textual warrant.

I have tried to distinguish what Aristotle seems to have said from what he probably meant by it; and though this distinction cannot always be sharp, I hope readers will usually be able to separate the translation from the translator's interpretations, especially from those interpretations that might be challenged by other translators or interpreters. Square brackets in the translation indicate some of the insertions that seem necessary or plausible to complete the sense, but have no direct rendering in the Greek (sometimes because of Greek idiom, sometimes because of Aristotle's compressed style). Not all such insertions are marked by square brackets; if the same insertion is repeated (e.g. 'science'; see note to

1094a18), it is mentioned in the notes or glossary but not marked in the text. In some particularly difficult and important passages I have offered a rather free and interpretative translation to bring out the sense, and supplied a more literal translation in the notes (see notes to 1095b6-8, 1097b16-20). Readers must not assume that all the controversial insertions are marked by square brackets in the translation; but those that are not marked should be discoverable from the notes.

Aristotle sometimes quotes from or alludes to literary and philosophical sources. These quotations and allusions are not usually very important. Their sources are collected together in a section called 'Aristotle's Literary References'. I have not thought it necessary to give references for the occasional historical or mythological allusions, since these can easily be traced in standard works of reference (see 'Further Reading') and they do not matter much for the understanding of the *Ethics*.

Irregularity in the marginal numbers indicates places where either (a) I have thought it better to alter the order of the Greek sentence (e.g. in i 5, where Aristotle has a long parenthesis), or (b) I have thought it plausible to suppose the Greek text we have is in the wrong order. Cases of (b) are marked in the 'Note on the Text'; they are especially frequent in Book v. In (b) I have not followed an ultra-conservative strategy; I have been willing to transpose passages when a transposition seemed probable, even if not certain. It should be remembered that a translator who finds a passage incoherent may simply have failed to understand it; and some of the transpositions in this translation may well be open to such a challenge.

The notes are intended to sketch the argument of particular passages, to mention parallels and cross-references, and only occasionally to suggest points about the argument and themes of the *Ethics* as a whole. There are some further suggestions of this sort in the longer entries in the glossary.

The numbers in the outer margins of the translation (e.g. '1094a1' = line one of column a of page 1094) refer to Immanuel Bekker's edition of the Greek text (Berlin, 1831). This is a standard form of reference to works of Aristotle. Since the numbers refer to lines of the Greek text, the numbers in an English translation correspond only roughly. The notes all refer to the Bekker pages of the Greek text. The outer margins of the translation also contain the capitulation most commonly used in editions, translations and citations (book numbers in roman numerals, chapter numbers in arabic).

Note on the Text

I have translated I. Bywater's text (Oxford, 1894), except for the variations noted below. Bywater's reading is indicated, where necessary, to the right of the slash marks //. Braces { } indicate the deletion of a passage found in the original manuscripts, and square brackets [ ] denote insertion of words not found in the manuscripts. Differences in punctuation are not recorded.

1094a13	ton auton de	//	kata ton auton dē
a14	hapasais dē	//	hapasais de
b4	praktikais	//	{ }
1098a12-16	anthrōpou . . . houtō	//	{ }
1101a10	outh'hupo	//	oud'hupo
1104a1	prakteon	//	prakton
1105b25	phobēthēnai	//	lupēthēnai
1106a8-9	{out'epainoumetha oute psegometha}		
b25	hamartanetai [kai psegetai] kai		
1107b5	{kai} peri		
1110b13	geloion dē	//	geloion de
1111a18	praxis [ho] kai		
1112a6	{ē tō(i) orthōs}		
a7	{alēthōs}		
a24	{kai} phusei		
a28-9	all'oude . . . bouleuetai: *insert after* a33, di' anthropou		

Note on the Text

b7	doxas	//	technas
b9	[to hōs dei] adihoriston		
b33	ouk ar'an	//	ou gar an
1113a12	boulēsin	//	bouleusin
b1	goun to	//	oun to
1114a12-13	ei de mē . . . an eiē: *insert after* a10, anaisthētou		
a15	kaitoi ei	//	kai ei
1114b3	mēdeis	//	mē, oudeis
b9	ei par'	//	kai ho par
b29-30	kai . . . prostaxē(i): *insert after* b28, hautas		
1115a22	gunaikas	//	gunaika
1116a7-9	kai hoi . . . hēsuchioi: *insert after* 1115b33, hupomenousin		
1117a4-5	phusikōtatē . . . einai: *insert after* a9, echousi ti		
a27	ho dē	//	ho de
1121b30	areskein	//	areskei
1122a7	{kai ho lē(i)stēs}		
1122b18	{megaloprepeia}		
1123a12	{haplōs}		
b24-26	ho de . . . megalopsouchon: *insert after* b15, elleipousin		
1123b23	hoi megaloi	//	{ }
b31	g'an	//	t'an
1124a29	{kai hoi}		
b7	mikrokindunos, oude puknokindunos, dia to oliga timān, oude philokindunos, megalokindunos // mikrokindunos, oude philokindunos dia to oliga timān, megalokindunos		
b27	melein	//	amelein
1126a28	timōrias kai	//	timōrias ē
1127a13	{kai eironeias}		
b12	hōs {ho}		
b20	sophon [ē] iatron		
1128a29	tauta kan	//	tauta kai
1129b15	{ē tois aristois}		

b16	kat' aretēn	//	{ }
b31	hoti {tēs teleias} aretēs [teleia] chrēsis		
1130a7	all'ho	//	alla
b23	prattomena	//	prostattomena
1131a16	pros tinas	//	pros ti kai tisin
a20	{ta pragmata}		
a21	{ta en hois}		
1132a29-30	to d'ison . . . analogian: *insert after* a32, dichastēs		
1132b11	elēluthe . . . kerdainein (b18): *insert after* 1132a14, kerdos		
1133a22	{ē trophēn}		
1133a23-24	{ē trophēn}		
1133b29- 1134a23	*insert after* 1135a5, hē aretē		
1134b13	auta	//	hauton
b33	dēlon [de] kai epi tōn allōn [kai] ho		
1137b4-5	{ou dikaion}		
1138a6	eā(i)	//	keleuei
a7	{ha de mē keleuei apagoreuei}		
b11	heautou	//	heauton
1139a8	ta hōn endechontai	//	ta endechomena
1139b28	archēs	//	arche
1140a5	kai	//	diho
a11	technazein {kai}		
1141a22	d'	//	dē
a26	phaien an	//	phēsi
	epitrepseian an	//	epitrepsei
b26	hōs {ta}		
b34	{gnōseōs}		
1142a28	en tois mathēmatikois	//	{ }
a30	ē [hē] phronēsis		
b16	{hē boulē}		
1143b28	chrēsimon	//	phronimon
b30	ousin	//	echousin
1144a26	autōn	//	autou

a28	kai [tous] panourgous		
1145a2	ousē(i)	//	huparchousē(i)
1146a23	entuchōsin	//	epituchōsin
b18-19	{epeit' . . . ē ou}		
1150a19	hē(i)	//	ē
a20	kai dia	//	ē dia
1151a3-5	homoios . . . polloi: *insert after* 1150b35, ponēria		
b20	hēdu	//	kalon
1152a10-14	ton de . . . prohairesin: *insert after* a8, on		
b31	[aei]	//	[haplōs]
1153a2	{hēdei}		
a3	kai [ēdē]		
a30	{haplōs} kai pōs ouk agathai [haplōs]		
b2	pē(i) tō(i)	//	tō(i) pē(i)
1154a1	mē [hē]		
a2	kai {hē}		
b1	hai dē	//	hai de
1155b15-16	{eirētai . . . emprosthen}		
1156a16	estin [hosper estin]		
b22	homoioi	//	homoia
1158a13	pollois	//	pollous
a14	agathon	//	agathous
1160a19-20	enioi . . . sunousias	//	{ }
1161a35	{kai . . . doulon}		
1163a2	kai hekonti	//	{ }
1166a21	ekeino to genomenon	//	{ }
b12	{kai} dia		
b12	. . . misousi te	//	misountai
1169a6	{ē} tou kalou		
1173a2	ōregeto	//	oregetai
a3	ti [to] legomenon		
a4	{phusikon agathon}		
b12	kenoumenos	//	temnomenos

1174a20	oikodomia	//	oikodomikē
a21	{ē} toutō(i)		
b10	tēs hēdonēs	//	tēn hēdonēn
1177a9	ouk ar'	//	ou gar
1178b12	*no lacuna*		
1179b17	ethesi	//	ēthesi
1180a32	[kai drān auto dunasthai] ē		
1181a11	sunētheias mallon	//	politikēs sunētheias

Abbreviations

In the Introduction, Notes, and Glossary, passages from the *EN* are cited by Bekker pages and lines. Other works of Aristotle are cited by Bekker pages and lines and abbreviated titles. (The Bekker pages are continuous throughout the Aristotelian corpus.) The abbreviations should be intelligible from the list of the traditional Latin or English titles below. Square brackets indicate dubious or spurious works. Some of the less obvious abbreviations are indicated in parentheses.

Analytica Posteriora

Analytica Priora

Categories

De Anima

De Caelo

De Generatione Animalium (GA)

De Generatione et Corruptione (GC)

De Interpretatione

De Motu Animalium (MA)

De Partibus Animalium (PA)

Ethica Eudemia

Ethica Nicomachea

Historia Animalium

[Magna Moralia]

Metaphysics

Parva Naturalia

Physics

Poetics

Politics

[Problems]

Rhetoric

Topics

The dialogues of Plato are cited by abbreviated title and the standard Stephanus pages.

Fragments of some Greek authors are cited from standard collections as follows:

DK = Diels, H., and Kranz, W., eds., *Die Fragmente der Vorsokratiker* (6th ed., Berlin, 1951).

Diehl = Diehl, E., ed., *Anthologia Lyrica Graeca* (3rd ed., Leipzig, 1949-52).

Kaibel = Kaibel, G., ed., *Comicorum Graecorum Fragmenta* (Berlin, 1899).

Kock = Kock, T., ed., *Comicorum Atticorum Fragmenta* (Leipzig, 1880-8).

TGF = Nauck, A., ed., *Tragicorum Graecorum Fragmenta* (2nd ed., Leipzig, 1899).

Nicomachean Ethics

1. The Highest Good: Happiness

1.1 The Highest Good is Supreme in the Hierarchy of Goods

Goods correspond to ends

Every craft and every investigation, and likewise every action and decision, seems to aim at some good; hence the good has been well described as that at which everything aims.

However, there is an apparent difference among the ends aimed at. For the end is sometimes an activity, sometimes a product beyond the activity; and when there is an end be- 5 yond the action, the product is by nature better than the activity.

The hierarchy of goods corresponds to the hierarchy of ends

Since there are many actions, crafts and sciences, the ends turn out to be many as well; for health is the end of medicine, a boat of boatbuilding, victory of generalship, and wealth of household management. 10

But whenever any of these sciences are subordinate to some one capacity — as e.g. bridlemaking and every other science producing equipment for horses are subordinate to horseman-

1

ship, while this and every action in warfare are in turn subordinate to generalship, and in the same way other sciences
are subordinate to further ones – in each of these the end of
15 the ruling science is more choiceworthy than all the ends
subordinate to it, since it is the end for which those ends are
also pursued. And here it does not matter whether the ends
of the actions are the activities themselves, or some product
beyond them, as in the sciences we have mentioned.

The highest good

i 2   Suppose, then, that (a) there is some end of the things we
pursue in our actions which we wish for because of itself,
and because of which we wish for the other things; and (b)
20 we do not choose everything because of something else,
since (c) if we do, it will go on without limit, making desire
empty and futile; then clearly (d) this end will be the good,
i.e. the best good.

*1.2   The Ruling Science Studying the Highest
Good is Political Science*

*The importance of finding the science
of the highest good*

Then surely knowledge of this good is also of great importance for the conduct of our lives, and if, like archers,
we have a target to aim at, we are more likely to hit the right
25 mark. If so, we should try to grasp, in outline at any rate,
what the good is, and which science or capacity is concerned
with it.

The relevant science is political science

It seems to concern the most controlling science, the one
that, more than any other, is the ruling science. And political
science apparently has this character.
(1) For it is the one that prescribes which of the sciences

2

ought to be studied in cities, and which ones each class in | 1094b
the city should learn, and how far.

(2) Again, we see that even the most honoured capacities,
e.g. generalship, household management and rhetoric, are
subordinate to it.

(3) Further, it uses the other sciences concerned with
action, and moreover legislates what must be done and what | 5
avoided.

Hence its end will include the ends of the other sciences,
and so will be the human good.

[This is properly called political science;] for though admittedly the good is the same for a city as for an individual,
still the good of the city is apparently a greater and more
complete good to acquire and preserve. For while it is satisfactory to acquire and preserve the good even for an indi-
vidual, it is finer and more divine to acquire and preserve | 10
it for a people and for cities. And so, since our investigation
aims at these [goods, for an individual and for a city], it is
a sort of political science.

1.3 The Method of Political Inquiry

The demand for exactness must be limited
by the nature of ethics

Our discussion will be adequate if its degree of clarity fits | i 3
the subject-matter; for we should not seek the same degree
of exactness in all sorts of arguments alike, any more than
in the products of different crafts.

Moreover, what is fine and what is just, the topics of in- | 15
quiry in political science, differ and vary so much that they
seem to rest on convention only, not on nature. Goods,
however, also vary in the same sort of way, since they cause
harm to many people; for it has happened that some people
have been destroyed because of their wealth, others because
of their bravery.

3

The proper aim of ethical theory

20   Since these, then, are the sorts of things we argue from and about, it will be satisfactory if we can indicate the truth roughly and in outline; since [that is to say] we argue from and about what holds good usually [but not universally], it will be satisfactory if we can draw conclusions of the same sort.

How to judge an ethical theory

Each of our claims, then, ought to be accepted in the same way [as claiming to hold good usually], since the educated person seeks exactness in each area to the extent that the

25   nature of the subject allows; for apparently it is just as mistaken to demand demonstrations from a rhetorician as to accept [merely] persuasive arguments from a mathematician.

Further, each person judges well what he knows, and is

1095a   a good judge about that; hence the good judge in a particular area is the person educated in that area, and the unconditionally good judge is the person educated in every area.

Qualifications of the student of ethics

This is why a youth is not a suitable student of political science; for he lacks experience of the actions in life which political science argues from and about.

Moreover, since he tends to be guided by his feelings, his

5   study will be futile and useless; for its end is action, not knowledge. And here it does not matter whether he is young in years or immature in character, since the deficiency does not depend on age, but results from being guided in his life and in each of his pursuits by his feelings; for an immature person, like an incontinent person, gets no benefit from his knowledge.

10   If, however, we are guided by reason in forming our desires and in acting, then this knowledge will be of great benefit.

4

These are the preliminary points about the student, about the way our claims are to be accepted, and about what we intend to do.

1.4   Common Beliefs About the Highest Good are Inadequate

1.41   Most people identify the good with happiness, but disagree about the nature of happiness

Let us, then, begin again. Since every sort of knowledge and decision pursues some good, what is that good which we say is the aim of political science? What [in other words] is the highest of all the goods pursued in action?

As far as its name goes, most people virtually agree [about what the good is], since both the many and the cultivated call it happiness, and suppose that living well and doing well are the same as being happy. But they disagree about what happiness is, and the many do not give the same answer as the wise.

For the many think it is something obvious and evident, e.g. pleasure, wealth or honour, some thinking one thing, others another; and indeed the same person keeps changing his mind, since in sickness he thinks it is health, in poverty wealth. And when they are conscious of their own ignorance, they admire anyone who speaks of something grand and beyond them.

[Among the wise,] however, some used to think that besides these many goods there is some other good that is something in itself, and also causes all these goods to be goods.

i 4
15

20

25

1.42   Ethical method

We must examine these common beliefs;
but we must not take for granted our first
principles, since we are arguing towards them,
not from them

Presumably, then, it is rather futile to examine all these
beliefs, and it is enough to examine those that are most current or seem to have some argument for them.

We must notice, however, the difference between arguments from origins and arguments towards origins. For indeed Plato was right to be puzzled about this, when he used
to ask if [the argument] set out from the origins or led towards
them—just as on a race course the path may go from the
starting-line to the far end, or back again.

To argue towards first principles we must begin
from common beliefs that are familiar to us

For while we should certainly begin from origins that are
known, things are known in two ways; for some are known
to us, some known unconditionally [but not necessarily
known to us]. Presumably, then, the origin *we* should begin
from is what is known to *us*.

To become familiar with common beliefs
we need a good upbringing

This is why we need to have been brought up in fine habits
if we are to be adequate students of what is fine and just,
and of political questions generally. For the origin we begin
from is the belief that something is true, and if this is apparent enough to us, we will not, at this stage, need the reason
why it is true in addition; and if we have this good upbringing, we have the origins to begin from, or can easily acquire
them. Someone who neither has them nor can acquire them
should listen to Hesiod: 'He who understands everything

6

himself is best of all; he is noble also who listens to one who
has spoken well; but he who neither understands it himself
nor takes to heart what he hears from another is a useless
man.'

1.43   Three conceptions of the best life
reflect common beliefs about the good, but
face criticism from other common beliefs

But let us begin again from [the common beliefs] from
which we digressed. For, it would seem, people quite reasonably reach their conception of the good, i.e. of happiness,
from the lives [they lead]; for there are roughly three most
favoured lives – the lives of gratification, of political activity, and, third, of study.

i 5
15
17, 18
19
16

The life of gratification: pleasure

The many, the most vulgar, would seem to conceive the
good and happiness as pleasure, and hence they also like the
life of gratification. Here they appear completely slavish,
since the life they decide on is a life for grazing animals;
and yet they have some argument in their defence, since many
in positions of power feel the same way as Sardanapallus
[and also choose this life].

17
19
20

The life of action: honour or virtue

The cultivated people, those active [in politics], conceive
the good as honour, since this is more or less the end [nor-
mally pursued] in the political life. This, however, appears
to be too superficial to be what we are seeking, since it
seems to depend more on those who honour than on the one
honoured, whereas we intuitively believe that the good is
something of our own and hard to take from us.

25

Further, it would seem, they pursue honour to convince
themselves that they are good; at any rate, they seek to be
honoured by intelligent people, among people who know

them, and for virtue. It is clear, then, that in the view of active people at least, virtue is superior [to honour].

Perhaps, indeed, one might conceive virtue more than honour to be the end of the political life. However, this also is apparently too incomplete [to be the good]. For, it seems, someone might possess virtue but be asleep or inactive throughout his life; or, further, he might suffer the worst evils and misfortunes; and if this is the sort of life he leads, no one would count him happy, except to defend a philosopher's paradox. Enough about this, since it has been adequately discussed in the popular works also.

The life of study
The third life is the life of study, which we will examine in what follows.

The life of money-making may be safely ignored
The money-maker's life is in a way forced on him [not chosen for itself]; and clearly wealth is not the good we are seeking, since it is [merely] useful, [choiceworthy only] for some other end. Hence one would be more inclined to suppose that [any of] the goods mentioned earlier is the end, since they are liked for themselves. But apparently they are not [the end] either; and many arguments have been presented against them. Let us, then, dismiss them.

1.44 A philosophical conception of the good: Plato's theory of 'Forms' or 'Ideas'
Presumably, though, we had better examine the universal good, and puzzle out what is meant in speaking of it. This sort of inquiry is, to be sure, unwelcome to us, when those who introduced the Forms were friends of ours; still, it presumably seems better, indeed only right, to destroy even what is close to us if that is the way to preserve the truth. And we must especially do this when we are philosophers,

8

[lovers of wisdom]; for though we love both the truth and our friends, piety requires us to honour the truth first.

1.441   Objections to the Form as a universal

(1)   There are no universals for ordered series

Those who introduced this view did not mean to produce an Idea for any [series] in which they spoke of prior and posterior [members]; that was why they did not mean to establish an Idea [of number] for [the series of] numbers. But the good is spoken of both in the [category of] what-it-is [i.e. substance], and in [the categories of] quality and relative; and what is in itself, i.e. substance, is by nature prior to what is relative, since a relative would seem to be an appendage and coincident of being. And so there is no common Idea over these. | 20

(2)   There is no universal good across the categories

Further, good is spoken of in as many ways as being is spoken of. For it is spoken of in [the category of] what-it-is, as god and mind; in quality, as the virtues; in quantity, as the measured amount; in relative, as the useful; in time, as the opportune moment; in place, as the [right] situation; and so on. Hence it is clear that the good cannot be some common [nature of good things] that is universal and single; for if it were, it would be spoken of in only one of the categories, not in them all. | 25

(3)   There is no single Idea across different sciences

Further, if a number of things have a single Idea, there is also a single science of them; hence [if there were an Idea of Good] there would also be some single science of all goods. But in fact there are many sciences even of the goods under | 30

one category; for the science of the opportune moment, e.g.
in war is generalship, in disease medicine. And similarly the
science of the measured amount in food is medicine, in ex-
ertion gymnastics. [Hence there is no single science of the
good, and so no Idea.]

1.442   Objections to the Form as separated

(4)   Separation is pointless for
understanding goodness
    One might be puzzled about what [the believers in Ideas]
35 really mean in speaking of The So-and-So Itself, since Man
1096b Itself and man have one and the same account of man; for
in so far as each is man, they will not differ at all. If that
is so, then [Good Itself and good have the same account of
good]; hence they also will not differ at all in so far as each
is good, [hence there is no point in appealing to Good Itself].

(5)   The eternity of the Form is irrelevant
    Moreover, Good Itself will be no more of a good by be-
ing eternal; for a white thing is no whiter if it lasts a long
5 time than if it lasts a day.

(6)   The Pythagorean view
    The Pythagoreans seemingly have a more plausible view
about the good, since they place the One in the column of
goods. Indeed, Speusippus seems to have followed them. But
let us leave this for another discussion.

1.443   Further objections to the Form, arising
from the diversity of goods

(7)   There is no Form even for intrinsic goods
    A dispute emerges about what we have said: 'The argu-
10 ments [in favour of the Idea] are not concerned with every

sort of good. Goods pursued and liked in themselves are spoken of as one species of goods, while those that in some way tend to produce or preserve these goods, or to prevent their contraries, are spoken of as goods because of these and in a different way; clearly, then, goods are spoken of in two ways, and some are goods in themselves, others goods because of these. [And it is claimed only that there is a single Form for all goods in themselves.]'

Let us, then, separate the goods in themselves from the [merely] useful goods, and consider whether goods in themselves are spoken of in correspondence to a single Idea.   15

Well, what sorts of goods may be regarded as goods in themselves? (a) Perhaps they are those that are pursued even on their own, e.g. intelligence, seeing, some types of pleasures, and honours; for even if we also pursue these because of something else, they may still be regarded as goods in themselves. (b) Or perhaps nothing except the Idea is good in itself.   20

[If (b) is true], then the Form will be futile, [since it will not explain the goodness of anything. But if (a) is true], then, since these other things are also goods in themselves, the same account of good will have to turn up in all of them, just as the same account of whiteness turns up in snow and in chalk. In fact, however, honour, intelligence and pleasure have different and dissimilar accounts, precisely in so far   25
as they are goods. Hence the good is not something common which corresponds to a single Idea.

(8)   Though goods are not homonymous by
chance, the connection between their definitions
does not imply the existence of a single Form

But how after all, then, is good spoken of? For [these goods have different accounts, i.e. are homonymous, and yet] are seemingly not homonymous by mere chance. Perhaps they are homonymous by all being derived from a single source,

11

or by all referring to a single focus. Or perhaps instead they are homonymous by analogy; for example, as sight is to body, so understanding is to soul, and so on for other cases.

1.444   The irrelevance of the Form to ethics

(9)   It is irrelevant to action

30   Presumably, though, we should leave these questions for now, since their exact treatment is more appropriate for another [branch of] philosophy. And the same is true about the Idea. For even if the good predicated in common is some single thing, or something separated, itself in itself, clearly it is not the sort of good a human being can pursue in action
35   or possess; but that is just the sort we are looking for in our present inquiry.

(10)   The sciences pay no attention to the Form

'But,' it might seem to some, 'it is better to get to know
1097a   the Idea with a view to the goods that we can possess and pursue in action; for if we have this as a sort of pattern, we shall also know better about the goods that are goods for us, and if we know about them, we shall hit on them.'

This argument does indeed have some plausibility, but
5   it would seem to clash with the sciences. For each of these, though it aims at some good and seeks to supply what is lacking, proceeds without concern for knowledge of the Idea; and if the Idea were such an important aid, surely it would not be reasonable for all craftsmen to be ignorant and not even to look for it.

(11)   And they are right, for the Form is useless to sciences

Moreover, it is a puzzle to know what the weaver or carpenter will gain for his own craft from knowing this Good

Itself, or how anyone will be better at medicine or generalship   10
from having gazed on the Idea Itself. For what the doctor
appears to consider is not even health [universally, let alone
good universally], but human beings' health, and even more
than that, presumably, this human being's health, since it is
particular patients he treats.

So much, then, for these questions.

1.5   Our Own View of the Good Takes Account of These Objections to Common Beliefs

1.51   Characteristics of the good

(1)   The good is the end of action   i 7
But let us return once again to the good we are looking   15
for, and consider just what it could be, since it is apparently
one thing in one action or craft, and another thing in another;
for it is one thing in medicine, another in generalship, and
so on for the rest.

What, then, is the good in each of these cases? Surely it
is that for the sake of which the other things are done; and
in medicine this is health, in generalship victory, in house-   20
building a house, in another case something else, but in every
action and decision it is the end, since it is for the sake of
the end that everyone does the other things.

And so, if there is some end of everything that is pursued
in action, this will be the good pursued in action; and if there
are more ends than one, these will be the goods pursued in
action.

Our argument has progressed, then, to the same conclusion [as before, that the highest end is the good]; but we must   25
try to clarify this still more.

(2)   The good is complete
Though apparently there are many ends, we choose some
of them, e.g. wealth, flutes and, in general, instruments,

because of something else; hence it is clear that not all ends
are complete. But the best good is apparently something
complete. Hence, if only one end is complete, this will be
what we are looking for; and if more than one are com-
30   plete, the most complete of these will be what we are looking for.

Criteria for completeness
An end pursued in itself, we say, is more complete than
an end pursued because of something else; and an end that
is never choiceworthy because of something else is more
complete than ends that are choiceworthy both in themselves
and because of this end; and hence an end that is always
[choiceworthy, and also] choiceworthy in itself, never because of something else, is unconditionally complete.

(3)   Happiness meets the criteria for
completeness, but other goods do not
Now happiness more than anything else seems uncondi-
1097b   tionally complete, since we always [choose it, and also]
choose it because of itself, never because of something else.
Honour, pleasure, understanding and every virtue we certainly choose because of themselves, since we would choose
each of them even if it had no further result, but we also
5   choose them for the sake of happiness, supposing that through
them we shall be happy. Happiness, by contrast, no one ever
chooses for their sake, or for the sake of anything else at all.

(4)   The good is self-sufficient; so is happiness
The same conclusion [that happiness is complete] also appears to follow from self-sufficiency, since the complete good
seems to be self-sufficient.
Now what we count as self-sufficient is not what suffices
for a solitary person by himself, living an isolated life, but
10   what suffices also for parents, children, wife and in general

14

for friends and fellow-citizens, since a human being is a naturally political [animal]. Here, however, we must impose some limit; for if we extend the good to parents' parents and children's children and to friends of friends, we shall go on without limit; but we must examine this another time.

Anyhow, we regard something as self-sufficient when all by itself it makes a life choiceworthy and lacking nothing; and that is what we think happiness does.

(5)   What is self-sufficient is most choiceworthy;
so is happiness

Moreover, we think happiness is most choiceworthy of all goods, since it is not counted as one good among many. If it were counted as one among many, then, clearly, we think that the addition of the smallest of goods would make it more choiceworthy; for [the smallest good] that is added becomes an extra quantity of goods [so creating a good larger than the original good], and the larger of two goods is always more choiceworthy. [But we do not think any addition can make happiness more choiceworthy; hence it is most choiceworthy.]

Happiness, then, is apparently something complete and self-sufficient, since it is the end of the things pursued in action.

1.52   A clearer account of the good:
the human soul's activity expressing virtue

But presumably the remark that the best good is happiness is apparently something [generally] agreed, and what we miss is a clearer statement of what the best good is.

(1)   If something has a function, its good
depends on its function

Well, perhaps we shall find the best good if we first find the function of a human being. For just as the good, i.e. [do-

15

20

25

ing] well, for a flautist, a sculptor, and every craftsman, and,
in general, for whatever has a function and [characteristic]
action, seems to depend on its function, the same seems to
be true for a human being, if a human being has some
function.

(2)   What sorts of things have functions?

Then do the carpenter and the leatherworker have their
30 functions and actions, while a human being has none, and
is by nature idle, without any function? Or, just as eye, hand,
foot and, in general, every [bodily] part apparently has its
functions, may we likewise ascribe to a human being some
function besides all of theirs?

(3)   The human function

What, then, could this be? For living is apparently shared
with plants, but what we are looking for is the special func-
1098a tion of a human being; hence we should set aside the life
of nutrition and growth. The life next in order is some sort
of life of sense-perception; but this too is apparently shared,
with horse, ox and every animal. The remaining possibility, then, is some sort of life of action of the [part of the
soul] that has reason.

Clarification of 'has reason' and 'life'

Now this [part has two parts, which have reason in different ways], one as obeying the reason [in the other part],
5 the other as itself having reason and thinking. [We intend
both.] Moreover, life is also spoken of in two ways [as capacity and as activity], and we must take [a human being's special
function to be] life as activity, since this seems to be called
life to a fuller extent.

16

(4)   The human good is activity
expressing virtue

(a) We have found, then, that the human function is the
soul's activity that expresses reason [as itself having reason]
or requires reason [as obeying reason]. (b) Now the function
of F, e.g. of a harpist, is the same in kind, so we say, as
the function of an excellent F, e.g. an excellent harpist. (c)
The same is true unconditionally in every case, when we | 10
add to the function the superior achievement that expresses
the virtue; for a harpist's function, e.g. is to play the harp,
and a good harpist's is to do it well. (d) Now we take the
human function to be a certain kind of life, and take this life
to be the soul's activity and actions that express reason. (e)
[Hence by (c) and (d)] the excellent man's function is to do
this finely and well. (f) Each function is completed well when | 15
its completion expresses the proper virtue. (g) Therefore [by
(d), (e) and (f)] the human good turns out to be the soul's
activity that expresses virtue.

(5)   The good must also be complete

And if there are more virtues than one, the good will express the best and most complete virtue. Moreover, it will
be in a complete life. For one swallow does not make a
spring, nor does one day; nor, similarly, does one day or a | 20
short time make us blessed and happy.

1.6   Defence of the Account of the Good, from
Principles of Ethical Method

1.61   It is reasonable that our account is
only a sketch

This, then, is a sketch of the good; for, presumably, the
outline must come first, to be filled in later. If the sketch
is good, then anyone, it seems, can advance and articulate
it, and in such cases time is a good discoverer or [at least]

25   a good co-worker. That is also how the crafts have improved,
     since anyone can add what is lacking [in the outline].

     *1.62   The inexactness of our account suits
     the subject-matter*
        However, we must also remember our previous remarks,
     so that we do not look for the same degree of exactness in
     all areas, but the degree that fits the subject-matter in each
     area and is proper to the investigation. For the carpenter's
30   and the geometer's inquiries about the right angle are dif-
     ferent also; the carpenter's is confined to the right angle's
     usefulness for his work, whereas the geometer's concerns
     what, or what sort of thing, the right angle is, since he studies
     the truth. We must do the same, then, in other areas too,
     [seeking the proper degree of exactness], so that digressions
     do not overwhelm our main task.

     *1.63 Having found a first principle, we should
     not demand a further principle beyond it*
1098b   Nor should we make the same demand for an explanation
     in all cases. Rather, in some cases it is enough to prove that
     something is true without explaining why it is true. This is
     so, e.g. with origins, where the fact that something is true
     is the first principle, i.e. the origin.
        Some origins are studied by means of induction, some by
     means of perception, some by means of some sort of habitua-
5   tion, and others by other means. In each case we should try
     to find them out by means suited to their nature, and work
     hard to define them well. For they have a great influence
     on what follows; for the origin seems to be more than half
     the whole, and makes evident the answer to many of our
     questions.

18

1.7   Defence of the Account of the Good, from Common Beliefs

However, we should examine the origin not only from
the conclusion and premises [of a deductive argument], but
also from what is said about it; for all the facts harmonize
with a true account, whereas the truth soon clashes with a
false one.

1.71   A common classification of goods

Goods are divided, then, into three types, some called external, some goods of the soul, others goods of the body;
and the goods of the soul are said to be goods to the fullest
extent and most of all, and the soul's actions and activities
are ascribed to the soul. Hence the account [of the good] is
sound, to judge by this belief anyhow—and it is an ancient
belief agreed on by philosophers.

Our account is also correct in saying that some sort of actions and activities are the end; for then the end turns out
to be a good of the soul, not an external good.

1.72   A common conception of happiness

The belief that the happy person lives well and does well
in action also agrees with our account, since we have virtually said that the end is a sort of living well and doing well
in action.

1.73   Commonly accepted features of happiness

Further, all the features that people look for in happiness
appear to be true of the end described in our account. For
to some people it seems to be virtue; to others intelligence;
to others some sort of wisdom; to others again it seems to
be these, or one of these, involving pleasure or requiring
its addition; and others add in external prosperity as well.

Some of these views are traditional, held by many, while

19

others are held by a few reputable men; and it is reasonable for each group to be not entirely in error, but correct on one point at least, or even on most points.

Virtue

30   First, our account agrees with those who say happiness is virtue [in general] or some [particular] virtue; for activity expressing virtue is proper to virtue. Presumably, though, it matters quite a bit whether we suppose that the best good consists in possessing or in using, i.e. in a state or in an activity [that actualizes the state]. For while someone may be in a state that achieves no good, if, e.g., he is asleep or inactive in some other way, this cannot be true of the activity; for it will necessarily do actions and do well in them. And just as Olympic prizes are not for the finest and strongest, but for contestants, since it is only these who win; so also in life [only] the fine and good people who act correctly win the prize.

Pleasure

Moreover, the life of these [active] people is also pleasant in itself. For being pleased is a condition of the soul, [hence included in the activity of the soul]. Further, each type of person finds pleasure in whatever he is called a lover of, so that a horse, e.g. pleases the horse-lover, a spectacle the lover of spectacles, and similarly what is just pleases the lover of justice, and in general what expresses virtue pleases the lover of virtue. Hence the things that please most people conflict, because they are not pleasant by nature, whereas the things that please lovers of what is fine are things pleasant by nature; and actions expressing virtue are pleasant in this way; and so they both please lovers of what is fine and are pleasant in themselves.

Hence their life does not need pleasure to be added [to virtuous activity] as some sort of ornament; rather, it has its

20

pleasure within itself. For besides the reasons already given, someone who does not enjoy fine actions is not good; for no one would call him just, e.g., if he did not enjoy doing just actions, or generous if he did not enjoy generous actions, and similarly for the other virtues. If this is so, then actions expressing the virtues are pleasant in themselves.

Hence our account satisfies traditional ideals

Moreover, these actions are good and fine as well as pleasant; indeed, they are good, fine and pleasant more than anything else, since on this question the excellent person has good judgement, and his judgement agrees with our conclusions.

Happiness, then, is best, finest and most pleasant, and these three features are not distinguished in the way suggested by the Delian inscription: 'What is most just is finest; being healthy is most beneficial; but it is most pleasant to win our heart's desire.' For all three features are found in the best activities, and happiness we say is these activities, or [rather] one of them, the best one.

External goods

Nonetheless, happiness evidently also needs external goods to be added [to the activity], as we said, since we cannot, or cannot easily, do fine actions if we lack the resources.

For, first of all, in many actions we use friends, wealth and political power just as we use instruments. Further, deprivation of certain [externals] – e.g. good birth, good children, beauty – mars our blessedness; for we do not altogether have the character of happiness if we look utterly repulsive or are ill-born, solitary or childless, and have it even less, presumably, if our children or friends are totally bad, or were good but have died.

And so, as we have said, happiness would seem to need this sort of prosperity added also; that is why some people

21

identify happiness with good fortune, while others [reacting from one extreme to the other] identify it with virtue.

1.8 The Place of Virtue and of External Goods in Happiness

1.81 How is happiness acquired?

i 9   This [question about the role of fortune] raises a puzzle: Is happiness acquired by learning, or habituation, or by some

10   other form of cultivation? Or is it the result of some divine fate, or even of fortune?

Is happiness a gift of the gods?

First, then, if the gods give any gift at all to human beings, it is reasonable for them to give happiness also; indeed, it is reasonable to give happiness more than any other human [good], in so far as it is the best of human [goods]. Presumably, however, this question is more suitable for a different inquiry.

Happiness is acquired by virtue, and hence by our own actions, not by fortune

15   But even if it is not sent by the gods, but instead results from virtue and some sort of learning or cultivation, happiness appears to be one of the most divine things, since the prize and goal of virtue appears to be the best good, something divine and blessed.

Moreover [if happiness comes in this way] it will be widely shared; for anyone who is not deformed [in his capacity] for virtue will be able to achieve happiness through some sort

20   of learning and attention.

And since it is better to be happy in this way than because of fortune, it is reasonable for this to be the way [we become] happy. For whatever is natural is naturally in the finest state possible, and so are the products of crafts and of every other

22

cause, especially the best cause; and it would be seriously
inappropriate to entrust what is greatest and finest to fortune.

The answer to our question is also evident from our ac-   25
count [of happiness]. For we have said it is a certain sort
of activity of the soul expressing virtue, [and hence not a
product of fortune]; and some of the other goods are necessary conditions [of happiness], others are naturally useful
and cooperative as instruments [but are not parts of it].

Further, this conclusion agrees with our opening remarks.
For we took the goal of political science to be the best good;   30
and most of its attention is devoted to the character of the
citizens, to make them good people who do fine actions,
[which is reasonable if happiness depends on virtue, not on
fortune].

It is not surprising, then, that we regard neither ox nor
horse nor any other kind of animal as happy, since none of
them can share in this sort of activity. And for the same   1100a
reason a child is not happy either, since his age prevents him
from doing these sorts of actions; and if he is called happy,
he is being congratulated because of anticipated blessedness,
since, as we have said, happiness requires both complete vir-
tue and a complete life.   5

But fortune still affects happiness

[Happiness needs a complete life.] For life includes many
reversals of fortune, good and bad, and the most prosperous
person may fall into a terrible disaster in old age, as the Trojan stories tell us about Priam; but if someone has suffered
these sorts of misfortunes and comes to a miserable end, no
one counts him happy.

1.82   Is it correct to call someone happy only
when he is dead?

Then should we count no human being happy during his   i 10
lifetime, but follow Solon's advice to wait to see the end?   10

23

And if we should hold that, can he really be happy during
the time after he has died? Surely that is completely absurd,
especially when we say happiness is an activity.

Is his happiness assured even then?

15   We do not say, then, that someone is happy during the
time he is dead, and Solon's point is not this [absurd one],
but rather that when a human being has died, we can safely
pronounce [that he was] blessed [before he died], on the assumption that he is now finally beyond evils and misfortunes.

Still, even this claim is disputable. For if a living person
20   has good or evil of which he is not aware, then a dead person also, it seems, has good or evil when, e.g., he receives
honours or dishonours, and his children, and descendants
in general, do well or suffer misfortune. [Hence, apparently,
what happens after his death can affect whether or not he
was happy before his death.]

However, this view also raises a puzzle. For even if someone has lived in blessedness until old age, and has died appropriately, many fluctuations of his descendants' fortunes
25   may still happen to him; for some may be good people and
get the life they deserve, while the contrary may be true of
others, and clearly they may be as distantly related to their
ancestor as you please. Surely, then, it would be an absurd
result if the dead person's condition changed along with the
fortunes of his descendants, so that at one time he became
happy [in his lifetime] and at another time miserable. But
30   it would also be absurd if the condition of descendants did
not affect their ancestors at all or for any length of time.

These puzzles reflect the belief that happiness
must be stable

But we must return to the previous puzzle, since that will
perhaps also show us the answer to our present question.

If, then, we must wait to see the end, and must then count

24

someone blessed, not as being blessed [during the time he is dead] but because he previously was blessed, surely it is absurd if at the time when he is happy we will not truly ascribe to him the happiness he has.   35

[We hesitate] out of reluctance to call him happy during   1100b
his lifetime, because of the variations, and because we suppose happiness is enduring and definitely not prone to fluctuate, whereas the same person's fortunes often turn to and
fro. For clearly, if we are guided by his fortunes, so that   5
we often call him happy and then miserable again, we will
be representing the happy person as a kind of chameleon,
insecurely based.

Virtue is a stable and controlling element
in happiness

But surely it is quite wrong to be guided by someone's fortunes. For his doing well or badly does not rest on them;
though a human life, as we said, needs these added, it is the
activities expressing virtue that control happiness, and the   10
contrary activities that control its contrary.

Indeed, the present puzzle is further evidence for our account [of happiness]. For no human achievement has the
stability of activities that express virtue, since these seem
to be more enduring even than our knowledge of the sciences;
and the most honourable of the virtues themselves are more   15
enduring [than the others] because blessed people devote their
lives to them more fully and more continually than to anything
else—for this [continual activity] would seem to be the reason
we do not forget them.

It follows, then, that the happy person has the [stability]
we are looking for and keeps the character he has throughout
his life. For always, or more than anything else, he will do
and study the actions expressing virtue, and will bear for-   20
tunes most finely, in every way and in all conditions appropriately, since he is truly 'good, foursquare and blameless'.

25

Still, the virtuous person can lose happiness
because of misfortune

However, many events are matters of fortune, and some
are smaller, some greater. Hence, while small strokes of good
25   or ill fortune clearly will not influence his life, many great
strokes of good fortune will make it more blessed, since in
themselves they naturally add adornment to it, and his use
of them proves to be fine and excellent. Conversely, if they
are great misfortunes, they oppress and spoil his blessedness,
30   since they involve pain and impede many activities.

And yet, even here what is fine shines through, whenever
someone bears many severe misfortunes with good temper,
not because he feels no distress, but because he is noble and
magnanimous.

And since it is activities that control life, as we said, no
blessed person could ever become miserable, since he will
35   never do hateful and base actions. For a truly good and
1101a   intelligent person, we suppose, will bear strokes of fortune
suitably, and from his resources at any time will do the finest actions, just as a good general will make the best use of
5   his forces in war, and a good shoemaker will produce the
finest shoe from the hides given him, and similarly for all
other craftsmen.

If this is so, then the happy person could never become
miserable. Still, he will not be blessed either, if he falls into
misfortunes as bad as Priam's. Nor, however, will he be in-
constant and prone to fluctuate, since he will neither be easily
10   shaken from his happiness nor shaken by just any misfortunes. He will be shaken from it, though, by many serious
misfortunes, and from these a return to happiness will take
no short time; at best, it will take a long and complete length
of time that includes great and fine successes.

This, then, is the partial truth in Solon's remark

Then why not say that the happy person is the one who

expresses complete virtue in his activities, with an adequate | 15
supply of external goods, not for just any time but for a complete life? Or should we add that he will also go on living
this way and will come to an appropriate end?

The future is not apparent to us, and we take happiness
to be the end, and altogether complete in every way; hence
we will say that a living person who has, and will keep, the | 20
goods we mentioned is blessed, but blessed as a human being is. So much for a determination of this question.

What happens after our deaths can affect the
happiness we had in our lives
Still, it is apparently rather unfriendly and contrary to the | i 11
[common] beliefs to claim that the fortunes of our descendants and all our friends contribute nothing. But since they
can find themselves in many and various circumstances, some
of which affect us more, some less, it is apparently a long, | 25
indeed endless, task to differentiate all the particular cases,
and perhaps a general outline will be enough of an answer.

Misfortunes, then, even to the person himself, differ, and
some have a certain weight and influence on his life, while
others would seem to be lighter. The same is true for the | 30
misfortunes of his friends; and it matters whether they happen to living or to dead people – much more than it matters
whether lawless and terrible crimes are committed before
a tragic drama begins or in the course of it. In our reasoning, then, we should also take account of this difference,
and even more, presumably, of the puzzle about whether | 35
the dead share in any good or evil. | 1101b

But neither gains nor losses are decisive for
the presence or absence of happiness
For if we consider this, anything good or evil penetrating
to the dead would seem to be weak and unimportant, either
unconditionally or for them; and even if it is not, still its

27

5 size and character are not enough to make people happy who are not happy, or to take away the blessedness of those who are happy. And so, when friends do well, and likewise when they do badly, it appears to contribute something to the dead, but of a character and size that neither makes happy people not happy nor anything else of this sort.

1.83   The insufficiency of virtue for happiness
is supported by other common beliefs, showing
i 12   *that happiness is honoured, not praised*
10   Now that we have determined these points, let us consider whether happiness is something praiseworthy, or instead something honourable; for clearly it is not a capacity [which is neither praiseworthy nor honourable].

Whatever is praiseworthy appears to be praised for its character and its state in relation to something. We praise, e.g., the just and the brave person, and in general the good person and virtue, for their actions and achievements; and
15 we praise the strong person, the good runner and each of the others because he naturally has a certain character and is in a certain state in relation to something good and excellent. This is clear also from praises of the gods; for these praises appear ridiculous because they are referred to us, but
20 they are referred to us because, as we said, praise depends on such a reference.

If praise is for these sorts of things, then clearly for the best things there is no praise, but something greater and better. And indeed this is how it appears. For the gods and the most godlike of men are [not praised, but] congratulated for
25 their blessedness and happiness. And the same is true of goods; for we never praise happiness, as we praise justice, but count it blessed, as something better and more godlike [than anything that is praised].

Indeed, Eudoxus seems to have used the correct argument for the victory of pleasure. By not praising pleasure though

28

it is a good, we indicate, so he thought, that it is superior
to everything praiseworthy; and [only] the god and the good   30
have this superiority since the other goods are [praised] by
reference to them.

[Here he seems to have argued correctly.] For praise is
given to virtue, since it makes us do fine actions; but celebrations are for [successful] achievements, either of body or of
soul. But an exact treatment of this is presumably more proper
for specialists in celebrations. For us, anyhow, it is clear   35
from what has been said that happiness is something hon-   1102a
ourable and complete.

*Our conclusions are supported by other claims
about happiness*
A further reason why this would seem to be correct is that
happiness is an origin; for the origin is what we all aim at
in all our other actions; and we take the origin and cause
of goods to be something honourable and divine.

1.9   Introduction to the Account of Virtue

*1.91   An account of happiness requires an
account of virtue*   i 13
Since happiness is an activity of the soul expressing com-   5
plete virtue, we must examine virtue; for that will perhaps
also be a way to study happiness better.

Moreover, the true politician seems to have spent more
effort on virtue than on anything else, since he wants to make
the citizens good and law-abiding. We find an example of   10
this in the Spartan and Cretan legislators and in any others
with their concerns. Since, then, the examination of virtue
is proper for political science, the inquiry clearly suits our
original decision [to pursue political science].

1.92   A discussion of virtue requires a
discussion of the soul

It is clear that the virtue we must examine is human virtue, since we are also seeking the human good and human
15 | happiness. And by human virtue we mean virtue of the soul,
not of the body, since we also say that happiness is an activity of the soul. If this is so, then it is clear that the politician must acquire some knowledge about the soul, just as
20 | someone setting out to heal the eyes must acquire knowledge
about the whole body as well. This is all the more true to
the extent that political science is better and more honourable
than medicine – and even among doctors the cultivated ones
devote a lot of effort to acquiring knowledge about the body.
Hence the politician as well [as the student of nature] must
study the soul.

But he must study it for the purpose [of inquiring into vir-
25 | tue], as far as suffices for what he seeks; for a more exact
treatment would presumably take more effort than his purpose requires. [We] have discussed the soul sufficiently [for
our purposes] in [our] popular works as well [as our less
popular], and we should use this discussion.

1.93   The rational and nonrational parts
of the soul

We have said, e.g., that one [part] of the soul is nonrational, while one has reason. Are these distinguished as parts
30 | of a body and everything divisible into parts are? Or are they
two only in account, and inseparable by nature, as the con-
vex and the concave are in a surface? It does not matter for
present purposes.

The nonrational part: (a) One part of it is
unresponsive to reason

Consider the nonrational [part]. One [part] of it, i.e. the
cause of nutrition and growth, is seemingly plant-like and

30

shared [with other living things]: for we can ascribe this capacity of the soul to everything that is nourished, including embryos, and the same one to complete living things, since this is more reasonable than to ascribe another capacity to them.

Hence the virtue of this capacity is apparently shared, not [specifically] human. For this part and capacity more than others seem to be active in sleep, and here the good and the bad person are least distinct, which is why happy people are said to be no better off than miserable people for half their lives.

And this lack of distinction is not surprising, since sleep is inactivity of the soul in so far as it is called excellent or base, unless to some small extent some movements penetrate [to our awareness], and in this way the decent person comes to have better images [in dreams] than just any random person has. Enough about this, however, and let us leave aside the nutritive part, since by nature it has no share in human virtue.

(b)   Another part is also nonrational

Another nature in the soul would also seem to be nonrational, though in a way it shares in reason.

[Clearly it is nonrational.] For in the continent and the incontinent person we praise their reason, i.e. the [part] of the soul that has reason, because it exhorts them correctly and towards what is best; but they evidently also have in them some other [part] that is by nature something besides reason, conflicting and struggling with reason.

For just as paralysed parts of a body, when we decide to move them to the right, do the contrary and move off to the left, the same is true of the soul; for incontinent people have impulses in contrary directions. In bodies, admittedly, we see the part go astray, whereas we do not see it in the soul; nonetheless, presumably, we should suppose that the soul

1102b

5

10

15

20

25 | also has a [part] besides reason, contrary to and countering reason. The [precise] way it is different does not matter.

But it is responsive to reason

However, this [part] as well [as the rational part] appears, as we said, to share in reason. At any rate, in the continent person it obeys reason; and in the temperate and the brave person it presumably listens still better to reason, since there it agrees with reason in everything.

Hence it differs both from the wholly
unresponsive part . . .

The nonrational [part], then, as well [as the whole soul] apparently has two parts. For while the plant-like [part] shares
30 | in reason not at all, the [part] with appetites and in general desires shares in reason in a way, in so far as it both listens to reason and obeys it.

It listens in the way in which we are said to 'listen to reason' from father or friends, not in the way in which we ['give the reason'] in mathematics.

The nonrational part also [obeys and] is persuaded in some way by reason, as is shown by chastening, and by every sort
1103a | of reproof and exhortation.

And from the wholly rational part

If we ought to say, then, that this [part] also has reason, then the [part] that has reason, as well [as the nonrational part] will have two parts, one that has reason to the full extent by having it within itself, and another [that has it] by listening to reason as to a father.

1.94 The division of the virtues corresponds
to the parts of the soul

The distinction between virtues also reflects this difference.
5 | For some virtues are called virtues of thought, other virtues

32

of character; wisdom, comprehension and intelligence are called virtues of thought, generosity and temperance virtues of character.

For when we speak of someone's character we do not say that he is wise or has good comprehension, but that he is gentle or temperate. [Hence these are the virtues of character.] And yet, we also praise the wise person for his state, and the states that are praiseworthy are the ones we call virtues. [Hence wisdom is also a virtue.]   10

2.   Virtues of Character in General

2.1   How a Virtue of Character is Acquired

Virtue, then, is of two sorts, virtue of thought and virtue   ii 1
of character. Virtue of thought arises and grows mostly from   15
teaching, and hence needs experience and time. Virtue of character [i.e. of *ēthos*] results from habit [*ethos*]; hence its name 'ethical', slightly varied from '*ethos*'.

Virtue comes about, not by a process of nature,
but by habituation

Hence it is also clear that none of the virtues of character arises in us naturally.

(1)   What is natural cannot be changed
by habituation

For if something is by nature [in one condition], habitua-   20
tion cannot bring it into another condition. A stone, e.g., by nature moves downwards, and habituation could not make it move upwards, not even if you threw it up ten thousand times to habituate it; nor could habituation make fire move downwards, or bring anything that is by nature in one condition into another condition.

Thus the virtues arise in us neither by nature nor against

33

25   nature. Rather, we are by nature able to acquire them, and reach
      our complete perfection through habit.

*(2)   Natural capacities are not acquired
by habituation*
      Further, if something arises in us by nature, we first have
      the capacity for it, and later display the activity. This is clear
      in the case of the senses; for we did not acquire them by
30   frequent seeing or hearing, but already had them when we
      exercised them, and did not get them by exercising them.
      Virtues, by contrast, we acquire, just as we acquire crafts,
      by having previously activated them. For we learn a craft
      by producing the same product that we must produce when
      we have learned it, becoming builders, e.g., by building and
      harpists by playing the harp; so also, then, we become just
1103b by doing just actions, temperate by doing temperate actions,
      brave by doing brave actions.

(3)   Legislators concentrate on habituation
      What goes on in cities is evidence for this also. For the
      legislator makes the citizens good by habituating them, and
5   this is the wish of every legislator; if he fails to do it well
      he misses his goal. [The right] habituation is what makes
      the difference between a good political system and a bad one.

*(4)   Virtue and vice are formed by good and
bad actions*
      Further, just as in the case of a craft, the sources and means
      that develop each virtue also ruin it. For playing the harp
      makes both good and bad harpists, and it is analogous in the
10   case of builders and all the rest; for building well makes good
      builders, building badly, bad ones. If it were not so, no
      teacher would be needed, but everyone would be born a good
      or a bad craftsman.
      It is the same, then, with the virtues. For actions in deal-

34

ings with [other] human beings make some people just, | 15
some unjust; actions in terrifying situations and the acquired
habit of fear or confidence make some brave and others cowardly. The same is true of situations involving appetites and
anger; for one or another sort of conduct in these situations
makes some people temperate and gentle, others intemperate | 20
and irascible.

Conclusion: The importance of habituation

To sum up, then, in a single account: A state [of character]
arises from [the repetition of] similar activities. Hence we
must display the right activities, since differences in these imply corresponding differences in the states. It is not unimportant, then, to acquire one sort of habit or another, right from
our youth; rather, it is very important, indeed all-important. | 25

2.12   What is the right sort of habituation?

*This is an appropriate question, for the aim of
ethical theory is practical*

Our present inquiry does not aim, as our others do, at | ii 2
study; for the purpose of our examination is not to know
what virtue is, but to become good, since otherwise the in-
quiry would be of no benefit to us. Hence we must examine | 30
the right way to act, since, as we have said, the actions also
control the character of the states we acquire.

First, then, actions should express correct reason. That is a
common [belief], and let us assume it; later we will say what
correct reason is and how it is related to the other virtues.

But let us take it as agreed in advance that every account | 1104a
of the actions we must do has to be stated in outline, not
exactly. As we also said at the start, the type of accounts
we demand should reflect the subject-matter; and questions
about actions and expediency, like questions about health,
have no fixed [and invariable answers].

5   And when our general account is so inexact, the account
of particular cases is all the more inexact. For these fall under
no craft or profession, and the agents themselves must consider in each case what the opportune action is, as doctors
and navigators do.

10   The account we offer, then, in our present inquiry is of
this inexact sort; still, we must try to offer help.

The right sort of habituation must avoid excess
and deficiency

First, then, we should observe that these sorts of states
naturally tend to be ruined by excess and deficiency. We see
this happen with strength and health, which we mention because we must use what is evident as a witness to what is

15   not. For both excessive and deficient exercises ruin strength;
and likewise, too much or too little eating or drinking ruins
health, while the proportionate amount produces, increases
and preserves it.

The same is true, then, of temperance, bravery and the

20   other virtues. For if, e.g., someone avoids and is afraid of
everything, standing firm against nothing, he becomes cowardly, but if he is afraid of nothing at all and goes to face
everything, he becomes rash. Similarly, if he gratifies himself
with every pleasure and refrains from none, he becomes intemperate, but if he avoids them all, as boors do, he becomes

25   some sort of insensible person. Temperance and bravery,
then, are ruined by excess and deficiency but preserved by
the mean.

The same actions, then, are the sources and causes both of
the emergence and growth of virtues and of their ruin; but
further, the activities of the virtues will be found in these

30   same actions. For this is also true of more evident cases,
e.g. strength, which arises from eating a lot and from with-
standing much hard labour, and it is the strong person who
is most able to do these very things. It is the same with the

virtues. Refraining from pleasures make us become temper-
ate, and when we have become temperate we are most able | 35
to refrain from pleasures. And it is similar with bravery; | 1104b
habituation in disdaining what is fearful and in standing firm
against it makes us become brave, and when we have become
brave we shall be most able to stand firm.

2.13   Pleasure and pain are important
in habituation

But [actions are not enough]; we must take as a sign of | ii 3
someone's state his pleasure or pain in consequence of his
action. For if someone who abstains from bodily pleasures | 5
enjoys the abstinence itself, then he is temperate, but if he
is grieved by it, he is intemperate. Again, if he stands firm
against terrifying situations and enjoys it, or at least does
not find it painful, then he is brave, and if he finds it painful, he is cowardly.

[Pleasures and pains are appropriately taken as signs] because virtue of character is concerned with pleasures and
pains.

Virtue is concerned with pleasure and pain

(1) For it is pleasure that causes us to do base actions, | 10
and pain that causes us to abstain from fine ones. Hence we
need to have had the appropriate upbringing—right from early
youth, as Plato says—to make us find enjoyment or pain in
the right things; for this is the correct education.

(2) Further, virtues are concerned with actions and feelings; but every feeling and every action implies pleasure or
pain; hence, for this reason too, virtue is concerned with | 15
pleasures and pains.

(3) Corrective treatment [for vicious actions] also indicates
[the relevance of pleasure and pain], since it uses pleasures
and pains; it uses them because such correction is a form

of medical treatment, and medical treatment naturally operates through contraries.

(4) Further, as we said earlier, every state of soul is naturally related to and concerned with whatever naturally makes it better or worse; and pleasures and pains make people worse, from pursuing and avoiding the wrong ones, at the wrong time, in the wrong ways, or whatever other distinctions of that sort are needed in an account.

These [bad effects of pleasure and pain] are the reason why people actually define the virtues as ways of being unaffected and undisturbed [by pleasures and pains]. They are wrong, however, because they speak [of being unaffected] unconditionally, not of being unaffected in the right or wrong way, at the right or wrong time, and the added specifications.

We assume, then, that virtue is the sort of state [with the appropriate specifications] that does the best actions concerned with pleasures and pains, and that vice is the contrary. The following points will also make it evident that virtue and vice are concerned with the same things.

(5) There are three objects of choice — fine, expedient and pleasant — and three objects of avoidance — their contraries, shameful, harmful and painful. About all these, then, the good person is correct and the bad person is in error, and especially about pleasure. For pleasure is shared with animals, and implied by every object of choice, since what is fine and what is expedient appear pleasant as well.

(6) Further, since pleasure grows up with all of us from infancy on, it is hard to rub out this feeling that is dyed into our lives; and we estimate actions as well [as feelings], some of us more, some less, by pleasure and pain. Hence, our whole inquiry must be about these, since good or bad enjoyment or pain is very important for our actions.

(7) Moreover, it is harder to fight pleasure than to fight emotion, [though that is hard enough], as Heracleitus says. Now both craft and virtue are concerned in every case with

38

what is harder, since a good result is even better when it | 10
is harder. Hence, for this reason also, the whole inquiry,
for virtue and political science alike, must consider pleasures
and pains; for if we use these well, we shall be good, and
if badly, bad.

In short, virtue is concerned with pleasures and pains; the
actions that are its sources also increase it or, if they are done | 15
differently, ruin it; and its activity is concerned with the same
actions that are its sources.

2.14 But our claims about habituation raise a
puzzle: How can we become good without
being good already?

However, someone might raise this puzzle: 'What do you | ii 4
mean by saying that to become just we must first do just actions and to become temperate we must first do temperate
actions? For if we do what is grammatical or musical, we
must already be grammarians or musicians. In the same way, | 20
then, if we do what is just or temperate, we must already
be just or temperate.'

First reply: Conformity versus understanding

But surely this is not so even with the crafts, for it is possible to produce something grammatical by chance or by following someone else's instructions. To be a grammarian,
then, we must both produce something grammatical and pro-
duce it in the way in which the grammarian produces it, i.e. | 25
expressing grammatical knowledge that is in us.

Second Reply: Crafts versus virtues

Moreover, in any case what is true of crafts is not true
of virtues. For the products of a craft determine by their own
character whether they have been produced well; and so it
suffices that they are in the right state when they have been
produced. But for actions expressing virtue to be done tem-

39

perately or justly [and hence well] it does not suffice that
30 | they are themselves in the right state. Rather, the agent must
also be in the right state when he does them. First, he must
know [that he is doing virtuous actions]; second, he must
decide on them, and decide on them for themselves; and,
third, he must also do them from a firm and unchanging
state.

1105b | As conditions for having a craft these three do not count,
except for the knowing itself. As a condition for having a
virtue, however, the knowing counts for nothing, or [rather]
for only a little, whereas the other two conditions are very
important, indeed all-important. And these other two condi-
5 | tions are achieved by the frequent doing of just and temperate
actions.

Hence actions are called just or temperate when they are
the sort that a just or temperate person would do. But the
just and temperate person is not the one who [merely] does
these actions, but the one who also does them in the way
in which just or temperate people do them.

10 | It is right, then, to say that a person comes to be just from
doing just actions and temperate from doing temperate actions; for no one has even a prospect of becoming good from
failing to do them.

*Virtue requires habituation, and therefore
requires practice, not just theory*

The many, however, do not do these actions but take refuge
in arguments, thinking that they are doing philosophy, and
that this is the way to become excellent people. In this they
15 | are like a sick person who listens attentively to the doctor,
but acts on none of his instructions. Such a course of treatment will not improve the state of his body; any more than
will the many's way of doing philosophy improve the state
of their souls.

2.2 A Virtue of Character is a State Intermediate between Two Extremes, and Involving Decision

2.21 The genus

Feelings, capacities, states

   Next we must examine what virtue is. Since there are three | ii 5
conditions arising in the soul – feelings, capacities and states – | 20
virtue must be one of these.

   By feelings I mean appetite, anger, fear, confidence, envy, joy, love, hate, longing, jealousy, pity, in general whatever implies pleasure or pain.

   By capacities I mean what we have when we are said to be capable of these feelings – capable of, e.g., being angry | 25
or afraid or feeling pity.

   By states I mean what we have when we are well or badly off in relation to feelings. If, e.g., our feeling is too intense or slack, we are badly off in relation to anger, but if it is intermediate, we are well off; and the same is true in the other cases.

Virtue is not a feeling . . .

   First, then, neither virtues nor vices are feelings. (a) For we are called excellent or base in so far as we have virtues | 30
or vices, not in so far as we have feelings. (b) We are neither praised nor blamed in so far as we have feelings; for we do not praise the angry or the frightened person, and do not blame the person who is simply angry, but only the person | 1106a
who is angry in a particular way. But we are praised or blamed in so far as we have virtues or vices. (c) We are angry and afraid without decision; but the virtues are decisions of some kind, or [rather] require decision. (d) Besides, in so far as we have feelings, we are said to be moved; but in so | 5
far as we have virtues or vices, we are said to be in some condition rather than moved.

Or a capacity . . .

For these reasons the virtues are not capacities either; for we are neither called good nor called bad in so far as we are simply capable of feelings. Further, while we have capacities by nature, we do not become good or bad by nature; we have discussed this before.

But a state

If, then, the virtues are neither feelings nor capacities, the remaining possibility is that they are states. And so we have said what the genus of virtue is.

2.22 The differentia

But we must say not only, as we already have, that it is a state, but also what sort of state it is.

Virtue and the human function

It should be said, then, that every virtue causes its possessors to be in a good state and to perform their functions well; the virtue of eyes, e.g., makes the eyes and their functioning excellent, because it makes us see well; and similarly, the virtue of a horse makes the horse excellent, and thereby good at galloping, at carrying its rider and at standing steady in the face of the enemy. If this is true in every case, then the virtue of a human being will likewise be the state that makes a human being good and makes him perform his function well.

We have already said how this will be true, and it will also be evident from our next remarks, if we consider the sort of nature that virtue has.

The numerical mean and the mean relative to us

In everything continuous and divisible we can take more, less and equal, and each of them either in the object itself or relative to us; and the equal is some intermediate between excess and deficiency.

By the intermediate in the object I mean what is equidistant from each extremity; this is one and the same for everyone. But relative to us the intermediate is what is neither superfluous nor deficient; this is not one, and is not the same for everyone.

If, e.g., ten are many and two are few, we take six as intermediate in the object, since it exceeds [two] and is exceeded [by ten] by an equal amount, [four]; this is what is intermediate by numerical proportion. But that is not how we must take the intermediate that is relative to us. For if, e.g., ten pounds [of food] are a lot for someone to eat, and two pounds a little, it does not follow that the trainer will prescribe six, since this might also be either a little or a lot for the person who is to take it—for Milo [the athlete] a little, but for the beginner in gymnastics a lot; and the same is true for running and wrestling. In this way every scientific expert avoids excess and deficiency and seeks and chooses what is intermediate—but intermediate relative to us, not in the object.

Virtue seeks the mean relative to us: Argument
from craft to virtue

This, then, is how each science produces its product well, by focusing on what is intermediate and making the product conform to that. This, indeed, is why people regularly comment on well-made products that nothing could be added or subtracted, since they assume that excess or deficiency ruins a good [result] while the mean preserves it. Good craftsmen also, we say, focus on what is intermediate when they produce their product. And since virtue, like nature, is better and more exact than any craft, it will also aim at what is intermediate.

43

Arguments from the nature of virtue of character

By virtue I mean virtue of character; for this [pursues the mean because] it is concerned with feelings and actions, and these admit of excess, deficiency and an intermediate condition. We can be afraid, e.g., or be confident, or have appetites, or get angry, or feel pity, in general have pleasure or pain, both too much and too little, and in both ways not well; but [having these feelings] at the right times, about the right things, towards the right people, for the right end, and in the right way, is the intermediate and best condition, and this is proper to virtue. Similarly, actions also admit of excess, deficiency and the intermediate condition.

Now virtue is concerned with feelings and actions, in which excess and deficiency are in error and incur blame, while the intermediate condition is correct and wins praise, which are both proper features of virtue. Virtue, then, is a mean, in so far as it aims at what is intermediate.

Moreover, there are many ways to be in error, since badness is proper to what is unlimited, as the Pythagoreans pictured it, and good to what is limited; but there is only one way to be correct. That is why error is easy and correctness hard, since it is easy to miss the target and hard to hit it. And so for this reason also excess and deficiency are proper to vice, the mean to virtue; 'for we are noble in only one way, but bad in all sorts of ways.'

2.23 Definition of virtue

Virtue, then, is (a) a state that decides, (b) [consisting] in a mean, (c) the mean relative to us, (d) which is defined by reference to reason, (e) i.e., to the reason by reference to which the intelligent person would define it. It is a mean between two vices, one of excess and one of deficiency.

It is a mean for this reason also: Some vices miss what is right because they are deficient, others because they are

excessive, in feelings or in actions, while virtue finds and | 5
chooses what is intermediate.

Hence, as far as its substance and the account stating its
essence are concerned, virtue is a mean; but as far as the
best [condition] and the good [result] are concerned, it is an
extremity.

The definition must not be misapplied to cases
in which there is no mean   "linguistic term for an"

But not every (action or feeling) admits of the mean. For
the names of some automatically include baseness, e.g. spite, | 10
shamelessness, envy [among feelings], and adultery, theft,
murder, among actions. All of these and similar things are
called by these names because they themselves, not their excesses or deficiencies, are base.

Hence in doing these things we can never be correct, but
must invariably be in error. We cannot do them well or not | 15
well—e.g. by committing adultery with the right woman at
the right time in the right way; on the contrary, it is true
unconditionally that to do any of them is to be in error.

[To think these admit of a mean], therefore, is like thinking that unjust or cowardly or intemperate action also ad-
mits of a mean, an excess and a deficiency. For then there | 20
would be a mean of excess, a mean of deficiency, an excess
of excess and a deficiency of deficiency.

Rather, just as there is no excess or deficiency of
temperance or of bravery, since the intermediate is a sort
of extreme [in achieving the good], so also there is no mean,
and no excess or deficiency, of these [vicious actions] either,
but whatever way anyone does them, he is in error. For in | 25
general there is no mean of excess or of deficiency, and no
excess or deficiency of a mean.

2.3   The Definition of Virtue as a Mean
Applies to the Individual Virtues

ii 7   However, we must not only state this general account but
also apply it to the particular cases. For among accounts
30   concerning actions, though the general ones are common to
more cases, the specific ones are truer, since actions are about
particular cases, and our account must accord with these.
Let us, then, find these from the chart.

2.31   Classification of virtues of character

Virtues concerned with feelings

(1) First, in feelings of fear and confidence the mean is
1107b   bravery. The excessively fearless person is nameless (and
in fact many cases are nameless), while the one who is excessively confident is rash; the one who is excessively afraid
and deficient in confidence is cowardly.
5   (2) In pleasures and pains, though not in all types, and in
pains less than in pleasures, the mean is temperance and the
excess intemperance. People deficient in pleasure are not
often found, which is why they also lack even a name; let
us call them insensible.

Virtues concerned with external goods

(3) In giving and taking money the mean is generosity,
10   the excess wastefulness and the deficiency ungenerosity. Here
the vicious people have contrary excesses and defects; for
the wasteful person spends to excess and is deficient in taking, whereas the ungenerous person takes to excess and is
deficient in spending. At the moment we are speaking in
15   outline and summary, and that suffices; later we shall define
these things more exactly.
(4) In questions of money there are also other conditions.
Another mean is magnificence; for the magnificent person
differs from the generous by being concerned with large mat-

ters, while the generous person is concerned with small. The
excess is ostentation and vulgarity, and the deficiency nig-   20
gardliness, and these differ from the vices related to generosity in ways we shall describe later.

(5) In honour and dishonour the mean is magnanimity,
the excess something called a sort of vanity, and the deficiency pusillanimity.

(6) And just as we said that generosity differs from mag-   25
nificence in its concern with small matters, similarly there
is a virtue concerned with small honours, differing in the
same way from magnanimity, which is concerned with great
honours. For honour can be desired either in the right way
or more or less than is right. If someone desires it to excess,
he is called an honour-lover, and if his desire is deficient
he is called indifferent to honour, but if he is intermediate   30
he has no name. The corresponding conditions have no name
either, except the condition of the honour-lover, which is
called honour-loving.

This is why people at the extremes claim the intermediate
area. Indeed, we also sometimes call the intermediate person an honour-lover, and sometimes call him indifferent to
honour; and sometimes we praise the honour-lover, some-   1108a
times the person indifferent to honour. We will mention later
the reason we do this; for the moment, let us speak of the
other cases in the way we have laid down.

Virtues concerned with social life

(7) Anger also admits of an excess, deficiency and mean.   5
These are all practically nameless; but since we call the intermediate person mild, let us call the mean mildness. Among
the extreme people let the excessive person be irascible, and
the vice be irascibility, and let the deficient person be a sort
of inirascible person, and the deficiency be inirascibility.

There are three other means, somewhat similar to one   10
another, but different. For they are all concerned with asso-

ciation in conversations and actions, but differ in so far as
one is concerned with truth-telling in these areas, the other
two with sources of pleasure, some of which are found in
amusement, and the others in daily life in general. Hence
we should also discuss these states, so that we can better
observe that in every case the mean is praiseworthy, while
the extremes are neither praiseworthy nor correct, but blameworthy. Most of these cases are also nameless, and we must
try, as in the other cases also, to make names ourselves, to
make things clear and easy to follow.

(8) In truth-telling, then, let us call the intermediate person truthful, and the mean truthfulness; pretence that over-
states will be boastfulness, and the person who has it boastful;
pretence that understates will be self-deprecation, and the
person who has it self-deprecating.

(9) In sources of pleasure in amusements let us call the
intermediate person witty, and the condition wit; the excess
buffoonery and the person who has it a buffoon; and the deficient person a sort of boor and the state boorishness.

(10) In the other sources of pleasure, those in daily life,
let us call the person who is pleasant in the right way friendly,
and the mean state friendliness. If someone goes to excess
with no [further] aim he will be ingratiating; if he does it
for his own advantage, a flatterer. The deficient person,
unpleasant in everything, will be a sort of quarrelsome and
ill-tempered person.

Mean states that are not virtues
(11) There are also means in feelings and concerned with
feelings: shame, e.g., is not a virtue, but the person prone
to shame as well as the virtuous person we have described
receives praise. For here also one person is called intermediate, and another — the person excessively prone to shame,
who is ashamed about everything — is called excessive; the
person who is deficient in shame or never feels shame at all

48

is said to have no sense of disgrace; and the intermediate
one is called prone to shame.

(12) Proper indignation is the mean between envy and spite;
these conditions are concerned with pleasure and pain at what
happens to our neighbours. For the properly indignant person feels pain when someone does well undeservedly; the
envious person exceeds him by feeling pain when anyone   5
does well, while the spiteful person is so deficient in feeling
pain that he actually enjoys [other people's misfortunes].

There will also be an opportunity elsewhere to speak of
these [means that are not virtues].

Justice

We must consider justice after these other conditions, and,
because it is not spoken of in one way only, we shall distinguish its two types and say how each of them is a mean.

Similarly, we must consider the virtues that belong to   10
reason.

2.32   *The relations between means and extremes*

The mean is opposed to each extreme

Among these three conditions, then, two are vices — one   ii 8
of excess, one of deficiency — and one — the mean — is virtue.
In a way each of them is opposed to each of the others, since
each extreme is contrary both to the intermediate condition
and to the other extreme, while the intermediate is contrary
to the extremes. For as the equal is greater in comparison   15
to the smaller, and smaller in comparison to the greater, so
also the intermediate states are excessive in comparison to
the deficiencies and deficient in comparison to the excesses —
both in feelings and in actions.

For the brave person, e.g., appears rash in comparison   20
to the coward, and cowardly in comparison to the rash person; similarly, the temperate person appears intemperate in

comparison to the insensible person, and insensible in comparison with the intemperate person, and the generous person appears wasteful in comparison to the ungenerous, and ungenerous in comparison to the wasteful person. That is why each of the extreme people tries to push the intermediate

25 person to the other extreme, so that the coward, e.g., calls the brave person rash, and the rash person calls him a coward, and similarly in the other cases.

*Extremes are more opposed to each other than
to the mean*

Because these conditions of soul are opposed to each other in these ways, the extremes are more contrary to each other than to the intermediate. For they are further from each other than from the intermediate, just as the large is further from

30 the small, and the small from the large, than either is from the equal.

Moreover, sometimes one extreme, e.g. rashness or wastefulness, appears somewhat like the intermediate state, e.g. bravery or generosity; but the extremes are most unlike one another; and the things that are furthest apart from each other

35 are defined as contraries. Hence also the things that are further apart are more contrary.

*Sometimes one extreme is more opposed than
the other to the mean*

1109a   In some cases the deficiency, in others the excess, is more opposed to the intermediate condition; e.g. it is cowardice, the deficiency, not rashness, the excess, that is more opposed to bravery; on the other hand, it is intemperance, the excess, not insensibility, the deficiency, that is more opposed

5 to temperance. This happens for two reasons.

One reason is derived from the object itself. Since sometimes one extreme is closer and more similar to the intermediate condition, we oppose the contrary extreme, more

than this closer one, to the intermediate condition. Since rashness, e.g., seems to be closer and more similar to bravery,
and cowardice less similar, we oppose cowardice more than
rashness to bravery; for what is further from the intermediate
condition seems to be more contrary to it. This, then, is one
reason, derived from the object itself. | 10

The other reason is derived from ourselves. For when we
ourselves have some natural tendency to one extreme more
than the other, this extreme appears more opposed to the intermediate condition; since, e.g., we have more of a natural
tendency to pleasure, we drift more easily towards intemper- | 15
ance than towards orderliness. Hence we say that an extreme
is more contrary if we naturally develop more in that direction; and this is why intemperance is more contrary to temperance, since it is the excess.

2.33 Practical advice on ways to achieve
the mean | ii 9

We have said enough, then, to show that virtue of char- | 20
acter is a mean and what sort of mean it is; that it is a mean
between two vices, one of excess and one of deficiency; and
that it is a mean because it aims at the intermediate condition in feelings and actions.

Hence it is hard work to be excellent, since in each case
it is hard work to find what is intermediate; e.g. not everyone, | 25
but only one who knows, finds the midpoint in a circle. So
also getting angry, or giving and spending money, is easy
and anyone can do it; but doing it to the right person, in the
right amount, at the right time, for the right end, and in the
right way is no longer easy, nor can everyone do it. Hence
[doing these things] well is rare, praiseworthy and fine. | 30

Avoid the more opposed extreme

Hence if we aim at the intermediate condition we must first
of all steer clear of the more contrary extreme, following

51

the advice that Calypso also gives—'Hold the ship outside the spray and surge.' For since one extreme is more in error, the other less, and since it is hard to hit the intermediate extremely accurately, the second-best tack, as they say, is
35   to take the lesser of the evils. We shall succeed best in this
1109b   by the method we describe.

Avoid the easier extreme

We must also examine what we ourselves drift into easily. For different people have different natural tendencies towards different goals, and we shall come to know our own tenden-
5   cies from the pleasure or pain that arises in us. We must drag ourselves off in the contrary direction; for if we pull far away from error, as they do in straightening bent wood, we shall reach the intermediate condition.

Be careful with pleasures

And in everything we must beware above all of pleasure and its sources; for we are already biased in its favour when we come to judge it. Hence we must react to it as the elders
10   reacted to Helen, and on each occasion repeat what they said; for if we do this, and send it off, we shall be less in error.

*These rules do not give exact and
detailed guidance*

In summary, then, if we do these things we shall best be able to reach the intermediate condition. But no doubt this is hard, especially in particular cases, since it is not easy to
15   define the way we should be angry, with whom, about what, for how long; for sometimes, indeed, we ourselves praise deficient people and call them mild, and sometimes praise quarrelsome people and call them manly. Still, we are not blamed if we deviate a little in excess or deficiency from
20   doing well, but only if we deviate a long way, since then we are easily noticed.

52

But how far and how much we must deviate to be blamed
is not easy to define in an account; for nothing perceptible
is easily defined, and [since] these [circumstances of virtuous
and vicious action] are particulars, the judgement about them
depends on perception. (*judgement*)

All this makes it clear, then, that in every case the in-
termediate state is praised, but we must sometimes incline | 25
towards the excess, sometimes towards the deficiency; for
that is the easiest way to succeed in hitting the intermediate
condition and [doing] well.

3.   The Preconditions of Virtue

3.1   Voluntary Action

3.11   Praise and blame require voluntary action | iii 1

Virtue, then, is about feelings and actions. These receive | 30
praise or blame when they are voluntary, but pardon, sometimes even pity, when they are involuntary. Hence, presumably, in examining virtue we must define the voluntary and
the involuntary. This is also useful to legislators, both for
honours and for corrective treatments. | 35

3.12   Force makes an action involuntary

What comes about by force or because of ignorance seems | 1110a
to be involuntary. What is forced has an external origin, the
sort of origin in which the agent or victim contributes nothing—if, e.g., a wind or human beings who control him were
to carry him off.

3.13   Duress does not make an action involuntary

Actions under duress sometimes seem forced,
sometimes not

But now consider actions done because of fear of greater

5 evils, or because of something fine. Suppose, e.g., a tyrant tells you to do something shameful, when he has control over your parents and children, and if you do it, they will live, but if not, they will die. These cases raise dispute about whether they are voluntary or involuntary.

However, the same sort of thing also happens with throw-
10 ing cargo overboard in storms; for no one willingly throws cargo overboard, unconditionally, but anyone with any sense throws it overboard [under some conditions] to save him-self and the others.

Such an action is a mixture of voluntary and
involuntary, but, taken as a whole, it is voluntary

These sorts of actions, then, are mixed. But they would seem to be more like voluntary actions. For at the time they are done they are choiceworthy, and the goal of an action reflects the occasion; hence also we should call the action voluntary or involuntary with reference to the time when he
15 does it. Now in fact he does it willingly; for in these sorts of actions he has within him the origin of the movement of the limbs that are the instruments [of the action], and when the origin of the actions is in him, it is also up to him to do them or not to do them. Hence actions of this sort are voluntary, though presumably the actions without [the ap-propriate] condition are involuntary, since no one would choose any action of this sort in itself.

Praise and blame for mixed actions assumes
they are voluntary

20 For such [mixed] actions people are sometimes actually praised, whenever they endure something shameful or pain-ful as the price of great and fine results; and if they do the reverse, they are blamed, since it is a base person who en-dures what is most shameful for nothing fine or for only some moderately fine result.

In some cases there is no praise, but there is pardon, whenever someone does a wrong action because of conditions of a sort that overstrain human nature, and that no one would endure. But presumably there are some things we cannot be compelled to do, and rather than do them we should suffer the most terrible consequences and accept death; for the things that [allegedly] compelled Euripides' Alcmaeon to kill his mother appear ridiculous. 25

It is sometimes hard, however, to judge what [goods] should be chosen at the price of what [evils], and what [evils] should be endured as the price of what [goods]. And it is even harder to abide by our judgment, since the results we expect [when we endure] are usually painful, and the actions we are compelled [to endure, when we choose] are usually shameful. That is why those who have been compelled or not compelled receive praise and blame. 30

1110b

Hence actions under duress are not forced, and our definition of force is not undermined

What sorts of things, then, should we say are forced? Perhaps we should say that something is forced unconditionally whenever its cause is external and the agent contributes nothing. Other things are involuntary in themselves, but choiceworthy on this occasion and as the price of these [goods], and their origin is in the agent. These are involuntary in themselves, but, on this occasion and as the price of these [goods], voluntary. Still, they would seem to be more like voluntary actions, since actions involve particular [conditions], and [in mixed actions] these [conditions] are voluntary. But what sort of thing should be chosen as the price of what [good] is not easy to answer, since there are many differences in particular [conditions]. 5

3.14   What is pleasant or fine does not make
an action involuntary

But suppose someone says that pleasant things and fine
10   things force us, since they are outside us and compel us. It
will follow that for him everything is forced, since everyone
in every action aims at something fine or pleasant.

Moreover, if we are forced and unwilling to act, we find
it painful; but if something pleasant or fine is its cause, we
do it with pleasure.

It is ridiculous, then, for [our opponent] to ascribe responsibility to external [causes] and not to himself, when he is
15   easily snared by such things; and ridiculous to take responsibility for fine actions himself, but to hold pleasant things
responsible for his shameful actions.

What is forced, then, would seem to be what has its origin
outside the person forced, who contributes nothing.

3.15   Ignorance without regret does not make
an action involuntary

Everything caused by ignorance is non-voluntary, but what
is involuntary also causes pain and regret. For if someone's
20   action was caused by ignorance, but he now has no objection to the action, he has done it neither willingly, since he
did not know what it was, nor unwillingly, since he now feels
no pain. Hence, among those who act because of ignorance,
the agent who now regrets his action seems to be unwilling,
while the agent with no regrets may be called non-willing,
since he is another case — for since he is different, it is better
if he has his own special name.

3.16   Action done in ignorance but not caused
by ignorance is not necessarily involuntary

25   Further, action caused by ignorance would seem to be different from action done in ignorance. For if the agent is
drunk or angry, his action seems to be caused by drunken-

ness or anger, not by ignorance, though it is done in ignorance, not in knowledge.

[This ignorance does not make an action involuntary.] Certainly every vicious person is ignorant of the actions he must
do or avoid, and this sort of error makes people unjust, and
in general bad. But talk of involuntary action is not meant | 30
to apply to [this] ignorance of what is beneficial.

3.17 Ignorance of particulars makes an action involuntary

For the cause of involuntary action is not [this] ignorance
in the decision, which causes vice; it is not [in other words]
ignorance of the universal, since that is a cause for blame.
Rather, the cause is ignorance of the particulars which the | 1111a
action consists in and is concerned with; for these allow both
pity and pardon, since an agent acts involuntarily if he is
ignorant of one of these particulars.

The varieties of ignorance of particulars

Presumably, then, it is not a bad idea to define these particulars, and say what they are, and how many. They are:
(1) who is doing it; (2) what he is doing; (3) about what or
to what he is doing it; (4) sometimes also what he is doing | 5
it with, e.g. the instrument; (5) for what result, e.g. safety;
(6) in what way, e.g. gently or hard.

Now certainly someone could not be ignorant of *all* of these
unless he were mad. Nor, clearly, (1) could he be ignorant
of who is doing it, since he could hardly be ignorant of
himself. But (2) he might be ignorant of what he is doing,
as when someone says that [the secret] slipped out while he
was speaking, or, as Aeschylus said about the mysteries, that
he did not know it was forbidden to reveal it; or, like the
person with the catapult, that he let it go when he [only] | 10
wanted to demonstrate it. (3) Again, he might think that his
son is an enemy, as Merope did; or (4) that the barbed spear

has a button on it, or that the stone is pumice-stone. (5) By giving someone a drink to save his life we might kill him; (6) and wanting to touch someone, as they do in sparring, we might wound him.

There is ignorance about all of these [particulars] that the action consists in. Hence someone who was ignorant of one of these seems to have done an action unwillingly, especially when he was ignorant of the most important of them; these seem to be (2) what he is doing, and (5) the result for which he does it.

Hence it is action called involuntary with reference to *this* sort of ignorance [that we meant when we said that] the agent must, in addition, feel pain and regret for his action.

3.18   The definition of voluntary action

Since, then, what is involuntary is what is forced or is caused by ignorance, what is voluntary seems to be what has its origin in the agent himself when he knows the particulars that the action consists in.

3.19   Reply to an objection

[Our definition is sound.] For, presumably, it is not correct to say that action caused by emotion or appetite is involuntary.

For, first of all, on this view none of the other animals will ever act voluntarily; nor will children. [But clearly they do.]

Next, among all the actions caused by appetite or emotion do we do none of them voluntarily? Or do we do the fine actions voluntarily and the shameful involuntarily? Surely [the second answer] is ridiculous when one and the same thing [i.e. appetite or emotion] causes [both fine and shameful actions]. And presumably it is also absurd to say [as the first answer implies] that things we ought to desire are involuntary; and in fact we ought both to be angry at some things and to have an appetite for some things, e.g. for health and learning.

Again, what is involuntary seems to be painful, whereas what expresses our appetite seems to be pleasant.

Moreover, how are errors that express emotion any less voluntary than those that express rational calculation? For both sorts of errors are to be avoided; and since nonrational feelings seem to be no less human [than rational calculation], actions resulting from emotion or appetite are also proper to a human being; it is absurd, then, to regard them as involuntary.

1111b

3.2 *Decision*

Now that we have defined what is voluntary and what involuntary, the next task is to discuss decision; for decision seems to be most proper to virtue, and to distinguish characters from one another better than actions do.

Decision, then, is apparently voluntary, but not the same as what is voluntary, which extends more widely. For children and the other animals share in what is voluntary, but not in decision; and the actions we do on the spur of the moment are said to be voluntary, but not to express decision.

iii 2

5

10

3.21 *What decision is not*

Those who say decision is appetite or emotion or wish or some sort of belief would seem to be wrong.

It is not appetite

For decision is not shared with nonrational [animals], but appetite and emotion are shared with them.

Further, the incontinent person acts on appetite, not on decision, but the continent person does the reverse and acts on decision, not on appetite.

Again, appetite is contrary to decision, but not to appetite.

15

Further, appetite's concern is what is pleasant and what
is painful, but neither of these is the concern of decision.

It is not emotion
Still less is emotion decision; for actions caused by emotion seem least of all to express decision.

It is not wish
But further, it is not wish either, though it is apparently
close to it.

For, first, we do not decide to do what is impossible, and
anyone claiming to decide to do it would seem a fool; but
we do wish for what is impossible, e.g. never to die, as well
[as for what is possible].

Further, we wish [not only for results we can achieve],
but also for results that are [possible, but] not achievable
through our own agency, e.g. victory for some actor or
athlete. But what we decide to do is never anything of that
sort, but what we think would come about through our own
agency.

Again, we wish for the end more [than for what promotes
it], but we decide to do what promotes the end. We wish,
e.g. to be healthy, but decide to do what will make us healthy;
and we wish to be happy, and say so, but could not appropriately say we decide to be happy, since in general what
we decide to do would seem to be what is up to us.

It is not belief in general . . .
Nor is it belief.

For, first, belief seems to be about everything, no less about
what is eternal and what is impossible [for us] than about
what is up to us.

Moreover, beliefs are divided into true and false, not into
good and bad, but decisions are divided into good and bad
more than into true and false.

60

. . . or any specific kind of belief

Now presumably no one even claims that decision is the | 1112a
same as belief in general. But it is not the same as any kind
of belief either.

For it is our decisions to do what is good or bad, not our
beliefs, that make the characters we have.

Again, we decide to take or avoid something good or bad.
We believe what it is, whom it benefits or how; but we do | 5
not exactly believe to take or avoid.

Further, decision is praised more for deciding on what is
right, whereas belief is praised for believing rightly.

Moreover, we decide on something [even] when we know
most completely that it is good; but [what] we believe [is]
what we do not quite know.

Again, those who make the best decisions do not seem to
be the same as those with the best beliefs; on the contrary,
some seem to have better beliefs, but to make the wrong | 10
choice because of vice.

We can agree that decision follows or implies belief. But
that is irrelevant, since it is not the question we are asking;
our question is whether decision is the *same* as some sort
of belief.

3.22 Decision requires deliberation

Then what, or what sort of thing, is decision, since it is
none of the things mentioned? Well, apparently it is volun-
tary, but not everything voluntary is decided. Then perhaps | 15
what is decided is the result of prior deliberation. For decision involves reason and thought, and even the name itself
would seem to indicate that [what is decided, *prohaireton*]
is chosen [*haireton*] before [*pro*] other things.

3.23 Not everything is open to deliberation

But do we deliberate about everything, and is everything | iii 3
open to deliberation, or is there no deliberation about some

61

20 things? By 'open to deliberation', presumably, we should mean what someone with some sense, not some fool or madman, might deliberate about.

Now no one deliberates about eternal things, e.g. about the universe, or about the incommensurability of the sides and the diagonal; nor about things that are in movement but
25 always come about the same way, either from necessity or by nature or by some other cause, e.g. the solstices or the rising of the stars; nor about what happens different ways at different times, e.g. droughts and rains; nor about what
30 results from fortune, e.g. the finding of a treasure. For none of these results could be achieved through our agency.

We deliberate about what is up to us, i.e. about the actions we can do; and this is what is left [besides the previous cases]. For causes seem to include nature, necessity and for-
33 tune, but besides them mind and everything [operating] through human agency.

28 However, we do not deliberate about all human affairs;
29 no Spartan, e.g., deliberates about how the Scythians might
33 have the best political system. Rather, each group of human beings deliberates about the actions *they* can do.

1112b Now there is no deliberation about the sciences that are exact and self-sufficient, e.g. about letters, since we are in no doubt about how to write them [in spelling a word]. Rather, we deliberate about what results through our agency, but in different ways on different occasions, e.g. about questions
5 of medicine and money-making; more about navigation than about gymnastics, to the extent that it is less exactly worked out, and similarly with other [crafts]; and more about beliefs than about sciences, since we are more in doubt about them.

Deliberation concerns what is usually [one way rather than another], where the outcome is unclear and the right way
10 to act is undefined. And we enlist partners in deliberation on large issues when we distrust our own ability to discern [the right answer].

62

We deliberate not about ends, but about what promotes ends; a doctor, e.g., does not deliberate about whether he will cure, or an orator about whether he will persuade, or a politician about whether he will produce good order, or any other [expert] about the end [that his science aims at].   15

3.24   The scope and method of deliberation

Rather, we first lay down the end, and then examine the ways and means to achieve it. If it appears that any of several [possible] means will reach it, we consider which of them will reach it most easily and most finely; and if only one [possible] means reaches it, we consider how that means will reach it, and how the means itself is reached, until we come to the first cause, the last thing to be discovered.

For a deliberator would seem to inquire and analyse in the   20 way described, as though analysing a diagram. [The comparison is apt, since], apparently, all deliberation is inquiry, though not all inquiry, e.g. in mathematics, is deliberation. And the last thing [found] in the analysis is the first that comes to be.

If we encounter an impossible step – e.g. we need money   25 but cannot raise it – we desist; but if the action appears possible, we undertake it. What is possible is what we could achieve through our agency [including what our friends could achieve for us]; for what our friends achieve is, in a way, achieved through our agency, since the origin is in us. [In crafts] we sometimes look for instruments, sometimes [for the way] to use them; so also in other cases we sometimes   30 look for the means to the end, sometimes for the proper use of the means or for the means to that proper use.

As we have said, then, a human being would seem to originate action; deliberation is about the actions he can do; and actions are for the sake of other things; hence we deliberate about what promotes an end, not about the end.

Nor do we deliberate about particulars, e.g. about whether   1113a

63

this is a loaf or is cooked the right amount; for these are questions for perception, and if we keep on deliberating at each
stage we shall go on without end.

3.25 Final account of decision

What we deliberate about is the same as what we decide
to do, except that by the time we decide to do it, it is definite;
for what we decide to do is what we have judged [to be right]
5 as a result of deliberation. For each of us stops inquiring
how to act as soon as he traces the origin to himself, and
within himself to the dominant part; for this is the part that
decides. This is also clear from the ancient political systems
described by Homer; there the kings would first decide and
then announce their decision to the people.

10 We have found, then, that what we decide to do is whatever
action among those up to us we deliberate about and desire
to do. Hence also decision will be deliberative desire to do
an action that is up to us; for when we have judged [that it
is right] as a result of deliberation, our desire to do it expresses our wish.

So much, then, for an outline of the sort of thing decision
is about; it is about what promotes the end.

iii 4 ### 3.3 Rational Wish for the End
15 Wish, we have said, is for the end. But to some it seems
that wish is for the good, to others that it is for the apparent
good.

3.31 Do we wish for the good?

For those who say the good is what is wished, it follows
that what someone wishes if he chooses incorrectly is not
wished at all. For if it is wished, then [on this view] it is
good; but what he wishes is in fact bad, if it turns out that
20 way. [Hence what he wishes is not wished, which is self-
contradictory.]

3.32   Or for the apparent good?

For those, on the other hand, who say the apparent good is wished, it follows that there is nothing wished by nature. To each person what is wished is what seems [good to him]; but different things, and indeed contrary things, if it turns out that way, appear good to different people. [Hence contrary things will be wished and nothing will be wished by nature.]

3.33   Solution

If, then, these views do not satisfy us, should we say that, unconditionally and in reality, what is wished is the good, but to each person what is wished is the apparent good?

The excellent person is the standard

To the excellent person, then, what is wished will be what | 25
is wished in reality, while to the base person what is wished is whatever it turns out to be [that appears good to him]. Similarly in the case of bodies, really healthy things are healthy to people in good condition, while other things are healthy to sickly people, and the same is true of what is bitter, sweet, hot, heavy and so on.

For the excellent person judges each sort of thing correctly, | 30
and in each case what is true appears to him. For each state [of character] has its own special [view of] what is fine and pleasant, and presumably the excellent person is far superior because he sees what is true in each case, being a sort of standard and measure of what is fine and pleasant.

In the many, however, pleasure would seem to cause deception, since it appears good when it is not; at any rate, | 1113b
they choose what is pleasant because they assume it is good, and avoid pain because they assume it is evil.

3.4   Virtue and Vice are in Our Power

3.41   The relevant actions are in our power

iii 5   We have found, then, that we wish for the end, and deliberate and decide about what promotes it; hence the actions
  5   concerned with what promotes the end will express a decision and will be voluntary. Now the activities of the virtues
are concerned with [what promotes the end]; hence virtue
is also up to us, and so is vice.

For when acting is up to us, so is not acting, and when
No is up to us, so is Yes. Hence if acting, when it is fine,
is up to us, then not acting, when it is shameful, is also up
  10   to us; and if not acting, when it is fine, is up to us, then acting, when it is shameful, is also up to us. Hence if doing,
and likewise not doing, fine or shameful actions is up to us;
and if, as we saw, [doing or not doing them] is [what it is]
to be a good or bad person; then it follows that being decent
or base is up to us.

  15   The claim that no one is willingly bad or unwillingly
blessed would seem to be partly true but partly false. For
while certainly no one is unwillingly blessed, vice is voluntary. If it is not, we must dispute the conclusion just reached,
that a human being originates and fathers his own actions
as he fathers his children. But if our conclusion appears true,
  20   and we cannot refer [actions] back to other origins beyond
those in ourselves, then it follows that whatever has its origin
in us is itself up to us and voluntary.

3.42   Our practices of reward and punishment
imply that virtue and vice are up to us

There would seem to be testimony in favour of our views
not only in what each of us does as a private citizen, but also
in what legislators themselves do. For they impose corrective treatments and penalties on anyone who does vicious
  25   actions, unless his action is forced or is caused by ignorance

66

that he is not responsible for; and they honour anyone who does fine actions; they assume that they will encourage the one and restrain the other. But no one encourages us to do anything that is not up to us and voluntary; people assume it is pointless to persuade us not to get hot or distressed or hungry or anything else of that sort, since persuasion will not stop it happening to us.

3.43   We punish for some types of ignorance, assuming that they are up to us

Indeed, legislators also impose corrective treatments for | 30
the ignorance itself, if the person seems to be responsible for the ignorance. A drunk, e.g., pays a double penalty; for the origin is in him, since he controls whether he gets drunk, and his getting drunk is responsible for his ignorance.

They also impose corrective treatment on someone who [does a vicious action] in ignorance of some provision of law that he is required to know and that is not hard [to know]. And they impose it in other cases likewise for any other ig- | 1114a
norance that seems to be caused by the agent's inattention; they assume it is up to him not to be ignorant, since he controls whether he pays attention.

3.44   And we are right, since our characters are up to us

But presumably his character makes him inattentive. Still, he is himself responsible for having this character, by living carelessly, and similarly for being unjust by cheating, or be- | 5
ing intemperate by passing his time in drinking and the like; for each type of activity produces the corresponding character. This is clear from those who train for any contest or action, since they continually practise the appropriate activities. [Only] a totally insensible person would not know that | 10
each type of activity is the source of the corresponding state;

12
13
   hence if someone does what he knows will make him unjust, he is willingly unjust.

Our responsibility is clear from the parallel
between character and health

11
12
13
   Moreover, it is unreasonable for someone doing injustice not to
wish to be unjust, or for someone doing intemperate action not to
wish to be intemperate. This does not mean, however, that if he is
unjust and wishes to stop, he will stop and will be just.

15
   For neither does a sick person recover his health [simply
by wishing]; nonetheless, he is sick willingly, by living incontinently and disobeying the doctors, if that was how it
happened. At that time, then, he was free not to be sick,
though no longer free once he has let himself go, just as it
was up to us to throw a stone, since the origin was in us,
though we can no longer take it back once we have thrown
it.

20
   Similarly, then, the person who is [now] unjust or intemperate
was originally free not to acquire this character, so that he has it
willingly, though once he has acquired the character, he is no
longer free not to have it [now].

   It is not only vices of the soul that are voluntary; vices
of the body are also voluntary for some people, and we actually censure them. For we never censure someone if nature
causes his ugliness; but if his lack of training or attention
25
causes it, we do censure him. The same is true for weakness
or maiming; for everyone would pity, not reproach someone
if he were blind by nature or because of a disease or a wound,
but would censure him if his heavy drinking or some other
form of intemperance made him blind.

   Hence bodily vices that are up to us are censured, while
30
those not up to us are not censured. If so, then in the other
cases also the vices that are censured will be up to us.

68

3.45   *But is our character really up to us?*

Objection

But someone may say, 'Everyone aims at the apparent good, and does not control how it appears; on the contrary, his character controls how the end appears to him.'

First reply

First, then, if each person is in some way responsible for his own state [of character], then he is also himself in some way responsible for how [the end] appears.

Consequences of the objection

Suppose, on the other hand, that no one is responsible for acting badly, but one does so because one is ignorant of the end, and thinks this is the way to gain what is best for oneself. One's aiming at the end will not be one's own choice, but one needs a sort of natural, inborn sense of sight, to judge finely and to choose what is really good. Whoever by nature has this sense in a fine condition has a good nature. For this sense is the greatest and finest thing, and one cannot acquire it or learn it from another; rather, its natural character determines his later condition, and when it is naturally good and fine, that is true and complete good nature.

If all this is true, then, surely virtue will be no more voluntary than vice? For how the end appears is laid down, by nature or in whatever way, for the good and the bad person alike, and they trace all the other things back to the end in doing whatever actions they do.

Second reply

Suppose, then, that it is not nature that makes the end appear however it appears to each person, but something also

5

10

15

69

depends on him; or, alternatively, suppose that [how] the end [appears] is natural, but virtue is voluntary because the virtuous person does the other things voluntarily. In either
20 case vice will be no less voluntary than virtue; for the bad person, no less than the good, is responsible for his own actions, even if not for [how] the end [appears].

Now the virtues, as we say, are voluntary, since in fact we are ourselves in a way jointly responsible for our states of character, and by having the sort of character we have we lay down the sort of end we do. Hence the vices will
25 also be voluntary, since the same is true of them.

3.46 Summary of the account of virtue

We have now discussed the virtues in general. We have described their genus in outline; they are means, and they are states. Certain actions produce them, and they cause us to do these same actions, expressing the virtues themselves, in the way that correct reason prescribes. They are up to us and voluntary.

30 Actions and states, however, are not voluntary in the same way. For we are in control of actions from the origin to the end, when we know the particulars. With states, however,
1115a we are in control of the origin, but do not know, any more than with sicknesses, what the cumulative effect of particular actions will be; none the less, since it was up to us to exercise a capacity either this way or another way, states are voluntary.

Let us now take up the virtues again, and discuss each
5 singly. Let us say what they are, what sorts of thing they are concerned with, and how they are concerned with them; it will also be clear at the same time how many virtues there are.

70

4. The Individual Virtues of Character

4.1 Bravery

4.11 Its scope: Frightening conditions

First let us discuss bravery. We have already made it apparent that there is a mean about feelings of fear and confidence. What we fear, clearly, is what is frightening, and such things are, speaking without qualification, bad things; hence people define fear as expectation of something bad.

Bravery is not concerned with fear of every
sort of danger

Now while we certainly fear all bad things, e.g. bad reputation, poverty, sickness, friendlessness, death, they do not all seem to concern the brave person. For fear of some bad things, e.g. bad reputation, is actually right and fine, and lack of fear is disgraceful; for if someone fears bad reputation, he is decent and properly prone to shame, and if he has no fear of it, he has no feeling of disgrace. Some, however, call this fearless person brave, by a transference [of the name], since he has some similarity to the brave person, in that the brave person is also a type of fearless person.

Presumably, though, it is wrong to fear poverty or sickness or, in general, [bad things] that are not the results of vice or caused by ourselves; still, someone who is fearless about these is not thereby brave. He also is called brave by similarity, since some people who are cowardly in the dangers of war are nonetheless generous, and face with confidence the [danger of] losing money.

Again, if someone is afraid of committing wanton aggression on children or women, or of being envious or anything of that sort, that does not make him cowardly. Nor again, if someone is confident when he is going to be whipped [for his crimes] does that make him brave.

iii 6

10

15

20

71

It is concerned with the fear of death

25   Then what sorts of frightening conditions concern the brave person? Surely the most frightening; for no one stands firmer against terrifying conditions. Now death is most frightening of all, since it is a boundary, and when someone is dead nothing beyond it seems either good or bad for him any more. Still, not even death in all conditions, e.g. on the sea or in sickness, seems to be the brave person's concern.

It is concerned specifically with the fear of
death in war

In what conditions, then, is death his concern? Surely in
30   the finest conditions. Now such deaths are those in war, since they occur in the greatest and finest danger; and this judgment is endorsed by the honours given in cities and by monarchs. Hence someone is called brave to the fullest extent if he is intrepid in facing a fine death and the immediate
35   dangers that bring death—and this is above all true of the dangers of war.

1115b   Certainly the brave person is also intrepid on the sea and in sicknesses, but not in the same way as seafarers are. For he has given up hope of safety, and objects to this sort of death [with nothing fine in it], but seafarers' experience makes them hopeful. Moreover, we act like brave men on occa-
5   sions when we can use our strength, or when it is fine to be killed; and neither of these is true when we perish on the sea.

4.12   The brave person's state of character

What does he find frightening?

iii 7   Now what is frightening is not the same for everyone. We do say, however, that some things are too frightening for a human being to resist; these, then, are frightening for everyone, at least for everyone with any sense. What is

72

frightening, but not irresistible for a human being, varies in
its seriousness and degree; and the same is true of what inspires confidence.

Now the brave person is unperturbed, as far as a human
being can be. Hence, though he will fear even the sorts of
things that are not irresistible, he will stand firm against
them, in the right way, as prescribed by reason, for the sake
of what is fine, since this is the end aimed at by virtue.

It is possible to be more or less afraid of these frightening
things, and also possible to be afraid of what is not frightening as though it were frightening. The cause of error may
be fear of the wrong thing, or in the wrong way, or at the
wrong time, or something of that sort; and the same is true
for things that inspire confidence.

Hence whoever stands firm against the right things and
fears the right things, for the right end, in the right way,
at the right time, and is correspondingly confident, is the
brave person; for the brave person's actions and feelings
reflect what something is worth and what reason [prescribes].

His motive: He aims at what is fine
Every activity aims at actions expressing its state of character, and to the brave person bravery is fine; hence the end
it aims at is also fine, since each thing is defined by its end.
The brave person, then, aims at what is fine when he expresses bravery in his standing firm and acting.

4.13 Bravery contrasted with its
corresponding vices
Consider now those who go to excess.

The person who is excessively fearless has no name — we
said earlier that many states have no names. He would be
some sort of madman, or incapable of feeling distress, if he
feared nothing, neither earthquake nor waves, as they say
about the Celts.

30 The person who is excessively confident about frightening things is rash. The rash person also seems to be a boaster, and a pretender to bravery. At any rate, the attitude to frightening things that the brave person really has is the attitude that the rash person wants to appear to have; hence he imitates the brave person where he can. That is why most of them are rash cowards; for rash though they are on these [occasions for imitation], they do not stand firm against any-

1116a7 thing frightening. Moreover, rash people are impetuous, and
8 wish for dangers before they arrive, but shrink from them
9 when they come; brave people, on the contrary, are eager when in action, but keep quiet until then.

1115b34 The person who is excessively afraid is the coward, since
35 he fears the wrong things, and in the wrong way, and so on.
1116a Though indeed he is also deficient in confidence, it is more his excessive pain that clearly distinguishes him. Hence, since he is afraid of everything, he is a despairing sort. The brave person, on the contrary, is hopeful, since [he is confident and] confidence is proper to a hopeful person.

5 Hence the coward, the rash person and the brave person are all concerned with the same things, but have different states related to them; the others are excessive or defective,
7 but the brave person has the intermediate and right state.

The brave person's motive is crucial

10 As we have said, then, bravery is a mean about what inspires confidence and about what is frightening in the conditions we have described; it chooses and stands firm because that is fine or because anything else is shameful. Dying to avoid poverty or erotic passion or something painful is proper to a coward, not to a brave person; for try-
15 ing to avoid burdens is softness, and such a person stands firm [in the face of death] to avoid an evil, not because it is fine.

74

*4.14   Five states that must be distinguished
from genuine bravery*

Bravery, then, is something of this sort. But other states, five of them, are also called bravery.

The bravery of citizens

Citizens' bravery comes first, since it looks most like bravery. For citizens seem to stand firm against dangers with the aim of avoiding reproaches and legal penalties and of winning honours; that is why the bravest seem to be those who hold cowards in dishonour and do honour to brave people. That is how Homer also describes them when he speaks of Diomede and Hector. [Hector says,] 'Polydamas will be the first to heap disgrace on me', and [Diomede says,] 'For sometime Hector speaking among the Trojans will say "The son of Tydeus fled from me." '

This is most like the [genuine] bravery described above, since it is caused by a virtue; for its cause is shame and desire for something fine – for honour – and aversion from reproach, which is disgraceful.

In this class we might also place those compelled by their superiors. However, they are worse to the extent that their behaviour is caused by fear, not by shame, by aversion from what is painful, not from what is disgraceful. For those who control them compel them, as Hector does; 'If I notice anyone shrinking back from the battle, nothing will help him to escape the dogs.' Commanders who strike the troops if they give ground and those who post them in front of ditches and suchlike do the same thing, since they all compel them. However, we must be brave because it is fine, not because we are compelled.

Experience and expertise

Experience about each situation also seems to be bravery;
5   that is why Socrates actually thought that bravery is scientific knowledge. Different people in different conditions
have this sort [of apparent courage], and in the conditions
of war the professional soldiers have it; for there seem to
be many groundless alarms in war, and the professionals
are the most familiar with these, and hence appear brave,
since others do not know that the alarms are groundless.

Moreover, their experience makes them most capable in
10   attack and defence, since they are capable users of their
weapons, and have the weapons that are best for attack and
defence. The result is that in fighting non-professionals
they are like armed troops fighting unarmed, or like trained
athletes fighting ordinary people; for in these contests also
the best fighters are the strongest and physically fittest, not
15   the bravest.

However, professional soldiers turn out to be cowards
when the danger overstrains them and they are inferior in
numbers and equipment. For they are the first to run, whereas
the citizen troops stand firm and get killed; this was what
happened at the temple of Hermes. For the citizens find it
20   shameful to run, and find death more choiceworthy than
safety at this cost. But the professionals from the start were
facing the danger on the assumption of their superiority, and
once they learn their mistake, they run, since they are more
afraid of being killed than of doing something shameful; and
that is not the brave person's character.

Emotion

Emotion is also counted as bravery; for those who act on
25   emotion also seem to be brave — as beasts seem to be when
they attack those who have wounded them — because brave
people are also full of emotion. For emotion is most eager
to run and face dangers; hence Homer's words, 'put strength

76

in his emotion', 'aroused strength and emotion', 'keen strength in his nostril', and 'his blood boiled'. All these would seem to signify the arousal and the impulse of emotion. | 30

Now brave people act because of what is fine, and their emotion cooperates with them. But beasts act because of pain; for [they attack only] because they have been wounded or frightened, since they do not approach us in a forest. They are not brave, then, since distress and emotion drives them in an impulsive rush to meet danger, foreseeing none | 35 of the terrifying prospects. For if they were brave, hungry asses would also be brave, since they stay feeding even if | 1117a they are beaten; and adulterers also do many daring actions because of appetite.

Human beings as well [as beasts] find it painful to be | 5 angered, and pleasant to exact a penalty. But those who fight for these reasons are not brave, though they are good fighters; for they fight because of their feelings, not because of what is fine or as reason [prescribes]. Still, they have something similar [to bravery]. The [bravery] caused | 4 by emotion would seem to be the most natural sort, and is [real] bravery once decision and the goal have been added | 5 to it.

Hopefulness
Hopeful people are not brave either, since it is their many | 9 victories over many opponents that make them confident in | 10 dangers. They are somewhat similar to brave people, since both are confident; but while brave people are confident for the reason given earlier, the hopeful are confident because they think they are stronger and nothing could happen to them—and drunks do the same sort of thing, since they be- | 15 come hopeful. And when things turn out differently for them, they run; but, as we saw, it is proper to the brave person to stand firm against what is and appears frightening to

a human being, because it is fine to stand firm and shameful to fail.

Indeed, that is why someone who is unafraid and unperturbed in a sudden alarm seems braver than [someone who is unafraid only] in dangers that are obvious in advance; for

20 what he does is more the result of his state of character, since it is less the outcome of preparation. If an action is foreseen, we might decide to do it [not only because of our state of character, but] also by reason and rational calculation; but when we have no warning, [our decision to act] expresses our state of character.

Ignorance

Those who act in ignorance also appear brave, and indeed they are close to hopeful people, though inferior to them in so far as they lack hopeful people's self-esteem.

25 That is why the hopeful stand firm for some time, whereas if ignorant people have been deceived and then realize or suspect that things are different, they run — that was what happened to the Argives when they stumbled on the Spartans and took them for Sicyonians.

We have described, then, the character of brave people and of the people who seem to be brave.

4.15   The relation of bravery to confidence

iii 9 *and fear, pleasure and pain*

30 Bravery is about feelings of confidence and fear, not, however, about both in the same way, but more about frightening things; for someone is brave if he is undisturbed and in the right state about these, more than if he is in this state about things inspiring confidence. As we said, then, standing firm against what is painful makes us call people brave; that is why bravery is both painful and justly praised, since

35 it is harder to stand firm against something painful than to refrain from something pleasant.

78

None the less, the end that bravery aims at seems to be $\quad$ 1117b
pleasant, though obscured by its surroundings. This is what
happens in athletic contests. For boxers find that the end
they aim at, the crown and the honours, is pleasant, but, being made of flesh, they find it distressing and painful to take $\quad$ 5
the punches and to bear all the hard work; and because
there are so many of these painful things, the end, being
small, appears to have nothing pleasant in it. And so, if this
is also true for bravery, the brave person will find death and
wounds painful, and suffer them unwillingly, but he will
stand firm against them because that is fine or because failure is shameful.

Indeed, the more he has every virtue and the happier $\quad$ 10
he is, the more pain he will feel at the prospect of death.
For this sort of person, more than anyone, finds it worth
while to be alive, and is knowingly deprived of the greatest
goods, and this is painful. But he is no less brave for all
that; presumably, indeed, he is all the braver, because he
chooses what is fine in war at the cost of all these goods. $\quad$ 15

Hence it is not true that the active exercise of every virtue
is pleasant; it is pleasant only in so far as we attain the end.

However, it is quite possible for brave people not to be
the best soldiers. Perhaps the best will be those who are less
brave, but possess no other good; for they are ready to face
dangers, and they sell their lives for small gains. $\quad$ 20

So much for bravery. It is easy to grasp what it is, in
outline at least, from what we have said.

4.2 Temperance

4.21 The pleasures and pains that concern it

Let us discuss temperance next, since bravery and tem- $\quad$ iii 10
perance seem to be the virtues of the non-rational parts.
Temperance, then, is a mean concerned with pleasures, as $\quad$ 25
we have already said; for it is concerned less, and in a dif-

nt way, with pains. Intemperance appears in this same
a too. Let us, then, now distinguish the specific pleasures
t concern them.

It is not concerned with non-bodily pleasures . . .

First, let us distinguish pleasures of the soul from those
of the body. Love of honour and of learning, e.g., are
among the soul's pleasures; for though a lover of one of
30 these enjoys it, only his thought, not his body, is at all affected. Those concerned with such pleasures are called
neither temperate nor intemperate. The same applies to
those concerned with any of the other non-bodily pleasures;
35 for lovers of tales, story-tellers, those who waste their days
on trivialities, are called babblers, but not intemperate. Nor
1118a do we call people intemperate if they feel pain over money
or friends.

. . . or with all bodily pleasures

Temperance, then, will be about bodily pleasures, but not
even about all of these. For those who enjoy what they
notice through sight, e.g. colours, shapes, a painting, are
5 called neither temperate nor intemperate, even though it
would also seem possible to enjoy these both in the right
way and excessively or deficiently. The same is true for
hearing; no one is ever called intemperate for the excessive
enjoyment of songs or play-acting, or temperate for the
right enjoyment of them.

Nor is this said about someone enjoying smells, except
10 coincidentally. For someone is called intemperate not for
enjoying the smell of apples or roses or incense, but rather
for enjoying the smell of perfumes or cooked delicacies.
For these are the smells an intemperate person enjoys
because they remind him of the objects of his appetite; and
15 we can see that others also enjoy the smells of food if they
are hungry. It is the enjoyment of the things [that he is re-

80

minded of by these smells] that is proper to an intemperate person, since these are the objects of his appetite.

Nor do other animals find pleasures from these senses, except coincidentally. What a hound enjoys, e.g., is not the smell of a hare, but eating it; but the hare's smell made the hound perceive it. And what a lion enjoys is not the sound | 20 of the ox, but eating it; but since the ox's sound made the lion perceive that it was near, the lion appears to enjoy the sound. Similarly, what pleases him is not the sight of 'a deer or a wild goat', but the prospect of food.

It is concerned with the pleasures of touch
and taste . . .

The pleasures that concern temperance and intemperance are those that are shared with the other animals, and so | 25 appear slavish and bestial. These pleasures are touch and taste. However, they seem to deal even with taste very little or not at all. For taste discriminates flavours—the sort of thing that wine-tasters and cooks savouring food do; but people, or intemperate people at any rate, do not much en- | 30 joy this. Rather, they enjoy the gratification that comes entirely through touch, in eating and drinking and in what are called the pleasures of sex. That is why a glutton actually prayed for his throat to become longer than a crane's, show- | 1118b ing that he took pleasure in the touching.

. . . and primarily of touch

And so the sense that concerns intemperance is the most widely shared, and seems justifiably open to reproach, since we have it in so far as we are animals, not in so far as we are human beings. To enjoy these things, then, and to like them most of all is bestial. For indeed the most civi- lized of the pleasures coming through touch, e.g. those pro- | 5 duced by rubbing and warming in gymnasia, are excluded from intemperance, since the touching that is proper to the intemperate person concerns only some parts of the body, not all of it.

4.22 The state of the temperate person

Distinction among appetites

iii 11   Some appetites seem to be shared [by everyone], while others seem to be additions that are special [to different peo-
10 ple]. The appetite for nourishment, e.g., is natural, since everyone who lacks nourishment, dry or liquid, has an appetite for it, sometimes for both; and, as Homer says, the young in their prime [all] have an appetite for sex. On the other hand, not everyone has an appetite for a particular sort of food or drink or sex, or for the same things; hence that sort of appetite seems to be special to [each of] us. Still, this also includes a natural element, since different sorts of people find different sorts of things pleasanter, and there are some things that are pleasanter for everyone than things chosen at random would be.
15   In natural appetites few people are in error, and only in one direction, towards excess. Eating indiscriminately or drinking until we are too full is exceeding the quantity that suits nature, since [the object of] natural appetite is the filling of a lack. Hence these people are called 'gluttons',
20 showing that they glut their bellies past what is right; that is how extra-slavish people turn out.

The vice of excess: Intemperance

   With the pleasures that are special to different people, many make errors and in many ways; for people are called lovers of something if they enjoy the wrong things, or if they enjoy something more than most people enjoy it, or if they enjoy something in the wrong way. And in all these
25 ways intemperate people go to excess. For some of the things they enjoy are hateful, and hence the wrong things;

and any special pleasures it is right to enjoy they enjoy more than is right, and more than most people enjoy them.

Clearly, then, with pleasures excess is intemperance, and is blameworthy. With pains, however, we are not called temperate, as we are called brave, for standing firm against them, or intemperate for not standing firm. Rather, some- | 30
one is intemperate because he feels more pain than is right at failing to get pleasant things; and even this pain is produced by the pleasure [he takes in them]. And someone is temperate because he does not feel pain at the absence of what is pleasant, or at refraining from it.

The intemperate person, then, has an appetite for all | 1119a
pleasant things, or rather for the pleasantest of them, and his appetite leads him to choose these at the cost of every-thing else. Hence he also feels pain both when he fails to get something and when he has an appetite for it, since appetite is associated with pain; it would seem absurd, though, to | 5
suffer pain because of pleasure.

The vice of deficiency

People who are deficient in pleasures and enjoy them less than is right are not found very much. For that sort of insen-sibility is not human; indeed, even the other animals dis-criminate among foods, enjoying some but not others; and if someone finds nothing pleasant, or preferable to anything else, he is far from being human. And the reason he has no | 10
name is that he is not found much.

The mean state: Temperance

The temperate person has an intermediate state in relation to these [bodily pleasures]. For he finds no pleasure in what most pleases the intemperate person, but finds it disagree-able; he finds no pleasure at all in the wrong things; and he finds no intense pleasure in any [bodily pleasures], suffers no pain at their absence, and has no appetite for them, or

15 only a moderate appetite, not to the wrong degree or at the wrong time or anything else at all of that sort.

If something is pleasant and conducive to health or fitness, he will desire this moderately and in the right way; and he will desire in the same way anything else that is pleasant if it is no obstacle to health and fitness, does not deviate from what is fine, and does not exceed his means. For the [opposite] sort of person likes these pleasures more

20 than they are worth, and that is not the temperate person's character; on the contrary, he likes them as correct reason [prescribes].

4.23 Intemperance compared with cowardice

iii 12 Intemperance looks more like a voluntary condition than cowardice does, since it is caused by pleasure, which is choiceworthy, while cowardice is caused by pain, which is to be avoided. Moreover, pain disturbs and ruins the nature of the sufferer, while pleasure does nothing of the sort; in-

25 temperance, then, is more voluntary.

Hence it is also more open to reproach. For it is also easier to acquire the habit of facing pleasant things, since our life includes many of them and we can acquire the habit with no danger; but with frightening things the reverse is true.

However, cowardice seems to be more voluntary than particular cowardly actions. For cowardice itself involves no pain, but the particular actions disturb us because of the pain

30 [that causes them], so that we actually throw away our weapons and do all the other disgraceful actions; and hence these actions even seem to be forced [and hence involuntary].

For the intemperate person the reverse is true. The particular actions are the result of his appetite and desire, and so they are voluntary; but the whole condition is less voluntary [than the actions], since no one has an appetite to be intemperate.

4.24 *Different uses of 'intemperance'*

We also apply the name of intemperance to the errors of children, since they have some similarity. Which gets its name from which does not matter for present purposes, but clearly the posterior is called after the prior. | 1119b

The name would seem to be quite appropriately transferred. For what needs to be tempered is what desires shameful things and tends to grow large; and this is the character | 5
of appetites and of children above all, since children also live by appetite, and the desire for what is pleasant is found more in them than in anyone else.

If, then, [the child or the appetitive part] is not obedient and subordinate to its rulers, it will go far astray. For when someone lacks understanding, his desire for what is pleasant is insatiable, and seeks its satisfaction from anywhere; the [repeated] active exercise of appetite increases the appetite he already had from birth; and if the appetites are | 10
large and intense, they actually expel rational calculation.

This is why appetites must be moderate and few, and never contrary to reason; this is the condition we call obedient and temperate. And just as the child's life must follow the instructions of his guide, so too the appetitive part must follow reason. | 15

Hence the temperate person's appetitive part must agree with reason; for both [his appetitive part and his reason] aim at what is fine, and the temperate person's appetites are for the right things, in the right ways, at the right times, which is just what reason also prescribes.

So much, then, for temperance.

4.3 *Generosity*

4.31 *Its scope*

It is concerned with wealth

Next let us discuss generosity. It seems, then, to be the | iv 1
mean about wealth; for the generous person is praised not

25 in conditions of war, nor in the conditions in which the temperate person is praised, nor in judicial verdicts, but in the
giving and taking of wealth, and more especially in the giving.
We call wealth anything whose worth is measured by money.

Each one of wastefulness and ungenerosity is both an excess and a deficiency about wealth. Ungenerosity is always
30 ascribed to those who take wealth more seriously than is
right. But when wastefulness is attributed to someone, several vices are sometimes combined. For incontinent people
and those who spend money on intemperance are called
wasteful; and since these have many vices at the same time,
they make wasteful people seem the basest.

In fact, however, these people are not properly called
wasteful. For the wasteful person is meant to have the single
1120a vicious feature of ruining his property; for someone who
causes his own destruction ['lays waste' to himself, and so]
is wasteful, and ruining one's own property seems to be a
sort of self-destruction, on the assumption that our living
depends on our property. This, then, is how we understand
wastefulness.

*It is concerned primarily with giving
rather than taking*

5 Whatever has a use can be used either well or badly; riches
are something useful; and the best user of something is the
person who has the virtue concerned with it. Hence the best
user of riches will be the person who has the virtue concerned
with wealth; and this is the generous person.

Now using wealth seems to consist in spending and giving, while taking and keeping seem to be possessing rather
10 than using. Hence it is more proper to the generous person
to give to the right people than to take from the right sources
and not from the wrong sources. For it is more proper to
virtue to do good than to receive good, and more proper to
do fine actions than not to do shameful ones; and clearly [the

right sort of] giving implies doing good and doing fine actions, while [the right sort of] taking implies receiving well | 15
or not doing something shameful.

Moreover, thanks go to the one who gives, not to the one who fails to take, and praise goes more [to the giver].

Besides, not taking is easier than giving, since people part with what is their own less readily than they avoid taking what is another's.

Further, those who are called generous are those who give | 20
[rightly]. Those who avoid taking [wrongly] are not praised for generosity, though they are praised none the less for justice, while those who take [rightly] are not much praised at all.

Besides, generous people are loved more than practically any others who are loved because of their virtue; that is because they are beneficial; and they are beneficial in their giving.

4.32 The generous person's state

He aims at what is fine

Actions expressing virtue are fine, and aim at what is fine. Hence the generous person as well [as every other virtuous person] will aim at what is fine in his giving and will give | 25
correctly; for he will give to the right people, the right amounts, at the right time, and all the other things that are implied by correct giving.

He takes pleasure in giving

He will do this, moreover, with pleasure or [at any rate] without pain; for action expressing virtue is pleasant or [at any rate] painless, and least of all is it painful. If someone gives to the wrong people, or does not aim at what is fine, but gives for some other reason, he will not be called generous, but some other sort of person. Nor will he be called

30 generous if he finds it painful to give; for such a person would choose wealth over fine action, and that is not proper to the generous person.

*In his attitude to acquisition he is neither mean
nor wasteful*

Nor will he take wealth from the wrong sources; since he does not honour wealth, this way of taking it is not for him. Nor will he be ready to ask for favours; since he is the one who benefits others, receiving benefits readily is not for him.

1120b He will, however, acquire wealth from the right sources, e.g. from his own possessions, regarding taking not as fine, but as necessary to provide something to give. Nor will he neglect his own possessions, since he wants to use them to assist people. And he will avoid giving to just anyone, so that he will have something to give to the right people, at the right time, and where it is fine.

He gives without stint

It is also very definitely proper to the generous person to
5 exceed so much in giving that he leaves less for himself, since it is proper to a generous person not to look out for himself.

However, [the reference to 'exceeding' must not mislead us. For] in speaking of generosity we refer to generosity that fits one's property. For what is generous does not depend on the quantity of what is given, but on the state of the giver, and that kind of giving fits one's property. Hence one who gives less [than another] may still be more generous, if he
10 has less to give.

Those who have not acquired their property by their own efforts, but have inherited it, seem to be more generous; for they have had no experience of shortage, and, besides, everyone likes his own products more than [other people's], as parents and poets do.

88

He is not concerned with wealth

It is not easy for a generous person to grow rich, since he is ready to spend, not to take or keep, and honours wealth for the sake of giving, not for itself. Indeed fortune is denounced for this reason, that those who most deserve to grow rich actually do so least. In fact, however, this is not an unreasonable result, since someone cannot possess wealth, any more than other things, if he pays no attention to possessing it.

However, he does not give indiscriminately

Still, he does not give to the wrong people, at the wrong time and so on. For if he did, his actions would no longer express generosity, and if he spent his resources on the wrong sort of giving, he would have nothing left to spend for the right purposes. For, as we have said, the generous person is the one whose spending fits his means, and for the right purposes, while the one who spends to excess is wasteful. Hence tyrants are not called wasteful, since it seems they will have difficulty giving and spending in excess of their possessions.

He achieves the mean in pleasures and pains

Since generosity, then, is a mean concerned with the giving and the taking of wealth, the generous person will both give and spend the right amount for the right purposes, in small and large matters alike, and do this with pleasure. He will also take the right amounts from the right sources; for since the virtue is a mean about both giving and taking, he will do both in the right way. For decent giving implies decent taking, and the other sort of taking is contrary to the decent sort; hence the states implying each other are present at the same time in the same subject, while the contrary states clearly are not.

If the generous person does find that his spending deviates from what is fine and right, he will feel pain, but moderately and in the right way; for it is proper to virtue to feel both pleasure and pain in the right things and in the right way.

The generous person is also an easy partner to associate with in dealings that involve money; for he can easily be treated unjustly, since he does not honour money, and is more grieved if he has failed to spend what it was right to spend than if he has spent what it was wrong to spend—here he disagrees with Simonides.

The wasteful person is in error here too, since he feels neither pleasure nor pain at the right things or in the right way; this will be more evident as we go on.

4.33   The vice of excess: Wastefulness

We have said that wastefulness and ungenerosity are excesses and deficiencies in two things, in giving and taking—for we also count spending as giving. Now wastefulness is excessive in giving and not taking, but deficient in taking. Ungenerosity is deficient in giving and excessive in taking, but in small matters.

Wastefulness without ungenerosity

Now the features of wastefulness are not very often combined; for it is not easy to take from nowhere and give to everyone, since private citizens soon outrun their resources in giving, and private citizens are the ones who seem to be wasteful. However, such a person seems to be quite a lot better than the ungenerous person, since he is easily cured, both by growing older and by poverty, and is capable of reaching the intermediate condition. For he has the features proper to the generous person, since he gives and does not take, though he does neither rightly or well. If, then, he is changed, by habituation or some other means, so that he does them rightly and well, he will be generous; for then he will give to the right people and will not take from the wrong sources. This is why the wasteful person seems not to be base in his character; for excess in giving without taking is proper to a foolish person, not to a vicious or ignoble one.

Someone who is wasteful in this way, then, seems to be much better than the ungenerous person, both for the reasons we have given and because he benefits many, whereas the ungenerous person benefits no one, not even himself.

Wastefulness combined with ungenerosity

Most wasteful people, however, as we have said, [not only | 30 give wrongly, but] also take from the wrong sources, and to this extent are ungenerous. They become acquisitive because they wish to spend, but cannot do this readily, since they soon exhaust all they have; hence they are compelled to provide from elsewhere. At the same time they care noth- | 1121b ing for what is fine, and so take from any source without scruple; for they have an appetite for giving, and the way or source does not matter to them.

This is why their ways of giving are not generous either, since they are not fine, do not aim at what is fine, and are not done in the right way. Rather, these people sometimes | 5 enrich people who ought to be poor, and would give nothing to people with sound characters, but would give much to flatterers or to those providing some other pleasure.

Hence most of these people are also intemperate. For since they part with money lightly, they also spend it lavishly on intemperance; and because their lives do not aim at what is | 10 fine, they decline towards pleasures.

If, then, the wasteful person has been left without a guide, he changes into this; but if he receives attention, he might reach the intermediate and the right state.

4.34 The vice of deficiency: Ungenerosity

Ungenerosity, on the other hand, is incurable, since old age and every incapacity seem to make people ungenerous. And it comes more naturally to human beings than wastefulness; for the many are money-lovers rather than givers. | 15

Moreover, it extends widely and has many species, since there seem to be many ways of being ungenerous. For it consists in two conditions, deficiency in giving and excess in taking; but it is not found as a whole in all cases. Sometimes the two conditions are separated, and some people go to excess in taking while others are deficient in giving.

Ungenerosity in giving too little
The people called misers, tight-fisted, skinflints and so on, are all deficient in giving, but they do not go after other people's goods and do not wish to take them.

With some people the reason for this is some sort of decency in them, and a concern to avoid what is shameful. For some people seem—at least, this is what they say—to hold on to their money so that they will never be compelled to do anything shameful. These include the cheeseparer, and everyone like that; he is so called from his excessive refusal to give anything.

Others refrain from other people's property because they are afraid, supposing that it is not easy for them to take other people's property without other people taking theirs too; hence, they say, they are content if they neither take from others nor give to them.

Acquisitive ungenerosity
Other people, by contrast, go to excess in taking, by taking anything from any source—those, e.g., who work at degrading occupations, pimps and all such people, and usurers who lend small amounts at high interest; for all of these take the wrong amounts from the wrong sources.

Shameful love of gain is apparently their common feature, since they all put up with reproaches for some gain, indeed for a small gain. For those who take the wrong things from the wrong sources on a large scale, e.g. tyrants who sack cities and plunder temples, are called wicked, impious and unjust, but not ungenerous.

92

The ungenerous, however, include the gambler and the robber, since these are shameful lovers of gain. For in pursuit of gain both go to great efforts and put up with reproaches; the robber faces the greatest dangers to get his | 10
haul, while the gambler takes his gains from his friends, when they are the ones he ought to be giving to. Both of them, then, are shameful lovers of gain, because they wish to acquire gains from the wrong sources; and all these methods of acquisition are ungenerous.

It is plausibly said that ungenerosity is contrary to generosity. For it is a greater evil than wastefulness; and error in | 15
this direction is more common than the error of wastefulness, as we have described it.

So much, then, for generosity and the vices opposed to it.

4.4 Magnificence

4.41 Magnificence contrasted with generosity

Next, it seems appropriate to discuss magnificence also. | iv 2
For it seems to be, like generosity, a virtue concerned with wealth, but it extends not, as generosity does, to all the ac- | 20
tions involving wealth, but only to those involving heavy expenses, and in them it exceeds generosity in its large scale.

For just as the name [*megaloprepeia*] itself suggests, magnificence is expenditure that is fitting [*prepousa*] in its large scale [*megethos*]. But large scale is large relative to something; for the expenses of a warship-captain and of a leader of a delegation are not the same. Hence what is fit- | 25
ting is also relative to oneself, the circumstances and the purpose.

Someone is called magnificent only if he spends the worthy amount on a large purpose, not on a trivial or an ordinary purpose like the one who 'gave to many a wanderer'; for the magnificent person is generous, but generosity does not imply magnificence.

4.42   The vices opposed to magnificence

30   The deficiency of this state is called niggardliness. The excess is called vulgarity, poor taste and such things. These are excesses not because they spend an excessively great amount on the right things, but because they show off in the wrong circumstances and in the wrong way. We shall discuss these vices later.

4.43   The actions of the magnificent person

The magnificent person, in contrast to these, is like a scien-
35   tific expert, since he is able to observe what will be the fitting amount, and to spend large amounts in an appropriate way.

1122b   For, as we said at the start, a state is defined by its activities and its objects; now the magnificent person's expenditures are large and fitting; so also, then, must the achievements be, since that is what makes the expense large and fitting to the achievement. Hence the achievement must be
5   worthy of the expense, and the expense worthy of, or even in excess of, the achievement.

4.44   His state

In this sort of spending the magnificent person will aim at what is fine, since that is a common feature of the virtues. Moreover, he will spend gladly and readily, since it is niggardly to count every penny; and he will think more about the finest and most fitting way to spend than about the
10   cost or about the cheapest way to do it.

4.45   Magnificence and generosity: The large
scale of magnificence

Hence the magnificent person must also be generous; for the generous person too will spend what is right in the right way. But it is in this spending that the large scale of the magnificent person, his greatness, is found, since his magnificence is a sort of large scale of generosity in these things; and from an expense that is equal [to a non-magnificent person's] he will make the achievement more magnificent.

[The achievement may be more magnificent even if the | 15
expense is equal.] For a possession and an achievement have different sorts of excellence; the most honoured [and hence most excellent] possession is the one worth most, for example gold, but the most honoured achievement is the one that is great and fine, since that is what is admirable to behold. Now what is magnificent is admirable, and the excellence of the achievement consists in its large scale.

The appropriate sphere of magnificence: Public expenditures

This sort of excellence is found in the sorts of expenses called honourable, e.g. in expenses for the gods – dedications, | 20
temples, sacrifices and so on for everything divine – and in expenses that provoke a good competition for honour, to the benefit of the community – if, e.g., some city thinks a splendid chorus or warship or a feast for the city must be provided.

But in all cases, as we have said, we fix the right amount by reference to the agent [as well as the task] – by who he | 25
is and what resources he has; for the amounts must be worthy of these, fitting the producer as well as the product.

These expenditures require wealth

Hence a poor person could not be magnificent, since he lacks the means for large and fitting expenditures; and if he attempts it, he is foolish, since he spends more than what is worthy and right for him, when in fact it is correct spending that expresses virtue.

But large spending befits those who have the means, ac- | 30
quired through their own efforts or their ancestors or connections, or are well-born or reputable, and so on; for each of these conditions includes greatness and reputation for worth.

95

This, then, above all is the character of the magnificent person, and magnificence is found in these sorts of expenses, as we have said, since these are the largest and most honoured.

35

The secondary sphere of magnificence in large private expenditures

It is found also in those private expenses that arise only once, e.g. a wedding and the like, and in those that concern the whole city, or the people in it with a reputation for worth – the receiving of foreign guests and sending them off, gifts and exchanges of gifts; for the magnificent person spends money on the common good, not on himself, and the gifts have some similarity to dedications.

1123a

5

It is also proper to the magnificent person to build a house befitting his riches, since this is also a suitable adornment; and to spend more readily on long-lasting achievements, since these are the finest, and in each case on what is fitting. For what suits gods does not suit human beings, and what suits a temple does not suit a tomb.

10

And since each great expense is great in relation to a particular kind of object, the most magnificent will be a great expense on a great object, and what is magnificent in a particular area will be what is great in relation to the particular kind of object. Moreover, greatness in the achievements is not the same as greatness in an expense, since the finest ball or oil-bottle has the magnificence proper to a gift for a child, but its value is small and paltry. And so it is proper to the magnificent person, whatever kind of thing he produces, to produce it magnificently, since this is not easily exceeded, and to produce something worthy of the expense.

15

This, then, is what the magnificent person is like.

4.46 The vice of excess

The vulgar person who exceeds [the mean] exceeds by spending more than is right, as has been said. For in small

20

expenses he spends a lot, and puts on an inappropriate display. He gives his club a dinner party in the style of a wedding banquet, and when he supplies a chorus for a comedy, he brings them on stage dressed in purple, as they do at Megara. In all this he aims not at what is fine, but at the display of his wealth and at the admiration he thinks he wins in this way. And so where a large expense is right, he spends a little, and spends a lot where a small expense is right.

4.47 The vice of deficiency

The niggardly person will be deficient in everything. After spending the largest amounts, he will refuse a small amount, and so destroy a fine result. Whatever he does, while he is doing it he will hesitate and consider how he can spend the smallest possible amount; he will even moan about spending this, and will always think he is doing something on a larger scale than is right.

These states, vulgarity and niggardliness, are vices. But they do not bring reproaches, since they do no harm to one's neighbours and are not too disgraceful.

4.5   Magnanimity

4.51   The virtue compared with the vices
contrary to it

Magnanimity seems, even going by the name alone, to be concerned with great things. Let us see first the sorts of things it is concerned with. It does not matter whether we consider the state itself or the person who expresses it.

The magnanimous person, then, seems to be the one who thinks himself worthy of great things and is really worthy of them. For if someone is not worthy of them but thinks he is, he is foolish, and no virtuous person is foolish or senseless; hence the magnanimous person is the one we have mentioned. Someone who is worthy of little and thinks so is

25

30

iv 3
35
1123b

5

temperate, but not magnanimous; for magnanimity is found
in greatness, just as beauty is found in a large body, and
small people can be attractive and well-proportioned, but not
beautiful.

Someone who thinks he is worthy of great things when
he is not is vain; but not everyone who thinks he is worthy
of greater things than he is worthy of is vain.

10 Someone who thinks he is worthy of less than he is worthy
of is pusillanimous, whether he is worthy of great or of
moderate things; and even if he is worthy of little, he thinks
he is worthy of still less than that. The one who seems most
pusillanimous is the one who is worthy of great things; for
consider how little he would think of himself if he were worthy of less.

The magnanimous person, then, is at the extreme in so
far as he makes great claims. But in so far as he makes them
rightly, he is intermediate; for what he thinks he is worthy
15 of reflects his real worth, while the others are excessive or
24 deficient. The pusillanimous person is deficient both in rela-
25 tion to himself [i.e. his worth] and in relation to the magnanimous person's estimate of his own worth, while the vain
26 person makes claims that are excessive for himself, but not
for the magnanimous person.

4.52   The scope of magnanimity: Honour

15 If, then, he thinks he is worthy of great things, and is worthy of them, especially of the greatest things, he has one concern above all. Worth is said to [make one worthy of] external goods; and we would suppose that the greatest of these is
the one we award to the gods, the one above all that is the aim
of people with a reputation for worth, the prize for the finest
20 [achievements]. All this is true of honour, since it is called
the greatest of the external goods. Hence the magnanimous
person has the right concern with honours and dishonours.

And even without argument it appears that magnanimous
people are concerned with honour. For the great think them-

selves worthy of honour most of all, and honour befits their worth.

4.53   The state of the magnanimous person

Magnanimity requires complete virtue

Since the magnanimous person is worthy of the greatest things, he is the best person. For in every case the better person is worthy of something greater, and the best person is worthy of the greatest things; and hence the truly magnanimous person must be good.

Greatness in each virtue also seems proper to the magnanimous person. And surely it would not at all fit a magnanimous person to run away [from danger when a coward would], swinging his arms [to get away faster], or to do injustice. For what goal will make him do shameful actions, when none [of their goals] is great to him? And examination of particular cases makes the magnanimous person appear altogether ridiculous if he is not good. | 30

Nor would he be worthy of honour if he were base. For honour is the prize of virtue, and is awarded to good people. | 35

Magnanimity, then, looks like a sort of adornment of the virtues; for it makes them greater, and it does not arise without them. Hence it is hard to be truly magnanimous, since it is not possible without being fine and good. | 1124a

Hence he has a discriminating attitude
to honour . . .

The magnanimous person, then, is concerned especially with honours and dishonours. And when he receives great honours from excellent people, he will be moderately pleased, thinking he is getting what is proper to him, or even less. For there can be no honour worthy of complete virtue; but still he will accept [excellent people's] honours, since they have nothing greater to award him. | 5

But if he is honoured by just anyone, or for something | 10

99

small, he will entirely disdain it; for that is not what he is worthy of. And similarly he will disdain dishonour; for it will not be justly attached to him.

. . . And to other goods of fortune

As we have said, then, the magnanimous person is concerned especially with honours. Still, he will also have a moderate attitude to riches and power and every sort of good
15 and bad fortune, however it turns out. He will be neither excessively pleased by good fortune nor excessively distressed by ill fortune, since he does not even regard honour as the greatest good.

For positions of power and riches are choiceworthy for their honour; at any rate their possessors wish to be honoured on account of them. Hence the magnanimous person who counts honour for little will also count these other goods for
20 little, which is why he seems arrogant.

The results of good fortune, however, seem to contribute to magnanimity. For the well-born and the powerful or rich are thought worthy of honour, since they are in a superior position, and everything superior in some good is more honoured. Hence these things also make people more magnanimous, since some people honour their possessors for these goods.
25 In reality, however, it is only the good person who is honourable. Still, anyone who has both virtue and these goods is more readily thought worthy of honour.

This attitude distinguishes him from pretenders
to magnanimity

Those who lack virtue but have these other goods are not justified in thinking themselves worthy of great things, and are not correctly called magnanimous; that is impossible without complete virtue. However, they become arrogant and
30 wantonly aggressive when they have these other goods. For without virtue it is hard to bear the results of good fortune
1124b suitably, and when these people cannot do it, but suppose

they are superior to other people, they despise everyone else, and do whatever they please.

They do this because they are imitating the magnanimous person though they are not really like him. They imitate him where they can; hence they do not do actions expressing virtue, but they despise other people. For the magnanimous person is justified when he despises, since his beliefs are true; but the many despise with no good reason.   5

His attitude to danger

He does not face dangers in a small cause, and does not face them frequently, since he honours few things, and is no lover of danger. But he faces them in a great cause, and whenever he faces them he is unsparing of his life, since he does not think life at all costs is worthwhile.

His attitude to giving and receiving benefits

He is the sort of person who does good but is ashamed   10
when he receives it; for doing good is proper to the superior person, and receiving it to the inferior. He returns more good than he has received; for in this way the original giver will be repaid, and will also have incurred a new debt to him, and will be the beneficiary.

Magnanimous people seem to remember the good they do, but not what they receive, since the recipient is inferior to the giver, and the magnanimous person wishes to be superior. And they seem to find pleasure in hearing of the good they   15
do, and none in hearing what they receive – that also seems to be why Thetis does not tell Zeus of the good she has done him, and the Spartans do not tell of the good they have done the Athenians, but only of the good received from them.

Again, it is proper to the magnanimous person to ask for nothing, or hardly anything, but to help eagerly.

His attitude to other people

When he meets people with good fortune or a reputation

20 for worth, he displays his greatness, since superiority over
them is difficult and impressive, and there is nothing ignoble in trying to be impressive with them. But when he meets
ordinary people he is moderate, since superiority over them
is easy, and an attempt to be impressive among inferiors is
as vulgar as a display of strength against the weak.

He stays away from what is commonly honoured, and from
areas where others lead; he is inactive and lethargic except
25 for some great honour or achievement. Hence his actions
are few, but great and renowned.

Moreover, he must be open in his hatreds and his friendships, since concealment is proper to a frightened person.
He is concerned for the truth more than for people's opinion.
He is open in his speech and actions, since his disdain makes
30 him speak freely. And he speaks the truth, except [when he
speaks less than the truth] to the many, [because he is mod-
erate], not because he is self-deprecating.

1125a He cannot let anyone else, except a friend, determine his
life. For that would be slavish; and this is why all flatterers
are servile and inferior people are flatterers.

He is not prone to marvel, since he finds nothing great;
or to remember evils, since it is not proper to a magnanimous
person to nurse memories, especially not of evils, but to
5 overlook them.

He is no gossip. For he will not talk about himself or about
another, since he is not concerned to have himself praised
or other people blamed. Nor is he given to praising people.
Hence he does not speak evil even of his enemies, except
[when he responds to their] wanton aggression.

10 He especially avoids laments or entreaties about necessities
or small matters, since these attitudes are proper to someone
who takes these things seriously.

He is the sort of person whose possessions are fine and
unproductive rather than productive and advantageous, since
that is more proper to a self-sufficient person.

The magnanimous person seems to have slow movements,

102

a deep voice and calm speech. For since he takes few things seriously, he is in no hurry, and since he counts nothing great, he is not strident; and these [attitudes he avoids] are the causes of a shrill voice and hasty movements.

This, then, is the character of the magnanimous person.

4.54 *The vices of excess and deficiency*

The deficient person is pusillanimous, and the person who goes to excess is vain. [Like the vulgar and the niggardly person] these also seem not to be evil people, since they are not evil-doers, but to be in error.

Pusillanimity

For the pusillanimous person is worthy of goods, but deprives himself of the goods he is worthy of, and would seem to have something bad in him because he does not think he is worthy of the goods. Indeed he would seem not to know himself; for if he did, he would aim at the things he is worthy of, since they are goods. For all that, such people seem hesitant rather than foolish.

But this belief of theirs actually seems to make them worse. For each sort of person seeks what [he thinks] he is worth; and these people hold back from fine actions and practices, and equally from external goods, because they think they are unworthy of them.

Vanity

Vain people, on the other hand, are foolish and do not know themselves; and they make this obvious. For they undertake commonly honoured exploits, but are not worthy of them, and then they are found out. They adorn themselves with clothes and ostentatious style and that sort of thing; and since they both wish for good fortune and wish it to be evident, they talk about it, thinking it will bring them honour.

Pusillanimity is more opposed than vanity to magnanimity; for it arises more often, and is worse.

103

35   Magnanimity, then, as has been said, is the virtue con-
      cerned with *great* honour.

4.6   The Virtue Concerned With Small Honours

iv 4   ### 4.61   A distinct virtue must be recognized here

1125b   But, as we said in the first discussion, [just as there is
      a virtue for small-scale giving], there would also seem to
      be a virtue concerned with honour whose relation to mag-
      nanimity seems similar to the relation of generosity to
      magnificence.

      For it abstains, just as generosity does, from anything great,
5   but forms the right attitude in us on medium and small mat-
      ters; and just as the taking and giving of money admits of
      a mean, an excess and a deficiency, so also we can desire
      honour more or less than is right, and we can desire it from
      the right sources and in the right way.

4.62   There is excess and deficiency in relation
to honour

10   For we blame the honour-lover for aiming at honour more
      than is right, and from the wrong sources; and we blame
      someone indifferent to honour for deciding not to be honoured
      even for fine things. Sometimes, however, we praise the
      honour-lover for being manly and a lover of what is fine;
      and again we praise the indifferent person for being moderate
      and temperate, as we said in the first discussion.

      Clearly, however, since we speak in several ways of lov-
      ing something, what we regard as love of honour is not the
15   same attitude in every case. Rather, when we praise it, we
      regard it as loving honour more than the many do; and when
      we blame it, we regard it as loving honour more than is
      right.

      But when the mean has no name, the extremes look like
      rivals for it, as though it were unclaimed.

104

4.63   Hence there is a mean

Nonetheless, where there is excess and deficiency there is also an intermediate condition; and since people desire honour both more and less than is right, it is also possible | 20
to desire it in the right way. This state, then, a nameless mean concerned with honour, is praised.

When compared with love of honour, it appears as indifference to honour; when compared with indifference, it appears as love of honour; and when compared with both, it appears in a way as both. This would seem to be true with the other virtues too; but in this case the extreme people ap- | 25
pear to be opposed [only to each other] because the intermediate person has no name.

4.7   Mildness

4.71   The mean concerned with anger

Mildness is the mean concerned with anger. Since the mean | iv 5
is nameless, and the extremes are practically nameless too, we call the intermediate condition mildness, inclining towards the deficiency, which is also nameless. The excess might be called a kind of irascibility; for the relevant feeling is anger, | 30
though its sources are many and varied.

The person who is angry at the right things and towards the right people, and also in the right way, at the right time and for the right length of time, is praised. This, then, will be the mild person, since it is his mildness that is praised; for being a mild person means being undistured, not led by feeling, but irritated at whatever reason prescribes and | 35
for the length of time it prescribes. And he seems to err more | 1126a
in the direction of deficiency, since the mild person is ready to pardon, not eager to exact a penalty.

4.72   The deficiency

The deficiency — a sort of inirascibility or whatever it is — is blamed, since people who are not angered by the right things, | 5 or in the right way, or at the right times, or towards the right people, all seem to be foolish. For such a person seems to be insensible and to feel no pain. Since he is not angered, he does not seem to be the sort to defend himself; and such willingness to accept insults to oneself and to overlook insults to one's family and friends is slavish.

4.73 Different types of excess

The excess arises in all these ways — in anger towards the wrong people, at the wrong times, more than is right, more hastily than is right, and for a longer time. However, they are not all found in the same person; for they could not all exist together, since evil destroys itself as well as other things, and if it is present as a whole it becomes unbearable.

Irascible people get angry quickly, towards the wrong people, at the wrong times and more than is right; but they stop soon, and this is their best feature. They do all this because they do not contain their anger, but their quick temper makes them pay back the offence without concealment, and then stop.

Choleric people are quick-tempered to extreme, and irascible about everything and at everything; that is how they get their name.

Bitter people, however, are hard to reconcile, and stay angry for a long time, since they contain their emotion. It stops, however, when they pay back the offence; for the exaction of the penalty produces pleasure in place of pain, and so puts a stop to the anger. But if this does not happen, they hold their grudge; for no one else persuades them out of it, since it is not obvious, and digesting anger in oneself takes time. This sort of person is most troublesome to himself and to his closest friends.

The people we call irritable are those who are irritated by the wrong things, more severely and for longer than is right, and are not reconciled until [the offender has suffered] a penalty and corrective treatment.

We regard the excess as more opposed [than the deficiency] to mildness. For it is more widespread, since it comes more naturally to human beings to exact a penalty from the offender [than to overlook an offence]; and moreover irritable people are harder to live with. | 30

4.74 Difficulty of finding the mean

These remarks also make clear a previous point of ours. For it is hard to define how, against whom, about what, and how long we should be angry, and up to what point someone is acting correctly or in error.

For someone who deviates a little towards either excess | 35
or deficiency is not blamed. For sometimes we praise deficient people and say they are mild; and sometimes we say | 1126b
that people who get irritated are manly because we think they are capable of ruling others.

How far, then, and in what way must someone deviate to be open to blame? It is not easy to answer in a [general] account, since these are particular cases, and the judgement depends on perception.

However, this much at least is clear: the intermediate state | 5
is to be praised, and it is expressed in being angry towards the right people, about the right things, in the right way and so on. The excesses and deficiencies are to be blamed, lightly if they go a little way, more if they go further, and strongly if they go far. Clearly, then, we must keep to the intermediate state.

So much, then, for the states concerned with anger. | 10

4.8 Friendliness in social intercourse

4.81 The mean and the extremes | iv 6

In meeting people, living together and associating in conversations and actions, some people seem to be ingratiating;

these are the ones who praise everything to please us and never cross us, but think they must cause no pain to those they meet. In contrast to these, people who oppose us on every point and do not care in the least about causing pain are called cantankerous and quarrelsome.

4.82   The mean

Clearly, the states we have mentioned are blameworthy, and the state intermediate between them is praiseworthy; this state is expressed in accepting and objecting to things when it is right and in the right way.

This state has no name, but it would seem to be most like friendship; for the character of the person in the intermediate state is just what we mean in speaking of a decent friend, except that the friend is also fond of us. It differs from friendship in not requiring any special feeling or any fondness for the people we meet. For this person takes each thing in the right way because that is his character, not because he is a friend or an enemy.

For he will behave this way to new and old acquaintances, to familiar companions and strangers without distinction, except that he will also do what is suitable for each; for the proper ways to spare or to hurt the feelings of familiar companions are not the proper ways to treat strangers.

Attitude to causing pleasure and pain

We have said, then, that in general he will treat people in the right way when he meets them. [More exactly], he will aim to avoid causing pain or to share pleasure, while always referring to what is fine and beneficial.

For he would seem to be concerned with the pleasures and pains that arise in meeting people; and if it is not fine, or it is harmful, for him to share one of these pleasures, he will object and will decide to cause pain instead. Further, if the other person will suffer no slight disgrace or harm from do-

ing an action, and only slight pain if he is opposed, the virtuous person will object to the action and not accept it.

When he meets people with a reputation for worth his at- | 35
titude will be different from his attitude to just anyone; he
will take different attitudes to those he knows better and those | 1127a
he knows less well; and similarly with the other differences,
according what is suitable to each sort of person.

What he will choose in itself [if he need not consider the
consequences], is to share pleasure and avoid causing pain.
But he will be guided by consequences—i.e. by what is fine | 5
and what is expedient—if they are greater; and, moreover,
to secure great pleasure in the future he will cause slight pain.

This, then, is the character of the intermediate person,
though he has no name.

4.83   The extremes

Among those who share pleasure the person who tries to
be pleasant with no ulterior purpose is ingratiating, and the
one who does it for some advantage in money and what
money can buy is the flatterer. The one who objects to | 10
everything is, as we have said, the cantankerous and quarrelsome person. However, the extremes appear to be opposite
[only] to each other, because the intermediate condition has
no name.

4.9   Truthfulness in Social Life

4.91   It is useful to discuss nameless virtues

The mean belonging to boastfulness is also concerned with | iv 7
practically these same [conditions of social life]; and it too
is nameless.

It is a good idea to examine the nameless virtues as well | 15
as the others. For if we discuss particular aspects of character
one at a time, we will acquire a better knowledge of them;
and if we survey the virtues and see that in each case the

virtue is a mean, we will have more confidence in our belief
that the virtues are means.

4.92   The extremes and the mean

As concerns social life, then, having discussed those who
aim at giving pleasure or pain when they meet people, let
us now discuss those who are truthful and false, both in words
and in actions, i.e. in their claims [about themselves].

First, then, the boaster seems to claim qualities that win
reputation, when he either lacks them altogether or has less
than he claims. And the self-deprecator, by contrast, denies
or belittles his actual qualities. The intermediate person,
however, is straightforward, truthful in what he says and
does, since he acknowledges the qualities he has without be-
littling or exaggerating.

Here as elsewhere the mean is praiseworthy

Each of these things may be done with or without an
ulterior purpose; and someone's character determines what
he says and does and the way he lives, if he is not acting
for an ulterior purpose. Now in itself [when no ulterior purpose is involved], falsehood is base and blameworthy, and
truth is fine and praiseworthy; hence the truthful person, like
other intermediate people, is praiseworthy, and both the
tellers of falsehoods are blameworthy, the boaster to a higher
degree.

4.93   The mean

Before we discuss each type of blameworthy person let
us discuss the truthful person. Here we do not mean someone
who is truthful in agreements and in matters of justice and
injustice, since these concern a different virtue, but someone
who is truthful both in what he says and in how he lives,
when nothing about justice is at stake, simply because that
is his state of character.

110

Someone with this character seems to be a decent person. For a lover of the truth who is truthful even when nothing is at stake will be still keener to tell the truth when something | 5 is at stake, since he will avoid falsehood as shameful [when something is at stake], having already avoided it in itself [when nothing was at stake]. And this sort of person is praiseworthy.

He inclines to tell less, rather than more, than the truth; for this appears more suitable, since excesses are oppressive.

4.94 The excess

If someone claims to have more than he has, with no | 10 ulterior purpose, he certainly looks as though he is a base person, since otherwise he would not enjoy telling falsehoods; but apparently he is pointlessly foolish rather than bad.

Among those who do it with an ulterior purpose, the one who does it for reputation or honour is not to be blamed too much as a boaster. But the one who does it for money or for means to making money is more disgraceful.

It is not a person's capacity, but his decision, that makes him a boaster; for his state of character makes a person a | 15 boaster, just as it makes a person a liar. And [boasters differ in their states of character]; one is a boaster because he enjoys telling falsehoods in itself, another because he pursues reputation or gain.

Boasters who aim at reputation, then, claim the qualities that win praise or win congratulation for happiness. Boasters who aim at profit claim the qualities that gratify other people and that allow someone to avoid detection when he claims | 20 to be what he is not, e.g. a wise diviner or doctor. That is why most people claim these sorts of things and boast about them; for they have the features just mentioned.

4.95 The deficiency

Self-deprecators underestimate themselves in what they say, and so appear to have more cultivated characters. For

25 they seem to be avoiding bombast, not looking for profit, in what they say; and the qualities that win reputation are the ones that these people especially disavow, as Socrates also used to do.

On the other hand, those who disavow small and obvious qualities are called humbugs, and are more readily despised; sometimes, indeed, this even appears a form of boastfulness, as the Spartans' [austere] dress

30 does—for the extreme deficiency, as well as the excess, is boastful.

But those who are moderate in their self-deprecation and confine themselves to qualities that are not too commonplace or obvious appear sophisticated.

It is the boaster [rather than the self-deprecator] who appears to be opposed to the truthful person, since he is the worse [of the two extremes].

4.10   Wit

iv 8   *4.101   Its scope*

Since life also includes relaxation, and in this we pass our

1128a time with some form of amusement, here also it seems possible to behave appropriately in meeting people, and to say and listen to the right things and in the right way. The company we are in when we speak or listen also makes a difference. Clearly, then, it is possible here also to exceed the intermediate condition or to be deficient.

5   *4.102   The extremes*

Those who go to excess in raising laughs seem to be vulgar buffoons. They stop at nothing to raise a laugh, and care more about that than about saying what is seemly and avoiding pain to the victims of the joke.

Those who would never say anything themselves to raise a laugh, and even object when other people do it, seem to be boorish and stiff.

112

4.103 The mean

Those who joke in appropriate ways are called witty, or, in other words, agile-witted, since these sorts of jokes seem to be movements of someone's character, and characters are judged, as bodies are, by their movements. Since there are always opportunities at hand for raising a laugh, and most people enjoy amusements and jokes more than they should, buffoons are also called witty because they are thought cultivated; nonetheless, they differ, and differ considerably, from witty people, as our account has made clear.

Dexterity is also proper to the intermediate state. It is proper to the dexterous person to say and listen to what suits the decent and civilized person. For some things are suitable for this sort of person to say and listen to by way of amusement; and the civilized person's amusement differs from the slavish person's, and the educated person's from the uneducated person's. This can also be seen from old and new comedies; for what people used to find funny was shameful abuse, but what they now find funny instead is innuendo, which is considerably more seemly.

Then should the person who jokes well be defined by his making remarks not unsuitable for a civilized person, or by his avoiding pain and even giving pleasure to the hearer? Perhaps, though, this [avoiding pain and giving pleasure] is indefinable, since different people find different things hateful or pleasant.

The remarks he is willing to hear made are of the same sort, since those he is prepared to hear made seem to be those he is prepared to make himself.

Hence he will not be indiscriminate in his remarks. For since a joke is a type of abuse, and legislators prohibit some types of abuse, they would presumably be right to prohibit some types of joke too. Hence the cultivated and civilized person, as a sort of law to himself, will take this [discriminating] attitude.

This, then, is the character of the intermediate person, whether he is called dexterous or witty.

4.104   The vice of excess: Buffoonery

35

1128b

The buffoon cannot resist raising a laugh, and spares neither himself nor anyone else if he can cause laughter, even by making remarks that the sophisticated person would never make, and some that the sophisticated person would not even be willing to hear made.

4.105   The vice of deficiency: Boorishness

The boor is useless when he meets people in these circumstances. For he contributes nothing himself, and objects to everything, even though relaxation and amusement seem to be necessary in life.

5

We have spoken, then, of three means in life, all concerned with association in certain conversations and actions. They differ in so far as one is concerned with truth, the others with what is pleasant. One of those concerned with pleasure is found in amusements, and the other in our behaviour in the other aspects of life when we meet people.

4.11   Shame

iv 9

10

4.111   It is a feeling, not a virtue

Shame is not properly regarded as a virtue, since it would seem to be more like a feeling than like a state [of character]. It is defined, at any rate, as a sort of fear of disrepute, and its expression is similar to that of fear of something terrifying; for a feeling of disgrace makes people blush, and fear of death makes them turn pale. Hence both [types of fear] appear to be in some way bodily [reactions], which seem to be more characteristic of feelings than of states.

15

114

4.112 It is suitable for young people

Further, the feeling of shame is suitable for youth, not for every time of life. For we think it right for young people to be prone to shame, since they live by their feelings, and hence often go astray, but are restrained by shame; and hence we praise young people who are prone to shame. No one, | 20
by contrast, would praise an older person for readiness to feel disgrace, since we think it wrong for him to do any action that causes a feeling of disgrace.

4.113 But it is not suitable for a
virtuous person

For a feeling of disgrace is not proper to the decent person either, if it is caused by base actions; for these should not be done. And if some actions are really disgraceful and others are base [only] in [his] belief, that does not matter, since neither should be done, and so he should not feel dis- | 25
grace. It is proper to a base person to have a character that makes him do disgraceful action.

Further, if someone is in a state that would make him feel disgrace if he were to do a disgraceful action, and because of this thinks he is decent, that is absurd. For shame is concerned with what is voluntary, and the decent person will never willingly do base actions. Shame might, however, be decent on an assumption; for if [the decent person] were to | 30
do [these disgraceful actions], he would feel disgrace; but this does not apply to the virtues.

And if we grant that it is base to feel no disgrace or shame at disgraceful actions, it still does not follow that to do such actions and then to feel disgrace at them is decent.

Continence is not a virtue either. It is a sort of mixed state. We will explain about it in what we say later. Now let us | 35
discuss justice.

5. Justice

5.1   The Definition of Justice

v 1
1129a

5.11   Justice as a state of character

The questions we must examine about justice and injustice are these: What sorts of actions are they concerned with? What sort of mean is justice? What are the extremes between which justice is intermediate? Let us examine them by the same type of investigation that we used in the topics discussed before.

We see that the state everyone means in speaking of justice is the state that makes us doers of just actions, that makes us do justice and wish what is just. In the same way they mean by injustice the state that makes us do injustice and wish what is unjust. Let us also, then, [follow the common beliefs and] begin by assuming this in outline.

*Since justice is a state, its relation to just
actions is different from the relation of a
capacity to its activities*

For what is true of sciences and capacities is not true of states. For while one and the same capacity or science seems to have contrary activities, a state that is a contrary has no contrary activities. Health, e.g., only makes us do healthy actions, not their contraries; for we say we are walking in a healthy way if [and only if] we are walking in the way a healthy person would.

*States may be studied by reference to
their contraries*

Often one of a pair of contrary states is recognized from the other contrary; and often the states are recognized from their subjects. For if, e.g., the good state is evident, the bad state becomes evident too; and moreover the good state be-

116

comes evident from the things that have it, and the things from the state. For if, e.g., the good state is thickness of flesh, then the bad state will necessarily be thinness of flesh, and the thing that produces the good state will be what produces thickness of flesh.

It follows, usually, that if one of a pair of contraries is spoken of in more ways than one, so is the other; if, e.g., what is just is spoken of in more ways than one, so is what is unjust.

5.12   The two types of justice and injustice
Now it would seem that justice and injustice are both spoken of in more ways than one, but since the different ways are closely related, their homonymy is unnoticed, and is less clear than it is with distant homonyms where the distance in appearance is wide (e.g., the bone below an animal's neck and what we lock doors with are called keys homonymously).

5.13   Justice as lawfulness and justice as fairness
Let us, then, find the number of ways an unjust person is spoken of. Both the lawless person and the greedy and unfair person seem to be unjust; and so, clearly, both the lawful and the fair person will be just. Hence what is just will be both what is lawful and what is fair, and what is unjust will be both what is lawless and what is unfair.

5.14   The goods and evils relevant to fairness
Since the unjust person is greedy, he will be concerned with goods—not with all goods, but only with those involved in good and bad fortune, goods which are, [considered] unconditionally, always good, but for this or that person not always good. Though human beings pray for these and pursue them, they are wrong; the right thing is to pray that

what is good unconditionally will also be good for us, but to choose [only] what is good for us.

Now the unjust person [who chooses these goods] does not choose more in every case; in the case of what is bad unconditionally he actually chooses less. But since what is
10 less bad also seems to be good in a way, and greed aims at more of what is good, he seems to be greedy. In fact he is unfair; for unfairness includes [all these actions], and is a common feature [of his choice of the greater good and of the lesser evil].

5.2 General Justice

5.21 It requires observance of law

Since, as we saw, the lawless person is unjust and the lawful person is just, it clearly follows that whatever is lawful is in some way just; for the provisions of legislative science are lawful, and we say that each of them is just.
15 Now in every matter they deal with the laws aim either at the common benefit of all, or at the benefit of those in control, whose control rests on virtue or on some other such basis. And so in one way what we call just is whatever produces and maintains happiness and its parts for a political community.

5.22 The scope of law extends to all the virtues . . .

20 Now the law instructs us to do the actions of a brave person—not to leave the battle-line, e.g., or to flee, or to throw away our weapons; of a temperate person—not to commit adultery or wanton aggression; of a mild person—not to strike or revile another; and similarly requires actions that express the other virtues, and prohibits those that express
25 the vices. The correctly established law does this correctly, and the less carefully framed one does this worse.

118

5.23 . . . and hence general justice is
complete virtue

This type of justice, then, is complete virtue, not complete virtue unconditionally, but complete virtue in relation to another. And this is why justice often seems to be supreme among the virtues, and 'neither the evening star nor the morning star is so marvellous', and the proverb says 'And in justice all virtue is summed up.'   30

Moreover, justice is complete virtue to the highest degree because it is the complete exercise of complete virtue. And it is the complete exercise because the person who has justice is able to exercise virtue in relation to another, not only in what concerns himself; for many are able to exercise virtue in their own concerns but unable in what relates to another.

And hence Bias seems to have been correct in saying that   1130a
ruling will reveal the man, since a ruler is automatically related to another, and in a community. And for the same reason justice is the only virtue that seems to be another person's good, because it is related to another; for it does what   5
benefits another, either the ruler or the fellow-member of the community.

The worst person, therefore, is the one who exercises his vice towards himself and his friends as well [as towards others]. And the best person is not the one who exercises virtue [only] towards himself, but the one who [also] exercises it in relation to another, since this is a difficult task.

This type of justice, then, is the whole, not a part, of virtue, and the injustice contrary to it is the whole, not a part,   10
of vice.

At the same time our discussion makes clear the difference between virtue and this type of justice. For virtue is the same as justice, but what it is to be virtue is not the same as what it is to be justice. Rather, in so far as virtue is related to another, it is justice, and in so far as it is a certain sort of state unconditionally it is virtue.

5.3   Special Justice Contrasted With General

5.31   Special justice must be a virtue distinct from general justice

v 2

15   But we are looking for the type of justice, since we say there is one, that consists in a part of virtue, and correspondingly for the type of injustice that is a part [of vice].

Here is evidence that there is this type of justice and injustice:

First, if someone's activities express the other vices — if, e.g., cowardice made him throw away his shield, or irritability made him revile someone, or ungenerosity made him fail to help someone with money — what he does is unjust, but

20   not greedy. But when one acts from greed, in many cases his action expresses none of these vices — certainly not all of them; but it still expresses some type of wickedness, since we blame him, and [in particular] it expresses injustice. Hence there is another type of injustice that is a part of the whole, and a way for a thing to be unjust that is a part of the whole that is contrary to law.

25   Moreover, if A commits adultery for profit and makes a profit, while B commits adultery because of his appetite, and spends money on it to his own loss, B seems intemperate rather than greedy, while A seems unjust, not intemperate. Clearly, then, this is because A acts to make a profit.

Further, we can refer every other unjust action to some

30   vice — to intemperance if he committed adultery, to cowardice if he deserted his comrade in the battle-line, to anger if he struck someone. But if he made an [unjust] profit, we can refer it to no other vice except injustice.

Hence evidently (a) there is another type of injustice, special injustice, besides the whole of injustice; and (b) it is synonymous with the whole, since the definition is in the

1130b   same genus. For (b) both have their area of competence in relation to another. But (a) special injustice is concerned with

120

honour or wealth or safety, or whatever single name will
include all these, and aims at the pleasure that results from
making a profit; but the concern of injustice as a whole is
whatever concerns the excellent person.   5

Clearly, then, there is more than one type of justice, and
there is another type besides [the type that is] the whole of
virtue; but we must still grasp what it is, and what sort of
thing it is.

5.32 *The distinction reflects the distinction*
between what is lawless and what is unfair

What is unjust is divided into what is lawless and what
is unfair, and what is just into what is lawful and what is
fair. The [general] injustice previously described, then, is   10
concerned with what is lawless. But what is unfair is not the
same as what is lawless, but related to it as part to whole,
since whatever is unfair is lawless, but not everything lawless is unfair. Hence also the type of injustice and the way
for a thing to be unjust [that expresses unfairness] are not
the same as the type [that expresses lawlessness], but differ
as parts from wholes. For this injustice [as unfairness] is a   15
part of the whole of injustice, and similarly justice [as fair-
ness] is a part of the whole of justice.

Hence we must describe special [as well as general] justice
and injustice, and equally this way for a thing to be just or
unjust.

5.33 *A detailed description of general justice is*
unnecessary, since it is simply the whole of virtue

Let us, then, set to one side the type of justice and injustice   20
that corresponds to the whole of virtue, justice being the exercise of the whole of virtue, and injustice of the whole of
vice, in relation to another.

And it is evident how we must distinguish the way for a
thing to be just or unjust that expresses this type of justice

and injustice; for the majority of lawful actions, we might say, are the actions resulting from virtue as a whole. For the law instructs us to express each virtue, and forbids us to express each vice, in how we live. Moreover, the actions producing the whole of virtue are the lawful actions that the laws prescribe for education promoting the common good.

We must wait till later, however, to determine whether the education that makes an individual an unconditionally good man is a task for political science or for another science; for, presumably, being a good man is not the same as being every sort of good citizen.

5.34 But a detailed description of special justice is needed

Special justice, however, and the corresponding way for something to be just [must be divided].

One species is found in the distribution of honours or wealth or anything else that can be divided among members of a community who share in a political system; for here it is possible for one member to have a share equal or unequal to another's.

Another species concerns rectification in transactions. This species has two parts, since one sort of transaction is voluntary, and one involuntary. Voluntary transactions include selling, buying, lending, pledging, renting, depositing, hiring out —these are called voluntary because the origin of these transactions is voluntary. Some involuntary ones are secret, e.g. theft, adultery, poisoning, pimping, slave-deception, murder by treachery, false witness; others are forcible, e.g. assault, imprisonment, murder, plunder, mutilation, slander, insult.

5.4 Justice in Distribution

5.41 Justice, fairness and equality

Since the unjust person is unfair, and what is unjust is unfair, there is clearly an intermediate between the unfair [extremes], and this is what is fair; for in any action where too much and too little are possible, the fair [amount] is also possible. And so if what is unjust is unfair, what is just is fair (*ison*), as seems true to everyone even without argument.

And since what is equal (*ison*) [and fair] is intermediate, what is just is some sort of intermediate. And since what is equal involves at least two things [equal to each other], it follows that what is just must be intermediate and equal, and related to some people. In so far as it is intermediate, it must be between too much and too little; in so far as it is equal, it involves two things; and in so far as it is just, it is just for some people. Hence what is just requires four things at least; the people for whom it is just are two, and the [equal] things that are involved are two.

5.42 *How equality is determined*

Equality for the people involved will be the same as for the things involved, since [in a just arrangement] the relation between the people will be the same as the relation between the things involved. For if the people involved are not equal, they will not [justly] receive equal shares; indeed, whenever equals receive unequal shares, or unequals equal shares, in a distribution, that is the source of quarrels and accusations.

This is also clear from considering what fits a person's worth. For everyone agrees that what is just in distributions must fit some sort of worth, but what they call worth is not the same; supporters of democracy say it is free citizenship, some supporters of oligarchy say it is wealth, others good birth, while supporters of aristocracy say it is virtue.

5.43 *Justice is proportionate equality*

Hence what is just [since it requires equal shares for equal people] is in some way proportionate. For proportion is

15

20

25

30

special to number as a whole, not only to numbers consisting
of [abstract] units, since it is equality of ratios and requires
at least four terms.

Now divided proportion clearly requires four terms. But
so does continuous proportion, since here we use one term
as two, and mention it twice. When, e.g., line A is to line
B as B is to C, B is mentioned twice; and so if B is introduced twice, the terms in the proportion will be four.

What is just will also require at least four terms, with the
same ratio [between the pairs], since the people [A and B]
and the items [C and D] involved are divided in the same
way. Term C, then, is to term D as A is to B, and, taking
them alternately, B is to D as A is to C. Hence there will
also be the same relation of whole [A and C] to whole [B
and D]; this is the relation in which the distribution pairs
them, and it pairs them justly if this is how they are combined.

Hence the combination of term A with C and of B with
D is what is just in distribution, and this way of being just
is intermediate, while what is unjust is contrary to what is
proportionate. For what is proportionate is intermediate, and
what is just is proportionate.

This is the sort of proportion that mathematicians call
geometrical, since in geometrical proportion the relation of
whole to whole is the same as the relation of each [part] to
each [part]. But this proportion [involved in justice] is not
continuous, since there is no single term for both the person
and the item.

What is just, then, is what is proportionate, and what is
unjust is what is counter-proportionate. Hence [in an unjust
action] one term becomes more and the other less; and this
is indeed how it turns out in practice, since the one doing
injustice has more of the good, and the victim less. With an
evil the ratio is reversed, since the lesser evil, compared to
the greater, counts as a good; for the lesser evil is more

choiceworthy than the greater, what is choiceworthy is good,
and what is more choiceworthy is a greater good.

This, then, is the first species of what is just.

5.5   Justice in Rectification

5.51   It is distinct from distributive justice

The other way of being just is the rectificatory, found in
transactions both voluntary and involuntary; and this way
of being just belongs to a different species from the first.

For what is just in distribution of common assets will
always fit the proportion mentioned above, since distribution from common funds will also fit the ratio to one another
of different people's deposits. Similarly, the way of being
unjust that is opposed to this way of being just is what is
counter-proportionate. On the other hand, what is just in
transactions is certainly equal in a way, and what is unjust
is unequal; but still it fits numerical proportion, not the [geo-
metrical] proportion of the other species.

5.52   It involves numerical proportion
and equality

For here it does not matter if a decent person has taken
from a base person, or a base person from a decent person,
or if a decent or a base person has committed adultery.
Rather, the law looks only at differences in the harm [in-
flicted], and treats the people involved as equals, when one
does injustice while the other suffers it, and one has done
the harm while the other has suffered it. Hence the judge
tries to restore this unjust situation to equality, since it is
unequal.

These apply to other wrongs besides theft

For [not only both when one steals from another but also]
and when one is wounded and the other wounds him, or one

kills and the other is killed, the action and the suffering are
unequally divided [with profit for the offender and loss for
10   the victim]; and the judge tries to restore the [profit and] loss
to a position of equality, by subtraction from [the offender's]
profit. For in such cases, stating it without qualification, we
speak of profit for, e.g., the attacker who wounded his victim, even if that is not the proper word for some cases, and
of loss for the victim who suffers the wound. At any rate,
when what was suffered has been measured, one part is called
the [victim's] loss, and the other the [offender's] profit.

1132b11   In fact, however, these names 'loss' and 'profit' are derived
from voluntary exchange. For having more than one's own
share is called making a profit, and having less than what
15   one had at the beginning is called suffering a loss, e.g. in
buying and selling and in other transactions permitted by
law. And when people get neither more nor less, but precisely what belongs to them, they say they have their own
share, and make neither a loss nor a profit.

5.53   Hence rectificatory justice is a mean
1132a14   Hence what is equal is intermediate between more and
less; profit and loss are more and less in contrary ways,
since more good and less evil is profit, and the contrary is
loss; and the intermediate area between [profit and loss],
we have found, is what is equal, which we say is just. Hence
what is just in rectification is what is intermediate between
loss and profit.

*This is confirmed by the judge's rectificatory
role in justice*
20   Hence parties to a dispute resort to a judge, and an appeal
to a judge is an appeal to what is just; for the judge is intended to be a sort of living embodiment of what is just.
Moreover, they seek the judge as an intermediary, and in
some cities they actually call judges mediators, assuming that

126

if they are awarded an intermediate amount, the award will
be just. If, then, the judge is an intermediary, what is just
is in some way intermediate.

5.54 *Rectificatory justice is administered by*
restoring numerical equality

The judge restores equality, as though a line [AB] had been | 25
cut into unequal parts [AC and CB], and he removed from
the larger part [AC] the amount [DC] by which it exceeds
the half [AD] of the line [AB], and added this amount [DC]
to the smaller part [CB]. And when the whole [AB] has
been halved [into AD and DB], then they say that each person has what is properly his own, when he has got an equal
share. This is also why it is called just (*dikaion*), because | 31
it is a bisection (*dicha*), as though we said bisected (*dichaion*),
and the judge (*dikastes*) is a bisector (*dichastes*).

What is equal [in this case] is intermediate, by numerical | 29
proportion, between the larger [AC] and the smaller line | 30
[CB]. For when [the same amount] is subtracted from one | 32
of two equal things and added to the other, then the one part
exceeds the other by the two parts; for if a part had been
subtracted from the one, but not added to the other, the larger | 1132b
part would have exceeded the smaller by just one part. Hence
the larger part exceeds the intermediate by one part, and the
intermediate from which [a part] was subtracted [exceeds the
smaller] by one part.

In this way, then, we will recognize what we must subtract from the one who has more and add to the one who
has less [to restore equality]; for to the one who has less we
must add the amount by which the intermediate exceeds what
he has, and from the greatest amount [which the one who | 5
has more has] we must subtract the amount by which it exceeds the intermediate. Let lines AA', BB' and CC' be
equal; let AE be subtracted from AA' and CD be added to
CC', so that the whole line DCC' will exceed the line EA'

by the parts CD and CF [where CF equals AE]; it follows that DCC′ exceeds BB′ by CD.

18

Hence what is just is intermediate between a certain kind of loss and gain, since it is having the equal amount both

20

before and after [the transaction].

5.6 Justice in Exchange

5.61 Justice is not simple reciprocity

v 5

It seems to some people, however, that reciprocity is also unconditionally just. This was the Pythagoreans' view, since their definition stated unconditionally that what is just is reciprocity with another.

The truth is that reciprocity suits neither distributive nor

25

rectificatory justice, though people take even Rhadamanthys' [primitive] conception of justice to describe rectificatory justice: 'If he suffered what he did, upright justice would be done.'

For in many cases reciprocity conflicts [with rectificatory justice]. If, e.g., a ruling official [exercising his office] wounded someone else, he must not be wounded in retalia-

30

tion, but if someone wounded a ruling official, he must not only be wounded but also receive corrective treatment. Moreover, the voluntary or involuntary character of the action makes a great difference.

5.62 But justice in exchange is proportionate reciprocity

In associations for exchange, however, this way of being just, reciprocity that is proportionate rather than equal, holds people together; for a city is maintained by proportionate reciprocity. For people seek to return either evil for evil,

1133a

since otherwise [their condition] seems to be slavery, or good for good, since otherwise there is no exchange; and they are maintained [in an association] by exchange.

Indeed, that is why they make a temple of the Graces prominent, so that there will be a return of benefits received. For
this is what is special to grace; when someone has been
gracious to us, we must do a service for him in return, and
also ourselves take the lead in being gracious again.   5

5.63   How proportionate reciprocity is secured

It is diagonal combination that produces proportionate exchange. Let A be a builder, B a shoemaker, C a house, D
a shoe. The builder must receive the shoemaker's product
from him, and give him the builder's own product in return.   10
If, then, first of all, proportionate equality is found, and,
next, reciprocity is also achieved, then the proportionate
return will be reached. Otherwise it is not equal, and the exchange will not be maintained, since the product of one may
well be superior to the product of the other. These products,
then, must be equalized.

This is true of the other crafts also; for they would have
been destroyed unless the producer produced the same   15
thing, of the same quantity and quality as the thing affected
underwent.

For no association [for exchange] is formed from two doctors. It is formed from a doctor and a farmer, and, in general,
from people who are different and unequal and who must
be equalized.

5.64   Money is designed to secure proportionate
reciprocity, by facilitating exchange

This is why all items for exchange must be comparable
in some way. Currency came along to do exactly this, and   20
in a way it becomes an intermediate, since it measures everything, and so measures excess and deficiency – how many
shoes are equal to a house.

Hence, as builder is to shoemaker, so must the number
of shoes be to a house; for if this does not happen, there will

25 be no exchange and no association, and the proportionate equality will not be reached unless they are equal in some way. Everything, then, must be measured by some one measure, as we said before.

Exchange rests on need, and hence is facilitated by money

In reality, this measure is need, which holds everything together; for if people required nothing, or needed things to different extents, there would be either no exchange or not the same exchange. And currency has become a sort of

30 pledge of need, by convention; in fact it has its name (*nomisma*) because it is not by nature, but by the current law (*nomos*), and it is within our power to alter it and to make it useless.

Reciprocity will be secured, then, when things are equalized, so that the shoemaker's product is to the farmer's as

1133b the farmer is to the shoemaker. However, they must be introduced into the figure of proportion not when they have already exchanged and one extreme has both excesses, but when they still have their own; in that way they will be equals and associates, because this sort of equality can be found in

5 them. Let A be a farmer, C food, B a shoemaker and D his product that has been equalized; if this sort of reciprocity were not possible, there would be no association.

Now clearly need holds [an association] together as a single unit, since people with no need of each other, both of them or either one, do not exchange, as they exchange whenever another requires what one has oneself, e.g. wine, when they

10 allow the export of corn. This, then, must be equalized.

If an item is not required at the moment, currency serves to guarantee us a future exchange, guaranteeing that the item will be there for us if we require it; for it must be there for us to take if we pay. Now the same thing happens to currency [as to other goods], and it does not always count for

130

the same; still, it tends to be more stable. Hence everything must have a price; for in that way there will always be ex- | 15
change, and then there will be association.

Currency, then, by making things commensurate as a measure does, equalizes them; for there would be no association without exchange, no exchange without equality, no equality without commensurability. And so, though things so different cannot become commensurate in reality, they can become commensurate enough in relation to our needs. | 20
Hence there must be some single unit fixed [as current] by a stipulation. This is why it is called currency; for this makes everything commensurate, since everything is measured by currency.

Let A, for instance, be a house, B ten minae, C a bed. A is half of B if a house is worth five minae or equal to them; and C, the bed, is a tenth of B. It is clear, then, how many | 25
beds are equal to one house — five. This is clearly how exchange was before there was currency; for it does not matter whether a house is exchanged for five beds or for the currency for which five beds are exchanged.

5.7   Political Justice

5.71   Conditions for political justice   v 6
We have previously described, then, the relation of reci- | 1134a23
procity to what is just. We must now notice that we are look- | 25
ing not only for what is just unconditionally but also for what is just in a political association. This is found among associates in a life aiming at self-sufficiency, who are free and either proportionately or numerically equal.

Hence those who lack these features have nothing politically just in their relations, though they have something just in so far as it is similar [to what is politically just].

For what is just is found among those who have law in | 30
their relations. Where there is law, there is injustice, since

the judicial process is judgement that distinguishes what is just from what is unjust. Where there is injustice there is also doing injustice, though where there is doing injustice there need not also be injustice. And doing injustice is awarding to oneself too many of the things that, [considered] unconditionally, are good, and too few of the things that, [considered] unconditionally, are bad.

5.72   The nature of political justice explains
why individuals are tempted to do injustice

35
1134b

This is why we allow only reason, not a human being, to be ruler; for a human being awards himself too many goods and becomes a tyrant, but a ruler is a guardian of what is just and hence of what is equal [and so must not award himself too many goods].

If a ruler is just, he seems to profit nothing by it. For since he does not award himself more of what, [considered] unconditionally, is good if it is not proportionate to him, he

5

seems to labour for another's benefit; that is why justice is said, as we also remarked before, to be another person's good. Hence some payment [for ruling] should be given; this is honour and privilege, and the people who are unsatisfied by these are the ones who become tyrants.

5.73   Forms similar to political justice

What is just for a master and a father is similar to this,

10

not the same. For there is no unconditional injustice in relation to what is one's own; one's own possession, or one's child until it is old enough and separated, is as though it were a part of oneself, and no one decides to harm himself. Hence there is no injustice in relation to them, and so nothing politically unjust or just either. For we found that what is politically just must conform to law, and apply to those who

15

are naturally suited for law, hence to those who have equality in ruling and being ruled. [Approximation to this equal-

132

ity] explains why relations with a wife more than with children or possessions allow something to count as just – for
that is what is just in households; still, this too is different
from what is politically just.

5.74 Justice by nature and by law

One part of what is politically just is natural, and the other   v 7
part legal. What is natural is what has the same validity everywhere alike, independent of its seeming so or not. What is   20
legal is what originally makes no difference [whether it is
done] one way or another, but makes a difference whenever
people have laid down the rule – e.g. that a mina is the price
of a ransom, or that a goat rather than two sheep should be
sacrificed; and also laws passed for particular cases, e.g. that
sacrifices should be offered to Brasidas; and enactments by
decree.

Variations may seem to show there is no natural justice

Now it seems to some people that everything just is merely
legal, since what is natural is unchangeable and equally valid   25
everywhere – fire, e.g. burns both here and in Persia – while
they see that what is just changes [from city to city].

However, variations are consistent with the existence of natural justice

This is not so, though in a way it is so. With us, though
presumably not at all with the gods, there is such a thing
as what is natural, but still all is changeable; despite the   30
change there is such a thing as what is natural and what is not.

What sort of thing that [is changeable and hence] admits
of being otherwise is natural, and what sort is not natural,
but legal and conventional, if both natural and legal are
changeable? It is clear in other cases also, and the same
distinction [between the natural and the unchangeable] will

35   apply; for the right hand, e.g., is naturally superior, even
     though it is possible for everyone to become ambidextrous.
         The sorts of things that are just by convention and expe-
1135a diency are like measures. For measures for wine and for corn
     are not of equal size everywhere, but in wholesale markets
     they are bigger, and in retail smaller. Similarly, the things
     that are just by human [enactment] and not by nature differ
5   from place to place, since political systems also differ; still,
     only one system is by nature the best everywhere.

5.8   The Relation of Justice to Just Action

5.81   Justice as a mean; injustice as excess and deficiency

1133b29   We have now said what it is that is unjust and just. And
     now that we have defined them, it is clear that doing justice
     is intermediate between doing injustice and suffering in-
     justice, since doing injustice is having too much and suffer-
     ing injustice is having too little.
         Justice is a mean, not as the other virtues are, but because
1134a it concerns an intermediate condition, while injustice con-
     cerns the extremes. Justice is the virtue that the just person
     is said to express in the just actions expressing his decision,
     distributing good things and bad, both between himself and
     others and between others. He does not award too much of
5   what is choiceworthy to himself and too little to his neigh-
     bour (and the reverse with what is harmful), but awards what
     is proportionately equal; and he does the same in distributing
     between others.
         Injustice, on the other hand, is related [in the same way]
     to what is unjust. What is unjust is disproportionate excess
     and deficiency in what is beneficial or harmful; hence in-
     justice is excess and deficiency because it concerns excess
10   and deficiency. The unjust person awards himself an excess
     of what is beneficial, [considered] unconditionally, and a de-

134

ficiency of what is harmful, and speaking as a whole, he acts similarly [in distributions between] others, but deviates from proportion in either direction. In an unjust action getting too little good is suffering injustice, and getting too much is doing injustice.

So much, then, for the nature of justice and the nature   15
of injustice, and similarly for what is just and unjust in general.

5.82   The difference between just action and just character

Since it is possible to do injustice without thereby being unjust, what sort of injustice must someone do to be unjust by having one of the different types of injustice, e.g. as a thief or adulterer or brigand?

But perhaps it is not the type of action that makes the difference [between merely doing injustice and being unjust]. For someone might lie with a woman and know who she is,   20
but the origin might be feeling rather than decision; in that case he is not unjust, though he does injustice – e.g. not a thief, though he stole, not an adulterer though he committed adultery, and so on in the other cases.

5.83   Just actions as universals and particulars

Each [type of] just and lawful [action] is related as a uni-   1135a5
versal to the particulars [that embody it]; for the [particular] actions that are done are many, but each [type] is one, since it is universal.

An act of injustice is different from what is unjust, and an act of justice from what is just. For what is unjust is unjust by nature or enactment; and when this has been done,   10
it is an act of injustice, but until then it is only unjust.

The same applies to an act of justice [in contrast to what is just]. Here, however, the general [type of action contrary to an act of injustice] is more usually called a just act, and what is called an act of justice is the [specific type of just act] that rectifies an act of injustice.

Later we must examine each of these actions, to see what sorts of species, and how many, they have, and what they are concerned with.

15

5.9 The Relation of Voluntary Action to Just Action and to Justice

5.91 Particular acts of injustice must be voluntary

v 8   Given this account of just and unjust actions, someone does injustice or does justice whenever he does them willingly, and does neither justice nor injustice whenever he does them unwillingly, except coincidentally, since the actions he does are coincidentally just or unjust.

20   Further, an act of injustice and a just act are defined by what is voluntary and what is involuntary. For when the action is voluntary, the agent is blamed, and thereby also it is an act of injustice. Hence something will be unjust without thereby being an act of injustice, if it is not also voluntary.

5.92 Voluntary action is defined by the appropriate sort of knowledge

And as I said before, I say that an action is voluntary under these conditions:

(1) It is up to the agent.

25   (2) He does it in knowledge, and [hence] not in ignorance of the person, instrument and goal, e.g. whom he is striking, with what, and for what goal.

(3) He [does] each of these neither coincidentally nor by force; if, e.g., someone seized your hand and struck another [with it], you [would not have struck the other] willingly, since it was not up to you.

136

5.93   Clarifications

Knowledge and ignorance

However [the question about knowledge is more complicated. For] it is possible that the victim is your father, and you know he is a human being or a bystander, but do not know he is your father. The same distinction must be made | 30 for the goal and for the action as a whole.

Actions in the agent's power

Actions are involuntary, then, if they are done in ignorance; or not done in ignorance, but not up to the agent; or done by force. For we also do or undergo many of our natural | 1135b [actions and processes], e.g. growing old and dying, in knowledge; but none of them is either voluntary or involuntary.

Coincidental actions

Both unjust and just actions may also be coincidental in the same way. For if someone returned a deposit unwillingly and because of fear, we should say that he neither does | 5 anything just nor does justice, except coincidentally. And similarly if someone is under compulsion and unwilling when he fails to return the deposit, we should say that he coincidentally does injustice and does something unjust.

Voluntary actions contrasted with actions
on decisions

In some of our voluntary actions we act on a previous decision, and in some we act without any; we act on a previous | 10 decision when we act on previous deliberation, and without any when we act without previous deliberation.

5.94   These distinctions explain different ways
of observing and violating justice

Errors

Among the three ways of inflicting harms in an association, actions done with ignorance are errors if someone does
neither the action he supposed, nor to the person, nor with
the instrument, nor for the result he supposed. For he thought,
e.g., that he was not hitting, or not hitting this person, or
15 not for this result; but coincidentally the result that was
achieved was not what he thought (e.g. [he hit him] to graze,
not to wound), or the victim or the instrument was not the
one he thought.

If the infliction of harm violates reasonable expectation,
the action is a misfortune. If it does not violate reasonable
expectation, but is done without vice, it is an error. For someone is in error if the origin of the cause is in him, and unfortunate when it is outside.

Acts of injustice

20 If he does it in knowledge, but without previous deliberation, it is an act of injustice – e.g. actions caused by emotion
and other feelings that are natural or necessary for human
beings. For when someone inflicts these harms and commits
these errors, he does injustice and these are acts of injustice;
but he is not thereby unjust or wicked, since it is not vice
that causes him to inflict the harm.

Actions caused by unjust character

25 But when his decision is the cause, he is unjust and vicious.
Hence it is a sound judgment that actions caused by emotion
do not result from forethought [and hence do not result from
decision], since the origin is not the agent who acted on the
emotion, but the person who provoked him to anger.

Moreover [in these cases] the dispute is not about whether

138

[the action caused by anger] happened or not, but about whether it was just, since anger is a response to apparent injustice.

For they do not dispute about whether it happened or not, as they do in commercial transactions, where one party or the other must be vicious, unless forgetfulness is the cause of the dispute. Rather [in cases of anger] they agree about the fact and dispute about which action was just; but [in commercial transactions] the [cheater] who has plotted against his victim knows very well [that what he is doing is unjust]. Hence [in cases of anger the agent] thinks he is suffering injustice, while [in transactions the cheater] does not think so.

And if [the cheater's] decision causes him to inflict the harm, he does injustice, and in doing *this* sort of act of injustice the agent is unjust, if it violates proportion or equality. In the same way, a person is just if his decision causes him to do justice; but he [merely] does justice if he merely does it voluntarily.

5.95 Conditions justifying pardon

Some involuntary actions are to be pardoned, and some are not. For when someone's error is not only committed in ignorance, but also caused by ignorance, it is to be pardoned. But when it is committed in ignorance, but is caused by some feeling that is neither natural nor human, and not by ignorance, it is not to be pardoned.

5.10 Puzzles About Justice and Injustice

5.101 Can someone voluntarily suffer injustice?

If we have adequately defined suffering injustice and doing injustice, some puzzles might be raised.

First of all, are those bizarre words of Euripides correct, where he writes, ' "I killed my mother—a short tale to tell." "Were both of you willing or both unwilling?" '? For is it

30

1136a

5

v 9
10

15

really possible to suffer injustice willingly, or is it always involuntary, as doing injustice is always voluntary? And is it always one way or the other, or is it sometimes voluntary and sometimes involuntary?

The same question arises about receiving justice. Since doing justice is always voluntary [as doing injustice is], it is reasonable for the same opposition to apply in both cases, so that both receiving justice and suffering injustice will be either alike voluntary or alike involuntary. Now it seems absurd in the case of receiving justice as well [as in the case of suffering injustice] for it to be always voluntary, since some people receive justice, but not willingly.

We might also raise the following puzzle: Does everyone who has received something unjust suffer injustice, or is it the same with receiving as it is with doing? For certainly it is possible, in the case both of doing and of receiving, to have a share in just things coincidentally; and clearly the same is true of unjust things, since doing something unjust is not the same as doing injustice, and suffering something unjust is not the same as suffering injustice. The same is true of doing justice and receiving it; for it is impossible to suffer injustice if no one does injustice and impossible to receive justice if no one does justice.

Apparently the incontinent person voluntarily suffers injustice

Now if doing injustice is simply harming someone willingly (and doing something willingly is doing it with knowledge of the victim, the instrument and the way) with no further conditions; and if the incontinent person harms himself willingly; then he suffers injustice willingly. Hence someone can do injustice to himself; and one of our puzzles was just this, whether someone can do injustice to himself.

Moreover, someone's incontinence might cause him to be

140

willingly harmed by another who is willing, so that it would
be possible to suffer injustice willingly.

But in fact he does not
Perhaps, however, our definition [of doing injustice] was
incorrect, and we should add to 'harming with knowledge
of the victim, the instrument and the way', the condition
'against the wish of the victim'. If so, then someone is harmed   5
and suffers something unjust willingly, but no one suffers
injustice willingly. For no one wishes it, not even the incontinent, but he acts against his wish; for no one wishes
for what he does not think is excellent, and what the incontinent does is not what he thinks it is right [and hence ex-
cellent] to do.

And if someone gives away what is his own, as Homer
says Glaucus gave to Diomede 'gold for bronze, a hundred   10
cows' worth for nine cows' worth', he does not suffer injustice. For it is up to him to give them, whereas suffering
injustice is not up to him, but requires someone to do him
injustice.

Clearly, then, suffering injustice is not voluntary.

5.102   Further questions about injustice
Two further questions that we decided to discuss still re-   15
main: If A distributes to B more than B deserves, is it A,
the distributor, or B, who has more, who does injustice?
And is it possible to do injustice to oneself?

For if the first alternative is possible, and A rather than
B does injustice, then if A knowingly and willingly distributes more to B than to himself, A does injustice to himself.   20
And indeed this is what a moderate person seems to do; for
the decent person tends to take less than his share.

Perhaps, however, it is not true without qualification that
he takes less. For perhaps he is greedy for some other good,
e.g. for reputation or for what is unconditionally fine.

141

Moreover, our definition of doing injustice allows us to solve the puzzle. For since he suffers nothing against his own wish, he does not suffer injustice, at least not from his

25   distribution, but, at most, is merely harmed.

But it is evidently the distributor who does injustice, and the one who has more does not always do it. For the one who receives an unjust share does not do injustice, but rather the one who willingly does what is unjust, i.e. the one who originates the action; and he is the distributor, not the re-

30   cipient. Besides, doing is spoken of in many ways, and there is a way in which soulless things, or hands, or servants at someone else's order, kill; the recipient, then, does not do injustice, but does something that is unjust.

Further, if the distributor judged in ignorance, he does not do injustice in violation of what is legally just, and his judgement is not unjust; in a way, though, it is unjust, since what is legally just is different from what is primarily just.

If, however, he judged unjustly, and did it knowingly, then

1137a   he himself as well [as the recipient] is greedy—to win gratitude or exact a penalty. So someone who has judged unjustly for these reasons has also got more, exactly as though he got a share of the [profits of] the act of injustice. For if he gave judgement about some land, e.g., on this condition [that he would share the profits], and what he got was not land, but money.

5.103   Misconceptions about justice and injustice

5   Since human beings think that doing injustice is up to them, they think that being just is also easy, when in fact it is not. For while lying with a neighbour's wife, wound-ing a neighbour, bribing, are all easy and up to us, being in a certain state when we do them is not easy, and not up to us.

10   Similarly, people think it takes no wisdom to know the things that are just and unjust, because it is not hard to com-

142

prehend what the laws speak of. But these are not the things
that are just, except coincidentally. Knowing how actions
must be done, and how distributions must be made, if they
are to be just, takes more work than it takes to know about
healthy things. And even in the case of healthy things, know-
ing about honey, wine, hellebore, burning and cutting is |15
easy, but knowing how these must be distributed to produce
health, and to whom and when, takes all the work that it
takes to be a doctor.

For the same reason they think that doing injustice is no
less proper to the just than to the unjust person, because the
just person is no less, and even more, able to do each of the
actions. For he is able to lie with a woman, and to wound |20
someone; and the brave person, similarly, is able to throw
away his shield, and to turn and run this way or that.

In fact, however, doing acts of cowardice or injustice is
not doing these actions, except coincidentally; it is being in
a certain state when we do them. Similarly, practising
medicine or healing is not cutting or not cutting, giving
drugs or not giving them, but doing all these things in a cer- |25
tain way.

5.104 The scope of justice explains difficulties in deciding the just distribution

What is just is found among those who have a share in
things that [considered] unconditionally are good, who can
have an excess or a deficiency of them. Some (as, presumably, the gods) can have no excess of them; others, the incurably evil, benefit from none of them, but are harmed by
them all; others again benefit from these goods up to a |30
point; and this is why what is just is something human.

5.105 Decency and its relation to justice

The next task is to discuss how decency is related to jus- | v 10
tice and how what is decent is related to what is just.

143

*The puzzle about their relation: Decency seems
to conflict with justice*

For on examination they appear as neither unconditionally the same nor as states of different kinds. Sometimes we praise what is decent and the decent person, so that even when we praise someone for other things we transfer the term 'decent' and use it instead of 'good', making it clear that what is more decent is better.

And yet, sometimes, when we reason about the matter, it appears absurd for what is decent to be something beyond what is just, and still praiseworthy. For [apparently] either what is just is not excellent or what is decent is not excellent, if it is something other than what is just, or else, if they are both excellent, they are the same.

Explanation and solution of the puzzle

These, then, are roughly the claims that raise the puzzle about what is decent; but in fact they are all correct in a way, and none is contrary to any other. For what is decent is better than one way of being just, but it is still just, and not better than what is just by being a different genus. Hence the same thing is just and decent, and while both are excellent, what is decent is superior.

The puzzle arises because what is decent is just, but is not what is legally just, but a rectification of it. The reason is that all law is universal, but in some areas no universal rule can be correct; and so where a universal rule has to be made, but cannot be correct, the law chooses the [universal rule] that is usually [correct], well aware of the error being made. And the law is no less correct on this account; for the source of the error is not the law or the legislator, but the nature of the object itself, since that is what the subject-matter of actions is bound to be like.

Hence whenever the law makes a universal rule, but in this particular case what happens violates the [intended scope of]

144

the universal rule, here the legislator falls short, and has made
an error by making an unconditional rule. Then it is correct
to rectify the deficiency; this is what the legislator would
have said himself if he had been present there, and what he
would have prescribed, had he known, in his legislation.

Hence what is decent is just, and better than a certain way
of being just—not better than what is unconditionally just,   25
but better than the error resulting from the omission of any
condition [in the rule]. And this is the nature of what is
decent—rectification of law in so far as the universality of
law makes it deficient.

This is also the reason why not everything is guided by
law. For on some matters legislation is impossible, and so
a decree is needed. For the standard applied to what is indefinite is itself indefinite, as the lead standard is in Lesbian   30
building, where it is not fixed, but adapts itself to the shape
of the stone; likewise, a decree is adapted to fit its objects.

Definition of decency

It is clear from this what is decent, and clear that it is just,
and better than a certain way of being just. It is also evident from this who the decent person is; for he is the one   35
who decides for and does such actions, not an exact stickler   1138a
for justice in the bad way, but taking less than he might
even though he has the law on his side. This is the decent
person, and his state is decency; it is a sort of justice, and
not some state different from it.

5.106   Injustice to oneself

Is it possible to do injustice to oneself or not? The answer   v 11
is evident from what has been said.

General injustice

First of all, some just actions are the legal prescriptions   5
expressing each virtue; e.g., we are legally forbidden to kill

ourselves. Moreover, if someone illegally and willingly inflicts harm on another, not returning harm for harm, he does injustice (a person acting willingly is one who knows

10 the victim and the instrument). Now if someone murders himself because of anger, he does this willingly, in violation of correct reason, when the law forbids it; hence he does injustice. But injustice to whom? Surely to the city, not to himself, since he suffers it willingly, and no one willingly suffers injustice. That is why the city both penalizes him and inflicts further dishonour on him for destroying himself, on the assumption that he is doing injustice to the city.

Special injustice

Now consider the type of injustice doing which makes the

15 agent only unjust, not base generally. Clearly this type of unjust action is different from the first type. For one type of unjust person is wicked in the same [special] way as the coward is, not by having total wickedness; hence his acts of injustice do not express total wickedness either.

Here also one cannot do injustice to oneself. For if one could, the same person could lose and get the same thing at

20 the same time. But this is impossible; on the contrary, what is just or unjust must always involve more than one person.

Moreover, doing injustice is voluntary, and results from a decision, and strikes first, since a victim who retaliates does not seem to do injustice; but if someone does injustice to himself, he does and suffers the same thing at the same time.

Further, on this view, it would be possible to suffer injustice willingly.

Besides, no one does injustice without doing one of the

25 particular acts of injustice. But no one commits adultery with his own wife, or burgles his own house, or steals his own possessions.

146

And in general the puzzle about doing injustice to oneself is also solved by the distinction about voluntarily suffering injustice.

5.107 Is it worse to do or to suffer injustice?

Besides, it is evident that both doing and suffering injustice are bad, since one is having more, one having less, | 30 than the intermediate amount, in the same way as with what is healthy in medicine and what is fit in gymnastics [both more and less than the intermediate amount are bad]. But doing injustice is worse; for it is blameworthy, involving vice that is either complete and unconditional or close to it (since not all voluntary doing of injustice is combined with [the state of] injustice). Suffering injustice, however, involves no vice or injustice. | 35

| 1138b

In itself, then, suffering injustice is less bad; and though it might still be coincidentally a greater evil, that is no concern of a craft. Rather, the craft says that pleurisy is a worse illness than a stumble, even though a stumble might sometimes coincidentally turn out worse, e.g. if someone stumbled and by coincidence was captured by the enemy or | 5 killed because he fell.

5.108 Justice and injustice within the self

It is possible for there to be a justice, by similarity and transference, not of a person to himself, but of certain parts of a person — not every kind of justice, but the kind that belongs to masters or households. For in these discussions the part of the soul that has reason is distinguished from the non-rational part. People look at these and it seems to them | 10 that there is injustice to oneself, because in these parts it is possible to suffer something against one's own desire. Hence it is possible for those parts to be just to each other, as it is for ruler and ruled.

So much, then, for our definitions of justice and the other virtues of character.

6. Virtues of Thought

6.1   The Doctrine of the Mean,
Correct Reason, and Virtues of Thought

6.11   What is correct reason?

vi 1   Since we have said previously that we must choose the intermediate condition, not the excess or the deficiency, and
20   that the intermediate condition is as correct reason says, let
us now determine this, [i.e. what it says].

For in all the states of character we have mentioned, as
well as in the others, there is a target which the person who
has reason focuses on and so tightens or relaxes; and there
is a definition of the means, which we say are between
25   excess and deficiency because they express correct reason.

To say this is admittedly true, but it is not at all clear. For
in other pursuits directed by a science it is equally true that
we must labour and be idle neither too much nor too little,
but the intermediate amount prescribed by correct reason.
30   But knowing only this, we would be none the wiser, e.g.
about the medicines to be applied to the body, if we were
told we must apply the ones that medical science prescribes
and in the way that the medical scientist applies them.

Similarly, then, our account of the states of the soul must
not only be true up to this point; we must also determine
what correct reason is, i.e. what its definition is.

6.12   To answer this question we must
discuss the virtues of thought . . .

35   After we divided the virtues of the soul we said that some
1139a   are virtues of character and some of thought. And so, having finished our discussion of the virtues of character, let
us now discuss the others as follows, after speaking first
about the soul.

. . . And to discuss these we must distinguish
two rational parts of the soul

Previously, then, we said there are two parts of the soul,
one that has reason, and one nonrational. Now we should | 5
divide in the same way the part that has reason.

Let us assume there are two parts that have reason; one
with which we study beings whose origins do not admit of
being otherwise than they are, and one with which we study
beings whose origins admit of being otherwise. For when
the beings are of different kinds, the parts of the soul natu-
rally suited to each of them are also of different kinds, since | 10
the parts possess knowledge by being somehow similar and
appropriate [to their objects].

Let us call one of these the scientific part, and the other
the rationally calculating part, since deliberating is the same
as rationally calculating, and no one deliberates about what
cannot be otherwise. Hence the rationally calculating part
is one part of the part of the soul that has reason. | 15

Hence we should find the best state of the scientific and
the best state of the rationally calculating part; for this state
is the virtue of each of them. And since something's virtue
is relative to its own proper function [we must consider the
function of each part].

6.13   The virtuous person has correct decision
and therefore must have the virtue of
practical thought

There are three [capacities] in the soul—perception, under- | vi 2
standing, desire—that control action and truth. Of these three
perception clearly originates no action, since beasts have
perception, but no share in action. | 20

As assertion and denial are to thought, so pursuit and
avoidance are to desire. Now virtue of character is a state
that decides; and decision is a deliberative desire. If, then,

the decision is excellent, the reason must be true and the
25 | desire correct, so that what reason asserts is what desire
pursues.

This, then, is thought and truth concerned with action. By
contrast, when thought is concerned with study, not with action or production, its good or bad state consists [simply]
in being true or false. For truth is the function of whatever
30 | thinks; but the function of what thinks about action is truth
agreeing with correct desire.

Now the origin of an action—the source of the movement,
not the action's goal—is decision, and the origin of decision
is desire together with reason that aims at some goal. Hence
decision requires understanding and thought, and also a state
35 | of character, since doing well or badly in action requires both
thought and character.

Thought by itself, however, moves nothing; what moves
us is thought aiming at some goal and concerned with ac-
1139b | tion. For this is the sort of thought that also originates pro-
ductive thinking; for every producer in his production aims
at some [further] goal, and the unconditional goal is not the
product, which is only the [conditional] goal of some [pro-
duction], and aims at some [further] goal. [An unconditional
goal is] what we achieve in *action*, since doing well in action is the goal.

Now desire is for the goal. Hence decision is either un-
5 | derstanding combined with desire or desire combined with
thought; and what originates movement in this way is a human
being.

*6.14   Correct decision belongs to the rationally
calculating part of the soul, the part concerned
with what is not necessary*

We do not decide to do what is already past; no one decides, e.g, to have sacked Troy. For neither do we deliberate

about what is past, but only about what will be and admits
[of being or not being]; and what is past does not admit of
not having happened. Hence Agathon is correct to say 'Of
this alone even a god is deprived—to make what is all done   10
to have never happened.'

Hence the function of each of the understanding parts is
truth; and so the virtue of each part will be the state that makes
that part grasp the truth most of all.

6.15 The particular virtues of thought

Then let us begin over again, and discuss these states of   vi 3
the soul. Let us say, then, that there are five states in which   15
the soul grasps the truth in its affirmations or denials. These
are craft, scientific knowledge, intelligence, wisdom and understanding; for belief and supposition admit of being false.

6.2 Scientific Knowledge

6.21 It is concerned with what is necessary

What science is is evident from the following, if we must
speak exactly and not be guided by [mere] similarities.

For we all suppose that what we know scientifically does   20
not even admit of being otherwise; and whenever what admits of being otherwise escapes observation, we do not notice
whether it is or is not, [and hence we do not know about
it]. Hence what is known scientifically is by necessity. Hence
it is eternal; for the things that are by unconditional necessity are all eternal, and eternal things are ingenerable and
indestructible.

6.22 Its first principles cannot be
scientifically known

Further, every science seems to be teachable, and what   25
is scientifically knowable is learnable. But all teaching is from
what is already known, as we also say in the *Analytics*; for

151

some teaching is through induction, some by deductive inference, [which both require previous knowledge].

Induction [reaches] the origin, i.e. the universal, while
deductive inference proceeds from the universals. Hence
30 deductive inference has origins from which it proceeds, but
which are not themselves [reached] by deductive inference.
Hence they are [reached] by induction.

6.23   Hence scientific knowledge requires demonstration from indemonstrable premises

Scientific knowledge, then, is a demonstrative state, and
has all the other features that in the *Analytics* we add to the
definition. For someone has scientific knowledge when he
has the appropriate sort of confidence, and the origins are
known to him; for if they are not better known to him
35 than the conclusion, he will have scientific knowledge only
coincidentally.

So much for a definition of scientific knowledge.

6.3   Craft-knowledge

vi 4   ### 6.31   Production contrasted with action
1140a

What admits of being otherwise includes what is produced
and what is done in action. Production and action are different; about them we rely also on [our] popular discussions.
Hence the state involving reason and concerned with action
is different from the state involving reason and concerned
5 with production. Nor is one included in the other; for action
is not production, and production is not action.

6.32   Crafts are concerned with production, not with action

Now building, e.g., is a craft, and is essentially a certain
state involving reason concerned with production; there is
no craft that is not a state involving reason concerned with

production, and no such state that is not a craft. Hence a
craft is the same as a state involving true reason concerned | 10
with production.

Every craft is concerned with coming to be; and the exercise of the craft is the study of how something that admits
of being and not being comes to be, something whose origin
is in the producer and not in the product. For a craft is not
concerned with things that are or come to be by necessity;
or with things that are by nature, since these have their origin | 15
in themselves.

And since production and action are different, craft must
be concerned with production, not with action.

In a way craft and fortune are concerned with the same
things, as Agathon says: 'Craft was fond of fortune, and for-
tune of craft.' | 20

A craft, then, as we have said, is a state involving true
reason concerned with production. Lack of craft is the contrary state involving false reason and concerned with production. Both are concerned with what admits of being otherwise.

6.4   Intelligence

6.41   An intelligent person deliberates
about living well   vi 5

To grasp what intelligence is we should first study the | 25
sort of people we call intelligent.

It seems proper, then, to an intelligent person to be able
to deliberate finely about what is good and beneficial for
himself, not about some restricted area — e.g. about what promotes health or strength — but about what promotes living well
in general.

A sign of this is the fact that we call people intelligent about
some [restricted area] whenever they calculate well to pro-
mote some excellent end, in an area where there is no craft. | 30
Hence where [living well] as a whole is concerned, the deliberative person will also be intelligent.

6.42   The scope of intelligence distinguishes it from scientific knowledge and from craft-knowledge

Now no one deliberates about what cannot be otherwise or about what cannot be achieved by his action. Hence, if science involves demonstration, but there is no demonstration of anything whose origins admit of being otherwise, since every such thing itself admits of being otherwise; and if we cannot deliberate about what is by necessity; it follows that intelligence is not science nor yet craft-knowledge. It is not science, because what is done in action admits of being otherwise; and it is not craft-knowledge, because action and production belong to different kinds.

6.43   Definition of intelligence

The remaining possibility, then, is that intelligence is a state grasping the truth, involving reason, concerned with action about what is good or bad for a human being.

*It must be concerned with action,
not with production*

For production has its end beyond it; but action does not, since its end is doing well itself, [and doing well is the concern of intelligence].

6.44   The definition is confirmed by commonly recognized features of intelligence

Commonly recognized intelligent people

Hence Pericles and such people are the ones whom we regard as intelligent, because they are able to study what is good for themselves and for human beings; and we think that household managers and politicians are such people.

*The recognized connection between temperance
and intelligence*

This is also how we come to give temperance (*sōphrosunē*)
its name, because we think that it preserves intelligence,
(*sōzousan tēn phronēsin*). This is the sort of supposition that
it preserves. For the sort of supposition that is corrupted and
perverted by what is pleasant or painful is not every sort —
not, e.g., the supposition that the triangle does or does not | 15
have two right angles — but suppositions about what is done
in action.

For the origin of what is done in action is the goal it aims
at; and if pleasure or pain has corrupted someone, it follows
that the origin will not appear to him. Hence it will not
be apparent that this must be the goal and cause of all his
choice and action; for vice corrupts the origin. | 20

Hence [since intelligence is what temperance preserves,
and what temperance preserves is a true supposition about
action], intelligence must be a state grasping the truth, involving reason, and concerned with action about human goods.

*We recognize that intelligence cannot
be misused . . .*

Moreover, there is virtue [or vice in the use] of craft, but
not [in the use] of intelligence. Further, in a craft, someone
who makes errors voluntarily is more choiceworthy; but with
intelligence, as with the virtues, the reverse is true. Clearly,
then, intelligence is a virtue, not craft-knowledge. | 25

There are two parts of the soul that have reason. Intelligence is a virtue of one of them, of the part that has belief;
for belief is concerned, as intelligence is, with what admits
of being otherwise.

. . . And that it cannot be forgotten

Moreover, it is not only a state involving reason. A sign
of this is the fact that such a state can be forgotten, but intelligence cannot.

6.5   Understanding

6.51   There must be a virtue of thought concerned with first principles

vi 6

30   Scientific knowledge is supposition about universals, things that are by necessity. Further, everything demonstrable and every science have origins, since scientific knowledge involves reason.

Hence there can be neither scientific knowledge nor craft-knowledge nor intelligence about the origins of what is scien-
35   tifically known. For what is scientifically known is demon-strable, [but the origins are not]; and craft and intelligence
1141a   are about what admits of being otherwise. Nor is wisdom [exclusively] about origins; for it is proper to the wise person to have a demonstration of some things.

6.52   Since no other virtue of thought grasps first principles, understanding must grasp them

[The states of the soul] by which we always grasp the truth and never make mistakes, about what can or cannot
5   be otherwise, are scientific knowledge, intelligence, wisdom and understanding. But none of the first three – intelligence, scientific knowledge, wisdom – is possible about origins. The remaining possibility, then, is that we have understanding about origins.

6.6   Wisdom

6.61   It is concerned with scientific knowledge and with understanding, not with action

vi 7   We ascribe wisdom in crafts to the people who have the
10   most exact expertise in the crafts, e.g. we call Pheidias a wise stone-worker and Polycleitus a wise bronze-worker, signifying nothing else by wisdom than excellence in a craft. But we also think some people are wise in general, not wise

156

in some [restricted] area, or in some other [specific] way, as Homer says in the *Margites*: 'The gods did not make him a digger or a ploughman or wise in anything else.' Clearly, then, wisdom is the most exact [form] of scientific knowledge. | 15

Hence the wise person must not only know what is derived from the origins of a science, but also grasp the truth about the origins. Therefore wisdom is understanding plus scientific knowledge; it is scientific knowledge of the most honourable things that has received [understanding as] its coping-stone.

6.62 *It must be distinguished from intelligence and political science*

For it would be absurd for someone to think that political science or intelligence is the most excellent science, when the best thing in the universe is not a human being [and the most excellent science must be of the best things]. | 20

Moreover, what is good and healthy for human beings and for fish is not the same, but what is white or straight is always the same. Hence everyone would also say that the content of wisdom is always the same, but the content of intelligence is not. For the agent they would call intelligent is the one who studies well each question about his own [good], and he is the one to whom they would entrust such questions. Hence intelligence is also ascribed to some of the beasts, the ones that are evidently capable of forethought about their own life. | 25

It is also evident that wisdom is not the same as political science. For if people are to say that science about what is beneficial to themselves [as human beings] counts as wisdom, there will be many types of wisdom [corresponding to the different species of animals]. For if there is no one medical science about all beings, there is no one science about the good of all animals, but a different science about each specific good. [Hence there will be many types of wis- | 30 dom, contrary to our assumption that it has always the same content].

And it does not matter if human beings are the best among the animals. For there are other beings of a far more divine nature than human beings; e.g., most evidently, the beings composing the universe.

What we have said makes it clear that wisdom is both scientific knowledge and understanding about what is by nature most honourable. That is why people say that Anaxagoras or Thales or that sort of person is wise, but not intelligent, when they see that he is ignorant of what benefits himself. And so they say that what he knows is extraordinary, amazing, difficult and divine, but useless, because it is not human goods that he looks for.

6.7   Intelligence Compared with the Other Virtues of Thought

6.71   It is concerned with action, and hence with particulars

Intelligence, by contrast, is about human concerns, about what is open to deliberation. For we say that deliberating well is the function of the intelligent person more than anyone else; but no one deliberates about what cannot be otherwise, or about what lacks a goal that is a good achievable in action. The unconditionally good deliberator is the one whose aim expresses rational calculation in pursuit of the best good for a human being that is achievable in action.

Nor is intelligence about universals only. It must also come to know particulars, since it is concerned with action and action is about particulars. Hence in other areas also some people who lack knowledge but have experience are better in action than others who have knowledge. For someone who knows that light meats are digestible and healthy, but not which sorts of meats are light, will not produce health;

the one who knows that bird meats are healthy will be better at producing health. And since intelligence is concerned with action, it must possess both [the universal and the particular knowledge] or the [particular] more [than the universal]. Here too, however, [as in medicine] there is a ruling [science].

6.72   *Intelligence concerns both the individual and the community*

Political science and intelligence are the same state, but their being is not the same.   vi 8

One part of intelligence about the city is the ruling part; this is legislative science.   25

The part concerned with particulars [often] monopolizes the name 'political science' that [properly] applies to both parts in common. This part is concerned with action and deliberation, since [it is concerned with decrees and] the decree is to be acted on as the last thing [reached in deliberation]. Hence these people are the only ones who are said to be politically active; for these are the only ones who practise [politics] in the way that handcraftsmen practise [their craft].

It is a mistake to confine intelligence to knowledge of one's own good without reference to the community

Now likewise intelligence concerned with the individual himself seems most of all to be counted as intelligence; and   30
this [part of intelligence often] monopolizes the name 'intelligence' that [properly] applies [to all parts] in common. Of the other parts one is household science, another legislative, another political, one part of which is deliberative and another judicial.

For knowledge of one's own good requires
reference to the community

In fact knowledge of what is [good] for oneself is one species [of intelligence]. But there is much difference [in opinions] about it.

1142a   Someone who knows about himself, and spends his time on his own concerns, seems to be intelligent, while politicians seem to be too active. Hence Euripides says, 'Surely I cannot be intelligent, when I could have been inactive,
5   numbered among all the many in the army, and have had an equal share. . . . For those who go too far and are too active. . . .'

For people seek what is good for themselves, and suppose that this [inactivity] is the action required [to achieve their good]. Hence this belief has led to the view that these are the intelligent people.

Presumably, however, one's own welfare requires house-
10   hold management and a political system.

Moreover, [another reason for the difference of opinion is this]: it is unclear, and should be examined, how one must manage one's own affairs.

6.73 Intelligence is difficult because it
involves experience and deliberation

A sign of what has been said [about the unclarity of what intelligence requires] is the fact that whereas young people become accomplished in geometry and mathematics, and wise within these limits, intelligent young people do not seem to be found. The reason is that intelligence is concerned with particulars as well as universals, and particulars become
15   known from experience, but a young person lacks experience, since some length of time is needed to produce it.

Indeed [to understand the difficulty and importance of experience] we might consider why a boy can become accomplished in mathematics, but not in wisdom or natural science.

160

Surely it is because mathematical objects are reached through abstraction, whereas the origins in these other cases are reached from experience. Young people, then, [lacking experience], have no real conviction in these other sciences, but only say the words, whereas the nature of mathematical objects is clear to them. | 20

Moreover [intelligence is difficult because it is deliberative and] deliberation may be in error about either the universal or the particular. For [we may wrongly suppose] either that all sorts of heavy water are bad or that this water is heavy.

6.74   Since intelligence concerns particulars,
it is neither scientific knowledge
nor understanding

Intelligence is evidently not scientific knowledge; for, as we said, it concerns the last thing [i.e. the particular], since | 25
this is what is done in action. Hence it is opposed to understanding. For understanding is about the [first] terms, [those] that have no account of them; but intelligence is about the last thing, an object of perception, not of scientific knowledge.

This is not the perception of special objects, but the sort by which we perceive that the last among mathematical objects is a triangle; for it will stop here too. This is another species [of perception than perception of special objects]; | 30
but it is still perception more than intelligence is.

6.8   Good Deliberation

6.81   It must be distinguished from other
virtues of thought

Inquiry and deliberation are different, since deliberation | vi 9
is a type of inquiry. We must also grasp what good deliberation is, and see whether it is some sort of scientific knowledge, or belief, or good guessing, or some other kind of thing.

First of all, then, it is not scientific knowledge. For we
1142b   do not inquire for what we already know; but good deliberation is a type of deliberation, and a deliberator inquires and
rationally calculates.

Moreover, it is not good guessing either. For good guessing involves no reasoning, and is done quickly; but we deliberate a long time, and it is said that we must act quickly on
5   the result of our deliberation, but deliberate slowly. Moreover, quick thinking is different from good deliberation, and
quick thinking is a kind of good guessing.

Nor is good deliberation any sort of belief. Rather, since
the bad deliberator is in error, and the good deliberator deliberates correctly, good deliberation is clearly some sort of
correctness.

But it is not correctness in scientific knowledge or in belief.
10   For there is no correctness in scientific knowledge, since there
is no error in it either; and correctness in belief consists in
truth, [but correctness in deliberation does not].

Further, everything about which one has belief is already determined, [but what is deliberated about is not yet
determined].

6.82   It is a type of thought

However, good deliberation requires reason; hence the remaining possibility is that it belongs to thought. For thought
is not yet assertion; [and this is why it is not belief]. For belief
is not inquiry, but already an assertion; but in deliberating,
15   either well or badly, we inquire for something and rationally
calculate about it.

6.83   It must be correct thought

But since good deliberation is a certain sort of correctness
in deliberation, we must inquire what [this correctness] is
and what it is [correctness] about.

It must reach the correct conclusion . . .

Now since correctness has several types, clearly good deliberation will not be every type. For the incontinent or base person will use rational calculation to reach what he proposes to see, and so will have deliberated correctly [if that is all it takes], but will have got himself a great evil. Having deliberated well seems, on the contrary, to be some sort of good; for the sort of correctness in deliberation that makes it good deliberation is the sort that reaches a good. | 20

. . . By the correct process

However, we can reach a good by a false inference, as well [as by correct deliberation], so that we reach the right thing to do, but by the wrong steps, when the middle term is false. Hence this type of deliberation, leading us by the wrong steps to the right thing to do, is not enough for good deliberation either. | 25

Moreover, one person may deliberate a long time before reaching the right thing to do, while another reaches it quickly. Nor, then, is the first condition enough for good deliberation; good deliberation is correctness that reflects what is beneficial, about the right thing, in the right way and at the right time.

. . . And aiming at the correct end

Further, our deliberation may be unconditionally good or good only to the extent that it promotes some [limited] end. Hence unconditionally good deliberation is the sort that correctly promotes the unconditional end [i.e. the highest good], while the [limited] sort is the sort that correctly promotes some [limited] end. | 30

Hence, if having deliberated well is proper to an intelligent person, good deliberation will be the type of correctness that expresses what is expedient for promoting the end about which intelligence is true supposition.

6.9   Comprehension

6.91   It has the same subject matter
as intelligence

vi 10
1143a

Comprehension, i.e. good comprehension, makes people, as we say, comprehend and comprehend well. It is not
the same as scientific knowledge in general. Nor is it the
same as belief, since, if it were, everyone would have comprehension. Nor is it any one of the specific sciences [with
its own specific area], in the way that medicine is about
what is healthy or geometry is about magnitudes.

For comprehension is neither about what always is and
5   is unchanging nor about just anything that comes to be. It
is about what we might be puzzled about and might deliberate
about. Hence it is about the same things as intelligence.

6.92   But it is different from intelligence

Still, comprehension is not the same as intelligence. For
intelligence is prescriptive, since its end is what must be
done or not done in action, whereas comprehension only
10   judges. (For comprehension and good comprehension are
the same; and so are people with comprehension and with
good comprehension.)

Comprehension is neither having intelligence nor acquiring it. Rather, it is similar to the way learning is called comprehending when someone applies scientific knowledge. In
the same way comprehension consists in the application of
belief to judge someone else's remarks on a question that con-
15   cerns intelligence, and moreover it must judge them finely
since judging well is the same as judging finely. And that
is how the name 'comprehension' was attached to the comprehension that makes people have good comprehension. It
is derived from the comprehension found in learning; for we
often call learning comprehending.

164

6.10   Consideration and Considerateness

The [state] called consideration makes people, as we say, considerate and makes them have consideration; it is the correct judgement of the decent person. A sign of this is our saying that the decent person more than others is considerate, and that it is decent to be considerate about some things. Considerateness is the correct consideration that judges what is decent; and correct consideration judges what is true.

vi 11
20

6.11   Intelligence and the Other Virtues
of Thought Concerned with Particulars

6.111   The virtues that grasp particulars

It is reasonable for all these states to tend to the same point. For we ascribe consideration, comprehension, intelligence and understanding to the same people, and say that these have consideration, and thereby understanding, and that they are intelligent and comprehending. For all these capacities are about the last things, i.e. particulars. Moreover, someone has comprehension and good consideration, or has considerateness, in being able to judge about the matters that concern the intelligent person; for what is decent is the common concern of all good people in relations with other people.

25

30

[These states are all concerned with particulars because] whatever is done in action is one of the particular and last things. For the intelligent person also must recognize [what is done in action], while comprehension and consideration are concerned with what is done in action, and this is one of the last things.

35

6.112   Understanding must grasp particulars

Understanding is also concerned with the last things, and in both directions. For there is understanding, not a rational account, about the first terms and the last.

165

1143b   In demonstrations understanding is about the unchanging
        terms that are first.
           In [premises] about what is done in action understanding
        is about the last term, the one that admits of being otherwise,
        and hence about the minor premise. For these last terms are
        the origins of the end to be aimed at, since universals are
5   reached from particulars. We must, then, have perception
        of these particulars, and this perception is understanding.

*6.113   Since understanding requires the
perception of particulars, it requires experience*

It seems to grow naturally . . .
           Hence these states actually seem to grow naturally, so that
        while no one seems to have natural wisdom, people seem
        to have natural consideration, comprehension and judgement.
        A sign [of their apparent natural character] is our thinking
        that they also correspond to someone's age, and the fact that
        understanding and consideration belong to a certain age, as
10   though nature were the cause.

           . . . But in fact it requires experience
           We must attend, then, to the undemonstrated remarks and
        beliefs of experienced and older people or of intelligent peo-
        ple, no less than to demonstrations. For these people see cor-
        rectly because experience has given them their eye.
15   We have said, then, what intelligence and wisdom are;
        what each is about; and that each is the virtue of a different
        part of the soul.

6.12   Puzzles About Intelligence and Wisdom

6.121   What use are intelligence and wisdom?
vi 12   Someone might, however, be puzzled about what use they
        are.

166

First puzzle

For wisdom is not concerned with any sort of coming | 20
into being, and hence will not study any source of human
happiness.

Second puzzle

Admittedly intelligence will study this; but what do we need
it for? | 25

For knowledge of what is healthy or fit—i.e. of what | 26
results from the state of health, not of what produces
it—makes us no readier to act appropriately if we are
already healthy; for having the science of medicine or | 27
gymnastics makes us no readier to act appropriately. | 21
Similarly, intelligence is the science of what is just and
what is fine, and what is good for a human being; but
this is how the good man acts; and if we are already
good, knowledge of them makes us no readier to act | 25
appropriately, since virtues are states [activated in
actions].

Third puzzle

If we concede that intelligence is not useful for this, should | 28
we say it is useful for becoming good? In that case it will
be no use to those who are already excellent. Nor, however, | 30
will it be any use to those who are not. For it will not matter
to them whether they have it themselves or take the advice
of others who have it. The advice of others will be quite adequate for us, just as it is with health: we wish to be healthy,
but still do not learn medical science.

Fourth puzzle

Besides, it would seem absurd for intelligence, inferior as
it is to wisdom, to control it [as a superior. But this will | 35
be the result], since the science that produces also rules and
prescribes about its product.

6.122   Answer to the first two puzzles:
How wisdom and intelligence are valuable

We must discuss these questions; for so far we have only gone through the puzzles about them.

1144a   First of all, let us state that both intelligence and wisdom must be choiceworthy in themselves, even if neither produces anything at all; for each is the virtue of one of the two [rational] parts [of the soul].

Second, they do produce something. Wisdom produces happiness, not in the way that medical science produces health, but in the way that health produces [health]. For since

5   wisdom is a part of virtue as a whole, it makes us happy because it is a state that we possess and activate.

Further, we fulfil our function in so far as we have intelligence and virtue of character; for virtue makes the goal correct, and intelligence makes what promotes the goal [cor-

10   rect]. The fourth part of the soul, the nutritive part, has no such virtue [related to our function], since no action is up to it to do or not to do.

6.13   Answer to the Second and Third Puzzles:
The Relation Between Intelligence and
Virtue of Character

To answer the claim that intelligence will make us no readier to do fine and just actions, we must begin from a little further back [in our discussion].

6.131   Virtue requires the right decision

Here is where we begin. We say that some people who

15   do just actions are not yet thereby just, if, e.g., they do the actions prescribed by the laws, either unwillingly or because of ignorance or because of some other end, not because of the actions themselves, even though they do the right actions, those that the excellent person ought to do. Equally, however,

it would seem to be possible for someone to do each type
of action in the state that makes him a good person, i.e. be-
cause of decision and for the sake of the actions themselves. | 20

6.132 The right decision requires cleverness, but also virtue

Now virtue makes the decision correct; but the actions that
are naturally to be done to fulfil the decision are the concern
not of virtue, but of another capacity. We must get to know
them more clearly before continuing our discussion.

There is a capacity, called cleverness, which is such as
to be able to do the actions that tend to promote whatever | 25
goal is assumed and to achieve it. If, then, the goal is fine,
cleverness is praiseworthy, and if the goal is base, cleverness is unscrupulousness; hence both intelligent and
unscrupulous people are called clever.

6.133 Hence intelligence requires virtue

Intelligence is not the same as this capacity [of cleverness],
though it requires it. Intelligence, this eye of the soul, can- | 30
not reach its fully developed state without virtue, as we have
said and as is clear. For inferences about actions have an
origin: 'Since the end and the best good is this sort of thing',
whatever it actually is—let it be any old thing for the sake of
argument. And this [best good] is apparent only to the good per-
son; for vice perverts us and produces false views about the ori- | 35
gins of actions.

Evidently, then, we cannot be intelligent without being
good. | 1144b

6.134 The relation of virtue to intelligence is clearer when we distinguish natural virtue from full virtue

We must, then, also examine virtue over again. For vir- | vi 13
tue is similar [in this way] to intelligence; as intelligence is

related to cleverness, not the same but similar, so natural
virtue is related to full virtue.

For each of us seems to possess his type of character to
5   some extent by nature, since we are just, brave, prone to
temperance, or have another feature, immediately from birth.
However, we still search for some other condition as full
goodness, and expect to possess these features in another
way.

For these natural states belong to children and to beasts
as well [as to adults], but without understanding they are
10 evidently harmful. At any rate, this much would seem to be
clear: just as a heavy body moving around unable to see suffers a heavy fall because it has no sight, so it is with virtue.
[A naturally well-endowed person without understanding will
harm himself.] But if someone acquires understanding, he
improves in his actions; and the state he now has, though
still similar [to the natural one], will be virtue to the full
extent.

6.135   The distinction makes it clear that
full and complete virtue requires intelligence

And so, just as there are two sorts of conditions, cleverness
15 and intelligence, in the part of the soul that has belief, so
also there are two in the part that has character, natural virtue and full virtue. And of these full virtue cannot be acquired without intelligence.

6.136   Hence we can now correctly define the
relation of the virtues to intelligence

This is why some say that all the virtues are [instances of]
intelligence, and why Socrates' inquiries were in one way
correct, and in another way in error. For in that he thought
20 all the virtues are [instances of] intelligence, he was in error;
but in that he thought they all require intelligence, he was
right.

170

Here is a sign of this: Whenever people now define virtue, they all say what state it is and what it is related to, and then add that it is the state that expresses correct reason. Now correct reason is reason that expresses intelligence; it would seem, then, that they all in a way intuitively believe that the state expressing intelligence is virtue. | 25

But we must make a slight change. For it is not merely the state expressing correct reason, but the state involving correct reason, that is virtue. And it is intelligence that is correct reason in this area. Socrates, then, thought that the virtues are [instances of] reason because he thought they are all [instances of] knowledge, whereas we think they involve reason. | 30

What we have said, then, makes it clear that we cannot be fully good without intelligence, or intelligent without virtue of character.

6.137 The inseparability of the virtues

In this way we can also solve the dialectical argument that someone might use to show that the virtues are separated from each other. For, [it is argued], since the same person is not naturally best suited for all the virtues, someone will | 35
already have one virtue before he has got another.

This is indeed possible with the natural virtues. It is not possible, however, with the [full] virtues that someone must have to be called unconditionally good; for as soon as he | 1145a
has intelligence, which is a single state, he has all the virtues as well.

6.138 Conclusion on intelligence and virtue:
Another answer to the second puzzle

And clearly, even if intelligence were useless in action, we would need it because it is the virtue of this part of the soul, and because the decision will not be correct without intelligence or without virtue. For virtue makes us reach the | 5 end in our action, while intelligence makes us reach what promotes the end.

6.139 Conclusion on the relation of intelligence to wisdom: Answer to the fourth puzzle

Moreover, intelligence does not control wisdom or the better part of the soul, just as medical science does not control health. For it does not use health, but only aims to bring health into being; hence it prescribes for the sake of health,
10   but does not prescribe to health. Besides, [saying that intelligence controls wisdom] would be like saying that political science rules the gods because it prescribes about everything in the city.

7. Conditions Connected with Virtue and Vice: Continence and Incontinence

7.1 Conditions Superior to Virtue, Inferior to Vice, and
vii 1   Between Virtue and Vice
15   Next we should make a new beginning, and say that there are three conditions of character to be avoided — vice, incontinence and bestiality. The contraries of two of these are clear; we call one virtue and the other continence.

7.11 Superior and inferior conditions

The contrary to bestiality is most suitably called virtue
20   superior to us, a heroic, indeed divine, sort of virtue. Thus Homer made Priam say that Hector was remarkably good; 'nor did he look as though he were the child of a mortal man, but of a god.' Moreover, so they say, human beings become gods because of exceedingly great virtue.

Clearly, then, this is the sort of state that would be op-
25   posite to the bestial state. For indeed, just as a beast has

172

neither virtue nor vice, so neither does a god, but the god's state is more honourable than virtue, and the beast's belongs to some kind different from vice.

Now it is rare that a divine man exists. (This is what the Spartans habitually call him; whenever they very much admire someone, they say he is a divine man.) Similarly, the bestial person is also rare among human beings. He is most often found in foreigners; but some bestial features also result from diseases and deformities. We also use 'bestial' as a term of reproach for people whose vice exceeds the human level.

7.12   Conditions between vice and virtue

We must make some remarks about this condition later. We have discussed vice earlier. We must now discuss incontinence, softness and self-indulgence, and also continence and resistance; for we must not suppose that continence and incontinence are concerned with the same states as virtue and vice, or that they belong to a different kind.

7.13   Method of inquiry

As in the other cases we must set out the appearances, and first of all go through the puzzles. In this way we must prove the common beliefs about these ways of being affected — ideally, all the common beliefs, but if not all, then most of them, and the most important. For if the objections are solved, and the common beliefs are left, it will be an adequate proof.

7.2   Common Beliefs About Continence and Incontinence

Continence and resistance seem to be good and praiseworthy conditions, while incontinence and softness seem to be base and blameworthy conditions.

The continent person seems to be the same as one who abides by his rational calculation; and the incontinent person seems to be the same as one who abandons it.

The incontinent person knows that his actions are base, but does them because of his feelings, while the continent person knows that his appetites are base, but because of reason does not follow them.

People think the temperate person is continent and resistant. Some think that every continent and resistant person is temperate, while others do not. Some people say the incontinent person is intemperate and the intemperate incontinent, with no distinction; others say they are different.

Sometimes it is said that an intelligent person cannot be incontinent; but sometimes it is said that some people are intelligent and clever, but still incontinent.

Further, people are called incontinent about emotion, honour and gain.

These, then, are the things that are said.

7.3   Puzzles About the Common Beliefs

7.31   The incontinent person's knowledge

vii 2   We might be puzzled about the sort of correct supposition someone has when he acts incontinently.

Does he have knowledge?

First of all, some say he cannot have knowledge [at the time he acts]. For it would be terrible, Socrates thought, for knowledge to be in someone, but mastered by something else, and dragged around like a slave. For Socrates fought against the account [of incontinence] in general, in the belief that there is no incontinence; for no one, he thought, supposes while he acts that his action conflicts with what is best; our action conflicts with what is best only because we are ignorant [of the conflict].

This argument, then, contradicts things that appear mani-

festly. If ignorance causes the incontinent person to be affected as he is, then we must look for the type of ignorance
that it turns out to be; for it is evident, at any rate, that be-   30
fore he is affected the person who acts incontinently does
not think [he should do the action he eventually does].

Or only belief?
Some people concede some of [Socrates' points], but reject some of them. For they agree that nothing is superior
to knowledge, but deny that no one's action conflicts with
what has seemed better to him. Hence they say that when
the incontinent person is overcome by pleasure he has only
belief, not knowledge.   35

In that case, however, if he has belief, not knowledge, and
what resists is not a strong supposition, but only a mild one,   1146a
such as people have when they are in doubt, we will pardon
failure to abide by these beliefs against strong appetites. In
fact, however, we do not pardon vice, or any other blameworthy condition [and incontinence is one of these].

Or intelligence?
Then is it intelligence that resists, since it is the strongest?   5
This is absurd. For on this view the same person will be both
intelligent and incontinent; and no one would say that the
intelligent person is the sort to do the worst actions willingly.

Besides, we have shown earlier that the intelligent person
acts [on his knowledge], since he is concerned with the last
things, [i.e. particulars], and that he has the other virtues.

7.32 Must the continent person have bad desires?
Further, if the continent person must have strong and base   10
appetites, the temperate person will not be continent nor the
continent person temperate. For the temperate person is not
the sort to have either excessive or base appetites; but [the
continent person] must have both.

175

For if his appetites are good, the state that prevents him from following them must be base, so that not all continence is excellent. If, on the other hand, the appetites are weak and not base, continence is nothing impressive; and if they are base and weak, it is nothing great.

7.33   Is incontinence sometimes desirable?

Besides, if continence makes someone prone to abide by every belief, it is bad, if, e.g., it makes him abide by a false as well [as a true] belief.

And if incontinence makes someone prone to abandon every belief, there will be an excellent type of incontinence. Neoptolemus, e.g., in Sophocles' *Philoctetes* is praiseworthy when, after being persuaded by Odysseus, he does not abide by his resolve, because he feels pain at lying.

Besides, the sophistical argument is a puzzle. For [the sophists] wish to refute an [opponent, by showing] that his views have paradoxical results, so that they will be clever in encounters. Hence the inference that results is a puzzle; for thought is tied up, since it does not want to stand still because the conclusion is displeasing, but it cannot advance because it cannot solve the argument.

A certain argument, then, concludes that foolishness combined with incontinence is virtue. For incontinence makes someone act contrary to what he supposes [is right]; but since he supposes that good things are bad and that it is wrong to do them, he will do the good actions, not the bad.

7.34   Is incontinence worse than intemperance?

Further, someone who acts to pursue what is pleasant because this is what he is persuaded and decides to do, seems to be better than someone who acts not because of rational calculation, but because of incontinence.

For the first person is the easier to cure, because he might be persuaded otherwise; but the incontinent person illustrates

176

the proverb 'If water chokes us, what must we drink to wash | 35
it down?' For if he had been persuaded to do the action he | 1146b
does, he would have stopped when he was persuaded to act
otherwise; but in fact, though already persuaded to act otherwise, he still acts [wrongly].

7.35 *What is the scope of incontinence?*

Further, is there incontinence and continence about everything? If so, who is the simply incontinent? For no one has
all the types of incontinence, but we say that some people
are simply incontinent. | 5

7.36 *Our approach to the puzzles*

These, then, are the sorts of puzzles that arise. We must
undermine some of these claims, and leave others intact; for
the solution of the puzzle is the discovery [of what we are
seeking].

First, then, we must examine whether the incontinent has | vii 3
knowledge or not, and in what way he has it. Second, what
should we take to be the incontinent and the continent per- | 10
son's area of concern – every pleasure and pain, or some
definite subclass? Are the continent and the resistant person
the same or different? Similarly we must deal with the other
questions that are relevant to this study.

7.4 *The Scope of Incontinence*

We begin the examination with this question: Are the con- | 15
tinent and the incontinent person distinguished [from others]
(i) by their concerns, or (ii) by their attitudes to them? In
other words, is the incontinent person incontinent (i) only
by having these concerns, or instead (ii) by having this attitude; or instead (iii) by both?

[Surely (iii) is right.] For [(i) is insufficient] since the sim-
ple incontinent is not concerned with everything, but with | 20
the same things as the intemperate person. Moreover, [(ii)

is insufficient] since he is not incontinent simply by being inclined towards these things – that would make incontinence the same as intemperance. Rather [as (iii) implies], he is incontinent by being inclined towards them in this way. For the intemperate person acts on decision when he is led on, since he thinks it is right in every case to pursue the pleasant thing at hand; but the incontinent person thinks it is wrong to pursue it, yet still pursues it.

7.5 Solution to the First Puzzle:
What Sort of Knowledge Does the
Incontinent Person Have or Lack?

7.51 It does not matter whether he has
knowledge or belief

25   It is claimed that the incontinent person's action conflicts with true belief, not with knowledge. But whether it is knowledge or belief that he has does not matter for this argument. For some people with belief are in no doubt, but think they have exact knowledge.

If, then, it is the weakness of their conviction that makes people with belief, not people with knowledge, act in conflict with their supposition, it follows that knowledge will [for these purposes] be no different from belief; for, as Hera-
30 cleitus makes clear, some people's convictions about what they believe are no weaker than other people's convictions about what they know.

7.52 But it does matter whether knowledge is
actual or potential

7.521 It is merely potential if we are not
attending to it . . .

But we speak of knowing in two ways, and ascribe it both to someone who has it without using it and to someone who

178

is using it. Hence it will matter whether someone has the
knowledge that his action is wrong, without attending to his
knowledge, or both has and attends to it. For this second | 35
case seems extraordinary, but wrong action when he does
not attend to his knowledge does not seem extraordinary.

7.522 . . . Or if we lack the premise
about particulars

Besides, since there are two types of premises, someone's | 1147a
action may well conflict with his knowledge if he has both
types of premises, but uses only the universal premise and
not the particular premise. For [the particular premise states
the particulars and] it is particular actions that are done.

7.523 . . . Or if we lack a universal term
that we need

Moreover, [in both types of premises] there are different
types of universal, (a) one type referring to the agent himself,
and (b) the other referring to the object. Perhaps, e.g., some- | 5
one knows that (a1) dry things benefit every human being,
and that (a2) he himself is a human being, or that (b1) this
sort of thing is dry; but he either does not have or does not
activate the knowledge that (b2) this particular thing is of
this sort.

Hence these ways [of knowing and not knowing] make such
a remarkable difference that it seems quite intelligible [for
someone acting against his knowledge] to have the one sort
of knowledge [i.e. without (b2)], but astounding if he has
the other sort [including (b2)].

7.524 . . . Or if our condition precludes the
exercise of our knowledge

Besides, human beings may have knowledge in a way dif- | 10
ferent from those we have described. For we see that hav-

ing without using includes different types of having; hence some people, e.g. those asleep or mad or drunk, both have knowledge in a way and do not have it.

15 Moreover, this is the condition of those affected by strong feelings. For emotions, sexual appetites and some conditions of this sort clearly [both disturb knowledge and] disturb the body as well, and even produce fits of madness in some people.

And this is the case that is relevant
to incontinence

Clearly, then [since incontinents are also affected by strong feelings], we should say that they have knowledge in a way similar to these people.

Saying the words that come from knowledge is no sign [of fully having it]. For people affected in these ways even
20 recite demonstrations and verses of Empedocles. Further, those who have just learnt something do not yet know it, though they string the words together; for it must grow into them, and this needs time.

Hence we must suppose that incontinents say the words in the way that actors do.

7.53   How incontinence happens

Action requires the combination of universal
and particular beliefs

Further, we may also look at the cause in the following
25 way, referring to [human] nature. One belief (a) is universal; the other (b) is about particulars, and because they are particulars perception controls them. And in the cases where these two beliefs result in (c) one belief, it is necessary in purely theoretical beliefs for the soul to affirm what has been concluded, and in beliefs about production (d) to act at once on what has been concluded.

If, e.g., (a) everything sweet must be tasted, and (b) this, some one particular thing, is sweet, it is necessary (d) for someone who is able and unhindered also to act on this at the same time. |30

But the incontinent person's appetite causes
the normal combination to be disrupted

Suppose, then, that someone has (a) the universal belief, and it hinders him from tasting; he has (b) the second belief, that everything sweet is pleasant and this is sweet, and this belief (b) is active; and he also has appetite. Hence the belief (c) tells him to avoid this, but appetite leads him on, since |35 it is capable of moving each of the [bodily] parts.

The result, then, is that in a way reason and belief make |1147b him act incontinently. The belief (b) is contrary to correct reason (a), but only coincidentally, not in itself. For it is the appetite, not the belief, that is contrary [in itself to correct reason].

Hence beasts are not incontinent, because they have no universal supposition, but [only] appearance and memory of |5 particulars.

7.54 How incontinence involves ignorance

How is the ignorance resolved, so that the incontinent person recovers his knowledge? The same account that applies to someone drunk or asleep applies here too, and is not special to this way of being affected. We must hear it from the natural scientists.

And since the last premise (b) is a belief about something perceptible, and controls action, this must be what the in- |10 continent person does not have when he is being affected. Or rather the way he has it is not knowledge of it, but, as we saw, [merely] saying the words, as the drunk says the words of Empedocles.

Further, since the last term does not seem to be universal,

181

15 or expressive of knowledge in the same way as the universal term, even the result Socrates was looking for would seem to come about. For the knowledge that is present when someone is affected by incontinence, and that is dragged about because he is affected, is not the sort that seems to be knowledge to the full extent [in (c)], but only perceptual knowledge [in (b)].

So much, then, for knowing and not knowing, and for how it is possible to know and still to act incontinently.

7.6 Solution to the Fifth Puzzle:
vii 4 *Who is Simply Incontinent?*
20 Next we must say whether anyone is simply incontinent, or all incontinents are incontinent in some particular way; and if someone is simply incontinent, we must say what sorts of things he is incontinent about.

7.61 Types of pleasures
First of all, both the continent and resistant person and the incontinent and soft person are evidently concerned with pleasures and pains.

Some sources of pleasure are necessary; others are choice-
25 worthy in themselves, but can be taken to excess. The necessary ones are the bodily conditions, i.e. those that concern food, sexual intercourse, and the sorts of bodily conditions that we took to concern temperance and intemperance. Other sources of pleasure are not necessary, but are choice-
30 worthy in themselves, e.g. victory, honour, wealth and similar good and pleasant things.

7.62 Incontinents in particular ways
When people go to excess, in conflict with the correct reason in them, in the pursuit of these sources of pleasure, we do not call them simply incontinent, but add the condition that they are incontinent about wealth, gain, honour or

emotion, and not simply incontinent. For we assume that
they are different, and called incontinent [only] because of
a similarity, just as the Olympic victor named Human was   35
different, since for him the common account [of human be-   1148a
ing] was only a little different from his special one, but it
was different none the less.

A sign in favour of what we say is the fact that incontinence
is blamed not only as an error but as a vice, either unconditional or partial, while none of these conditions is blamed
as a vice.

7.63   Simple incontinents
Now consider the people concerned with the bodily grati-   5
fications, those that we take to concern the temperate and
the intemperate person. Some of these people go to excess
in pursuing these pleasant things and avoiding painful things —
hunger, thirst, heat, cold and all that concerns touch and
taste — not, however, because they have decided on it, but
in conflict with their decision and thought.

These are the people called simply incontinent, not with   10
the added condition that they are incontinent about, e.g.,
anger.

A sign of this is the fact that people are also called soft
about these [bodily] pleasures, but not about any of the non-
necessary ones.

7.64   The incontinent person and the
intemperate person
This is also why we include the incontinent and the intemperate person, and the continent and the temperate person, in the same class, but do not include any of those who
are incontinent in some particular way. It is because the in-   15
continent and the intemperate person are concerned in a way
with the same pleasures and pains. In fact they are concerned
with the same things, but not in the same way; the intem-

perate person decides on them, but the incontinent person
does not.

Hence, if someone has no appetites, or slight ones, for excesses, but still pursues them and avoids moderate pains, we
will take him to be more intemperate than the person who
20 does it because he has intense appetites. For think of the
lengths he would go to if he also acquired vigorous appetites
and felt severe pains at the lack of necessities.

7.65   Non-vicious incontinence
Some pleasant things are naturally choiceworthy, some
naturally the opposite, some in between, as we divided them
earlier. Hence some appetites and pleasures are for fine and
25 excellent kinds of things, e.g. wealth, profit, victory and
honour. About all these and about the things in between people are blamed not for feeling an appetite and love for them,
but for doing so in a particular way, namely to excess.

Some people are overcome by, or pursue, some of these
30 naturally fine and good things to an extent that conflicts with
reason, e.g. they take honour or children or parents more
seriously than is right. For though these are certainly good
and people are praised for taking them seriously, still excess about them is also possible. It is excessive if someone
fights, as Niobe did [for her children], even with the gods,
1148b or regards his father as Satyrus, nicknamed the Fatherlover,
did – for he seemed to be excessively silly about it.

There is no vice here, for the reason we have given, since
each of these things is naturally choiceworthy for itself,
though excess about them is bad and to be avoided. Simi-
5 larly, there is no incontinence here either, since incontinence
is not merely to be avoided, but also blameworthy [and these
conditions are not].

But because it is a similar way of being affected, people
call it incontinence, adding the condition that it is incontinence
about this or that. Just so they call someone a bad doctor

or a bad actor, though they would never call him simply bad,
since each of these conditions is not vice, but only similar | 10
to it by analogy.

It is likewise clear that the only condition we should take
to be continence or incontinence is the one concerned with
what concerns temperance and intemperance. We speak of
incontinence about emotion because of the similarity [to simple incontinence], and hence add the condition that someone
is incontinent about emotion, as we do with honour or gain.

7.66 *Simple incontinence must be distinguished from bestial and diseased states*

vii 5

Some things are naturally pleasant, and some of these are | 15
unconditionally pleasant, while others correspond to differences between kinds of animals and of human beings. Other
things are not naturally pleasant, but deformities or habits
or degenerate natures make them pleasant; and we can see
states concerned with each of these that are similar to [states
concerned with naturally pleasant things].

Bestiality

By bestial states I mean e.g. the female human being who | 20
is said to tear pregnant women apart and devour the children; or the pleasures of some of the savage people around
the Black Sea who are reputed to enjoy raw meat and human
flesh, while some trade their children to each other to feast
on; or what is said about Phalaris. These states are bestial.

Disease

Other states are caused by attacks of disease, and in some | 25
cases by fits of madness — e.g. the person who sacrificed his
mother and ate her, and the one who ate the liver of his
fellow-slave.

Other states result from diseased conditions or from habit —
e.g. plucking hairs, chewing nails, even coal and earth, and

besides these sexual intercourse between males. For in some
30 people these result from [a diseased] nature, in others from
habit, as, e.g., in those who have suffered wanton [sexual]
assault since their childhood.

These conditions allow only the qualified kind
of incontinence or vice

Whenever nature is the cause, no one would call these
people incontinent, any more than women would be called
incontinent for being mounted rather than mounting. The
same applies to those who are in a diseased state because
of habit.

1149a   Each of these states, then, is outside the limits of vice,
just as bestiality is. If someone who has them overcomes
them or is overcome by them, that is not simple [continence
or] incontinence, but the type so called from similarity, just
as someone who is overcome by emotion should be called
incontinent in relation to his feelings, but not [simply] incontinent.

5   Among all the excesses of foolishness, cowardice, intemperance and irritability some are bestial, some diseased. If,
e.g., someone's natural character makes him afraid of everything, even the noise of a mouse, he is a coward with a bestial sort of cowardice. Another person was afraid of a weasel
because of an attack of disease.

Among foolish people also those who naturally lack reason
10 and live only by perception are bestial, as some races of distant foreigners do. Those who are foolish because of attacks
of disease, e.g. epilepsy, or because of fits of madness, are
diseased.

Sometimes it is possible to have some of these conditions
without being overcome — e.g. if Phalaris had an appetite to
15 eat a child or for some bizarre sexual pleasure, but restrained
it. It is also possible to be overcome by these conditions and
not merely to have them.

186

The scope of incontinence

One sort of vice is human, and this is called simple vice; another sort is called vice with an added condition, and is said to be bestial or diseased vice, but not simple vice. Similarly, then, it is also clear that one sort of incontinence is bestial, another diseased, but only the incontinence corresponding to human intemperance is simple incontinence. | 20

It is clear, then, that incontinence and continence apply only to the concerns of intemperance and temperance, and for other things there is another form of incontinence, so called by transference of the name, and not simply.

7.7 Simple Incontinence is Worse than Incontinence in Emotion

7.71 Simple incontinence is less closely related to reason

Moreover, let us observe, incontinence about emotion is | vii 6
less shameful than incontinence about appetites. | 25

For, first of all, emotion would seem to hear reason a bit, but to mishear it. It is like over-hasty servants who run out before they have heard all their instructions, and then carry them out wrongly, or dogs who bark at any noise at all, before investigating to see if it is a friend. In the same way, since emotion is naturally hot and hasty, it hears, but | 30 does not hear the instruction, and rushes off to exact a penalty. For reason or appearance has shown that we are being slighted or wantonly insulted; and emotion, as though it had inferred that it is right to fight this sort of thing, is irritated at once. Appetite, however, only needs reason or perception | 35 to say that this is pleasant, and it rushes off for gratification.

Hence emotion follows reason in a way, but appetite does | 1149b not. Therefore [incontinence about appetite] is more shameful. For if someone is incontinent about emotion, he is over-

187

come by reason in a way; but if he is incontinent about appetite, he is overcome by appetite, not by reason.

7.72 *It is less natural*

Besides, it is more pardonable to follow natural desires, since it is also more pardonable to follow those natural appetites that are shared by everyone and to the extent that they are shared. Now emotion and irritability are more natural than the excessive and unnecessary appetites. It is just as the son said in his defence for beating his father: 'Yes, and he beat his father, and his father beat *his* father before that'; and pointing to his young son, he said, 'And he will beat me when he becomes a man; it runs in our family.' Similarly, the father being dragged by his son kept urging him to stop at the front door, since that was as far as he had dragged his own father.

7.73 *It involves more plotting*

Moreover, those who plot more are more unjust. But the emotional person does not plot, and neither does emotion; it is open. Appetite, however, is like what they say about Aphrodite, 'trick-weaving Cypris', and what Homer says about her embroidered girdle: 'Blandishment, which steals the wits even of the very intelligent.'

If, then, incontinence about appetite is more unjust and more shameful than incontinence about emotion, it is simple incontinence, and vice in a way.

7.74 *It more justly provokes anger*

Further, no one feels pain when he commits wanton aggression; but whatever someone does from anger, he does feeling pain when he does it, whereas the wanton aggressor does what he does with pleasure. Now if whatever more justly provokes anger is more unjust, incontinence caused by appetite is more unjust, since emotion involves no wanton aggression.

7.8   Incontinence Compared with Intemperance

7.81   We can grasp the scope of incontinence
by grasping the scope of intemperance

It is clear, then, how incontinence about appetites is more
shameful than incontinence about emotion, and that continence and incontinence are about bodily appetites and pleasures. Now we must grasp the varieties of these appetites
and pleasures.

As we said at the beginning, some appetites are human
and natural in kind and degree, some bestial, some caused
by deformities and diseases. Temperance and intemperance
are concerned only with the first of these.

This is also why we do not call beasts either temperate
or intemperate, except by transference of the name, if one
kind of animal exceeds another altogether in wanton aggression, destructiveness and ravenousness. For beasts have
neither decision nor rational calculation, but are outside
[rational] nature, as the madmen among human beings are.

Bestiality is less grave than vice, but more frightening; for
the best part is not corrupted, as it is in a human being, but
absent altogether. Hence a comparison between the two is
like a comparison between an inanimate and an animate being to see which is worse. For in each case the badness of
something that lacks an internal origin of its badness is less
destructive than the badness of something that has such an
internal origin; and understanding is such an internal origin.
It is similar, then, to a comparison between the injustice [of
a beast] and an unjust human being; for in a way each [of
these] is worse, since a bad human being can do innumer-
ably more bad things than a beast.

7.82   How intemperance differs from incontinence

Now consider the pleasures and pains arising through touch
and taste, and consider the appetites for these pleasures, and

25

30

35
1150a

5

vii 7
10

189

the aversions from these pains. Earlier we defined temperance and intemperance as concerned with these. It is possible for someone to be in the state where he is overcome,
even by [pleasure and pains] which most people overcome,
and possible to overcome even those that overcome most people. The person who is prone to be overcome by pleasures
is incontinent; the one who overcomes is continent; the one
overcome by pains is soft; and the one who overcomes them
15 is resistant. The state of most people is in between, though
indeed they may lean more towards the worse states.

Now some pleasures are necessary and some are not. [The
necessary ones are necessary] to a certain extent, while their
excesses and deficiencies are not. The same is true for appetites and pains.

One person pursues excesses of pleasant things because
20 they are excesses and because he decides on it, for themselves
and not for some further result. He is intemperate; for he
is bound to have no regrets, and so is incurable, since someone without regrets is incurable.

The one who is deficient is his opposite, while the intermediate one is temperate. The same is true for the one who
avoids bodily pains not because he is overcome, but because
he decides on it.

25 One of those who do not [act on] decision is led on because
of pleasure; the other is led on because he is avoiding the
pain that comes from appetite; hence these two differ from
each other.

Intemperance is worse than incontinence

Now it would seem to everyone that someone who does
a shameful action from no appetite or a weak one is worse
than if he does it from an intense appetite; and similarly if
he strikes another not from anger, he is worse than if he
30 strikes from anger. For [if he can do such evil when he is
unaffected by feeling], what would he have done if he had

190

been strongly affected? Hence the intemperate person is worse than the incontinent.

7.83   How incontinence differs from softness

One of the states mentioned [being overcome by pain] is more a species of softness, while the other person is intemperate. The continent person is opposed to the incontinent, and the resistant to the soft. For resistance consists in holding out, and continence in overcoming, but holding out | 35 is different from overcoming, just as not being defeated differs from winning; hence continence is more choiceworthy than resistance.

Someone who is deficient in withstanding what most people withstand, and are capable of withstanding, is soft and | 1150b self-indulgent; for self-indulgence is a kind of softness. This person trails his cloak to avoid the labour and pain of lifting it, and imitates an invalid, though he does not think he is | 5 miserable — he is [merely] similar to a miserable person.

It is similar with continence and incontinence also. For it is not surprising if someone is overcome by strong and excessive pleasures or pains; on the contrary, this is pardonable, provided he struggles against them — like Theodectes' Philoctetes bitten by the snake, or Carcinus' Cercyon in the | 10 *Alope*, and like those who are trying to restrain their laughter and burst out laughing all at once, as happened to Xenophantes. But it is surprising if someone is overcome by what most people can resist, and is incapable of withstanding it, not because of his hereditary nature or because of disease — as, e.g., the Scythian kings' softness is hereditary, and as the | 15 female is distinguished [by softness] from the male.

The lover of amusements also seems to be intemperate, but in fact he is soft. For amusement is a relaxation, since it is a release, and the lover of amusement is one of those who go to excess here.

191

7.84   Types of incontinence

One type of incontinence is impetuosity, while another is
20 weakness. For the weak person deliberates, but then his feeling makes him abandon the result of his deliberation; but
the impetuous person is led on by his feelings because he
has not deliberated. For some people are like those who do
not get tickled themselves if they tickle someone else first;
if they see and notice something in advance, and rouse themselves and their rational calculation, they are not overcome
25 by feelings, no matter whether something is pleasant or
painful.

Quick-tempered and ardent people are most prone to be
impetuous incontinents. For in quick-tempered people the
appetite is so fast, and in ardent people so intense, that
they do not wait for reason, because they tend to follow
appearance.

7.9   Answer to the Fourth Puzzle:
Why Intemperance is Worse than Incontinence

7.91   Incontinence is curable,
but intemperance is not

vii 8   The intemperate person, as we said, is not prone to regret,
30 since he abides by his decision [when he acts]. But every
incontinent is prone to regret. Hence the truth is not what
we said in raising the puzzles, but in fact the intemperate
person is incurable, and the incontinent curable.

For vice resembles diseases such as dropsy or consump-
tion, while incontinence is more like epilepsy; vice is a con-
1151a3 tinuous bad condition, while incontinence is not. For the in-
4 continent is similar to those who get drunk quickly from a
5 little wine, and from less than it takes for most people.
1150b35   And in general incontinence and vice are of different kinds.
for the vicious person does not notice that he is vicious, while
the incontinent person notices that he is incontinent.

Among the incontinent people themselves those who aban- don themselves [to desire, i.e. the impetuous] are better than those [i.e. the weak] who have reason but do not abide by it. For the second type are overcome by a less strong feel- ing, and do not act without having deliberated, as the first type do.

Evidently, then, incontinence is not a vice, though pre- sumably it is one in a way. For incontinence conflicts with decision, while vice expresses decision. All the same, it is similar to vice in its actions. Thus Demodocus attacks the Milesians: 'The Milesians are not stupid, but they do what stupid people would do'; and in the same way incontinents are not unjust, but will do injustice.

7.92   Intemperance destroys first principles, but incontinence does not

Moreover, the incontinent person is the sort to pursue ex- cessive bodily pleasures that conflict with correct reason, but not because he is persuaded [it is best]. The intemperate per- son, however, is persuaded, because he is the sort of person to pursue them. Hence the incontinent person is easily per- suaded out of it, while the intemperate person is not.

For virtue preserves the origin, while vice corrupts it; and in action the end we act for is the origin, as the assumptions are the origins in mathematics. Reason does not teach the origins either in mathematics or in actions; [with actions] it is virtue, either natural or habituated, that teaches correct belief about the origin.

The sort of person [with this virtue] is temperate, and the contrary sort intemperate. But there is also someone who because of his feelings abandons himself contrary to correct reason. They overcome him far enough so that his actions do not express correct reason, but not so far as to make him the sort of person to be persuaded that it is right to pursue such pleasures without restraint. This is the incontinent per-

5

10

15

20

25 son. He is better than the intemperate person, and is not unconditionally bad, since the best thing, the origin, is preserved in him.

Another sort of person is contrary to him. [This is the continent person] who abides [by reason] and does not abandon
himself, not because of his feelings at least. It is evident
from this that the continent person's state is excellent, and
the incontinent person's state is base.

7.10   Answer to the Third Puzzle:
The Continent Person's Decision

7.101   It must be the correct decision

vii 9   Now is someone continent if he abides by just any sort
30 of reason and any sort of decision, or must he abide by the
correct decision? And is someone incontinent if he fails to
abide by just any decision and any reason, or must it be reason that is not false, and the correct decision? This was the
puzzle raised earlier.

Perhaps in fact the continent person abides, and the incontinent fails to abide, by just any decision coincidentally,
but abides by the true reason and the correct decision in it-
35 self. For if someone chooses or pursues one thing because
1151b of a second, he pursues and chooses the second in itself and
the first coincidentally. Now when we speak of something
unconditionally, we speak of it in itself. Hence in one way
[i.e. coincidentally] the continent person abides by just any
opinion, and the incontinent abandons it; but unconditionally the continent person abides by the true opinion and the
incontinent person abandons it.

7.102   Continence must be distinguished from
undesirable states easily confused with it

5   Now there are some other people who tend to abide by
their belief. These are the people called stubborn, who are

194

hard to persuade into something and not easy to persuade out of it. These have some similarity to continent people, just as the wasteful person has to the generous, and the rash to the confident. But they are different on many points.

The continent person is not swayed because of feeling and appetite; [but he is not inflexible about everything] since he will be easily persuaded whenever it is appropriate. But stubborn people are not swayed by reason; for they acquire appetites, and many of them are led on by pleasures.

The stubborn include the opinionated, the ignorant and the boorish. The opinionated are as they are because of pleasure and pain. For they find enjoyment in winning [the argument] if they are not persuaded to change their views, and they feel pain if their opinions are voided, like decrees in the Assembly. Hence they are more like incontinent than like continent people.

7.103 *And incontinence must be distinguished from desirable states easily confused with it*

There are also some people who do not abide by their resolutions, but not because they are incontinent—Neoptolemus, e.g., in Sophocles' *Philoctetes*. Though certainly it was pleasure that made him abandon his resolution, it was a fine pleasure, since he found telling the truth pleasant, and Odysseus had persuaded him to lie. [He is not incontinent;] for not everyone who does something because of pleasure is either intemperate or base or incontinent, but only someone who does it because of a shameful pleasure.

7.104 *The deficiency corresponding to continence*

Now there is also the sort of person who enjoys bodily things less than is right, and does not abide by reason; hence the continent person is intermediate between this person and the incontinent. For the incontinent fails to abide by reason because of too much [enjoyment]; and the other person fails because of too little; while the continent person abides and is not swayed because of too much or too little.

30 If continence is excellent, then both of these contrary states must be base, as indeed they appear. However, the other state is evident in only a few people on a few occasions; and hence continence seems to be contrary only to incontinence, just as temperance seems to be contrary only to intemperance.

7.11 Answer to the Fourth Common Belief: Temperance and Continence

Now many things are called by some name because of similarity [to genuine cases]; this has happened also to the continence of the temperate person, because of similarity.
35 For the continent and the temperate person are both the sort to do nothing in conflict with reason because of bodily plea-
1152a sures; but the continent person has base appetites, and the temperate person lacks them. The temperate person is the sort to find nothing pleasant that conflicts with reason; the continent is the sort to find such things pleasant but not to be led by them.

The incontinent and the intemperate person are similar too;
5 though they are different, they both pursue bodily sources of pleasure, but the intemperate person [pursues them because he] also thinks it is right, while the incontinent person does not think so.

7.12 Answer to the Fifth Common Belief: Incontinence and Intelligence

7.121 An incontinent person cannot be intelligent
vii 10 Nor can the same person be at once both intelligent and incontinent.

For we have shown that an intelligent person must also
8 at the same time be excellent in character, [and the inconti-

196

nent person is not]. However, a clever person may well be   10
incontinent. Indeed, the reason people sometimes seem to
be intelligent but incontinent is that [really they are only   11
clever and] cleverness differs from intelligence in the way   12
we described in our first discussion; though they are closely   13
related in definition, they differ in [so far as intelligence re- 14
quires the right] decision.

Moreover, someone is not intelligent simply by knowing;   8
he must also act on his knowledge. But the incontinent per-   9
son does not.

Further, the incontinent person is not in the condition of   14
someone who knows and is attending [to his knowledge, as
he would have to be if he had intelligence], but in the condi-   15
tion of one asleep or drunk.

7.122   *But still, he is not vicious*

He acts willingly; for in a way he acts in knowledge both
of what he is doing and of the end he is doing it for. But he
is not base, since his decision is decent; hence he is half base.

Nor is he unjust, since he is not a plotter. For one type
of incontinent person [i.e. the weak] does not abide by the
result of his deliberation, while the ardent [i.e. impetuous]
person is not even prone to deliberate at all.

In fact the incontinent person is like a city that votes for   20
all the right decrees and has good laws, but does not apply
them, as in Anaxandrides' taunt, 'The city willed it, that cares
nothing for laws.' The base person, by contrast, is like a city
that applies its laws, but applies bad ones.

7.123   *Some varieties of incontinence are*
worse than others

Incontinence and continence are concerned with what ex-   25
ceeds the state of most people; the continent person abides
[by reason] more than most people are capable of doing, the
incontinent person less.

197

The [impetuous] type of incontinence found in ardent people is more easily cured than the [weak] type of incontinence
found in those who deliberate but do not abide by it.

Incontinents through habituation are more easily cured than
30 the natural incontinents; for habit is easier than nature to
change. Indeed the reason why habit is also difficult to change
is that it is like nature, as Euenus says, 'Habit, I say, is
longtime training, my friend, and in the end training is nature
for human beings.'

We have said, then, what continence and incontinence,
35 resistance and softness are, and how these states are related
to each other.

8. A Further Condition Connected with Virtue and Vice: Pleasure

8.1 Problems About Pleasure

vii 11   ### 8.11 Why pleasure is important
1152b
It is proper to the political philosopher to study pleasure
and pain, since he is the ruling craftsman of the end which
we refer to in calling something unconditionally bad or good.

Moreover, we must also examine them because we have
5 laid it down that virtue and vice of character are concerned
with pains and pleasures, and because most people think happiness involves pleasure; hence they call the blessed person
by that name (*makarios*) from enjoyment (*chairein*).

8.12 Beliefs about pleasure

(1) Now it seems to some people that no pleasure is a good,
either in itself or coincidentally, on the ground that the good
is not the same as pleasure.
10   (2) To others it seems that some pleasures are good, but
most are bad.

(3) Further, the third view is that even if every pleasure
is a good, the best good still cannot be pleasure.

198

8.13   Arguments for these beliefs

(1) Their reasons for thinking it is not a good at all are these:

(a) Every pleasure is a perceived becoming towards [the fulfillment of something's] nature; but no becoming is of the same kind as its end, e.g. no [process of] building is of the same kind as a house.   15

(b) Besides, the temperate person avoids pleasures.

(c) Besides, the intelligent person pursues what is painless, not what is pleasant.

(d) Besides, pleasures impede intelligent thinking, and impede it more the more we enjoy them; no one, e.g., while having sexual intercourse can think about anything.

(e) Besides, every good is the product of a craft, but there is no craft of pleasure.

(f) Besides, children and animals pursue pleasure.   20

(2) To show that not all pleasures are excellent things, people say (a) that some are shameful and reproached, and (b) that some are harmful, since some pleasant things cause disease.

(3) To show that the best good is not pleasure, people say that pleasure is not an end, but a becoming.

These, then, are roughly the things said about it.

8.2   Reply to the Arguments   vii 12

These arguments, however, do not show that pleasure is   25
not a good, or even that it is not the best good. This will be clear as follows.

8.21   Not all pleasures are unconditional
pleasures, and unconditional pleasures may
still be goods

First of all, since what is good may be good in either of two ways, as unconditionally good or as good for some particular thing or person, this will also be true for natures and states, and hence also for processes and becomings. And so among the [processes and becomings] that seem bad (i) some are bad unconditionally, but for some person not bad, and for this person actually choiceworthy. (ii) Some are not choiceworthy for him either, except sometimes and for a short time, not on each occasion. (iii) Some are not even pleasures, but appear to be; these are the [processes], e.g. in sick people, that involve pain and are means to medical treatment.

Further, since one sort of good is an activity and another sort is a state, the processes that restore us to our natural state are pleasant coincidentally. Here the activity in the appetites belongs to the rest of our state and nature [i.e. the part that is still undisturbed]. For there are also pleasures without pain and appetite, e.g. the pleasures of studying, those in which our nature lacks nothing.

A sign [that supports our distinction between pleasures] is the fact that we do not enjoy the same thing when our nature is being refilled that we enjoy when it is eventually fully restored. When it is fully restored, we enjoy things that are unconditionally pleasant; but when it is being refilled, we enjoy even the contrary things.

For we even enjoy sharp or bitter things, though none of these is pleasant by nature or unconditionally pleasant. Hence [these pleasures] are not [unconditional] pleasures either; for as pleasant things differ from each other, so the pleasures arising from them differ too.

8.22 Reply to (3): Pleasure may still be the best good

Further, it is not necesssary for something else to be better than pleasure, as the end, some say, is better than the becoming. For pleasures are not becomings, nor do they all even involve a becoming. They are activities, and an end [in themselves], and arise when we exercise [a capacity], not when we are coming to be [in some state]. And not all pleasures have something else as their end, but only those in people who are being led towards the completion of their nature.

8.23 Reply to (1a): Pleasure is not a perceived becoming

Hence it is also a mistake to call pleasure a perceived becoming. It should instead be called an activity of the natural state, and should be called not perceived, but unimpeded. The reason it seems to some people to be a becoming is that it is a good to the full extent [and hence an activity]; for they think activities are becomings, though in fact these are different things.

8.24 Reply to (2b): Pleasures with bad results

To say that pleasures are bad because some pleasant things cause disease is the same as saying that some healthy things are bad for money-making. To this extent both are bad; but that is not enough to make them bad, since even study is sometimes harmful to health.

8.25 Reply to (1d): Pleasures that impede

Neither intelligence nor any state is impeded by the pleasures arising from it, but only by alien pleasures. For the pleasures arising from study and learning will make us study and learn all the more.

8.26 Reply to (1e): Pleasure and craft

The fact that pleasure is not the product of a craft is quite reasonable; for a craft does not belong to any other activity either, but to a capacity. And yet, the crafts of perfumery and cooking do seem to be crafts of pleasure.

8.27 Reply to (1b), (1c), (1f): Varieties of pleasures

The claim that the temperate person avoids pleasure, that the intelligent person pursues the painless life, and that

children and beasts pursue pleasure – all these are solved by
the same reply. For we have explained in what ways pleasures
30 are good, and in what ways not all are unconditionally good;
and it is these pleasures [that are not unconditionally good]
that beasts and children pursue, while the intelligent person
pursues painlessness in relation to these. These are the pleasures associated with appetite and pain and the bodily pleasures (since these are associated with appetite and pain) and
their excesses, whose pursuit makes the intemperate person
intemperate. Hence the temperate person avoids these plea-
35 sures [but not all pleasures], since there are pleasures of the
temperate person too.

8.3 Further Reply to (1): Pleasure Still

vii 13 *Appears to be a Good*
1153b   Moreover, it is also agreed that pain is an evil, and is to
be avoided; for one kind of pain is unconditionally bad, and
another is bad in a particular way, by impeding [activities].
But the contrary to what is to be avoided, in so far as it is bad
and to be avoided, is a good; hence pleasure must be a good.
5   For Speusippus' solution – [that pleasure is contrary both to
pain and to the good] as the greater is contrary both to the
lesser and to the equal – does not succeed. For he would not
say [as his solution requires] that pleasure is essentially an evil.

8.4 Further Reply to (3): Pleasure May
Still Be the Best Good
      Besides, just as one science might well be the best good,
even though some sciences are bad, some pleasure might well
be the best good, even though most pleasures are bad.

8.41 This possibility is left open if happiness
is defined as unimpeded activity
10   Moreover, if each state has its unimpeded activities, and
happiness is the activity, if the activity is unimpeded, of all
states or of some one of them, then presumably it necessar-

ily follows that some unimpeded activity is most choiceworthy. But pleasure is an unimpeded activity; hence some
type of pleasure might be the best good even if most pleasures
turn out to be unconditionally bad.

8.42   This definition of happiness is supported
by common beliefs

This is why all think the happy life is pleasant and weave
pleasure into happiness, quite reasonably, since no activity | 15
is complete if it is impeded, and happiness is something
complete.

Hence the happy person needs to have goods of the body
and external goods added [to good activities], and needs fortune also, so that he will not be impeded in these ways. Some
maintain, on the contrary, that we are happy when we are
broken on the wheel, or fall into terrible misfortunes, pro-
vided that we are good. Willingly or unwillingly, these peo- | 20
ple are talking nonsense.

And because happiness needs fortune added, good fortune
seems to some people to be the same as happiness. But it
is not. For when it is excessive, it actually impedes happiness; and then, presumably, it is no longer rightly called
good fortune, since the limit [up to which it is good] is defined
in relation to happiness.

8.43   The widespread pursuit of pleasure
supports its claim to be the good

The fact that all, both beasts and human beings, pursue | 25
pleasure is some sign of its being in some way the best
good: 'No rumour is altogether lost which many peoples
[spread]. . . . ' But since the best nature and state neither
is nor seems to be the same for all, they also do not all pur- | 30
sue the same pleasure, though they all pursue pleasure. Presumably in fact they do pursue the same pleasure, and not
the one they think or would say they pursue; for all things
by nature have something divine [in them].

8.44   A one-sided choice of examples
should not mislead us

However, the bodily pleasures have taken over the name
35 because people most often aim at them, and all share in them;
and so, since these are the only pleasures they know, people
1154a suppose that they are the only pleasures.

8.5   Further Reply to (1): Since Pleasure Is
a Part of Happiness, It Must Be a Good

Evidently, moreover, if pleasure is not a good and an activity, it will not be true that the happy person lives pleasantly.
For what will he need pleasure for if it is not a good? Indeed, it will even be possible for him to live painfully; for
5 pain is neither an evil nor a good if pleasure is not, and why
then would he avoid it? So the life of the excellent person
will not be pleasanter if his activities are not also pleasanter.

8.6   Further Reply to (2):
Are Bodily Pleasures Bad?

vii 14   Those who maintain that some pleasures, e.g. the fine ones,
10 are highly choiceworthy, but the bodily pleasures that concern the intemperate person are not, should examine bodily
pleasures. If what they say is true, why are the pains contrary to these pleasures awful? For it is a good that is contrary to an evil.

Then are the necessary [bodily pleasures] good only in the
way that what is not bad is good? Or are they good up to
a point?

[In fact they are good up to a point.] For though some
states and processes allow no excess of what is better, and
hence no excess of the pleasure [in them] either, others do
15 allow excess of what is better, and hence also allow excess
of the pleasure in them too. Now the bodily goods allow excess. The base person is base because he pursues the excess,
but not because he pursues the necessary pleasures; for all

enjoy delicacies and wines and sexual relations in some way, though not all in the right way.

The contrary is true for pains. The base person avoids pain in general, not [only] an excess of it. For not [all] pain is | 20 contrary to excess [of pleasure], except to someone who pursues the excess [of pleasure].

8.7 Why People Hold Mistaken Views About Bodily Pleasures

We must, however, not only state the true view, but also explain the false view, since an explanation of that promotes confidence. For when we have an apparently reasonable explanation of why a false view appears true, that makes us | 25 more confident of the true view. Hence we should say why bodily pleasures appear more choiceworthy.

8.71 Bodily pleasures follow pains

First, then, it is because bodily pleasure pushes out pain. Excesses of pain make people seek a cure in the pursuit of excessive pleasure and of bodily pleasure in general. And these cures become intense—that is why they are pursued— | 30 because they appear next to their contraries.

And this explains some errors about pleasure

Indeed these are the two reasons why pleasure seems to be no excellent thing, as we have said.

First, some pleasures are the actions of a base nature— either base from birth, as in a beast, or base because of habit, e.g. the actions of base human beings.

Second, others are cures of something deficient, and it is better to be in a good state than to be coming into it. In fact | 1154b these pleasures coincide with our restoration to complete health, and so are excellent coincidentally.

8.72 Bodily pleasures are intense

Further, bodily pleasures are pursued because they are in-

tense, by people who are incapable of enjoying other pleasures. At any rate, these people induce some kinds of thirst
in themselves, which is blameless whenever the thirsts are
5   harmless, but base whenever they are harmful. And they do
this because they enjoy nothing else, and many people's nature
makes the neutral condition painful to them.

8.73   They are intense because of our
natural imperfections

For an animal is always suffering, as the natural scientists
also testify, since they maintain that seeing and hearing are
painful. However, we are used [to seeing and hearing] by
now, so they say, [and so feel no intense pain]. Indeed, the
10   [process of] growth makes young people's condition similar
to an intoxicated person's and hence youth is pleasant.

Naturally ardent people, by contrast, are always requiring
a cure, since their constitution causes their body continual
turmoil, and they are always having intense desires. A pain
is driven out by its contrary pleasure, indeed by any pleasure
15   at all that is strong enough; and this is why such people
become intemperate and base.

Pleasures without pains, however, have no excess. These
are pleasant by nature and not coincidentally. By coincidentally pleasant things I mean pleasant things that are curative;
for the [process of] being cured coincides with some action
of the part of us that remains healthy, and hence undergoing
20   a cure seems to be pleasant. Things are pleasant by nature,
however, when they produce action of a healthy nature.

8.74   The same natural imperfections explain
why pleasures need to be varied

The reason why no one thing is always pleasant is that our
nature is not simple, but has more than one constituent, in
so far as we are perishable; hence the action of one part is
contrary to nature for the other nature in us, and when they
are equally balanced, the action seems neither pleasant nor

painful. For if something has a simple nature the same ac- | 25
tion will always be pleasantest.

That is why the god always enjoys one simple pleasure
[without change]. For activity belongs not only to change
but also to unchangingness, and indeed there is pleasure in
rest more than in change. 'Variation in everything is sweet',
as the poet says, because of some inferiority; for just as it | 30
is the inferior human being who is prone to variation, so also
the nature that needs variation is inferior, since it is not simple or decent.

So much, then, for continence and incontinence and for
pleasure and pain, what each of them is, and in what ways
some [aspects] of them are good and others bad. It remains
for us to discuss friendship as well.

9. The Varieties of Friendship

9.1 The Problems

9.11 Common beliefs about friendship | viii 1
After that the next topic to discuss is friendship; for it is | 1155a
a virtue, or involves virtue, and besides is most necessary
for our life.

It is necessary in all external conditions . . .
For no one would choose to live without friends even if | 5
he had all the other goods. For in fact rich people and holders
of powerful positions, even more than other people, seem
to need friends. For how would one benefit from such prosperity if one had no opportunity for beneficence, which is
most often displayed, and most highly praised, in relation
to friends? And how would one guard and protect prosper- | 10
ity without friends, when it is all the more precarious the
greater it is? In poverty also, and in the other misfortunes,
people think friends are the only refuge.

207

In all times of life . . .

Moreover, the young need it to keep them from error. The old need it to care for them and support the actions that fail because of weakness. And those in their prime need it, to do fine actions; for 'when two go together . . .', they are more capable of understanding and acting.

And throughout nature . . .

Further, a parent would seem to have a natural friendship for a child, and a child for a parent, not only among human beings but also among birds and most kinds of animals. Members of the same race, and human beings most of all, have a natural friendship for each other; that is why we praise friends of humanity. And in our travels we can see how every human being is akin and beloved to a human being.

For communities as well as for individuals

Moreover, friendship would seem to hold cities together, and legislators would seem to be more concerned about it than about justice. For concord would seem to be similar to friendship and they aim at concord above all, while they try above all to expel civil conflict, which is enmity.

Further, if people are friends, they have no need of justice, but if they are just they need friendship in addition; and the justice that is most just seems to belong to friendship.

It is both necessary and fine

However, friendship is not only necessary, but also fine. For we praise lovers of friends, and having many friends seems to be a fine thing. Moreover, people think that the same people are good and also friends.

9.12 Puzzles about friendship

Still, there are quite a few disputed points about friendship. For some hold it is a sort of similarity and that similar people are friends. Hence the saying 'Similar to similar', and 'Birds of a feather', and so on. On the other hand it is said | 35 that similar people are all like the proverbial potters, quarrelling with each other.

On these questions some people inquire at a higher level, | 1155b more proper to natural science. Euripides says that when earth gets dry it longs passionately for rain, and the holy heaven when filled with rain longs passionately to fall into the earth; and Heracleitus says that the opponent cooperates, the finest | 5 harmony arises from discordant elements, and all things come to be in struggle. Others, e.g. Empedocles, oppose this view, and say that similar aims for similar.

Let us, then, leave aside the puzzles proper to natural science, since they are not proper to the present examination; and let us examine the puzzles that concern human [nature], and bear on characters and feelings. | 10

For instance, does friendship arise among all sorts of people, or can people not be friends if they are vicious?

Is there one species of friendship, or are there more? Some people think there is only one species because friendship allows more and less. But here their confidence rests on an inadequate sign; for things of different species also allow | 15 more and less.

9.2   General Account of Friendship

9.21   The object of friendship: What is lovable

Perhaps these questions will become clear once we find | viii 2 out what it is that is lovable. For, it seems, not everything is loved, but [only] what is lovable, and this is either good or pleasant or useful. However, it seems that what is useful is the source of some good or some pleasure; hence what | 20 is good and what is pleasant are lovable as ends.

Do people love what is good, or what is good for them? For sometimes these conflict; and the same is true of what

is pleasant. Each one, it seems, loves what is good for him;
and while what is good is lovable unconditionally, what is
25   lovable for each one is what is good for him. In fact each
one loves not what *is* good for him, but what *appears* good
for him; but this will not matter, since [what appears good
for him] will be what appears lovable.

Hence there are these three causes of love.

9.22 *Necessary conditions for friendship*

There is no friendship for soulless things

Love for a soulless thing is not called friendship, since
there is no mutual loving, and you do not wish good to it.
For it would presumably be ridiculous to wish good things
30   to wine; the most you wish is its preservation so that you
can have it. To a friend, however, it is said, you must wish
goods for his own sake.

Friendship is not mere goodwill . . .

If you wish good things in this way, but the same wish
is not returned by the other, you would be said to have [only]
goodwill for the other. For friendship is said to be *reciprocated* goodwill.

And not mere reciprocated goodwill

But perhaps we should add that friends are aware of the
35   reciprocated goodwill. For many a one has goodwill to peo-
1156a   ple whom he has not seen but supposes to be decent or useful,
and one of these might have the same goodwill towards him.
These people, then, apparently have goodwill to each other,
but how could we call them friends when they are unaware
of their attitude to each other?

Hence, [to be friends] they must have goodwill to each
5   other, wish goods and be aware of it, from one of the causes
mentioned above.

210

9.3   The Three Types of Friendship

9.31   Complete and incomplete species of
friendship correspond to the different objects
Now since these causes differ in species, so do the types
of loving and types of friendship. Hence friendship has three
species, corresponding to the three objects of love. For each
object of love has a corresponding type of mutual loving,
combined with awareness of it, and those who love each
other wish goods to each other in so far as they love each
other.

9.32   Friendships for utility and pleasure
are incomplete
Those who love each other for utility love the other not
in himself, but in so far as they gain some good for themselves
from him. The same is true of those who love for pleasure;
for they like a witty person not because of his character, but
because he is pleasant to themselves.
And so those who love for utility or pleasure are fond of
a friend because of what is good or pleasant for themselves,
not in so far as the beloved is who he is, but in so far as
he is useful or pleasant.
Hence these friendships as well [as the friends] are coincidental, since the beloved is loved not in so far as he is who
he is, but in so far as he provides some good or pleasure.
And so these sorts of friendships are easily dissolved, when
the friends do not remain similar [to what they were]; for
if someone is no longer pleasant or useful, the other stops
loving him.

9.33   Friendship for utility
What is useful does not remain the same, but is different
at different times. Hence, when the cause of their being

viii 3

10

15

20

friends is removed, the friendship is dissolved too, on the assumption that the friendship aims at these [useful results]. This sort of friendship seems to arise especially among older people, since at that age they pursue what is advantageous, not what is pleasant, and also among those in their prime or youth who pursue what is expedient.

Nor do such people live together very much. For sometimes they do not even find each other pleasant. Hence they have no further need to meet in this way if they are not advantageous [to each other]; for each finds the other pleasant [only] to the extent that he expects some good from him. The friendship of hosts and guests is taken to be of this type too.

9.34   Friendships for pleasure

The cause of friendship between young people seems to be pleasure. For their lives are guided by their feelings, and they pursue above all what is pleasant for themselves and what is near at hand. But as they grow up [what they find] pleasant changes too. Hence they are quick to become friends, and quick to stop; for their friendship shifts with [what they find] pleasant, and the change in such pleasure is quick. Young people are prone to erotic passion, since this mostly follows feelings, and is caused by pleasure; that is why they love and quickly stop, often changing in a single day.

These people wish to spend their days together and to live together; for this is how they gain [the good things] corresponding to their friendship.

9.35   Complete friendship is the friendship of good people

But complete friendship is the friendship of good people similar in virtue; for they wish goods in the same way to each other in so far as they are good, and they are good in themselves. [Hence they wish goods to each other for each other's own sake.] Now those who wish goods to their friend | 10 for the friend's own sake are friends most of all; for they have this attitude because of the friend himself, not coincidentally. Hence these people's friendship lasts as long as they are good; and virtue is enduring.

Each of them is both good unconditionally and good for his friend, since good people are both unconditionally good and advantageous for each other. They are pleasant in the same ways too, since good people are pleasant both uncon- | 15 ditionally and for each other. [They are pleasant for each other] because each person finds his own actions and actions of that kind pleasant, and the actions of good people are the same or similar.

It is reasonable that this sort of friendship is enduring, since it embraces in itself all the features that friends must have. For the cause of every friendship is good or pleasure, either | 20 unconditional or for the lover; and every friendship reflects some similarity. And all the features we have mentioned are found in this friendship because of [the nature of] the friends themselves. For they are similar in this way [i.e. in being good]. Moreover, their friendship also has the other things — what is unconditionally good and what is unconditionally pleasant; and these are lovable most of all. Hence loving and friendship are found most of all and at their best in these friends.

These kinds of friendships are likely to be rare, since such | 25 people are few. Moreover, they need time to grow accustomed to each other; for, as the proverb says, they cannot know each other before they have shared the traditional [peck of] salt, and they cannot accept each other or be friends until each appears lovable to the other and gains the other's confidence. Those who are quick to treat each other in friendly | 30 ways wish to be friends, but are not friends, unless they are also lovable, and know this. For though the wish for friendship comes quickly, friendship does not.

9.4   Differences and Similarities Between
Complete and Incomplete Friendship

9.41   The incomplete friendships resemble
the complete

viii 4

This sort of friendship, then, is complete both in time and in the other ways. In every way each friend gets the same things and similar things from each, and this is what must be true of friends. Friendship for pleasure bears some resemblance to this complete sort, since good people are also pleasant to each other. And friendship for utility also resembles it, since good people are also useful to each other.

Incomplete friendships endure to the extent that
they resemble complete friendships

With these [incomplete friends] also, the friendships are most enduring when they get the same thing—e.g. pleasure —from each other, and, moreover, get it from the same source, as witty people do. They must not be like the erotic lover and the boy he loves. For these do not take pleasure in the same things; the lover takes pleasure in seeing his beloved, while the beloved takes pleasure in being courted by his lover. When the beloved's bloom is fading, sometimes the friendship fades too; for the lover no longer finds pleasure in seeing his beloved, while the beloved is no longer courted by the lover.

Many, however, remain friends if they have similar characters and come to be fond of each other's characters from being accustomed to them. Those who exchange utility rather than pleasure in their erotic relations are friends to a lesser extent and less enduring friends.

Those who are friends for utility dissolve the friendship as soon as the advantage is removed; for they were never friends of each other, but of what was expedient for them.

214

*9.42   But the character of the friends in
complete friendship makes it more enduring*

Now it is possible for bad people as well [as good] to
be friends to each other for pleasure or utility, for decent
people to be friends to base people, and for someone with
neither character to be a friend to someone with any character. Clearly, however, only good people can be friends to
each other because of the other person himself; for bad people find no enjoyment in one another if they get no benefit.   20

Moreover, it is only the friendship of good people that is
immune to slander. For it is hard to trust anyone speaking
against someone whom we ourselves have found reliable for
a long time; and among good people there is trust, the belief
that he would never do injustice [to a friend], and all the
other things expected in a true friendship. But in the other
types of friendship [distrust] may easily arise.   25

*9.43   Hence incomplete friendships are
friendships only to a limited extent*

[These must be counted as types of friendship.] For people include among friends [not only the best type, but] also
those who are friends for utility, as cities are—since alliances
between cities seem to aim at expediency—and those who
are fond of each other, as children are, for pleasure. Hence
we must presumably also say that such people are friends,
but say that there are more species of friendship than one.   30

On this view, the friendship of good people in so far as
they are good is friendship in the primary way, and to the
full extent; and the others are friendships by similarity. They
are friends in so far as there is something good, and [hence]
something similar to [what one finds in the best kind]; for
what is pleasant is good to lovers of pleasure. But these [in-
complete] types of friendship are not very regularly combined, and the same people do not become friends for both
utility and pleasure. For things that [merely] coincide with   35
each other are not very regularly combined.

1157b Friendship has been assigned, then, to these species. Base people will be friends for pleasure or utility, since they are similar in that way. But good people will be friends because of themselves, since they are friends in so far as they are good. These, then, are friends unconditionally; the others

5 are friends coincidentally and by being similar to these.

9.44   Only complete friendship includes all the right states and activities

Friendship includes both states and activities

viii 5 Just as with the virtues some people are called good in their state of character, others good in their activity, the same is true of friendship. For some people find enjoyment in each other by living together, and provide each other with good things. Others, however, are asleep or separated by distance, and so are not active in these ways, but are in the state that

10 would result in the friendly activities; for distance does not dissolve the friendship unconditionally, but only its activity. But if the absence is long, it also seems to cause the friendship to be forgotten; hence the saying, 'Lack of conversation has dissolved many a friendship'.

The right activities require pleasure in living together

Older people and sour people do not appear to be prone

15 to friendship. For there is little pleasure to be found in them, and no one can spend his days with what is painful or not pleasant, since nature appears to avoid above all what is painful and to aim at what is pleasant.

Those who welcome each other but do not live together would seem to have goodwill rather than friendship. For

20 nothing is as proper to friends as living together; for while those who are in want desire benefit, blessedly happy people [who want for nothing], no less than the others, desire

216

to spend their days together, since a solitary life fits them least of all. But people cannot spend their time with each other if they are not pleasant and do not enjoy the same things, as they seem to in the friendship of companions.

And only the best kind of friendship includes
the appropriate activities and attitudes

It is the friendship of good people that is friendship most of all, as we have often said. For what is lovable and choice-worthy seems to be what is unconditionally good or pleasant, and what is lovable and choiceworthy for each person seems to be what is good or pleasant for him; and both of these make one good person lovable and choiceworthy for another good person. | 25

Loving would seem to be a feeling, but friendship a state. For loving occurs no less towards soulless things, but recip- | 30
rocal loving requires decision, and decision comes from a state; and what makes [good people] wish good to the be-loved for his own sake is their state, not their feeling.

Moreover, in loving their friend they love what is good for themselves; for when a good person becomes a friend he becomes a good for his friend. Each of them loves what | 35
is good for himself, and repays in equal measure the wish and the pleasantness of his friend; for friendship is said to be equality. And this is true above all in the friendship of | 1158a
good people.

9.45 The characteristics of friendship are
found in friendships for pleasure more
than in friendships for utility

Among sour people and older people friendship is found | viii 6
less often, since they are worse tempered and enjoy meeting people less, [and so lack] what seems to be most typical and most productive of friendship. That is why young people | 5
become friends quickly, but older people do not, since they

do not become friends with people in whom they find no enjoyment—nor do sour people. These people have goodwill to each other, since they wish goods and give help in time of need; but they scarcely count as friends, since they do not spend their days together or find enjoyment in each other, and these things seem to be above all typical of friendship.

9.46 The number of friends distinguishes the best kind of friendship

No one can have complete friendship for many people, just as no one can have an erotic passion for many at the same time; for [complete friendship, like erotic passion,] is like an excess, and an excess is naturally directed at a single individual. Moreover, just as it is hard for the same person to please many people intensely at the same time, it is also hard, presumably, to be good towards many people at the same time.

Besides, he must gain experience of the other too, and become accustomed to him, which is very difficult.

It is possible, however, to please many people when the friendship is for utility or pleasure, since many people can be pleased in these ways, and the services take little time.

9.47 Friendship for pleasure contrasted with friendship for utility

Of these other two types of friendship the friendship for pleasure is more like [real] friendship; for they get the same thing from each other, and they find enjoyment in each other or in the same things. This is what friendships are like among young people; for a generous [attitude] is found here more [than among older people], whereas it is mercenary people who form friendships for utility.

Moreover, blessedly happy people have no need of anything useful, but do need sources of pleasure. For they want

218

to spend their lives with companions, and though what is painful is borne for a short time, no one could continuously en-
dure even The Good Itself if it were painful to him; hence | 25
they seek friends who are pleasant. But, presumably, they
must also seek friends who are good as well [as pleasant],
and good for them too; for then they will have everything
that friends must have.

9.48   Evidence of the difference between the
two incomplete types of friendship
Someone in a position of power appears to have separate
groups of friends; for some are useful to him, others pleas-
ant, but the same ones are not often both. For he does not | 30
seek friends who are both pleasant and virtuous, or useful
for fine actions, but seeks one group to be witty, when he
pursues pleasure, and the other group to be clever in carrying out instructions; and the same person rarely has both
features.

Though admittedly, as we have said, an excellent person
is both pleasant and useful, he does not become a friend to
a superior [in power and position] unless the superior is also
superior in virtue; otherwise he does not reach [proportionate] | 35
equality by having a proportionate superior. And this superiority both in power and in virtue is not often found.

9.49   Summary: The extent to which
incomplete friendships are friendships
The friendships we have mentioned involve equality, since | 1158b
both friends get the same and wish the same to each other,
or exchange one thing for another, e.g. pleasure for benefit.
But, as we have said, they are friendships to a lesser ex-
tent, and less enduring. Because they are both similar and | 5
dissimilar to the same thing they seem both to be and not
to be friendships. For in so far as they are similar to the
friendship of virtue, they appear to be friendships; for that

type of friendship includes both utility and pleasure, and one of these types includes utility, the other pleasure. On the other hand, since the friendship of virtue is enduring and immune to slander, while these change quickly and differ from it in many other ways as well, they do not appear to be friendships, in so far as they are dissimilar to that [best] type.

9.5   Friendship Between Unequals

9.51   Types of friendship between unequals

A different species of friendship is the one that corresponds to superiority, e.g. of a father towards his son, and in general of an older person towards a younger, of a man towards a woman, and of any sort of ruler towards the one he rules.

These friendships also differ from each other. For friendship of parents to children is not the same as that of rulers to ruled; nor is friendship of father to son the same as that of son to father, or of man to woman as that of woman to man.

Explanation of the different types

For each of these friends has a different virtue and a different function, and there are different causes of love. Hence the ways of loving are different, and so are the friendships. Each does not get the same thing from the other, then, and must not seek it; but whenever children accord to their parents what they must accord to those who gave them birth, and parents accord what they must to their children, their friendship is enduring and decent.

9.52   Proportion and equality in friendship and in justice

In all the friendships corresponding to superiority, the loving must also be proportional, e.g. the better person, and

220

the more beneficial, and each of the others likewise, must be loved more than he loves; for when the loving reflects the comparative worth of the friends, equality is achieved in a way, and this seems to be proper to friendship.

Equality, however, does not appear to be the same in friendship as in justice. For in justice equality is equality primarily in worth and secondarily in quantity; but in friendship it is equality primarily in quantity and secondarily in worth. | 30

This is clear if friends come to be separated by some wide gap in virtue, vice, wealth, or something else; for then they are friends no more, and do not even expect to be. This is most evident with gods, since they have the greatest superiority in all goods. But it is also clear with kings, since far inferior people do not expect to be their friends; nor do worthless people expect to be friends to the best or wisest. | 35

1159a

When the right proportion and equality are lost,
the friendship is lost

Now in these cases there is no exact definition of how long people are friends. For even if one of them loses a lot, the friendship still endures; but if one is widely separated [from the other], as a god is [from a human being], it no longer endures. | 5

Hence there is this puzzle: do friends really wish their friend to have the greatest good, e.g. to be a god? For [if he becomes a god], *he* will no longer have friends, and hence no longer have goods, since friends are goods.

If, then, we have been right to say that one friend wishes good things to the other for the sake of the other *himself*, the other must remain whatever sort of being he is. Hence it is to the other as a human being that a friend will wish the greatest goods—though presumably not all of them, since each person wishes goods most of all to himself. | 10

221

9.53 *The value of friendship consists in loving more than in being loved*

The many might seem to value being loved simply as a means to honour

viii 8
15
It is because they love honour that the many seem to prefer being loved to loving; that is why they love flatterers. For the flatterer is a friend in an inferior position, or [rather] pretends to be one, and pretends to love more than he is loved; and being loved seems close to being honoured, which the many do indeed pursue.

But in fact they also value friendship apart from honour

20
It would seem, however, that they choose honour coincidentally, not in itself. For the many enjoy being honoured by powerful people because they expect to get whatever they need from them, and so enjoy the honour as a sign of this good treatment. Those who want honour from decent people with knowledge are seeking to confirm their own view of themselves, and so they are pleased because the judgment of those who say they are good makes them confident that they are good.

25
Being loved, on the contrary, they enjoy in itself. Hence it seems to be better than being honoured, and friendship seems choiceworthy in itself.

And loving, not being loved, is the more valuable aspect of friendship

But friendship seems to consist more in loving than in being loved. A sign of this is the enjoyment a mother finds in loving. For sometimes she gives her child away to be brought
30
up, and loves him as long as she knows about him; but she does not seek the child's love, if she cannot both [love and

be loved]. She would seem to be satisfied if she sees the child doing well, and she loves the child even if ignorance prevents him from according to her what befits a mother.

Friendship, then, consists more in loving; and people who love their friends are praised; hence, it would seem, loving is the virtue of friends. And so friends whose love corresponds to their friends' worth are enduring friends and have an enduring friendship. This above all is the way for unequals as well as equals to be friends, since this is the way for them to be equalized.

This explains why virtuous friendships endure

Equality and similarity, and above all the similarity of those who are similar in being virtuous, is friendship. For virtuous people are enduringly [virtuous] in themselves, and enduring [friends] to each other. They neither request nor provide assistance that requires base actions, but, you might even say, prevent this. For it is proper to good people to avoid error themselves and not to permit it in their friends.

Vicious people, by contrast, have no firmness, since they do not even remain similar to what they were, but become friends for a short time, enjoying each other's vice.

Useful or pleasant friends, however, last longer, for as long as they supply each other with pleasures or benefits.

9.54 It is only partly true that friendship is between contraries

The friendship that seems to arise most from contraries is friendship for utility, e.g. of poor to rich or ignorant to knowledgeable; for we aim at whatever we find we lack, and give something else in return.

Here we might also include the erotic lover and his beloved, and the beautiful and the ugly. Hence an erotic lover also sometimes appears ridiculous, when he expects to be

35

1159b

5

10

15

loved in the same way as he loves; that would presumably be a proper expectation if he were lovable in the same way, but it is ridiculous when he is not.

20   Presumably, however, contrary seeks contrary coincidentally, not in itself, and desire is for the intermediate. For what is good, e.g., for the dry is to reach the intermediate, not to become wet, and the same is true for the hot and so on. Let us, then, dismiss these questions, since they are rather extraneous to our concern.

9.6   Friendship in Communities

9.61   Friendship, like justice, is found in a community

viii 9
25   As we said at the beginning, friendship and justice would seem to have the same area of concern and to be found in the same people. For in every community there seems to be some sort of justice, and some type of friendship also. At any rate, fellow-voyagers and fellow-soldiers are called friends, and so are members of other communities. And the extent
30   of their community is the extent of their friendship, since it is also the extent of the justice found there. The proverb 'What friends have is common' is correct, since friendship involves community. But while brothers and companions have everything in common, what people have in common in other types of community is limited, more in some communities and less in others, since some friendships are also
35   closer than others, some less close.
1160a   What is just is also different, since it is not the same for parents towards children as for one brother towards another, and not the same for companions as for fellow-citizens, and similarly with the other types of friendship. Similarly, what is unjust towards each of these is also different, and becomes more unjust as it is practised on closer friends. It is more

224

shocking, e.g., to rob a companion of money than to rob | 5
a fellow-citizen, to fail to help a brother than a stranger, and
to strike one's father than anyone else. What is just also
naturally increases with friendship, since it involves the same
people and extends over an equal area.

9.62 Partial communities are subordinate
to the political community

All communities would seem to be parts of the political
community. For people keep company for some advantage | 10
and to supply something contributing to their life. Moreover,
the political community seems both to have been originally
formed and to endure for advantage; for legislators also aim
at advantage, and the common advantage is said to be just.

The other types of community aim at partial advantage.
Sea-travellers, e.g. seek the advantage proper to a journey, | 15
in making money or something like that, while fellow-
soldiers seek the advantage proper to war, desiring either
money or victory or a city; and the same is true of fellow-
tribesmen and fellow-demesmen. Some communities — re-
ligious societies and dining clubs — seem to arise for plea- | 20
sure, since these are, respectively, for religious sacrifices
and for companionship.

All these communities would seem to be subordinate to
the political community, since it aims not at some advantage
close at hand, but at advantage for the whole of life . . .
[For] in performing sacrifices and arranging gatherings for
these, people both accord honours to the gods and provide | 25
themselves with pleasant relaxations. For the long-established
sacrifices and gatherings appear to take place after the har-
vesting of the crops, as a sort of first-fruits, since this was
the time when people used to be most at leisure [and the time
when relaxation would be most advantageous for the whole
of life].

All the types of community, then, appear to be parts of
the political community, and these sorts of communities imply the appropriate sorts of friendships.

9.63 The types of political systems

There are three species of political system (*politeia*), and
an equal number of deviations, which are a sort of corruption of them. The first political system is kingship; the second aristocracy; and since the third rests on property (*timēma*)
it appears proper to call it a timocratic system, though most
people usually call it a polity (*politeia*). The best of these
is kingship and the worst timocracy.

The deviation from kingship is tyranny. For, though both
are monarchies, they show the widest difference, since the
tyrant considers his own advantage, but the king considers
the advantage of his subjects. For someone is a king only
if he is self-sufficient and superior in all goods; and since such
a person needs nothing more, he will consider the subjects'
benefit, not his own. For a king who is not like this would
be only some sort of titular king. Tyranny is contrary to this;
for the tyrant pursues his own good.

It is more evident that [tyranny] is the worst [deviation
than that timocracy is the worst political system]; but the
worst is contrary to the best; [hence kingship is the best].

The transition from kingship is to tyranny. For tyranny
is the degenerate condition of monarchy, and the vicious king
becomes a tyrant.

The transition from aristocracy [rule of the best people]
is to oligarchy [rule of the few], resulting from the badness
of the rulers. They distribute the city's goods in conflict with
people's worth, so that they distribute all or most of the goods
to themselves, and always assign ruling offices to the same
people, counting wealth for most. Hence the rulers are few,
and they are vicious people instead of the most decent.

226

The transition from timocracy is to democracy [rule by the people], since these border on each other. For timocracy is also meant to be rule by the majority, and all those with the property-qualification are equal; [and majority-rule and equality are the marks of democracy]. Democracy is the least vicious [of the deviations]; for it deviates only slightly from | 20 the form of a [genuine] political system.

These, then, are the most frequent transitions from one political system to another, since they are the smallest and easiest.

9.64   These correspond to types of communities

Resemblances to these – indeed, a sort of pattern of them – can also be found in households. For the community of a father and his sons has the structure of kingship, since the | 25 father is concerned for his children. Indeed that is why Homer also calls Zeus father, since kingship is meant to be paternal rule.

Among the Persians, however, the father's rule is tyrannical, since he treats his sons as slaves. The rule of a master over his slaves is also tyrannical, since it is the master's ad- | 30 vantage that is achieved in it. This, then, appears a correct form of rule, whereas the Persian form appears erroneous, since the different types of rule suit different subjects.

The community of man and woman appears aristocratic. For the man's rule in the area where it is right corresponds to the worth [of each], and he commits to the woman what is fitting for her. If, however, the man controls everything, | 35 he changes it into an oligarchy; for then his action conflicts with the worth [of each], and does not correspond to his | 1161a superiority. Sometimes, indeed, women rule because they are heiresses; and these cases of rule do not reflect virtue, but result from wealth and power, as is true in oligarchies.

The community of brothers is like a timocratic [system], since they are equal except in so far as they differ in age; | 5

227

and hence, if they differ very much in age, the friendship is no longer brotherly.

Democracy is found most of all in dwellings without a master, since everyone there is on equal terms; and also in those where the ruler is weak and everyone is free [to do what he likes].

9.65 *Different types of friendship and justice are found in different communities*

viii 11

10

Friendship appears in each of the political systems, to the extent that justice appears also. A king's friendship to his subjects involves superior beneficence. For he benefits his subjects, since he is good and attends to them to ensure that they do well, as a shepherd attends to his sheep; hence Homer also called Agamemnon shepherd of the peoples.

15

Paternal friendship resembles this, but differs in conferring a greater benefit, since the father is the cause of his children's being, which seems to be the greatest benefit, and of their nurture and education. These benefits are also ascribed to ancestors; and by nature father is ruler over sons, ancestors over descendants, and king over subjects.

20

All these are friendships of superiority; that is why parents are also honoured. And what is just in these friendships is not the same in each case, but corresponds to worth; for so does the friendship.

The friendship of man to woman is the same as in an aristocracy. For it reflects virtue, in assigning more good to the better, and assigning what is fitting to each. The same is true for what is just here.

25

The friendship of brothers is similar to that of companions, since they are equal and of an age, and such people usually have the same feelings and characters. Friendship in a timocracy is similar to this. For there the citizens are meant to be equal and decent, and so rule in turn and on equal terms.

30

The same is true, then, of their friendship.

9.66 Without community there is no friendship

In the deviations, however, justice is found only to a slight degree; and hence the same is true of friendship. There is least of it in the worst deviation; for in a tyranny there is little or no friendship.

For where ruler and ruled have nothing in common, they have no friendship, since they have no justice either. This is true for a craftsman in relation to his tool, and for the soul in relation to the body. For in all these cases the user benefits what he uses, but there is neither friendship nor justice towards soulless things.

Nor is there any towards a horse or cow, or towards a slave, in so far as he is a slave. For master and slave have nothing in common, since a slave is a tool with a soul, while a tool is a slave without a soul. In so far as he is a slave, then, there is no friendship with him.

But there is friendship with him in so far as he is a human being. For every human being seems to have some relations of justice with everyone who is capable of community in law and agreement. Hence there is also friendship, to the extent that a slave is a human being.

Hence there are friendships and justice to only a slight degree in tyrannies also, but to a much larger degree in democracies; for there people are equal, and so have much in common.

9.7 Friendship Within Families

As we have said, then, every friendship is found in a community. But we should set apart the friendship of families and that of companions. The friendship of citizens, tribesmen, voyagers and suchlike are more like friendships in a community, since they appear to reflect some sort of agreement; and among these we may include the friendship of host and guest.

9.71   The primacy of paternal friendship

Friendship in families also seems to have many species, but they all seem to depend on paternal friendship. For a parent is fond of his children because he regards them as something of himself; and children are fond of a parent because they regard themselves as coming from him.

20 A parent knows better what has come from him than the children know that they are from the parent; and the parent regards his children as his own more than the product regards the maker as its own. For a person regards what comes from him as his own, as the owner regards his tooth or hair or anything; but what has come from him regards its owner as its own not at all, or to a lesser degree.

25 The length of time also matters. For a parent becomes fond of his children as soon as they are born, while children become fond of the parent when time has passed and they have acquired some comprehension or [at least] perception. And this also makes it clear why mothers love their children more [than fathers do].

A parent loves his children as [he loves] himself. For what has come from him is a sort of other himself; [it is other because] it is separate. Children love a parent because they regard themselves as having come from him.

9.72   Other friendships in families are derived from relations between brothers, and hence from paternal friendship

30 Brothers love each other because they have come from the same [parents]. For the same relation to the parents makes the same thing for both of them; hence we speak of the same blood, the same stock and so on. Hence they are the same thing in a way, in different [subjects]. Being brought up together and being of an age contributes largely to friendship; 35 for 'two of an age' [get on well], and those with the same character are companions. That is why the friendship of 1162a brothers and that of companions are similar.

230

Cousins and other relatives are akin by being related to brothers, since that makes them descendants of the same parents [i.e. the parents of these brothers]. Some are more akin, others less, by the ancestor's being near to or far from them.

9.73 Family friendships correspond to different types of friendships between equals and unequals

The friendship of children to a parent, like the friendship of human beings to a god, is friendship towards what is good | 5
and superior. For the parent conferred the greatest benefits, since he is the cause of their being and nurture and of their education once they have been born. This sort of friendship also includes pleasure and utility, more than the friendship of unrelated people does, to the extent that [parents and children] have more of a life in common.

Friendship between brothers has the features of friendship | 10
between companions, especially when [the companions] are decent, or in general similar. For brothers are that much more akin to each other [than ordinary companions], and are fond of each other from birth; they are that much more similar in character when they are from the same parents, nurtured together and educated similarly; and the proof of their reliability over time is fullest and firmest. | 15

Among other relatives too the features of friendship are proportional [to the relation].

9.74 Husbands and wives have different types of friendship

The friendship of man and woman also seems to be natural. For human beings naturally tend to form couples more than to form cities, to the extent that the household is prior to the city, and more necessary, and child-bearing is shared more widely among the animals.

20   With the other animals this is the extent of the community. Human beings, however, share a household not only for child-bearing, but also for the benefits in their life. For from the start their functions are divided, with different ones for the man and the woman; hence each supplies the other's needs by contributing a special function to the common good. Hence their friendship seems to include both utility and pleasure.

25   And it may also be friendship for virtue, if they are decent. For each has a proper virtue, and this will be a source of enjoyment for them. Children seem to be another bond, and that is why childless unions are more quickly dissolved; for children are a common good for both, and what is common holds them together.

*9.75   These different friendships impose
different obligations of justice*

30   How should a man conduct his life towards his wife, or, in general, toward a friend? That appears to be the same as asking what the just conduct of their lives is. For what is just is not the same for a friend towards a friend as towards a stranger, or the same towards a companion as towards a classmate.

10.   Problems and Difficulties in Friendships

10.1   Disputes in Friendships Between Equals

*10.11   Different questions arise in the
three types of friendship*

viii 13   There are three types of friendship, as we said at the beginning; and within each type some friendships rest on equality, while others correspond to superiority. For equally good people can be friends, but also a better and a worse person; and the same is true of friends for pleasure or utility,

35

1162b

232

since they may be either equal or unequal in their benefits.
Hence equals must equalize in loving and in the other things,
because of their equality; and unequals must make the return that is proportionate to the types of superiority.

10.12   Disputes among friends for utility
arise easily

Accusations and reproaches arise only or most often in | 5
friendship for utility. And this is reasonable. For friends for
virtue are eager to benefit each other, since this is proper
to virtue and to friendship; and if this is the achievement they
compete for, there are no accusations or fights. For no one
objects if the other loves and benefits him; if he is gracious, | 10
he retaliates by benefiting the other. And if the superior gets
what he aims at, he will not accuse his friend of anything,
since each of them desires what is good.

Nor are there many accusations among friends for pleasure.
For both of them get what they want at the same time if they
enjoy spending their time together; and someone who accused | 15
his friend of not pleasing him would appear ridiculous, when
he is free to spend his days without the friend's company.

Friendship for utility, however, is liable to accusations.
For these friends deal with each other in the expectation of
gaining benefits. Hence they always require more, thinking
they have got less than is fitting; and they reproach the other
because they get less than they require and deserve. And those
who confer benefits cannot supply as much as the recipients | 20
require.

10.13   Sources of the disputes

There are two ways of being just, one unwritten, and one
governed by rules of law. And similarly one type of friendship of utility would seem to depend on character, and the
other on rules. Accusations arise most readily if it is not the | 25
same sort of friendship when they dissolve it that it was when
they formed it.

Friendship dependent on rules is the type that is on explicit conditions. One type of this is entirely mercenary and requires immediate payment. The other is more generous and postpones the time [of repayment], but conforms to an agreement [requiring] one thing in return for another. In this sort of friendship it is clear and unambiguous what is owed, but the postponement is a friendly aspect of it. That is why some 30 cities do not allow legal actions in these cases, but think that people who have formed an arrangement on the basis of trust must put up with the outcome.

Inexplicit understandings leave room for disputes

Friendship [for utility] that depends on character is not on explicit conditions. Someone makes a present or whatever it is, as to a friend, but expects to get back as much or more, since he assumes that it is not a free gift, but a loan. And if he does not dissolve the friendship on the terms on which he formed it, he will accuse the other.

35 This happens because all or most people wish for what is fine, but decide to do what is beneficial; and while it is fine 1163a to do someone a good turn without the aim of receiving one in return, it is beneficial to receive a good turn.

10.2   Answers to the Disputes

10.21   We should make a fair return

We should, if we can, make a return worthy of what we have received, [if the other has undertaken the friendship] willingly. For we should never make a friend of someone who is unwilling, but must suppose that we were in error at the beginning, and received a benefit from the wrong per-5 son; for since it was not from a friend, and this was not why he was doing it, we must dissolve the arrangement as though we had received a good turn on explicit conditions. And we will agree to repay if we can. If we cannot repay, the giver would not even expect it. Hence we should repay if we can. We should consider at the beginning who is doing us a good turn, and on what conditions, so that we can put up with it on these conditions, or else decline it.

10.22   A fair return in a friendship for utility should be proportionate to utility

It is disputable whether we must measure [the return] by the benefit accruing to the recipient, and make the return proportional to that, or instead by the good turn done by the benefactor. For a recipient says that what he got was a small matter for the benefactor, and that he could have got it from someone else instead, and so he belittles it. But the benefactor says it was the biggest thing he had, that it could not be got from anyone else, and that he gave it when he was in danger or similar need. | 10

| 15

Since the friendship is for utility, surely the benefit to the recipient must be the measure [of the return]. For he was the one who required it, and the benefactor supplies him on the assumption that he will get an equal return. Hence the aid has been as great as the benefit received, and the recipient should return as much as he gained, or still more, since that is finer. | 20

10.23   Hence a different standard applies to friendships for virtue

But in friendships of virtue, there are no accusations. Rather, the decision of the benefactor would seem to be the measure, since the controlling element in virtue and character is found in decision.

10.3   Disputes in Friendships Between Unequals

10.31   Disputes arise from conflicting expectations

There are also disputes in friendships that correspond to superiority, since each friend expects to have more than the other, but whenever this happens the friendship is dissolved. | viii 14
| 25

For the better person thinks it is fitting for him to have more, on the ground that more is fittingly accorded to the good person. And the more beneficial person thinks the same. For it is wrong, people say, for someone to have an equal share when he is useless; a public service, not a friendship, 30 is the result if the benefits from the friendship do not correspond to the worth of the actions. [Each superior party says this] because he notices that in a financial association the larger contributors gain more, and he thinks the same thing is right in a friendship.

But the needy person, the inferior party in the friendship, takes the opposite view, saying it is proper to a virtuous friend to supply his needy [friends]. For what use is it, as 35 they say, to be an excellent or powerful person's friend if you are not going to gain anything by it?

10.32   Answer to the disputes

The conflicting expectations are partly mistaken
Well, each of them would seem to be correct in what he 1163b expects, and it is right for each of them to get more from the friendship — but not more of the same thing. Rather, the superior person should get more honour, and the needy person more profit, since honour is the reward of virtue and beneficence, while profit is what supplies need.

10.33   Political practice confirms our answer
5   This also appears to be true in political systems. For someone who provides nothing for the community receives no honour, since what is common is given to someone who benefits the community, and honour is something common. For it is impossible both to make money off the community and to receive honour from it at the same time; for no one 10 endures the smaller share of everything. Hence someone who

236

suffers a monetary loss [by holding office] receives honour
in return, while someone who accepts bribes [in office] receives money [but not honour]; for distribution that corresponds to worth equalizes and preserves the friendship, as
we have said.

10.34   Sometimes honour is the only possible
return to superiors

This, then, is how we should treat unequals. If we are
benefited in virtue or in money, we should return honour,
and thereby make what return we can. For friendship seeks   15
what is possible, not what corresponds to worth, since that
is impossible in some cases, e.g. with honour to gods and
parents. For no one could ever make a return corresponding to their worth, but someone who attends to them as far
as he is able seems to be a decent person.

10.35   Illustration from the relation of
father and son

That is why it seems that a son is not free to disavow his
father, but a father is free to disavow his son. For a debtor   20
should return what he owes, and since no matter what a
son has done he has not made a worthy return for what his
father has done for him, he is always the debtor. But the
creditor is free to remit the debt, and hence the father is free
to remit.

At the same time, however, it presumably seems that no
one would ever withdraw from a son who was not far gone
in vice. For, quite apart from their natural friendship, it is
human not to repel aid. The son, however, if he is vicious,   25
will want to avoid helping his father, or will not be keen on
it. For the many wish to receive benefits, but they avoid doing them because they suppose it is unprofitable. So much,
then, for these things.

10.4   Disputes Between Friends with Dissimilar Aims

10.41   Disputes arise from conflicting aims

ix 1   In all friendships of friends with dissimilar aims it is proportion that equalizes and preserves the friendship, as we
35   said; e.g. in political friendship the cobbler receives a worthy exchange for his shoes, and so do the weaver and the
1164a   others. Here money is supplied as a common measure; everything is related to this and measured by it.

In erotic friendships, however, sometimes the lover charges that he loves the beloved deeply and is not loved in return;
5   and in fact perhaps he has nothing lovable in him. The beloved, however, often charges that previously the lover was promising him everything, and now fulfils none of his promises.

These sorts of charges arise whenever the lover loves his beloved for pleasure while the beloved loves his lover for utility, and they do not both provide these. For when the friendship has these causes, it is dissolved whenever they
10   do not get what they were friends for; for each was not fond of the other himself, but only of what the other had, and since this was unstable, the friendships are unstable too.

Friendship of character, however, is friendship in itself, and endures, as we have said.

Friends quarrel when they get results different from those they want; for when someone does not get what he aims
15   at, it is like getting nothing. It is like the person who promised the lyre player a reward, and a greater reward the better he played; in the morning, when the player asked him to deliver on his promise, the other said he had paid pleasure for pleasure. Now if this was what each of them had wished, it would be quite enough. But if one wished for delight and the other for profit, and one has got his delight

238

and the other has not made his profit, the association is in | 20
no good state. For each person sets his mind on what he
finds he requires, and this will be his aim when he gives
what he gives.

10.42   To settle disputes we must decide
the value of a friend's services

Who should fix the worth [of a benefit], the giver or the
receiver? The giver would seem to leave it to the receiver,
as Protagoras is said to have done. For whenever he taught | 25
anything at all, he used to tell the pupil to estimate how much
the knowledge was worth, and that amount would be his payment. In such cases, however, some prefer the rule 'A man
should have his payment'.

But those who take the money first, and then do nothing
that they said they would do, because their promises were
excessive, are predictably accused, since they do not carry | 30
out what they agreed to. And presumably the sophists are
compelled to make excessive promises. For no one would
pay them money for the knowledge they really have; hence
they take the payment, and then do not do what they were
paid to do, and predictably are accused.

10.43   In the best friendship the friend's
intention is the standard

But where no agreement about services is made, friends
who give services because of the friend himself are not open | 35
to accusation, as we have said, since this is the character
of the friendship that reflects virtue. And the return should | 1164b
reflect the decision [of the original giver], since decision is
proper to a friend and to virtue.

And it would seem that the same sort of return should also
be made to those who have shared philosophy in common
with us. For its worth is not measured by money, and no

5 equivalent honour can be paid; but it is enough, presumably, to do what we can, as we do towards gods and parents.

10.44   In others the benefit received
must be the measure

If the giving is not of this sort, but on some specified condition, then presumably the repayment must be, ideally, what each of them thinks matches the worth of the gift. But if they do not agree on this, then it would seem not merely necessary, but also just, for the party who benefits first to fix the repay-
10 ment. For if the other receives in return as much benefit as the first received, or as much as he would have paid for the pleasure, he will have got the worthy return from him.

Indeed this is also how it appears in buying and selling. For in some cities there are actually laws prohibiting legal actions in voluntary bargains, on the assumption that if we have trusted someone we must dissolve the association with
15 him on the same terms on which we formed it. The law does this because it supposes that it is more just for the recipient to fix repayment than for the giver to fix it.

For usually those who have something and those who want it do not put the same price on it, since what they own and what they are giving appears to givers to be worth a lot. But nonetheless the return is made in the amount fixed by the
20 initial recipient. Presumably, however, the price must be not what it appears to be worth when he has got it, but the price he put on it before he got it.

10.5   Conflicts Between Different Types
of Friendships

10.51   Different types of friendships create
different obligations

ix 2   Here are some other questions that raise a puzzle. Must one accord [authority in] everything to his father, and obey

240

him in everything? Or must he trust the doctor when he is
sick, and should he vote for a military expert to be general?
Similarly, should someone serve his friend rather than an | 25
excellent person, and return a favour to a benefactor rather
than do a favour for a companion, if he cannot do both?

10.52   Usually we should return debts first

Surely it is not easy to define all these matters exactly.
For they include many differences of all sorts – in importance
and unimportance and in what is fine and what is necessary.
Clearly, however, not everything should be given to the same | 30
person, and usually we should return favours rather than do
favours for our companions, just as we should return a loan
to a creditor rather than lend to a companion.

10.53   But the general rule needs qualification

But presumably this is not always true. If, e.g., some-
one has rescued you from pirates, should you ransom him | 35
in return, no matter who he is? Or if he does not need to
be ransomed, but asks for his money back, should you re- | 1165a
turn it, or should you ransom your father instead? Here it
seems that you should ransom your father, rather than even
yourself.

As we have said, then, generally speaking we should return
what we owe. But if making a gift [to B] outweighs [return-
ing the money to A] by being finer or more necessary, we
should incline to [making the gift to B] instead.

For sometimes even a return of a previous favour is not | 5
fair [but an excessive demand], whenever [the original giver]
knows he is benefiting an excellent person, but [the recipient]
would be returning the benefit to someone he thinks is
vicious.

For sometimes you should not even lend in return to someone who has lent to you. For he expected repayment when

10 he lent to a decent person, whereas you have no hope of it from a bad person. If that is really so, then, the demand [for reciprocity] is not fair; and even if it is not so, but you think it is so, your refusal of the demand seems not at all absurd.

As we have often said, then, arguments about acting and being affected are no more definite than their subject matter.

10.54 Different benefits are owed
to different friends

Clearly, then, we should not give the same thing to every-
15 one, and we should not give our fathers everything, just as we should not make all our sacrifices to Zeus. And since different things should be given to parents, brothers, com-panions and benefactors, we should accord to each what is proper and suitable. This is what actually appears to be done; e.g. kinsfolk are the people invited to a wedding, since they
20 share the same family, and hence share in actions that con-cern it; and for the same reason it is thought that kinsfolk more than anyone must come to funerals.

It seems that we must supply means of support to parents more than anyone. For we suppose that we owe them this, and that it is finer to supply those who are the causes of our being than to supply ourselves in this way. And we should accord honour to our parents, just as we should to the gods,
25 but not every sort of honour; for we should not accord the same honour to father and to mother, nor accord them the honour due a wise person or a general. We should accord a father's honour to a father, and likewise a mother's to a mother.

We should accord to every older person the honour befit-ting his age, by standing up, giving up seats and so on. With companions and brothers we should speak freely, and have
30 everything in common. To kinsfolk, fellow-tribesmen, fellow-citizens and all the rest we should always try to accord what is proper, and should compare what belongs to each, as be-

fits closeness of relation, virtue or usefulness. Comparison
is easier with people of the same kind, and more difficult
with people of different kinds, but the difficulty is no rea-
son for giving up the comparison; rather, we should define | 35
as far as we can.

10.6 When Should Friendships Be Dissolved?

10.61 It is easy with friendships for
utility and pleasure
There is also a puzzle about dissolving or not dissolving | ix 3
friendships with friends who do not remain the same. With | 1165b
friends for utility or pleasure perhaps there is nothing absurd in dissolving the friendship whenever they are no longer
pleasant or useful. For they were friends of pleasure or utility;
and if these give out, it is reasonable not to love.

10.62 Supposed friendships for virtue
may also be dissolved
However, we might accuse a friend if he really liked us | 5
for utility or pleasure, and pretended to like us for our
character. For, as we said at the beginning, friends are most
at odds when they are not friends in the way they think they
are. And so, if we mistakenly suppose we are loved for our
character, when our friend is doing nothing to suggest this,
we must hold ourselves responsible. But if we are deceived | 10
by his pretence, we are justified in accusing him—even more
justified than in accusing debasers of the currency, to the
extent that his evildoing debases something more precious.

10.63 A change of character creates
special difficulties
But if we accept a friend as a good person, and then he
becomes vicious, and seems so, should we still love him?
Surely we cannot, if not everything, but only what is good,

15 | is lovable. What is bad is not lovable, and must not be loved; for we ought neither to love what is bad nor to become similar to a bad person, and we have said that similar is friend to similar.

Then should the friendship be dissolved at once [as soon as the friend becomes bad]? Surely not with everyone, but only with an incurably vicious person. If someone can be set right, we should try harder to rescue his character than

20 | his property, in so far as character is both better and more proper to friendship.

However, the friend who dissolves the friendship seems to be doing nothing absurd. For he was not the friend of a person of this sort; hence, if the friend has altered, and he cannot save him, he leaves him.

But if one friend stayed the same and the other became more decent and far excelled his friend in virtue, should the better person still treat the other as a friend? Surely he can-

25 | not. This becomes clear in a wide separation, such as we find in friendships beginning in childhood. For if one friend still thinks as a child, while the other becomes a most superior man, how could they still be friends, when they neither approve of the same things nor find the same things enjoyable or painful? For they do not even find it so in their life

30 | together and without that they cannot be friends, since they cannot live together—we have discussed this.

10.64   But the dissolution of a friendship
may not cancel all special relations

Then should the better person regard the other as though he had never become his friend? Surely he must keep some memory of the familiarity they had; and just as we think we must do kindnesses for friends more than for strangers, so

35 | also we should accord something to past friends because of the former friendship, whenever excessive vice does not cause the dissolution.

11.   The Sources and Justification of Friendship

11.1   Friendship May Be Understood
by Reference to Self-love

11.11   The features of friendship

The defining features of friendship that are found in friendships to one's neighbours would seem to be derived from
features of friendship towards oneself.

For a friend is taken to be (1) someone who wishes and
does goods or apparent goods to his friend for the friend's
own sake; or (2) one who wishes the friend to be and to live
for the friend's own sake — this is how mothers feel towards
their children, and how friends who have been in conflict
feel [towards each other]. (3) Others take a friend to be one
who spends his time with his friend, and (4) makes the same
choices; or (5) one who shares his friend's distress and
enjoyment — and this also is true especially of mothers. And
people define friendship by one of these features.

11.12   These Features of Friendship Reflect
the Virtuous Person's Love of Himself

Each of these features is found in the decent person's relation to himself, and it is found in other people in so far as
they suppose they are decent. As we have said, virtue and
the excellent person would seem to be the standard in each
case.

(4) The excellent person is of one mind with himself, and
desires the same things in his whole soul.

(1) Hence he wishes goods and apparent goods to himself,
and does them in his actions, since it is proper to the good
person to achieve the good. He wishes and does them for
his own sake, since he does them for the sake of his thinking part, and that is what each person seems to be.

(2) He wishes himself to live and to be preserved. And

he wishes this for the part by which he has intelligence more than for any other part. For being is a good for the good
20 person, and each person wishes for goods for himself. And no one chooses to become another person even if that other will have every good when he has come into being; for, as it is, the god has the good [but no one chooses to be replaced by a god]. Rather [each of us chooses goods] on condition that he remains whatever he is; and each person would seem to be the understanding part, or that most of all. [Hence the good person wishes for goods for the understanding part.]

(3) Further, such a person finds it pleasant to spend time with himself, and so wishes to do it. For his memories of
25 what he has done are agreeable, and his expectations for the future are good, and hence both are pleasant. And besides, his thought is well supplied with topics for study.

(5) Moreover, he shares his own distresses and pleasures, more than other people share theirs. For it is always the same thing that is painful or pleasant, not different things at different times. This is because he practically never regrets [what he has done].

30 The decent person, then, has each of these features in relation to himself, and is related to his friend as he is to himself, since the friend is another himself. Hence friendship seems to be one of these features, and people with these features seem to be friends.

Is there friendship towards oneself, or is there not? Let us dismiss that question for the present. However, there
35 seems to be friendship in so far as someone is two or more parts. This seems to be true from what we have said, and
1166b because an extreme degree of friendship resembles one's friendship to oneself.

*11.13   Vicious people are not capable
of the same self-love*

The many, base though they are, also appear to have these features. But perhaps they share in them only in so far as

246

they approve of themselves and suppose they are decent. For
no one who is utterly bad and unscrupulous either has these   5
features or appears to have them.

Indeed, even base people hardly have them.

(4) For they are at odds with themselves, and, like incontinent people, have an appetite for one thing and a wish for
another.

(1) For they do not choose things that seem to be good
for them, but instead choose pleasant things that are actually
harmful. And cowardice or laziness causes others to shrink   10
from doing what they think best for themselves.

(2) Those who have done many terrible actions hate and
shun life because of their vice, and destroy themselves.

(3) Besides, vicious people seek others to pass their days
with, and shun themselves. For when they are by themselves   15
they remember many disagreeable actions, and expect to do
others in the future; but they manage to forget these in other
people's company. These people have nothing lovable about
them, and so have no friendly feelings for themselves.

(5) Hence such a person does not share his own enjoyments
and distresses. For his soul is in conflict, and because he   20
is vicious one part is distressed at being restrained, and
another is pleased [by the intended action]; and so each part
pulls in a different direction, as though they were tearing
him apart. Even if he cannot be distressed and pleased at
the same time, still he is soon distressed because he was
pleased, and wishes these things had not become pleasant
to him; for base people are full of regret.   25

11.14 Both self-love and friendship
require virtue

Hence the base person appears not to have a friendly attitude even towards himself, because he has nothing lovable
about him.

If this state is utterly miserable, everyone should earnestly shun vice and try to be decent; for that is how someone will have a friendly relation to himself and will become a friend to another.

11.2 Goodwill is a Component of Friendship

11.21 Goodwill is not the same as friendship

Goodwill would seem to be a feature of friendship, but still it is not friendship. For it arises even towards people we do not know, and without their noticing it, whereas friendship does not. We have said this before also.

Nor is it loving, since it lacks intensity and desire, which are implied by loving. Moreover, while loving requires familiarity, goodwill can also arise in a moment, as it arises, e.g., [in a spectator] for contestants. For [the spectator] acquires goodwill for them, and wants what they want, but would not cooperate with them in any action; for, as we said, his good will arises in a moment and his fondness is superficial.

11.22 It is the basis of friendship . . .

In fact goodwill would seem to originate friendship in the way that pleasure coming through sight originates erotic passion. For no one has erotic passion for another without previous pleasure in his appearance. But still enjoyment of his appearance does not imply erotic passion for him; passion consists also in longing for him in his absence and an appetite for his presence. Similarly, though people cannot be friends without previous goodwill, goodwill does not imply friendship; for when they have goodwill people only wish goods to the other, and will not cooperate with him in any action, or go to any trouble for him.

Hence we might transfer [the name 'friendship'], and say that goodwill is inactive friendship, and that when it lasts some time and they grow accustomed to each other, it becomes friendship.

*11.23 . . . But only of the best kind
of friendship*

It does not, however, become friendship for utility or
pleasure, since these aims do not produce goodwill either.

For a recipient of a benefit does what is just when he re- | 15
turns goodwill for what he has received. But those who wish
for another's welfare because they hope to enrich themselves
through him would seem to have goodwill to themselves,
rather than to him. Likewise, they would seem to be friends
to themselves rather than to him, if they attend to him because he is of some use to them.

But in general goodwill results from some sort of virtue
and decency, whenever one person finds another to be
apparently fine or brave or something similar. As we said, | 20
this also arises in the case of contestants.

11.3   Concord is a Component of Friendship

*11.31   It requires agreement in beliefs
about goods . . .*

Now concord also appears to be a feature of friendship. | ix 6
Hence it is not merely sharing a belief, since this might happen among people who do not know each other. Nor are peo-
ple said to be in concord when they agree about just any- | 25
thing, e.g. on astronomical questions, since concord on these
questions is not a feature of friendship. Rather, a city is said
to be in concord when [its citizens] agree about what is advantageous, make the same decision, and act on their common resolution.

Hence concord concerns questions for action, and, more
exactly, large questions where both or all can get what they | 30
want. A city, e.g., is in concord whenever all the citizens
resolve to make offices elective, or to make an alliance with
the Spartans, or to make Pittacus ruler, when he is willing too.

. . . But especially about the distribution of goods

Whenever each person wants the same thing all to himself, as the people in the *Phoenissae* do, they are in conflict. For it is not concord when each merely has the same thing in mind, whatever it is, but each must also have the same thing in mind for the same person; this is true, e.g., whenever both the common people and the decent party want the best people to rule, since when that is so both sides get what they seek.

Concord, then, is apparently political friendship, as indeed it is said to be; for it is concerned with advantage and with what affects life [as a whole].

11.32   Hence it is largely confined to virtuous people

This sort of concord is found in decent people. For they are in concord with themselves and with each other, since they are practically of the same mind; for their wishes are stable, not flowing back and forth like a tidal strait. They wish for what is just and advantageous, and also seek it in common.

Base people, however, cannot be in concord, except to a small extent, just as they can be friends only to a small extent; for they are greedy for more benefits, and shirk labours and public services. And since each wishes this for himself, he interrogates and obstructs his neighbour; for when people do not look out for the common good, it is ruined. The result is that they are in conflict, trying to compel each other to do what is just, but not wishing to do it themselves.

11.4   Active and Unselfish Benevolence is a Component of Friendship

11.41   Why do benefactors love more than they are loved?

Now benefactors seem to love their beneficiaries more than the beneficiaries love them [in return], and this is discussed as though it were an unreasonable thing to happen.

250

11.42   The common explanation assumes
that the benefactor is purely selfish

Here is how it appears to most people. It is because the | 20
beneficiaries are debtors and the benefactors creditors: the
debtor in a loan wishes the creditor did not exist, while the
creditor even attends to the safety of the debtor. So also,
then, a benefactor wants the beneficiary to exist because he
expects gratitude in return, while the beneficiary is not at- | 25
tentive about making the return.

Now Epicharmus might say that most people say this because they 'take a bad person's point of view'. Still, it would
seem to be a human point of view, since the many are indeed forgetful, and seek to receive benefits more than to
give them.

But this explanation is refuted by the facts

However, it seems that the cause is more proper to [hu-
man] nature, and the case of creditors is not even similar.
For they do not love their debtors, but in wishing for their | 30
safety simply seek repayment; whereas benefactors love
and like their beneficiaries even if they are of no present or
future use to them.

11.43   The correct explanation assumes
that the benefactor is unselfish

The same is true with craftsmen; for each likes his own
product more than it would like him if it acquired a soul. | 35
Perhaps this is true of poets most of all, since they dearly | 1168a
like their own poems, and are fond of them as though they
were their children. This, then, is what the case of the
benefactor resembles; here the beneficiary is his product,
and hence he likes him more than the product likes its | 5
producer.

251

11.44   This explanation is justified by facts
about human nature

Active benevolence realizes human capacities
   The cause of this is as follows:
1. Being is choiceworthy and lovable for all.
2. We are in so far as we are actualized, since we are in
so far as we live and act.
3. The product is, in a way, the producer in his actualization.
4. Hence the producer is fond of the product, because he
loves his own being. And this is natural, since what he is
potentially is what the product indicates in actualization.

It is finest and pleasantest
10   At the same time, the benefactor's action is fine for him,
so that he finds enjoyment in the person he acts on; but the
person acted on finds nothing fine in the agent, but only,
at most, some advantage, which is less pleasant and lovable.
   What is pleasant is actualization in the present, expectation for the future, and memory of the past; but what is
15   pleasantest is the [action we do] in so far as we are actualized, and this is also most lovable. For the benefactor, then,
his product endures, since what is fine is long-lasting; but
for the person acted on, what is useful passes away.
   Besides, memory of something fine is pleasant, while
memory of [receiving] something useful is not altogether
pleasant, or is less pleasant – though the reverse would seem
to be true for expectation.

Benevolence is production
20   Moreover, loving is like production, while being loved is
like being acted on; and [the benefactor's] love and friendliness is the result of his greater activity.

252

Benevolence reflects the benefactor's own effort

Besides, everyone is fond of what has needed effort to produce it; e.g. people who have made money themselves are fonder of it than people who have inherited it. And while receiving a benefit seems to take no effort, giving one is hard work.

This is also why mothers love their children more [than | 25 fathers do], since giving birth is more effort for them, and they know better that the children are theirs. And this also would seem to be proper to benefactors.

11.5 Self-love is a Component of Friendship

11.51 The common view identifies
self-love with selfishness

There is also a puzzle about whether one ought to love | ix 8 oneself or someone else most of all; for those who like them- selves most are criticized and denounced as self-lovers, as | 30 though this were something shameful.

Indeed, the base person does seem to go to every length for his own sake, and all the more the more vicious he is; hence he is accused, e.g., of doing nothing of his own ac- cord. The decent person, on the contrary, acts for what is fine, all the more the better he is, and for his friend's sake, disregarding his own good. | 35

11.52 But facts about friendship
justify self-love

The facts, however, conflict with these claims, and that | 1168b is not unreasonable.

For it is said that we must love most the friend who is most a friend; and one person is most a friend to another if he wishes goods to the other for the other's sake, even if no one will know about it. But these are features most of all of one's relation to oneself; and so too are all the other defining features of a friend, since we have said that all the features of friendship extend from oneself to others.

All the proverbs agree with this too, e.g. speaking of 'one soul', 'what friends have is common', 'equality is friendship' and 'the knee is closer than the shin'. For all these are true most of all in someone's relations with himself, since one is a friend to himself most of all. Hence he should also love 10 himself most of all.

11.53   Hence we must distinguish good and bad forms of self-love

It is not surprising that there is a puzzle about which view we ought to follow, since both inspire some confidence; hence we must presumably divide these sorts of arguments, and distinguish how far and in what ways those on each side are true.

15 Perhaps, then, it will become clear, if we grasp how those on each side understand self-love.

11.54   The bad form of self-love is selfish, resting on an incorrect view of the self

Those who make self-love a matter for reproach ascribe it to those who award the biggest share in money, honours and bodily pleasures to themselves. For these are the goods desired and eagerly pursued by the many on the assumption that they are best; and hence they are also contested.

Those who are greedy for these goods gratify their ap-20 petites and in general their feelings and the non-rational part of the soul; and since this is the character of the many, the application of the term ['self-love'] is derived from the most frequent [kind of self-love], which is base. This type of self-lover, then, is justifiably reproached.

And plainly it is the person who awards himself these goods whom the many habitually call a self-lover. For if

someone is always eager to excel everyone in doing just or | 25
temperate actions or any others expressing the virtues, and
in general always gains for himself what is fine, no one will
call him a self-lover or blame him for it.

11.55   But the good form of self-love
rests on a correct view of the self

However, it is this more than the other sort of person who
seems to be a self-lover. At any rate he awards himself what
is finest and best of all, and gratifies the most controlling | 30
part of himself, obeying it in everything. And just as a city
and every other composite system seems to be above all its
most controlling part, the same is true of a human being;
hence someone loves himself most if he likes and gratifies
this part.

Similarly, someone is called continent or incontinent be-
cause his understanding is or is not the master, on the as- | 35
sumption that this is what each person is. Moreover, his | 1169a
own voluntary actions seem above all to be those involving
reason. Clearly, then, this, or this above all, is what each
person is, and the decent person likes this most of all.

Hence he most of all is a self-lover, but a different kind
from the self-lover who is reproached, differing from him
as much as the life guided by reason differs from the life | 5
guided by feelings, and as much as the desire for what is
fine differs from the desire for what seems advantageous.

11.56   Hence it leads to virtuous action

Those who are unusually eager to do fine actions are
welcomed and praised by everyone. And when everyone
contends to achieve what is fine and strains to do the finest
actions, everything that is right will be done for the com- | 10
mon good, and each person individually will receive the
greatest of goods, since that is the character of virtue.

255

Hence the good person must be a self-lover, since he will both help himself and benefit others by doing fine actions. But the vicious person must not love himself, since he will harm both himself and his neighbours by following his base feelings.

15   For the vicious person, then, the right actions conflict with those he does. The decent person, however, does the right actions, since every understanding chooses what is best for itself and the decent person obeys his understanding.

11.57   It even leads to costly sacrifices

Besides, it is true that, as they say, the excellent person labours for his friends and for his native country, and will
20 die for them if he must; he will sacrifice money, honours and contested goods in general, in achieving what is fine for himself. For he will choose intense pleasure for a short time over mild pleasure for a long time; a year of living finely over many years of undistinguished life; and a single fine
25 and great action over many small actions.

This is presumably true of one who dies for others; he does indeed choose something great and fine for himself. He is ready to sacrifice money as long as his friends profit; for the friends gain money, while he gains what is fine, and so he awards himself the greater good. He treats hon-
30 ours and offices the same way; for he will sacrifice them all for his friends, since this is fine and praiseworthy for him. It is not surprising, then, that he seems to be excellent, when he chooses what is fine at the cost of everything. It is also possible, however, to sacrifice actions to his friend, since it may be finer to be responsible for his friend's do-ing the action than to do it himself. In everything praise-
35 worthy, then, the excellent person evidently awards himself more of what is fine.

1169b   In this way, then, we must be self-lovers, as we have said. But in the way the many are, we ought not to be.

256

11.6   The Justification of Friendship

11.61   Friends do not seem to be needed
for happiness

There is also a dispute about whether the happy person
will need friends or not.

For it is said that blessedly happy and self-sufficient people have no need of friends. For they already have [all] the
goods, and hence, being self-sufficient, need nothing added. 5
But your friend, since he is another yourself, supplies what
your own efforts cannot supply. Hence it is said, 'When the
god gives well, what need is there of friends?'

11.62   But friends are the greatest
external good

However, in awarding the happy person all the goods it
would seem absurd not to give him friends; for having friends
seems to be the greatest external good.   10

11.63   We need friends for us to benefit

And it is more proper to a friend to confer benefits than
to receive them, and proper to the good person and to virtue
to do good; and it is finer to benefit friends than to benefit
strangers. Hence the excellent person will need people for
him to benefit. Indeed, that is why there is a question about
whether friends are needed more in good fortune than in ill-
fortune; for it is assumed that in ill-fortune we need people   15
to benefit us, and in good fortune we need others for us to
benefit.

11.64   Solitude makes happiness impossible

Surely it is also absurd to make the blessed person solitary. For no one would choose to have all [other] goods and
yet be alone, since a human being is political, tending by
nature to live together with others. This will also be true,

257

20   then, of the happy person; for he has the natural goods, and clearly it is better to spend his days with decent friends than with strangers of just any character. Hence the happy person will need friends.

11.65 *We can observe the actions of virtuous friends*

Then what are the other side saying, and in what way is it true? Surely they say what they say because the many think that it is the useful people who are friends. Certainly 25 the blessedly happy person will have no need of these, since he has [all] goods. Similarly, he will have no need, or very little, of friends for pleasure; for since his life is pleasant, it has no need of imported pleasures. Since he does not need these sorts of friends, he does not seem to need friends at all.

However, this conclusion is presumably not true:
(1) For we said at the beginning that happiness is a kind of 30 activity; and clearly activity comes into being, and does not belong [to someone all the time], as a possession does. Being happy, then, is found in living and being active.
(2) The activity of the good person is excellent, and [hence] pleasant in itself, as we said at the beginning.
(3) Moreover, what is our own is pleasant.
(4) We are able to observe our neighbours more than our-
35 selves, and to observe their actions more than our own.
(5) Hence a good person finds pleasure in the actions of ex-
1170a cellent people who are his friends, since these actions have both the naturally pleasant [features, i.e. they are good, and they are his own].
(6) The blessed person decides to observe virtuous actions that are his own; and the actions of a virtuous friend are of this sort.
(7) Hence he will need virtuous friends.

258

11.66 Friendship provides pleasure

Further, it is thought that the happy person must live pleasantly. But the solitary person's life is hard, since it is not easy for him to be continuously active all by himself; but in relation to others and in their company it is easier, and hence his activity will be more continuous. It is also pleasant in itself, as it must be in the blessedly happy person's case. For the excellent person, in so far as he is excellent, enjoys actions expressing virtue, and objects to actions caused by vice, just as the musician enjoys fine melodies and is pained by bad ones.

11.67 Friendship encourages virtue

Further, good people's life together allows the cultivation of virtue, as Theognis says.

11.68 Friendship realizes human capacities

If we examine the question more from the point of view of [human] nature, an excellent friend would seem to be choiceworthy by nature for an excellent person.

(1) For, as we have said, what is good by nature is good and pleasant in itself for an excellent person.

(2) For animals life is defined by the capacity for perception; for human beings it is defined by the capacity for perception or understanding.

(3) Every capacity refers to an activity, and a thing is present to its full extent in its activity.

(4) Hence living to its full extent would seem to be perceiving or understanding.

(5) Life is good and pleasant in itself. For it has definite order, which is proper to the nature of what is good.

(6) What is good by nature is also good for the decent person. That is why life would seem to be pleasant for everyone. Here, however, we must not consider a life that is vicious and corrupted, or filled with pains; for such a life

25 lacks definite order, just as its proper features do. (The truth about pain will be more evident in what follows.)

(7) Life itself, then, is good and pleasant. So it looks, at any rate, from the fact that everyone desires it, and decent and blessed people desire it more than others do; for their life is most choiceworthy for them, and their living is most blessed.

(8) Now someone who sees perceives that he sees; one who
30 hears perceives that he hears; and one who walks perceives that he walks.

(9) Similarly in the other cases also there is some [element] that perceives that we are active.

(10) Hence, if we are perceiving, we perceive that we are perceiving; and if we are understanding, we perceive that we are understanding.

(11) Now perceiving that we are perceiving or understanding is the same as perceiving that we are, since we agreed [in (4)] that being is perceiving or understanding.

1170b (12) Perceiving that we are alive is pleasant in itself. For life is by nature a good [from (5)], and it is pleasant to perceive that something good is present in us.

(13) And living is choiceworthy, for a good person most of all, since being is good and pleasant for him; for he is
5 pleased to perceive something good in itself together [with his own being].

(14) The excellent person is related to his friend in the same way as he is related to himself, since a friend is another himself.

(15) Therefore, just as his own being is choiceworthy for him, his friend's being is choiceworthy for him in the same or a similar way.

*11.69 Friendship includes shared life,
and hence shared conversation and thought*

We agreed that someone's own being is choiceworthy because he perceives that he is good, and this sort of percep-

260

tion is pleasant in itself. He must, then, perceive his friend's being together [with his own], and he will do this when they live together and share conversation and thought. For in the case of human beings what seems to count as living together is this sharing of conversation and thought, not sharing the same pasture, as in the case of grazing animals.

11.610   Conclusion: Friendship is needed for self-sufficiency

If, then, for the blessedly happy person, being is choice-worthy, since it is naturally good and pleasant; and if the being of his friend is closely similar to his own; then his friend will also be choiceworthy. Whatever is choiceworthy for him he must possess, since otherwise he will to this extent lack something, [and hence will not be self-suficient]. Anyone who is to be happy, then, must have excellent friends.

11.7   The Proper Number of Friends for a Happy Life

Then should we have as many friends as possible? Or is it the same as with the friendship of host and guest, where it seems to be good advice to 'have neither many nor none'? Is this also good advice in friendship, to have neither no friends nor many?

11.71   Friends for utility and pleasure should be limited

With friends for utility the advice seems very apt, since it is hard work to return many people's services, and life is too short for it. Indeed, more [such] friends than are adequate for one's own life are superfluous, and a hindrance to living finely; hence we have no need of them. A few friends for pleasure are enough also, just as a little seasoning on food is enough.

261

11.72 Friends for virtue must be limited by
the requirements of living together

Of excellent people, however, should we have as many
30   as possible as friends, or is there some proper measure of
their number, as of the number in a city? For a city could
not be formed from ten human beings, but it would be a city
no longer if it had ten myriads; presumably, though, the
right quantity is not just one number, but anything between
1171a certain defined limits. Hence there is also some limit defining the number of friends.

Presumably, this is the largest number with whom you
could live together, since we found that living together
seems to be most characteristic of friendship. And clearly
you cannot live with many people and distribute yourself
among them.

Besides, these many people must also be friends to each
5   other, if they are all to spend their days together; and this
is hard work for many people to manage. It also becomes
difficult for many to share each other's enjoyments and distresses as their own, since you are quite likely to find yourself sharing one friend's pleasure and another friend's grief
at the same time.

11.73 An excessive number of friends changes
the character of the friendship

Presumably, then, it is good not to seek as many friends
as possible, and good to have no more than enough for liv-
10   ing together; indeed it even seems impossible to be an extremely close friend to many people. For the same reason it
also seems impossible to be passionately in love with many
people, since passionate erotic love tends to be an excess of
friendship, and one has this for one person; hence also one
has extremely close friendship for a few people.

This would seem to be borne out in what people actually
do. For the friendship of companions is not found in groups

262

of many people, and the friendships celebrated in song are | 15
always between two people. By contrast, those who have
many friends and treat everyone as close to them seem to
be friends to no one, except in a fellow-citizen's way. These
people are regarded as ingratiating.

Certainly it is possible to be a friend of many in a fellow-
citizen's way, and still to be a truly decent person, not ingratiating; but it is impossible to be many people's friend
for their virtue and for themselves. We have reason to be | 20
satisfied if we can find even a few such friends.

11.8 The Role of Friends in Living Together, in Good Fortune and in Ill Fortune

Have we more need of friends in good fortune or in ill | ix 11
fortune? For in fact we seek them in both, since in ill fortune we need assistance, while in good fortune we need
friends to live with and to benefit, since then we wish to do
good.

Certainly it is more necessary to have friends in ill for-
tune, and hence useful friends are needed here. But it is | 25
finer to have them in good fortune, and hence we also seek
decent friends; for it is more choiceworthy to do good to
them and spend our time with them.

11.81 The good person will avoid causing pain to his friends

The very presence of friends is also pleasant, in ill fortune
as well as good fortune; for we have our pain lightened
when our friends share our distress. Hence indeed one might | 30
be puzzled about whether they take a part of it from us, as
though helping us to lift a weight, or, alternatively, their
presence is pleasant and our awareness that they share our
distress makes the pain smaller. Well, we need not discuss
whether it is this or something else that lightens our pain; at
any rate, what we have mentioned does appear to occur.

35
1171b However, the presence of friends would seem to be a mixture [of pleasure and pain]. For certainly the sight of our
friends in itself is pleasant, especially when we are in ill
fortune, and it gives us some assistance in removing our
pain. For a friend consoles us by the sight of him and by
conversation, if he is dexterous, since he knows our character and what gives us pleasure and pain. Nonetheless, aware-
5 ness of his pain at our ill fortune is painful to us, since
everyone tries to avoid causing pain to his friends.

That is why someone with a manly nature tries to prevent
his friend from sharing his pain. Unless he is unusually immune to pain, he cannot endure pain coming to his friends;
and he does not allow others to share his mourning at all,
10 since he is not prone to mourn himself either. Females, however, and effeminate men enjoy having people to wail with
them; they love them as friends who share their distress.
But in everything we clearly must imitate the better person.

*11.82   He will readily share his good fortune
with his friends*

In good fortune, by contrast, the presence of friends
makes it pleasant to pass our time and to notice that they
take pleasure in our own goods.

15 Hence it seems that we must eagerly call our friends to
share our good fortune, since it is fine to do good. But we
must hesitate to call them to share our ill fortune, since we
must share bad things with them as little as possible; hence
the saying 'My misfortune is enough'. We should invite them
20 most of all whenever they will benefit us greatly, with little
trouble to themselves.

*11.83   He will show them proper consideration
in their good and ill fortune*

Conversely, it is presumably appropriate to go eagerly,
without having to be called, to friends in misfortune. For

264

it is proper to a friend to benefit, especially to benefit a
friend in need who has not demanded it, since this is finer
and pleasanter for both friends. In good fortune he should
come eagerly to help him, since friends are needed for this
also; but he should be slow to come to receive benefits,
since eagerness to be benefitted is not fine. Presumably,   25
though, one should avoid getting a reputation for being a
killjoy, as sometimes happens, by refusing benefits.

Hence the presence of friends is apparently choiceworthy
in all conditions.

11.9   The Importance of Living Together
in Friendship

11.91   Living together is essential for
the best friendship

What the erotic lover likes most is the sight of his be-   ix 12
loved, and this is the sort of perception he chooses over the   30
others, supposing that this above all is what makes him fall
in love and remain in love. In the same way, surely, what
friends find most choiceworthy is living together. For friendship is community, and we are related to our friend as we
are related to ourselves. Hence, since the perception of our
own being is choiceworthy, so is the perception of our friend's
being. Perception is active when we live with him; hence,   35
not surprisingly, this is what we seek.   1172a

11.92   Living together includes the sharing
of valued pursuits

Whatever someone [regards as] his being, or the end for
which he chooses to be alive, that is the activity he wishes
to pursue in his friend's company. Hence some friends
drink together, others play dice, while others do gymnastics
and go hunting, or do philosophy. They spend their days   5
together on whichever pursuit in life they like most; for

since they want to live with their friends, they share the actions in which they find their common life.

11.93   Hence virtuous people have the
best life together

Hence the friendship of base people turns out to be vicious.
For they are unstable, and share base pursuits; and
10 by becoming similar to each other, they grow vicious. But
the friendship of decent people is decent, and increases the
more often they meet. And they seem to become still better
from their activities and their mutual correction. For each
moulds the other in what they approve of, so that '[you will
learn] what is noble from noble people'.
15   So much, then, for friendship. The next task will be to
discuss pleasure.

12.   Pleasure

12.1   The Right Approach to Pleasure

x 1 ### 12.11   Pleasure is of great ethical importance
20   The next task, presumably, is to discuss pleasure. For it
seems to be especially proper to our [animal] kind, and hence
when we educate children we steer them by pleasure and pain.
Besides, enjoying and hating the right things seems to be most
important for virtue of character. For pleasure and pain extend through the whole of our lives, and are of great impor-
25 tance for virtue and the happy life, since people decide to
do what is pleasant, and avoid what is painful. Least of all,
then, it seems, should these topics be neglected.
    This is especially true because they arouse much dispute.
For some say pleasure is the good, while others, on the contrary, say it is altogether base.

*12.12   But this should not tempt us
to exaggerate the badness of pleasure,
since such exaggeration is self-defeating*

Now presumably some who say it is base say so because
they are persuaded that it is so. Others, however, say it because they think it is better for the conduct of our lives to   30
present pleasure as base even if it is not. For, they say, since
the many lean towards pleasure and are slaves to pleasures,
we must lead them in the contrary direction, because that
is the way to reach the intermediate condition.

Surely, however, this is wrong. For arguments about ac-
tions and feelings are less credible than the facts; hence any   35
conflict between arguments and perceptible [facts] arouses
contempt for the arguments, and moreover undermines the   1172b
truth as well [as the arguments]. For if someone blames
pleasure, but then has been seen to seek it on *some* occasions, the reason for his lapse seems to be that he approves
of *every* type of pleasure; for the many are not the sort to
make distinctions.

True arguments, then, would seem to be the most useful,   5
not only for knowledge but also for the conduct of life. For
since they harmonize with the facts, they are credible, and
so encourage those who comprehend them to live by them.

Enough of this, then; let us now consider what has been
said about pleasure.

*12.2   The Case for Pleasure: No Sound
Argument Proves that It is the Good*

12.21   Eudoxus' arguments

Eudoxus thought that pleasure is the good.   x 2
(1) This was because (a) he saw that all [animals], both   10
rational and non-rational, seek it. (b) In everything, he says,
what is choiceworthy is decent, and what is most choiceworthy is supreme. (c) Each thing finds its own good, just

as it finds its own nourishment. (d) Hence, when all are drawn
to the same thing [i.e. pleasure], this indicates that it is best
15 for all. (e) And what is good for all, what all aim at, is the
good.

Eudoxus' arguments were found credible because of his
virtuous character, rather than on their own [merits]. For
since he seemed to be outstandingly temperate, he did not
seem to be saying this because he was a friend of pleasure;
rather, it seemed, what he said was how it really was.

(2) He thought it was no less evident from consideration
of the contrary. (a) Pain in itself is to be avoided for all.
20 (b) Similarly, then, its contrary is choiceworthy for all. (c)
What is most choiceworthy is what we choose not because
of, or for the sake of, anything else. (d) And it is agreed
that this is the character of pleasure, since we never ask
anyone what his end is in being pleased, on the assumption
that pleasure is choiceworthy in itself.

(3) Moreover, [he argued], when pleasure is added to any
other good, e.g. to just or temperate action, it makes that
25 good more choiceworthy; and good is increased by the addition of itself.

12.22 Discussion of Eudoxus' arguments

This [third] argument, at least, would seem to present pleasure as one good among others, no more a good than any
other. For the addition of *any* other good makes a good more
choiceworthy than it is all by itself.

Indeed Plato uses this sort of argument when he undermines the claim of pleasure to be the good. For, he argues,
30 the pleasant life is more choiceworthy when combined with
intelligence than it is without it; and if the mixed [good] is
better, pleasure is not the good, since nothing can be added
to the good to make it more choiceworthy.

Nor, clearly, could anything else be the good if it is made
more choiceworthy by the addition of anything that is good

in itself. Then what is the good that meets this condition, | 35
and that we share in also? That is what we are looking for.

12.3 The Case Against Pleasure:
No Sound Argument Proves that It
is not a Good

12.31 An exaggerated reply to Eudoxus'
first argument

When some object that what everything aims at is not good,
surely there is nothing in what they say. For if things seem | 1173a
[good] to all, we say they *are* [good]; and if someone undermines confidence in these, what he says will hardly inspire
more confidence in other things. For if [only] beings without
understanding desired these things, there would be something
in the objection; but if intelligent beings also desire them,
how can there be anything in it? And presumably even in
inferior [animals] there is something superior to themselves, | 5
that seeks their own proper good.

12.32 An exaggerated reply to Eudoxus'
second argument

The argument [offered against Eudoxus] about the contrary would also seem to be incorrect. For they argue that
if pain is an evil, it does not follow that pleasure is a good,
since evil is also opposed to evil, and both are opposed to
the neutral condition [without pleasure or pain].

The objectors' general point here is right, but what they
say in the case mentioned is false. For if both pleasure and | 10
pain were evils, we would also have to avoid both, and if
both were neutral, we would have to avoid neither, or else
avoid both equally. Evidently, however, we avoid pain as
an evil and choose pleasure as a good; hence this must also
be the opposition between them.

12.33   Pleasure and quality

x 3   Again, if [as the objectors argue] pleasure is not a quality, it does not follow [as they suppose] that it is not a good.
15   For neither are virtuous activities or happiness qualities.

12.34   Pleasure admits of degrees

They say that the good is definite, whereas pleasure is indefinite because it admits of more and less.

If their judgement rests on the actual condition of being
pleased, it must also hold for justice and the other virtues,
where evidently we are said to have a certain character more
20   and less, and to express the virtues more and less in our actions. For we may be more [and less] just or brave, and may
do just or temperate actions more and less.

If, on the other hand, their judgement rests on the [vari-
ety of] pleasures, then surely they fail to state the reason
[why pleasures admit of more and less], namely that some
are unmixed [with pain] and others are mixed.

25   Moreover, just as health admits of more and less, though
it is definite, why should pleasure not be the same? For not
every [healthy person] has the same proportion [of bodily
elements], nor does the same person always have the same,
but it may be relaxed and still remain up to a certain limit,
and may differ in more and less. The same is quite possible,
then, for pleasure also.

12.35   Pleasure is not a process

They hold that what is good is complete, whereas processes
30   and becomings are incomplete; and they try to show that
pleasure is a process and a becoming. It would seem, however, that they are wrong, and pleasure is not even a process.

Pleasures are not quick or slow

For quickness or slowness seems to be proper to every
process—if not in itself (as, e.g., with the universe), then

270

in relation to something else. But neither of these is true
of pleasure. For though certainly it is possible to become
pleased quickly, as it is possible to become angry quickly,   1173b
it is not possible to be pleased quickly, not even in relation
to something else. But this is possible for walking and growing and all such things [i.e. for processes]. It is possible,
then, to pass quickly or slowly into pleasure, but not possible to be [quickly or slowly] in the corresponding activity,
i.e. to be pleased quickly [or slowly].

*The relation of pleasure to pain is not suitable
for a process*
      And how could pleasure be a becoming? For not just any   5
random thing, it seems, comes to be from any other; but what
something comes to be from is what it is dissolved into. Hence
whatever pleasure is the becoming of, pain should be the
perishing of it.
      They do indeed say that pain is the emptying of the natural
[condition, and hence the perishing], and that pleasure is its
refilling, [and hence the becoming]. Emptying and filling happen to the body; if, then, pleasure is the refilling of something
natural, what has the refilling will also have the pleasure.   10
Hence it will be the body that has pleasure.
      This does not seem to be true, however. The refilling, then,
is not pleasure, though someone might be pleased while a
refilling is going on, and pained when he is becoming empty.
      This belief [that pleasure is refilling] seems to have arisen
from pains and pleasures in connection with food; for first
we are empty and suffer pain, and then take pleasure in the   15
refilling. However, the same is not true for all pleasures;
for pleasures in mathematics, and among pleasures in perception those through the sense of smell, and many sounds,
sights, memories and expectations as well, all arise without
[previous] pain. If this is so, what will they be comings-to-
be of? For since no emptiness of anything has come to be,   20
there is nothing whose refilling might come to be.

12.36   Good and bad pleasures:
Three different accounts

Some people cite the disgraceful pleasures [to show that pleasure is not a good].

(1) To them we might reply that these [sources of disgraceful pleasures] are not pleasant. If things are healthy or sweet or bitter to sick people, we should not suppose that they are also healthy, or sweet, or bitter, except to them; nor should we suppose that things appearing white to people with eye disease are white, except to them. Similarly, if things are pleasant to people in bad condition, we should not suppose that they are also pleasant, except to these people.

25 (2) Or we might say that the pleasures are choiceworthy, but not when they come from these sources, just as wealth is desirable, but not if you have to betray someone to get it, and health is desirable, but not if it requires you to eat anything and everything.

(3) Or perhaps pleasures differ in species. For those from fine sources are different from those from shameful sources;

30 and we cannot have the just person's pleasure without being just, any more than we can have the musician's without being musicians, and similarly in the other cases.

12.37   Arguments for the third account:
Pleasure is not the good

The difference between a friend and a flatterer seems to indicate that pleasure is not good, or else that pleasures differ in species. For in dealings with us the friend seems to aim at what is good, but the flatterer at what is pleasant;

1174a and the flatterer is reproached, whereas the friend is praised, on the assumption that in their dealings they have different aims.

Besides, no one would choose to live with a child's [level of] thought for his whole life, taking as much pleasure as possible in what pleases children, or to enjoy himself while doing some utterly shameful action, even if he would never suffer pain for it.

Moreover, there are many things that we would be eager for even if they brought no pleasure, e.g. seeing, remembering, knowing, having the virtues. Even if pleasures necessarily follow on them, that does not matter, since we would choose them even if no pleasure resulted from them.   5

It would seem to be clear, then, that pleasure is not the good, that not every pleasure is choiceworthy, and that some are choiceworthy in themselves, differing in species or in their sources [from those that are not]. So much, then, for the things that are said about pleasure and pain.   10

12.4   Pleasure is an Activity, not a Process

What, then, or what kind of thing, is pleasure? This will become clearer if we take it up again from the beginning.   x 4

12.41   Pleasure is complete at any time

Seeing seems to be complete at any time, since it has no need for anything else to complete its form by coming to be at a later time. And pleasure is also like this, since it is some sort of whole, and no pleasure is to be found at any time that will have its form completed by coming to be for a longer time. Hence pleasure is not a process either.   15

12.42   A process needs time for its completion . . .

For every process, e.g. constructing a building, takes time, and aims at some end, and is complete when it produces the product it seeks, or, [in other words, is complete] in the whole time [that it takes].   20

. . . And consists of dissimilar sub-processes

Moreover, each process is incomplete during the processes that are its parts, i.e. during the time it goes on; and it consists of processes that are different in form from the whole process and from each other.

For laying stones together and fluting a column are different processes; and both are different from the [whole] production of the temple. For the production of the temple is a complete production, since it needs nothing further [when it is finished] to achieve the proposed goal; but the production of the foundation or the triglyph is an incomplete production, since [when it is finished] it is [the production] of a part.

Hence [processes that are parts of larger processes] differ in form; and we cannot find a process complete in form at any time [while it is going on], but [only], if at all, in the whole time [that it takes].

The same is true of walking and the other [processes]. For if locomotion is a process from one place to another, it includes locomotions differing in form—flying, walking, jumping and so on. And besides these differences, there are differences in walking itself. For the place from which and the place to which are not the same in the whole racecourse as they are in a part of it, or the same in one part as in another; nor is traveling along one line the same as traveling along another, since what we cover is not just a line, but a line in a [particular] place, and this line and that line are in different places.

Hence it is not complete at every time

Now we have discussed process exactly elsewhere. But, at any rate, a process, it would seem, is not complete at every time; and the many [constituent] processes are incomplete, and differ in form, since the place from which and the place to which make the form of a process [and different processes begin and end in different places].

12.43   Hence pleasure is not a process

The form of pleasure, by contrast, is complete at any time. Cleary, then, it is different from a process, and is something whole and complete. This also seems true because a process must take time, but being pleased need not; for what [takes no time and hence is present] in an instant is a whole.

This also makes it clear that it is wrong to say there is a | 10
process or a coming-to-be of pleasure. For this is not said of everything, but only of what is divisible and not a whole; for seeing, or a point, or a unit, has no coming to be, and none of these is either a process or a becoming. But pleasure is a whole; hence it too has no coming to be.

12.5   Pleasure Completes an Activity

12.51   The best activity requires the faculty
in the best condition with the best object

Every faculty of perception is active in relation to its perceptible object, and completely active when it is in good | 15
condition in relation to the finest of its perceptible objects. For this above all seems to be the character of complete activity, whether it is ascribed to the faculty or to the subject that has it. Hence for each faculty the best activity is the activity of the subject in the best condition in relation to the best object of the faculty.

12.52   The best activity is pleasantest

This activity will also be the most complete and the pleas- | 20
antest. For every faculty of perception, and every sort of thought and study, has its pleasure; the pleasantest activity is the most complete; and the most complete is the activity of the subject in good condition in relation to the most excellent object of the faculty. Pleasure completes the activity.

12.53 *Pleasure completes an activity by being a consequent final cause*

But the way in which pleasure completes the activity is not the way in which the perceptible object and the faculty of perception complete it when they are both excellent—just as health and the doctor are not the cause of being healthy in the same way. For clearly a pleasure arises that corresponds to each faculty of perception, since we say that sights and sounds are pleasant; and clearly it arises above all whenever the faculty of perception is best, and is active in relation to the best sort of object. When this is the condition of the perceptible object and of the perceiving subject, there will always be pleasure, when the producer and the subject to be affected are both present.

Pleasure completes the activity—not, however, as the state does, by being present [in the activity], but as a sort of consequent end, like the bloom on youths.

Hence as long as the objects of understanding or perception and the subject that judges or attends are in the right condition, there will be pleasure in the activity. For as long as the subject affected and the productive [cause] remain similar and in the same relation to each other, the same thing naturally arises.

12.54 *Hence pleasure is not continuous because an activity is not continuous*

Then how is it that no one is continuously pleased? Is it not because we get tired? For nothing human is capable of continuous activity, and hence no continuous pleasure arises either, since pleasure is a consequence of the activity.

Again, some things delight us when they are new to us, but less later, for the same reason. For at first our thought is stimulated and intensely active towards them, as our sense of sight is when we look closely at something; but later the

276

activity becomes lax and careless, so that the pleasure fades | 10
also.

12.55 *The connection between pleasure and activity explains why we desire pleasure*

We might think that everyone desires pleasure, since every-one aims at being alive. Living is a type of activity, and each of us is active towards the objects he likes most and in the ways he likes most. The musician, e.g., activates his hear-ing in hearing melodies; the lover of learning activates his thought in thinking about objects of study; and so on for | 15
each of the others. Pleasure completes their activities, and hence completes life, which they desire. It is reasonable, then, that they also aim at pleasure, since it completes each person's life for him, and life is choiceworthy.

Do we choose life because of pleasure, or pleasure because of life? Let us set aside this question for now, since the two appear to be yoked together, and to allow no separation; for | 20
pleasure never arises without activity, and, equally, it com-pletes every activity.

12.6 *Pleasures Differ in Kind*

12.61 *Different activities require different pleasures to complete them*

Hence pleasures also seem to be of different species. For | x 5
we suppose that things of different species are completed by different things. That is how it appears, both with natural things and with artifacts, e.g. with animals, trees, a paint-ing, a statue, a house or an implement; and similarly, ac- | 25
tivities that differ in species are also completed by things that differ in species. Activities of thought differ in species from activities of the faculties of perception, and so do these from each other; so also, then, do the pleasures that complete them.

277

12.62 An activity is promoted by its proper pleasure

This is also apparent from the way each pleasure is proper
to the activity that it completes. For the proper pleasure increases the activity. For we judge each thing better and more
exactly when our activity is associated with pleasure. If,
e.g., we enjoy doing geometry, we become better geometers,
and understand each question better; and similarly lovers of
music, building and so on improve at their proper function
when they enjoy it.

Each pleasure increases the activity; what increases it is
proper to it; and since the activities are different in species,
what is proper to them is also different in species.

12.63 And conversely it is impeded by an alien pleasure

This is even more apparent from the way some activities
are impeded by pleasures from others. For lovers of flutes,
e.g., cannot pay attention to a conversation if they catch the
sound of someone playing the flute, because they enjoy flute-
playing more than their present activity; and so the pleasure
proper to flute-playing destroys the activity of conversation.

The same is true in other cases also, whenever we are
engaged in two activities at once. For the pleasanter activity
pushes out the other one, all the more if it is much pleasanter,
so that we no longer even engage in the other activity. Hence
if we are enjoying one thing intensely, we do not do another
very much. It is when we are only mildly pleased that we
do something else, e.g. people who eat nuts in theatres do
this most when the actors are bad.

Since, then, the proper pleasure makes an activity more
exact, longer and better, while an alien pleasure damages
it, clearly the two pleasures differ widely.

For an alien pleasure does virtually what a proper pain
does. The proper pain destroys activity, so that if, e.g.,

278

writing or rational calculation has no pleasure and is in fact
painful for us, we do not write or calculate, since the activity is painful. Hence the proper pleasures and pains have   20
contrary effects on an activity; and the proper ones are those
that arise from the activity in itself. And as we have said,
the effect of alien pleasures is similar to the effect of pain,
since they ruin the activity, though not in the same way as
pain.

12.7 Which Pleasures are Goods?

12.71 The goodness of the activity determines
the goodness of the pleasure

Since activities differ in degrees of decency and badness,
and some are choiceworthy, some to be avoided, some   25
neither, the same is true of pleasures; for each activity has
its own proper pleasure. Hence the pleasure proper to an excellent activity is decent, and the one proper to a base activity is vicious; for, similarly, appetites for fine things are
praiseworthy, and appetites for shameful things are blameworthy.

And in fact the pleasure in an activity is more proper to   30
it than the desire for it. For the desire is distinguished from
it in time and in nature; but the pleasure is close to the activity, and so little distinguished from it that disputes arise
about whether the activity is the same as the pleasure.

Still, pleasure is seemingly neither thought nor perception,
since that would be absurd. Rather, it is because [pleasure   35
and activity] are not separated that to some people they appear the same.

Hence, just as activities differ, so do the pleasures. Sight   1176a
differs from touch in purity, as hearing and smell do from
taste; hence the pleasures also differ in the same way. So
also do the pleasures of thought differ from these [pleasures
of sense]; and both sorts have different kinds within them.

12.72   The function of each kind of animal
determines its proper activity and its
proper pleasure

Each kind of animal seems to have its own proper pleasure, just as it has its own proper function; for the proper pleasure will be the one that corresponds to its activity.

5   This is apparent if we also study each kind. For a horse, a dog and a human being have different pleasures; and, as Heracleitus says, an ass would choose chaff over gold, since asses find food pleasanter than gold. Hence animals that differ in species also have pleasures that differ in species; and it would be reasonable for animals of the same species to have the same pleasures also.

12.73   The human function determines
the proper human pleasure, as measured
by the virtuous person

10   In fact, however, the pleasures differ quite a lot, in human beings at any rate. For the same things delight some people, and cause pain to others; and while some find them painful and hateful, others find them pleasant and lovable. The same is true of sweet things. For the same things do not seem sweet to a feverish and to a healthy person, or hot to an
15   enfeebled and to a vigorous person; and the same is true of other things.

But in all such cases it seems that what is really so is what appears so to the excellent person. If this is correct, as it seems to be, and virtue, i.e. the good person in so far as he is good, is the measure of each thing, then what appear pleasures to him will also *be* pleasures, and what is pleasant will be what he enjoys.

20   And if what he finds objectionable appears pleasant to someone, that is nothing surprising, since human beings suffer many sorts of corruption and damage. It is not pleasant, however, except to these people in these conditions.

Clearly, then, we should say that the pleasures agreed to be shameful are not pleasures at all, except to corrupted people.

But what about those pleasures that seem to be decent? Of these, which kind, or which particular pleasure, should | 25 we take to be the pleasure of a human being? Surely it will be clear from the activities, since the pleasures are consequences of these.

Hence the pleasures that complete the activities of the complete and blessedly happy man, whether he has one activity or more than one, will be called the human pleasures to the fullest extent. The other pleasures will be human in secondary and even more remote ways corresponding to the character of the activities.

13.   Happiness: Further Discussion

13.1   Recapitulation: Happiness is an End
in Itself, Consisting in Virtuous Action | x 6
We have now finished our discussion of the types of vir- | 30 tue; of friendship; and of pleasure. It remains for us to discuss happiness in outline, since we take this to be the end of human [aims]. Our discussion will be shorter if we first take up again what we said before.

We said, then, that happiness is not a state. For if it were, someone might have it and yet be asleep for his whole life, living the life of a plant, or suffer the greatest misfortunes. | 35 If we do not approve of this, we count happiness as an ac- | 1176b tivity rather than a state, as we said before.

Some activities are necessary, i.e. choiceworthy for some other end, while others are choiceworthy in themselves. Clearly, then, we should count happiness as one of those activities that are choiceworthy in themselves, not as one of | 5 those choiceworthy for some other end. For happiness lacks nothing, but is self-sufficient; and an activity is choiceworthy in itself when nothing further beyond it is sought from it.

281

This seems to be the character of actions expressing virtue; for doing fine and excellent actions is choiceworthy for itself.

13.2 Happiness is Virtuous Action, not Amusement

13.21 Amusement is popularly regarded as happiness

But pleasant amusements also [seem to be choiceworthy in themselves]. For they are not chosen for other ends, since they actually cause more harm than benefit, by causing neglect of our bodies and possessions.

Moreover, most of those people congratulated for their happiness resort to these sorts of pastimes. Hence people who are witty participants in them have a good reputation with tyrants, since they offer themselves as pleasant [partners] in the tyrant's aims, and these are the sort of people the tyrant requires. And so these amusements seem to have the character of happiness because people in supreme power spend their leisure in them.

13.22 But popular reputation is inadequate evidence

However, these sorts of people are presumably no evidence. For virtue and understanding, the sources of excellent activities, do not depend on holding supreme power. Further, these powerful people have had no taste of pure and civilized pleasure, and so they resort to bodily pleasures. But that is no reason to think these pleasures are most choiceworthy, since boys also think that what they honour is best. Hence, just as different things appear honourable to boys and to men, it is reasonable that in the same way different things appear honourable to base and to decent people.

282

As we have often said, then, what is honourable and pleas- | 25
ant is what is so to the excellent person; and to each type
of person the activity expressing his own proper state is most
choiceworthy; hence the activity expressing virtue is most
choiceworthy to the excellent person [and hence is most
honourable and pleasant].

13.23 *Happiness cannot be amusement*

Happiness, then, is not found in amusement; for it would
be absurd if the end were amusement, and our lifelong ef-
forts and sufferings aimed at amusing ourselves. For we | 30
choose practically everything for some other end—except for
happiness, since it is [the] end; but serious work and toil
aimed [only] at amusement appears stupid and excessively
childish. Rather, it seems correct to amuse ourselves so that
we can do something serious, as Anacharsis says; for amusement would seem to be relaxation, and it is because we can-
not toil continuously that we require relaxation. Relaxation, | 35
then, is not [the] end, since we pursue it [to prepare] for
activity. | 1177a

Further, the happy life seems to be a life expressing virtue, which is a life involving serious actions, and not consisting in amusement.

Besides, we say that things to be taken seriously are better than funny things that provide amusement, and that in
each case the activity of the better part and the better per- | 5
son is more serious and excellent; and the activity of what
is better is superior, and thereby has more the character of
happiness.

Moreover, anyone at all, even a slave, no less than the best
person, might enjoy bodily pleasures; but no one would allow
that a slave shares in happiness, if one does not [also allow
that the slave shares in the sort of] life [needed for happi-
ness]. Happiness, then, is found not in these pastimes, but
in the activities expressing virtue, as we also said previously. | 10

283

13.3 Theoretical Study is the Supreme Element of Happiness

x 7   If happiness, then, is activity expressing virtue, it is reasonable for it to express the supreme virtue, which will be the virtue of the best thing.

15   The best is understanding, or whatever else seems to be the natural ruler and leader, and to understand what is fine and divine, by being itself either divine or the most divine element in us.

Hence complete happiness will be its activity expressing its proper virtue; and we have said that this activity is the activity of study. This seems to agree with what has been said before, and also with the truth.

13.31   The activity of theoretical study is best

20   For this activity is supreme, since understanding is the supreme element in us, and the objects of understanding are the supreme objects of knowledge.

13.32   It is most continuous

Besides, it is the most continuous activity, since we are more capable of continuous study than of any continuous action.

13.33   It is pleasantest

We think pleasure must be mixed into happiness; and it is agreed that the activity expressing wisdom is the pleasantest

25   of the activities expressing virtue. At any rate, philosophy seems to have remarkably pure and firm pleasures; and it is reasonable for those who have knowledge to spend their lives more pleasantly than those who seek it.

13.34   It is most self-sufficient

Moreover, the self-sufficiency we spoke of will be found in study above all.

For admittedly the wise person, the just person and the other virtuous people all need the good things necessary for life. Still, when these are adequately supplied, the just per- | 30
son needs other people as partners and recipients of his just actions; and the same is true of the temperate person and the brave person and each of the others.

But the wise person is able, and more able the wiser he is, to study even by himself; and though he presumably does it better with colleagues, even so he is more self-sufficient | 1177b
than any other [virtuous person].

13.35   It aims at no end beyond itself
Besides, study seems to be liked because of itself alone, since it has no result beyond having studied. But from the virtues concerned with action we try to a greater or lesser extent to gain something beyond the action itself.

13.36   It involves leisure
Happiness seems to be found in leisure, since we accept | 5
trouble so that we can be at leisure, and fight wars so that we can be at peace. Now the virtues concerned with action have their activities in politics or war, and actions here seem to require trouble.

This seems completely true for actions in war, since no one chooses to fight a war, and no one continues it, for the sake of fighting a war; for someone would have to be a com- | 10
plete murderer if he made his friends his enemies so that there could be battles and killings.

But the actions of the politician require trouble also. Be- yond political activities themselves these actions seek posi- tions of power and honours; or at least they seek happiness for the politician himself and for his fellow-citizens, which is something different from political science itself, and clearly | 15
is sought on the assumption that it is different.

Hence among actions expressing the virtues those in poli-

tics and war are pre-eminently fine and great; but they require trouble, aim at some [further] end, and are choiceworthy for something other than themselves.

But the activity of understanding, it seems, is superior in excellence because it is the activity of study,
20   aims at no end beyond itself and has its own proper
pleasure, which increases the activity. Further, self-sufficiency, leisure, unwearied activity (as far as is possible for a human being), and any other features
ascribed to the blessed person, are evidently features of
this activity.

25   Hence a human being's complete happiness will be this activity, if it receives a complete span of life, since nothing
incomplete is proper to happiness.

13.37 It is a god-like life

Such a life would be superior to the human level. For someone will live it not in so far as he is a human being, but in
so far as he has some divine element in him. And the activity of this divine element is as much superior to the activity
expressing the rest of virtue as this element is superior to
30   the compound. Hence if understanding is something divine
in comparison with a human being, so also will the life that
expresses understanding be divine in comparison with human
life.

We ought not to follow the proverb-writers, and 'think
human, since you are human', or 'think mortal, since you
are mortal'. Rather, as far as we can, we ought to be pro-
immortal, and go to all lengths to live a life that expresses
1178a our supreme element; for however much this element may
lack in bulk, by much more it surpasses everything in power
and value.

13.38 It realizes the supreme element
in human nature

Moreover, each person seems to be his understanding, if
he is his controlling and better element; it would be absurd,

then, if he were to choose not his own life, but something else's.

And what we have said previously will also apply now. | 5
For what is proper to each thing's nature is supremely best and pleasantest for it; and hence for a human being the life expressing understanding will be supremely best and pleasantest, if understanding above all is the human being. This life, then, will also be happiest.

13.4 The Relation of Study to the Other Virtues in Happiness

13.41 The other virtues are human, not divine

The life expressing the other kind of virtue [i.e. the kind | x 8
concerned with action] is [happiest] in a secondary way because the activities expressing this virtue are human. | 10

For we do just and brave actions, and the others expressing the virtues, in relation to other people, by abiding by what fits each person in contracts, services, all types of actions, and also in feelings; and all these appear to be human conditions.

Indeed, some feelings actually seem to arise from the body; | 15
and in many ways virtue of character seems to be proper to feelings.

Besides, intelligence is yoked together with virtue of character, and so is this virtue with intelligence. For the origins of intelligence express the virtues of character; and correctness in virtues of character expresses intelligence. And since these virtues are also connected to feelings, they are con- | 20
cerned with the compound. Since the virtues of the compound are human virtues, the life and the happiness expressing these virtues is also human.

The virtue of understanding, however, is separated [from the compound]. Let us say no more about it, since an exact account would be too large a task for our present project.

13.42   The other virtues require more external
goods than study requires

Moreover, it seems to need external supplies very little,
25   or [at any rate] less than virtue of character needs them. For
grant that they both need necessary goods, and to the same
extent, since there will be only a very small difference even
though the politician labours more about the body and suchlike. Still, there will be a large difference in [what is needed]
for the [proper] activities [of each type of virtue].

For the generous person will need money for generous ac-
30   tions; and the just person will need it for paying debts, since
wishes are not clear, and people who are not just pretend
to wish to do justice. Similarly, the brave person will need
enough power, and the temperate person will need freedom
[to do intemperate actions], if they are to achieve anything
that the virtue requires. For how else will they, or any other
virtuous people, make their virtue clear?

35   Moreover, it is disputed whether it is decision or actions that is
more in control of virtue, on the assumption that virtue depends
1178b   on both. Well, certainly it is clear that what is complete depends
on both; but for actions many external goods are needed, and the
greater and finer the actions the more numerous are the external
goods needed.

But someone who is studying needs none of these goods,
for that activity at least; indeed, for study at least, we might
say they are even hindrances.

5   In so far as he is a human being, however, and [hence]
lives together with a number of other human beings, he
chooses to do the actions expressing virtue. Hence he will
need the sorts of external goods [that are needed for the vir-
tues], for living a human life.

13.43   Beliefs about the gods support the
supremacy of study

In another way also it appears that complete happiness is
some activity of study. For we traditionally suppose that the

288

gods more than anyone are blessed and happy; but what sorts | 10
of actions ought we to ascribe to them? Just actions? Surely
they will appear ridiculous making contracts, returning deposits and so on. Brave actions? Do they endure what [they
find] frightening and endure dangers because it is fine? Generous actions? Whom will they give to? And surely it would
be absurd for them to have currency or anything like that.
What would their temperate actions be? Surely it is vulgar | 15
praise to say that they do not have base appetites. When we
go through them all, anything that concerns actions appears
trivial and unworthy of the gods.

However, we all traditionally suppose that they are alive
and active, since surely they are not asleep like Endymion. | 20
Then if someone is alive, and action is excluded, and production even more, what is left but study? Hence the gods'
activity that is superior in blessedness will be an activity of
study. And so the human activity that is most akin to the gods'
will, more than any others, have the character of happiness.

A sign of this is the fact that other animals have no share
in happiness, being completely deprived of this activity of | 25
study. For the whole life of the gods is blessed, and human
life is blessed to the extent that it has something resembling
this sort of activity; but none of the other animals is happy,
because none of them shares in study at all. Hence happiness
extends just as far as study extends, and the more someone
studies, the happier he is, not coincidentally but in so far | 30
as he studies, since study is valuable in itself. And so [on
this argument] happiness will be some kind of study.

13.44 But a human being also needs
moderate external goods

However, the happy person is a human being, and so will
need external prosperity also; for his nature is not self-
sufficient for study, but he needs a healthy body, and needs | 35
to have food and the other services provided.

Still, even though no one can be blessedly happy without external goods, we must not think that to be happy we will need many large goods. For self-sufficiency and action do not depend on excess, and we can do fine actions even if we do not rule earth and sea; for even from moderate re-
5   sources we can do the actions expressing virtue. This is evident to see, since many private citizens seem to do decent actions no less than people in power do—even more, in fact. It is enough if moderate resources are provided; for the life of someone whose activity expresses virtue will be happy.

Traditional views held by the wise support us
10   Solon surely described happy people well, when he said they had been moderately supplied with external goods, had done what he regarded as the finest actions, and had lived their lives temperately. For it is possible to have moderate possessions and still to do the right actions.

And Anaxagoras would seem to have supposed that the happy person was neither rich nor powerful, since he said
15   he would not be surprised if the happy person appeared an absurd sort of person to the many. For the many judge by externals, since these are all they perceive.

Hence the beliefs of the wise would seem to accord with our arguments.

But theory must be tested in practice
These considerations do indeed produce some confidence. The truth, however, in questions about action is judged from
20   what we do and how we live, since these are what control [the answers to such questions]. Hence we ought to examine what has been said by applying it to what we do and how we live; and if it harmonizes with what we do, we should accept it, but if it conflicts we should count it [mere] words.

290

13.45   The person who studies is most
loved by the gods

The person whose activity expresses understanding and who takes care of understanding would seem to be in the best condition, and most loved by the gods. For if the gods pay some attention to human beings, as they seem to, it would | 25
be reasonable for them to take pleasure in what is best and most akin to them, namely understanding; and reasonable for them to benefit in return those who most of all like and honour understanding, on the assumption that these people attend to what is beloved by the gods, and act correctly and finely.

Clearly, all this is true of the wise person more than anyone | 30
else; hence he is most loved by the gods. And it is likely that this same person will be happiest; hence the wise person will be happier than anyone else on this argument too.

14.   Ethics, Moral Education and Politics

14.1   We Must Study Moral Education to See
How to Make People Virtuous

We have now said enough in outlines about happiness and | x 9
the virtues, and about friendship and pleasure also. Should we then think that our decision [to study these] has achieved | 35
its end? On the contrary, the aim of studies about action, | 1179b
as we say, is surely not to study and know about each thing, but rather to act on our knowledge. Hence knowing about virtue is not enough, but we must also try to possess and exercise virtue, or become good in any other way.

14.11   Argument alone is not enough

Now if arguments were sufficient by themselves to make | 5
people decent, the rewards they would command would justifiably have been many and large, as Theognis says, and rightly bestowed. In fact, however, arguments seem to have enough influence to stimulate and encourage the civilized ones

among the young people, and perhaps to make virtue take possession of a well-born character that truly loves what is fine; but they seem unable to stimulate the many towards being fine and good.

For the many naturally obey fear, not shame; they avoid what is base because of the penalties, not because it is disgraceful. For since they live by their feelings, they pursue their proper pleasures and the sources of them, and avoid the opposed pains, and have not even a notion of what is fine and [hence] truly pleasant, since they have had no taste of it.

What argument could reform people like these? For it is impossible, or not easy, to alter by argument what has long been absorbed by habit; but, presumably, we should be satisfied to achieve some share in virtue when we already have what we seem to need to become decent.

14.12 Nature, habit and teaching are all needed

Some think it is nature that makes people good; some think it is habit; some that it is teaching.

The [contribution] of nature clearly is not up to us, but results from some divine cause in those who have it, who are the truly fortunate ones.

Arguments and teaching surely do not influence everyone, but the soul of the student needs to have been prepared by habits for enjoying and hating finely, like ground that is to nourish seed. For someone whose life follows his feelings would not even listen to an argument turning him away, or comprehend it [if he did listen]; and in that state how could he be persuaded to change? And in general feelings seem to yield to force, not to argument.

Hence we must already in some way have a character suitable for virtue, fond of what is fine and objecting to what is shameful.

292

14.2   Moral Education Requires Legislation

14.21   Both children and adults need laws
But it is hard for someone to be trained correctly for virtue from his youth if he has not been brought up under correct laws, since the many, especially the young, do not find
it pleasant to live in a temperate and resistant way. Hence
laws must prescribe their upbringing and practices; for they | 35
will not find these things painful when they get used to them.

Presumably, however, it is not enough to get the correct | 1180a
upbringing and attention when they are young; rather, they
must continue the same practices and be habituated to them
when they become men. Hence we need laws concerned with
these things also, and in general with all of life. For the many
yield to compulsion more than to argument, and to sanctions | 5
more than to what is fine.

14.22   Hence the state legislates for morality
This, some think, is why legislators should urge people
towards virtue and exhort them to aim at what is fine, on
the assumption that anyone whose good habits have prepared
him decently will listen to them, but should impose corrective treatments and penalties on anyone who disobeys or lacks
the right nature, and completely expel an incurable. For the | 10
decent person, it is assumed, will attend to reason because
his life aims at what is fine, while the base person, since he
desires pleasure, has to receive corrective treatment by pain,
like a beast of burden; that is why it is said that the pains
imposed must be those most contrary to the pleasures he likes.

As we have said, then, someone who is to be good must | 15
be finely brought up and habituated, and then must live in
decent practices, doing nothing base either willingly or unwillingly. And this will be true if his life follows some sort
of understanding and correct order that has influence over
him.

14.23 A state is a better moral educator than an individual

A father's instructions, however, lack this influence and
20 compelling power; and so in general do the instructions of
an individual man, unless he is a king or someone like that.
Law, however, has the power that compels; and law is reason
that proceeds from a sort of intelligence and understanding.
Besides, people become hostile to an individual human being who opposes their impulses even if he is correct in op-
posing them; whereas a law's prescription of what is decent
is not burdensome.

14.24 But states neglect this task, and leave it to individuals

25 And yet, only in Sparta, or in a few other cities as well,
does the legislator seem to have attended to upbringing and
practices. In most other cities they are neglected, and each
individual citizen lives as he wishes, 'laying down the rules
for his children and wife', like a Cyclops.

It is best, then, if the community attends to upbringing,
30 and attends correctly. If, however, the community neglects
it, it seems fitting for each individual to promote the virtue
of his children and his friends — to be able to do it, or at least
to decide to do it.

14.3 Moral Education Needs Legislative Science

14.31 Both states and individuals need legislative science

From what we have said, however, it seems he will be
better able to do it if he acquires legislative science. For,
35 clearly, attention by the community works through laws, and
1180b decent attention works through excellent laws; and whether
the laws are written or unwritten, for the education of one
or of many, seems unimportant, as it is in music, gymnastics

294

and other practices. For just as in cities the provisions of
law and the [prevailing] types of character have influence,
similarly a father's words and habits have influence, and all   5
the more because of kinship and because of the benefits he
does; for his children are already fond of him and naturally
ready to obey.

14.32   Sometimes an individual can legislate
more accurately in individual cases

Moreover, education adapted to an individual is actually
better than a common education for everyone, just as indi-
vidualized medical treatment is better. For though generally
a feverish patient benefits from rest and starvation, presumably some patient does not; nor does the boxing instructor   10
impose the same way of fighting on everyone. Hence it seems
that treatment in particular cases is more exactly right when
each person gets special attention, since he then more often
gets the suitable treatment.

14.33   But he also needs universal
legislative science

Nonetheless a doctor, a gymnastics trainer and everyone
else will give the best individual attention if they also know
universally what is good for all, or for these sorts. For   15
sciences are said to be, and are, of what is common [to
many particular cases].

Admittedly someone without scientific knowledge may well
attend properly to a single person, if his experience has
allowed him to take exact note of what happens in each case,
just as some people seem to be their own best doctors, though
unable to help anyone else at all. None the less, presumably,   20
it seems that someone who wants to be an expert in a craft
and a branch of study should progress to the universal, and
come to know that, as far as possible; for that, as we have
said, is what the sciences are about.

Then perhaps also someone who wishes to make people

25 better by his attention, many people or few, should try to acquire legislative science, if we will become good through laws. For not just anyone can improve the condition of just anyone, or the person presented to him; but if anyone can it is the person with knowledge, just as in medical science and the others that require attention and intelligence.

14.4   Who Should Teach Legislative Science, and How?

30 Next, then, should we examine whence and how someone might acquire legislative science? Just as in other cases [we go to the practitioner], should we go to the politicians? For, as we saw, legislative science seems to be a part of political science.

14.41   Some of the obvious candidates lack experience, others lack theory

But is the case of political science perhaps apparently different from the other sciences and capacities? For evidently in others the same people, e.g. doctors or painters, who transmit the capacity to others actively practise it them-
35 selves. By contrast, it is the sophists who advertise that
1181a they teach politics but none of them practises it. Instead, those who practise it are the political activists, and they seem to act on some sort of capacity and experience rather than thought.

For evidently they neither write nor speak on such questions, though presumably it would be finer to do this than
5 to compose speeches for the law courts or the Assembly; nor have they made politicians out of their own sons or any other friends of theirs. And yet it would be reasonable for them to do this if they were able; for there is nothing better than the political capacity that they could leave to their cities, and nothing better that they could decide to produce in themselves, or, therefore, in their closest friends.

14.42   *Both experience and theory*
are necessary

Certainly experience would seem to contribute quite a lot; | 10
otherwise people would not have become better politicians by
familiarity with politics. Hence those who aim to know about
political science would seem to need experience as well.

By contrast, those of the sophists who advertise [that they
teach political science] appear to be a long way from teaching;
for they are altogether ignorant about the sort of thing political
science is, and the sorts of things it is about. For if they had
known what it is, they would not have taken it to be the same | 15
as rhetoric, or something inferior to it, or thought it an easy
task to assemble the laws with good reputations and then
legislate. For they think they can select the best laws, as
though the selection itself did not require comprehension,
and as though correct judgement were not the most important thing, as it is in music.

It is those with experience in each area who judge the prod- | 20
ucts correctly and who comprehend the method or way of
completing them, and what fits with what; for if we lack experience, we must be satisfied with noticing that the product
is well or badly made, as with painting. Now laws would
seem to be the products of political science; how, then, could | 1181b
someone acquire legislative science, or judge which laws are
best, from laws alone? For neither do we appear to become
experts in medicine by reading textbooks.

And yet doctors not only try to describe the [recognized]
treatments, but also distinguish different [physical] states,
and try to say how each type of patient might be cured and
must be treated. And what they say seems to be useful to | 5
the experienced, though useless to the ignorant.

Similarly, then, collections of laws and political systems
might also, presumably, be most useful if we are capable
of studying them and of judging what is done finely or in
the contrary way, and what sorts of [elements] fit with what.

10 Those who lack the [proper] state [of experience] when they
go through these collections will not manage to judge finely,
unless they can do it all by themselves [without training],
though they might come to comprehend them better by going through them.

14.43 The right approach to legislative science

Since, then, our predecessors have left the area of legislation uncharted, it is presumably better to examine it ourselves
instead, and indeed to examine political systems in general,
15 and so to complete the philosophy of human affairs, as far
as we are able.

First, then, let us try to review any sound remarks our
predecessors have made on particular topics. Then let us
study the collected political systems, to see from them what
sorts of things preserve and destroy cities, and political sys-
20 tems of different types; and what causes some cities to conduct politics well, and some badly.

For when we have studied these questions, we will perhaps
grasp better what sort of political system is best; how each
political system should be organized so as to be best; and
what habits and laws it should follow.

Let us discuss this, then, starting from the beginning.

Notes

Book I

1094a1-22 The *EN* seeks to describe and understand the highest good and to prescribe ways to achieve it. Here Aristotle explains what sort of thing the highest good will be, assuming for the moment that there is one (see ch. 2, 7). He calls it 'the good', 1094a22; for 'highest' see 1095a16.

There are subordinate and superordinate CRAFTS and SCIENCES with subordinate and superordinate ENDS; the highest superordinate end is the highest good. The argument is fuller at 1097a15.

1094a2 'seems to aim' We begin with an APPEARANCE.

'has been well described . . . ' cf. 1172b9. Aristotle need not agree that the description is completely accurate. If 'action and decision' refers to action on a decision, then he need not mean that every single thing we do aims at some good; for we do things that are not ACTIONS on a DECISION (cf. 1111b9-15).

1094a3 'difference' Cf. *Met.* 1050a21-b2. Here and in a16 the difference between ACTIVITIES with and without further products (see FUNCTION) corresponds to the later distinction between PRODUCTION and ACTION. In a5 'action' must have the sense noted in ACTION #2.

1094a10-18 'But whenever . . .' 'Sciences' is supplied except in 'sciences we have mentioned', a18. Aristotle refers to all the 'actions, crafts and sciences' of a7. None of these meets his most stringent conditions for a SCIENCE.

1094a23 'and if . . . right mark.' Or: 'like archers who have a target to aim at, we are more likely to hit what is right [if we know what the target is].' The version in the text implies that knowledge of the good gives us a target we would otherwise lack (cf. Plato, *Rep.* 519c2); the alternative version does not imply this.

1094a26 'It seems . . .' The argument is this:

(1) The highest good is the all-inclusive end.

299

(2) The all-inclusive end is the end of political science.

(3) Therefore the highest good is the end of political science.

This argument answers the question not answered in 1094a18-22, if we can continue:

(4) We pursue the end of political science in the way described in (a).

(5) Hence we pursue the highest good.

1094b11-1095a2   Having introduced political science and set himself the task (1094a22, 'Then surely . . .') of saying what its end is, Aristotle explains how he will proceed, and how he expects his success to be judged. Hence he now describes the method of ETHICS, and the limitations of the method.

1094b12 'fits the subject-matter'   See 1098a28, 1137b19.

1094b15 'difference and variation'   People see that what is JUST and FINE depends on circumstances—e.g. it is USUALLY but not always just to pay your debts (Plato, *Rep.* 331a); and they infer that there is no objective truth about what is just and fine. They think that these rest on convention (lit. 'are by convention', *nomos*—see LAW), and not on NATURE.

Aristotle remarks, at a16, that similar variations apply to goods, without inclining us to infer that goods are merely conventional. Aspirin, e.g., is not always good for a headache, but it is not a matter of convention that it is good for headaches on those occasions when it is. Hence the argument from variation to convention is invalid. See Plato, *Pr.* 334a-c, *Tht.* 172a, 177a-179b; and notes to 1113a29, 1134b27-30.

1095a2-10 'Hence a youth . . .'   Two reasons are given for excluding a youth (see HUMAN BEING #7) from these lectures ('student' lit. = 'hearer') on ethics. The first ('for he is . . .') is closely connected with the remarks about the EDUCATED person. The second ('Moreover . . .') relies more generally on the practical character of ETHICS #1, which has also been assumed in the restriction of ethics to USUAL truths. On upbringing, cf. 1095b4, 1179b25.

1095a14-28   We return to the question at 1094a24 ('we should try . . .'), and consider what the good might be. As usual, we begin with APPEARANCES: (a) Everyone thinks the good is HAPPINESS; Aristotle argues for this in 1097a34. (b) But we need some clearer account (see REASON) and DEFINITION of happiness—of the types of states and activities it consists in; and we begin with a survey of some common views.

1095a27   'In itself' here means 'in its own right', not dependent on anything else; hence it refers to the independence of the Platonic Form from its sensible instances.

1095a28-b13   To justify beginning with appearances Aristotle adds

300

a further remark on method. We must begin from ORIGINS known to us (see ETHICS #4). The translation tries to clarify Aristotle's different uses of 'origin' here. The 'belief that' which we begin from is probably something like 'It is just to pay debts' or 'Bravery is a good thing'. These are true or nearly true, but they need defence and justification from a first principle that explains why they are true.

1095b1 'far end' Lit. 'limit'. Aristotle thinks of a Greek stadium, in which the midpoint of the race is at the end farthest from the starting line.

1095b6-8 'For the . . . find them.' Lit. 'For the origin is the that, and if this appears adequately, he will not at all need in addition the because. Such a one has origins or would get them easily.' The origins we are looking for are those known UNCONDITIONALLY, and we do not have them simply as a result of good upbringing; these tell us the 'because' or 'reason why'. The origins we have from good upbringing are simply those that allow us to begin the inquiry. See 1095a2, 1179b25, EDUCATION.

1095b14-1096a2 Three traditional ways of life are discussed, since they embody three conceptions of the good and of happiness; cf. *EE* 1214a31, 1215a32-b14.

The criticisms of the three lives reflect Aristotle's own criteria for the good:

   (1) The good involves distinctively human activities, not those of 'grazing animals', b20.
   (2) It must be our own, not heavily dependent on external conditions.
   (3) It must be complete ('it appears . . .', b32).

For defence of these criteria see (1) 1097b33, 1118b1, 1170b12, 1174a1; (2) 1099b13; (3) 1097a28.

1095b14-19 'For, it would . . . slavish' Aristotle's sentences have been rearranged. Lit: 'For they would seem to conceive, not unreasonably, the good and happiness from the lives, the many and most vulgar as pleasure, whence they also like the life of gratification. For the most favoured lives are roughly three, the one just mentioned, the political life, and, third, the life of study. Now the many appear completely slavish . . .'

1095b19 The life of pleasure is rather brusquely dismissed as slavish (see HUMAN BEING #9). Aristotle discusses it more fully when he has examined pleasure; see note to 1176b9.

1095b22 Sardanapallus An Assyrian king who lived in legendary luxury.

1095b23 The proper value of HONOUR is more fully discussed in the account of magnanimity; see note to 1123a34. On the inadequacy of honour see 1159a22.

1095b26 'our own' *Oikeion*; see PROPER. Here Aristotle means that it must be some genuine intrinsic feature of ourselves, not simply the product of other people's attitudes towards us. **'Intuitively believe'** lit. 'divine'—cf. Plato, *Rep.* 505a1. We have not yet given a reason for our conviction.

1096a2 'philosopher's paradox' Lit. 'thesis' or 'position'. This is a dialectical term (ETHICS #4); see *Top.* 104b18. It is implied in the views of Socrates in *Gorg.* 470e, 507c (cf. *Rep.* 354a), and accepted by his professed followers, the Cynics. Cf. notes to 1106b24, 1153b19. Aristotle is himself committed to the claim (cf. *Rep.* 361d) that virtue makes someone happier than he would be by living any other way, not to the claim that virtue alone is sufficient for happiness.

1096a3 'the popular works' *(enkuklia)* Probably these are by Aristotle himself, and are the same as the 'popular' (or 'external', *exōterika*) works of 1102a26, 1140a3.

1096a11 Aristotle mentioned the Platonic belief in a universal and separated Form of the good at 1095a26, and now proceeds to criticize it at length (cf. *EE* i 8, *MM* i 1). Much of the discussion is important for Aristotle's general criticism of Plato (cf. esp. *Met.* i 9), but less important for ethics. Aristotle is primarily concerned to argue against the view that goodness is a single property. If it were one, then knowledge of what is good for human beings would ultimately rest on knowledge of the single type of goodness found throughout the universe, such as is expressed in Plato's Form of the Good (*Rep.* 508-9, 517c, 534bc). The effect of Aristotle's claim that goods are HOMONYMOUS is to sever ethical argument from general cosmological theories about goodness (cf. 1155b1-10).

1096a13 'friends' cf. note to 1164b1.

1096a23 'good is spoken of . . .' In (1) and (2) Aristotle considers the Platonic claims compared with his doctrine of the categories and his associated belief in the homonymy of being (cf. *Catg.* 4, *Top.* i 9, *Met.* v 7, vii 1). There is nothing that all beings are—i.e. there is no general answer to the question 'What is it?' for every being. The categories provide the most general answers that are available to this question. Since the goodness of any thing depends on the kind of thing it is, goodness can be no more of a unified property than being is. If the categories indicate ten ways of being a being, they must also indicate ten different ways of being good (cf. *Top.* 107a3).

1096a24 'as god . . .' Probably Aristotle means not just that these are examples of goods that are SUBSTANCES, but that they are what it is to be good in the category of substance.

1096a34 Arguments (4)-(7) object to the separation of the Forms as both paradigms and instances of the properties to which they correspond. In the Platonic view the Form of Just is perfectly just and is separable from sensible just things. See *Met.* 987a32, 1078b9-1079a4, 1086a24-b13, Plato, *Phd.* 74.

1096b1 'Man Itself and man' The second 'man' here probably refers to the universal that is immanent in particulars. (Less probably it means 'a man', i.e. a particular man.) Aristotle accuses Plato of pointlessly introducing separated, independent Forms when the immanent universals (good, man etc.) recognized by Aristotle are all that we need if we want to understand the natures of things.

1096b23 'Chalk' is not a translation; but Aristotle is just looking for another example of something white. The term he uses, *psimuthion*, refers to lead carbonate ('white lead') produced from lead, and used for whitening.

1096b27 'homonymous by mere chance' See HOMONYMY, note to 1129a27.

1096b27-9 'Perhaps they . . . in other cases.' Lit. 'Then by being from one thing or all contributing to one thing, or rather by analogy? For as sight in body, so mind in soul, and something else in something else.'

'All referring . . .' Cf. *Met.* 1003a27, *EE* 1236a14, b20. Analogy is the option that Aristotle apparently prefers for goods, judging by 1097b25; cf. *Phys.* 191a8, *Met.* 1048a37 on analogy.

1096b31 'is more appropriate' Cf. note to 1155b1.

1097a15 'But let us . . .' Aristotle begins from the diversity of goods that we apparently must recognize when we reject the Platonic attempt to find unity in goods. He wants to show that this diversity does not require us to reject unity in the human good. First (15-25) he repeats the argument of i 1; in a24 'the same conclusion' refers to i 2.

1097a25-b21 Here we make progress, with arguments to show that (1) the good satisfies some formal criteria (see note to 1095b14) and (2) happiness is the good, 1095a17, because it satisfies these criteria. They are formal criteria because Aristotle thinks (cf. Plato, *Phil.* 20d, and notes to 1172b26-35) that they are reasonable conditions for us to impose on the good before we consider the claims of specific candidates claiming to be the good.

The formal criteria require the good to be (a) complete, (b) self-sufficient, and (c) most choiceworthy, not counted as one good among many. Here (a) follows from our choosing the good only for its own sake and not also for the sake of something else; if there were some more comprehensive and complete end than the good, we would choose the good for the sake of that. The other two criteria explain what is required by completeness.

1097a28 'complete' *Teleion*; see HAPPINESS #2. *Teleion* is cognate with *telos,* 'end', and hence the translations 'final' and 'perfect' have also been proposed. But the close association of *teleion* with the other criteria for happiness, and its use in 1098a18, 1101a13, justify the translation 'complete'.

1097a30 Why is 'the most complete of these' rather than 'all of these' what we are seeking? Cf. 1098a17, 1099a30, *EE* 1219a35. Perhaps Aristotle means that we are not to pursue merely an unordered collection of ends, but the complete single end that is the whole formed by them.

1097a33 'and hence an end . . .' The supplement seems necessary to give the sense Aristotle intends for 'always choiceworthy in itself'. The weaker claim 'choiceworthy in itself on those occasions when we choose it' would not distinguish this case from the preceding case ('and an end that is never . . .').

1097b3 'for we would choose . . .' Since the highest good is comprehensive, it is composed of goods in themselves; if any of these were left out, we would not have found the final good. Being goods in themselves, these components of happiness are not chosen only for their contribution to happiness, but also for their own sakes. Cf. 1174a4. At the same time they are not merely instrumental means to happiness; see DECISION #2.

1097b6 Self-sufficiency See HAPPINESS #3, note to 1177a27. If happiness by itself makes life lacking in nothing, it must include all the intrinsic goods that a rational person chooses as part of his life.

1097b9 'solitary . . . political' See 1142a9, 1157b18, 1158a23, 1169b16, 1170b12, 1172a6, 1178b5, *Pol.* 1253a7, 1280b33.

1097b16-20 For argument (5) see note to 1172b26, *MM* 1184a8-30. An alternative translation is: '. . . of all goods, when it is not counted with other goods. When it is so counted, then, clearly, we think the addition of the smallest good to it makes it more choiceworthy . . .', implying that happiness does not embrace all intrinsic goods. This alternative is hard to reconcile with the demands for completeness and self-sufficiency. Cf. notes to 1170b17, 1172b26-35.

The demand for completeness must not be taken to imply the maximum quantity of each intrinsic good; see 1100b22-8, 1101b1-9.

1097b22-1098a20 Aristotle now offers his own account of the good, which ought to satisfy the formal criteria just presented. He appeals to the FUNCTION of a human being, found by consideration of the human

SOUL, 1097b34. The life of ACTION expressing REASON will be a life that includes other activities besides reasoning (just as a dog's life includes more than just PERCEPTION); but it is still guided by reasoning, as a dog's activities are guided by perception. Cf. note to 1166a13.

We may be surprised by Aristotle's move from function to life, and then to soul, first mentioned in 1098a7, 'the soul's activity'. But the connections between soul, life, activity, function and essence make the move legitimate. An organism's soul is the characteristic form and activity that defines the type of life that is essential to it.

1097b26 'depend on their function' Lit. 'in their function'. 'In' in Aristotle is often ambiguous between 'consists in' and 'depends on'; cf. *Phys.* 210a14-24. Since Aristotle takes good performance, not mere performance, of the function to be necessary for doing well, 'depends on' seems to be needed here.

1098a4 'obeying reason' Cf. 1102b26.

1098a4-8 'One as obeying the reason' (a4) = 'requires reason' — lit. 'not without reason' — (a8) and refers to the role of non-rational desires. **'Itself having reason and thinking'** (a4) = 'EXPRESSES reason' — lit. 'according to reason' — (a7) and refers to the role of reason and rational desires. On these rational and non-rational parts of the soul see 1102b26.

Here Aristotle recognizes that the human function includes activities that are distinct from reasoning. The task of adapting them to obey reason in the right way is a task for the moral training that is described in Book II. See also note to 1144b26.

1098a12 'do it well' Here (as in 1097b27, '[doing] well') 'well' must be understood to include more than competent or skilful performance; doing it well is achieving one's good as a harpist, i.e. one's good in so far as one is considered simply as a harpist. Similarly, the virtue that makes someone do well as a human being is the virtue that makes him achieve his own good as a human being; this matters more than his good as a harpist, since his essential function is to be a human being, not to be a harpist. Unless Aristotle is entitled to this connection between virtue, doing well, and achieving one's own good, he is not entitled to his argument from the actions of a good and virtuous human being to the good of a human being.

1098a17 'expresses virtue' A human being's good requires him to perform the function of a human being. But simply performing the function will not ensure his good; many people may live human lives, and in doing so perform human functions to some extent, and still may be badly off in their lives (*EE* 1215b27-31). In that case 'performing one's function' cannot be a sufficient account of a person's good. Aristotle sees this, and replies that in such cases people are not performing the human function well. He therefore insists that to achieve our good we must perform the human function well, and that to perform it well is to perform it in the way that expresses virtue. These claims are not very adventurous if 'well' means 'so as to achieve one's good', and 'virtue' means 'the sort of state that causes him to perform his function well' (cf. 1106a15). To make his claims more interesting Aristotle needs to answer these two additional questions: (1) What is a virtue? What states of a person meet the conditions for being virtues that are implied here? It will not do for Aristotle simply to assume that the states commonly called virtues really promote happiness; to show that they are really virtues he needs to show that they really promote happiness. He does try to show this through (a) the division of the soul (see note to 1102a25); (b) the general account of virtue of character (ii 6); and (c) its application to the individual virtues in iii 6–iv 9. A virtue is the state that allows the full, rationally-controlled, harmonious realization of human capacities. (Cf. 1170a13 ff.)

(2) Why is it so important to be virtuous? It is not made clear here, but it is assumed in i 8 and gradually explained in i 9-10, that the active expression of the virtues is a component of happiness that we never have good reason to sacrifice for the sake of any other good, even though it does not by itself guarantee happiness. Virtue has this dominant place in happiness because (a) happiness requires a life expressing reason, performing the human function well; and (b) the life of virtue is this sort of life, since it achieves the best sort of rational control over our lives. A proper defence of (b) requires a full account of the virtues; Aristotle summarizes his defence in ix 4.

1098a18 'complete life' See 1101a6, 1177b25, *EE* 1219b5, *MM* 1185a5. Complete virtue needs a complete life (which need not, however, be a whole lifetime; see 1101a6-13) because virtuous activities need time to develop and to express themselves fully. This is especially clear with friendship, 1157a10, 1158a14, and with intelligence, 1143b7. Here the enduring character of virtue is important; see notes to 1100b11, 1140b29, 1156b12.

1098a20-b8 The comments on method (1094b11, 1095a28) are now applied to the discussion of the highest good.

1098a31 'what or what sort' See DEFINITION #3.

1098b1-3 'Rather, in . . . i.e. the origin.' Lit. 'But it is enough in some cases for the that to be proved well, e.g. in the case of origins; and the that is first and origin.' Here Aristotle uses the phrase 'the that' for the ORIGINS known unconditionally, i.e., the first principles of his theory (in this case, the account of happiness), and not (as in 1095b6) for the origins known to us, the starting-points in our inquiry. Starting-points are beliefs that need some further 'because'. First principles provide the necessary 'because', and a further 'because' cannot be given for the first principles, since they are first, and themselves give the 'because'.

1098b7 'the origin seems . . .' A Greek proverb—i.e., 'well begun is more than half done'.

1098b9 'should examine the origin' Here Aristotle states a general method for evaluating claims to have found an origin. Following the method of considering APPEARANCES (see ETHICS #7), we appeal to common beliefs to confirm our claims. Here the origin in question is happiness (cf. 1102a2); we have reached an account of this origin, and now we appeal to common beliefs about happiness to confirm the conclusions stated in our account.

'From the conclusion . . .' refers to the method of argument in i 7, where Aristotle has been arguing from general formal features of the good and from the human function; though these are not rejected in common beliefs, they do not simply have the status of common beliefs in his account.

In **'what is said . . . facts . . . truth'** Aristotle seems to assume rather hastily that the beliefs he will consider are true. For a more discriminating attitude see 1145b1-7.

1098b12 By 'goods of the soul' Aristotle does not mean just 'good for the soul'; all three types of goods are good for the soul. He means 'goods that depend on the condition of the soul, rather than on the body or on conditions outside the agent'. Goods of the soul are preferable for the reason given in 1099b11-25.

1098b14 'are said' Lit. 'we say'; but Aristotle must be reporting it as a widely held belief.

1098b25 'involving . . . ' Lit. 'with pleasure or not without pleasure'. Aristotle seems to be distinguishing (a) life consisting of activities that are sources of pleasure in themselves, and (b) life consisting in activities that are not in themselves sources of pleasure, plus added sources of pleasure. The same distinction is assumed at 1099a15.

1099a7 On pleasure cf. 1104b3, note to 1175a21.

1099a12 'conflict' I.e., with each other. If I have an excessive desire for food, I may make myself sick by overeating, and so interfere with my other pleasures. **'Pleasant by nature'** Cf. 1153a5, 1176a19.

1099a16 'does not need . . .' Cf. 1169b26.

1099a30 'one of them' See note to 1097a30.

1099a31 On external goods, see GOOD.

1099b3 'character of happiness' (*eudaimonikos*) I.e., we are not good candidates for happiness. Cf. 1176b16, 1177a6, 1178b23.

1099b11-1100a5 Aristotle returns to the assumption in 1095b25 ('we believe intuitively'). His account shows that happiness depends largely on our own actions; we are not at the mercy of FORTUNE for the major components of our happiness. Happiness partly consists in virtuous actions; and being virtuous—so Aristotle will argue in iii 5—is up to us, not entirely dependent on fortune.

1099b32 Children, animals and happiness; see note to 1177a8; 1178b27; *Phys.*197b6. A different reason is given in *EE* 1219b5.

1100a10 Solon's question is reasonable if we consider the differences between Aristotle's conception of HAPPINESS (#1) and a conception that may seem more natural to us. Solon thinks of happiness as complete success; and someone lacks this complete success if his success does not last for his entire life. Since external conditions beyond his control can interfere with his success, we are wise to wait until the end of his life, when we can be sure that they have not interfered, before we say that he was happy.

1100a18 'Still, even . . . ' Aristotle suggests that the end of a person's life may be too soon to tell if he was or was not really successful in his aims. A happy person, according to the conception that Aristotle considers, is one who succeeds in fulfilling the aims that he sets himself; and if these include, e.g., the welfare of his children, then his success, and hence his happiness, depends on what happens after his death, when his children succeed or fail.

1100a27-30 'Surely, then . . .' Queen Victoria died in 1901; her descendant Czar Nicholas was deposed in 1917. The absurdity that Aristotle considers here is not (a) 'Victoria has now become unhappy' (said in 1917)—though he certainly thinks this is absurd (a14-15, 'we do not say . . .'). He considers the different absurdity (b) 'It has now become true that Victoria was (before 1901) unhappy'. What was true of her in her lifetime cannot be affected by every fluctuation of fortune after her death (though it can be altered by some such fluctuations; see previous note).

1100b7 'Surely it is not . . . ' Aristotle's reply urges that Solon's worry is mostly, but not entirely, wrong. A virtuous person's main aim will be to exercise his virtues in his life. He can succeed in this, and hence achieve the main component of his happiness, independently of fortune. However, some conditions of happiness do depend on fortune, and here, Aristotle admits, happiness is not entirely stable.

1100b11 The stability of virtue; see 1105a33; notes to 1140b29, 1156b12; 1159b2, 1164a12, 1172b9. The virtues deal with a person's life as a whole, and so he has reason to exercise them in all his dealings. This continuous exercise is supported by friendship. See 1170a7 (cf. 1154b20, 1175a3, 1177a21), 1172a1-8.

1100b26 The role for external goods suggested in 'add adornment', *sunepikosmein*, is illustrated in 1123a7, 1124a1.

1100b32 'magnanimous' See note to 1123b29. Because the virtuous person does not overestimate external goods, he will not be crushed by misfortune and will see no reason to give up his virtuous actions. See note to 1166a29.

On making the best of available resources, see *Pol.* 1332a19.

1101a16-21 'Or should we . . . human being is.' This translation assumes that 'who has and will keep' implies a 'complete life' that may be shorter than a whole lifetime. Hence Aristotle's answer to 'Or should we . . . ?' is 'No'.

An alternative translation would be 'an appropriate end, since the future . . . every way? Hence . . . '. This would suggest that the answer to 'Or should we . . . ?' is 'Yes'; but this would be strange when Aristotle has just answered 'No' in a6-16, where he says that we can be happy for something less than a complete lifetime. The alternative translation should therefore be rejected.

1101b10 Praise and honour *MM* 1183b20-38. Praise is accorded to what is FINE #3 because it is the agent's own achievement, resulting from his own voluntary effort under human conditions (hence it is inappropriate to the gods; 1178b16). Congratulation, however, belongs to success in action; this is what distinguishes happiness from virtuous action, which is not sufficient by itself for the complete success required in happiness (cf. note to 1177b18).

1101b24 'godlike' Or 'divine'. Cf. 1145a18-27.

1101b27 Eudoxus See 1172b9, note to 1094a2. Aristotle is endorsing Eudoxus' claim that some goods are too great to be praised, not the argument for hedonism that Eudoxus derives from this claim.

1102a2 'for the origin . . .' Lit. 'for for the sake of this we do all the other things'. The antecedent of 'this' is probably 'origin', and Aristotle's implicit premise is that we do all our actions for the sake of happiness. It is the ORIGIN, since our deliberation (see DECISION) begins from our conception of happiness as the highest good; and we aim at it as the END, since we try to find the action that will best realize our conception of happiness.

1102a5 In his account of happiness Aristotle has not yet said what the virtues are; see note to 1098a17. We still want to see whether happiness requires justice or injustice, kindness or cruelty, bravery or cowardice. Aristotle begins his answer to that question, according to the suggestion in 1098a3, by considering the human SOUL, and especially its division into rational and non-rational parts (see DESIRE). The condition that promotes happiness will be the proper relation between the rational and the nonrational parts.

1102a13 'decision' The decision made in i 2.

1102a26 'as well . . . ' Or perhaps 'even in the popular works', on which see note to 1096a3.

1102a30 'two in account' For this question about parts of the soul see *DA* 413b13-32, 432a15-b8, 433a31-b13. By 'two in account' Aristotle means what he means when he speaks of things that are 'the same, but their being is not the same'; cf. note to 1130a12.

1102b28 'for there it agrees . . . ' For this important difference between continence and virtue cf. 1111b14, 1115b10, 1119a11, 1151b34, and note to 1104b6.

1102b32 'listen to reason' Alternatively, 'take account' — lit., have *logos* (reason, account) — of father or friends, not in the way in which we [give an account]. . . .'

1103a3-10 'Virtue is distinguished . . .' This does not mean the virtues of character involve only the nonrational part; for they all require INTELLIGENCE, which belongs to the rational part. Moreover, some of the virtues of thought — intelligence, good deliberation, understanding and consideration — will require the right training of the nonrational part too; see vi 9, 11.

Book II

1103a18 'hence its name' Aristotle plays on the similarity between *ēthos* (character) and *ethos* (habit). On habit see EDUCATION #1. For etymological speculations cf. 1112a16, 1132a30, 1140b11, 1152b7; they are part of the appeal to ordinary language, which in turn is part of Aristotle's appeal to APPEARANCES.

1103a25 'reach our complete perfection (or just 'completion' or 'perfection', *teleiōsis*) **through habit'** NATURE (see #2) is not neutral, equally suited for virtue or vice, but appropriately completed by virtue. On 'complete' see note to 1097a28, HAPPINESS #2.

1103b3 'legislator' See LAW.

1103b22 'similar activities' The translation and supplement assume that 'similar' means 'similar to each other', i.e. that habituation involves the repetition of the same sort of activity in the same conditions. Alternatively, 'similar' might mean 'similar to the state resulting from them', assuming that, e.g., brave actions are similar to bravery.

1103b22 'Hence we must . . .' The account of moral EDUCATION strongly stresses habituation; the activities of the virtues (e.g. standing firm as an activity of bravery) must be practised, if we are to acquire the right STATE of character. (1) Habituation is needed because we need more than just the learning of instructions, 1103a15; nonrational desires must also be trained. (2) However, these activities are not caused by the state of which they are activities; although we do what the brave person does when we are being trained, we do not do it because of our bravery until the habituation is completed and we have become brave. (See ii 4.) (3) We do not learn simply to repeat the actions until they become automatic or 'second nature' (cf. 1152a32). We must also acquire the virtuous person's state and motive, 1105a32. Hence habituation must include more than simply becoming accustomed to a type of action.

1103b26 On practical results see ETHICS #1. True theories are nonetheless important; indeed they are all the more important when the practical purpose of ethics is considered; see note to 1172a27.

1103b31 'First, then . . .' Aristotle begins with an APPEARANCE, a common belief about virtue, which he gradually explains and defends; see 1107a1, 1138b18, 1144b21.

1104a13 For the maxim 'we must use . . .' cf. Anaxagoras, DK 59 B 21a.

1104a26 'the mean' The doctrine expounded in ii 6 is anticipated here. So far, however, Aristotle only argues that virtue is acquired by a mean — neither total repression nor total indulgence of a natural desire or FEELING. He later argues that virtue consists in an intermediate condition too.

1104b3 'take as a sign' Virtue requires the right kind of pleasure (1099a7) as a 'consequent' (cf. 1174b33). It is not simply that the virtuous person gets pleasure from virtuous action (he has come to feel the pleasure that in the early stages of his training was the result of some external reward); he must also take pleasure in the fact that the actions are virtuous — hence 'enjoys this [abstinence] itself'. See note to 1175a21.

1104b6 'someone who is grieved . . .' We might think that Aristotle is referring here to the continent (see INCONTINENT) person described at 1102b27, who suffers a conflict between the rational and non-rational parts of his soul. Here, however, Aristotle says that the person who is grieved at being denied the intemperate satisfaction of bodily appetites is intemperate, not continent. The two cases should be distinguished. (1) The continent person has been trained to have some of the virtuous person's desires, and hence he does not resent abstinence from improper pleasures; his trouble is just that he also has strong appetites for these pleasures. (2) The intemperate person may find that he has to refrain from an improper pleasure (e.g. if he sees that he cannot avoid detection if he commits adultery), and will be grieved and resentful if he has to deny himself such pleasures.

1104b24 'people actually define'   Probably SPEUSIPPUS (cf. Plato, *Phil.* 42e-51a; 1153a31) or the Cynics (cf. note to 1096a2).

1104b30 'three objects of choice'   Cf. 1126b29, 1155b18.

1105a17   On this puzzle see note to 1103b22. Aristotle explains why his account of habituation does not self-defeatingly assume the existence of the state that is supposed to result from the habituation. The objector's argument (1) rests on an alleged feature of the crafts, and hence (2) assumes that virtues are analogous to crafts in the relevant ways. Aristotle's first reply challenges (1), and argues that the crafts do not support the objection. The second reply is independent of the first, and challenges (2), insisting on an important difference between virtues and crafts.

1105a26   The second reply contrasts the value of acting from craft-knowledge—purely instrumental value, simply a means to the right product—with the value of acting from virtue.

1105a27 'For the products . . . produced well.'   Lit. 'the things coming to be by crafts have the well in themselves'. Aristotle is not taking back the point he has made in the first reply, that someone might produce a good product accidentally. He means that the goodness and badness of production is determined by its usefulness for producing the product; a better method of production is better because it is better at producing the right sort of product.

1105a28 'But for actions . . . '   The value of virtuous actions, as opposed to a craftsman's production (the process), is not simply efficiency in producing a product; it also has its characteristic motive. The value of virtue is intrinsic; virtuous action is not valuable simply as a means to some further result (e.g. acting kindly is not simply a means to making someone feel better). The intrinsic value of virtue reflects the virtuous person's motive, shown by the second condition in a32. The demand for a specific motive differentiates virtue from craft, and hence differentiates the training required for each of them; this is Aristotle's answer to the puzzle raised in the chapter. Virtuous action versus production; see note to 1106b8, ACTION #3.

1105b19 Aristotle sets out to define virtue by elimination. The three 'conditions' are the different conditions of soul concerned with action. Neither FEELINGS nor CAPACITIES are the same as virtues, because they are the raw material of virtue – they require training and organization, as 1104a20 implied.

1105b25-8 'By states . . . well off.' 'STATE', *hexis*, lit. 'having', is formed from *echein*, 'to have'. 'Well (badly) off' translates *echein* with the adverb, lit. 'have well (badly)'. (Greek says 'How do you have?' for the English 'How do you do?' or 'How are you?') Here Aristotle argues that a state is not *merely* a capacity. He does not deny, but indeed believes, that a state is a *type* of capacity; see e.g. 'able to' in 1104a32-b3, indicating the type of capacity that is included in the state of character.

1105b33 'simply' *haplōs*: see UNCONDITIONAL.

1106a2 'praised or blamed' Is this praise or blame ever justified? Aristotle answers in iii 5.

1106a15 'what sort' See DEFINITION #3.

1106a15-24 'It should . . .' The connection between virtue and FUNCTION was urged in 1098a7; cf. 1139a16; Plato, *Rep.* 352d. As i 13 argued, a virtue will require the right relation among different parts of the soul, so that someone's actions are guided by reason. Here Aristotle expands his earlier suggestion (see note to 1104a26) that guidance by reason requires neither total repression nor total indulgence of nonrational desires. Hence the connection between virtue and function leads directly into the doctrine of the mean.

1106a26-b35 Aristotle warns against any misleading suggestion that his appeal to a mean is intended to offer a precise, quantitative test for virtuous action that we can readily apply to particular cases – as though, e.g., we could decide that there is a proper, moderate degree of anger to be displayed in all conditions, or in all conditions of a certain precisely described type. The point of the doctrine, and of Aristotle's insistence on the 'intermediate relative to us', is that no such precise quantitative test can be found. It cannot be found because virtue expresses correct reason, as its relation to the FUNCTION of a human being requires; correct reason may require extreme anger at extreme injuries and slight anger at a trivial offence; in both cases moderate anger would be wrong. To find the mean relative to us is to find the state of character that correct reason requires, neither suppressing nor totally indulging nonrational desires.

1106b8 'product'   *Ergon*, also translated 'FUNCTION' in a16-24. Here Aristotle argues, as often, from crafts to virtues – from the way in which a craft achieves its *ergon*, product, to the way in which virtue achieves its *ergon*, function. On the different sorts of 'achievement' involved here see note to 1105a26.

1106b36 'virtue, then . . .'   Clause (a) has been anticipated at 1105a31, (d) at 1103b21; (e) might be derived from 1106b8-16, by taking the INTELLIGENT person to correspond to the craftsman finding the mean. But the clauses are defended only later. For (a), see 1111b5; for (d) and (e), 1138b18, 1144b21.

1107a9-27 'Now not every . . .'   We cannot find a virtue by taking just any description of a type of action or feeling, and claiming that there is a virtue in finding the mean in that – for the action or feeling may be a vicious one. How, then, do we decide which actions and feelings are suitable raw material for the doctrine of the mean? Aristotelian virtues include mean conditions of natural desires and tendencies. But they also include mean conditions of desires and tendencies (e.g. love of honour) that develop in normal forms of social life, and Aristotle must assume that such desires and tendencies should not be eliminated by altering the normal forms of social life. On the other hand, the fact that vicious desires tend to arise in normal forms of social life is not a reason for cultivating a mean condition of them (e.g. if legally enforced monogamy encourages the development of adulterous desires). Apparently, then, Aristotle must rely on some initial judgements about the goodness or badness of different desires, and the forms of social life that encourage or allow them, before he can say which desires are the appropriate material for virtue, and for which desires a mean condition should be cultivated. These initial judgements may be disputable, as we can see by considering some of the social virtues discussed in Book iv.

1107a11 'adultery, theft . . .'   Does Aristotle's theory justify him in his confidence that some types of action, in any circumstances, are always wrong? See note to 1127a4. We might say that we would not *call* anything theft or murder unless we thought it wrong. Aristotle might say the same of adultery (it is the unjust use of a wife who justly belongs to another man).

1107a28 'not only state . . .'   See PARTICULAR.

1107a34 'diagram'   See *EE* 1220b37, *DI* 22a22. This chapter anticipates the detailed argument of iii 6 – v, and in some ways makes its aim clearer: (1) The virtues are classified into groups. (2) Aristotle seeks to show that for every genuine virtue of character the doctrine of the mean explains why it is a virtue. (3) In some cases this is fairly easy,

314

where (as with bravery) Aristotle can find a trio of mean, excess and deficiency already recognized in ordinary beliefs. But sometimes it is hard, where we do not naturally think of a trio, and have no names for some of its alleged members. This is why Aristotle's remarks on the 'nameless' virtues are important (see 1107b2, VIRTUE). He wants to show that his doctrine applies here too, and hence that the trio is recognizable even where common beliefs have not yet recognized it.

1108b19 'For the brave . . .' The doctrine of the mean explains disputes about the virtues, and tells us, as a good theory should (1154a22), why people make mistakes about the virtues. Those who do not fully understand the requirements of the virtue identify it with one extreme, which is then open to legitimate criticism from the other extreme; cf. 1125b4-18, *Rhet.* 1367a32-b7.

1109a5 'One reason . . .' How is one extreme nearer than the other to the mean? Perhaps Aristotle means that the rash person has the same sort of attitude to fears that the brave person has, but goes too far with it, whereas the coward has not developed the right sort of attitude at all. Cf. 1121a20, 1122a13, 1125a32, 1127b31.

1109a30 'Hence, whoever . . . ' Aristotle offers practical advice, as he promised (1104a10), stressing that his doctrine does not offer precise answers to particular questions. See ETHICS #8, PERCEPTION.

1109a34 'extremely accurately' (*akrōs*) This is a pun on *akrōs* = 'extremely' and *akron* = 'extreme' (as opposed to intermediate); cf. perhaps 1107a8, 23 (the mean is, in one sense, an extremity).

1109b9 'the elders . . .' In Homer (*Il.* iii 156) the Trojan elders comment on Helen's beauty: 'Her face is uncannily like the faces of the immortal goddesses. But, beautiful though she is, let her depart in the ships; may she not be left behind to cause grief to us and our children' (158-60).

1109b22 'and [since] . . .' Lit. 'and such things are in particulars and the judgement (or 'discrimination') is in perception'. For 'in' see notes to 1097b26, 1111a1.

Book III

1109b30 As the first words show, iii 1-5 is part of the general discussion of virtues of character. (1) Aristotle has said that virtue is praiseworthy (1101b14, 1106a2), and now argues that the praise is justified. (2) Since DECISION is mentioned in the account of virtue, 1107a1, it needs to be discussed. (3) Most important, Aristotle has assumed that if happiness consists in virtuous activity, it will, to this extent, be up to us, not dependent on FORTUNE, 1099b13-25. He needs to show that virtue is up to us. (4) The reference to legislators, 1109b34, reflects the close relation between legislation (see LAW) and EDUCATION for virtue.

1109b35 'What comes . . .'   We begin with APPEARANCES, the two conditions that 'seem' to make action involuntary, and Aristotle argues that there are no other reasonable conditions of involuntariness.

1110a2 'victim'   (See FEELING.) Lit. 'the one affected'. Perhaps 'the one having the feeling' (cf. 'feelings and actions', 1109b30). But more probably Aristotle is remarking that if I break a window because the wind blows me into it, I am a passive victim rather than an agent.

'contributes nothing'   Do I contribute nothing if you force me to do something that I already want to do? We might say (a) Yes, since my wanting makes no difference to what actually happens; (b) No, since my wanting is a contribution, though it happens not to be used in this case. Aristotle probably intends (b); cf. 1110b11-13, 18-24; 1111a32; *EE* 1224b8.

1110a4 'But now consider . . .'   Aristotle rejects two possible claims about these 'mixed' actions: (1) they are forced, and hence involuntary; (2) they are not forced, but they are involuntary, so that Aristotle's initial two conditions for involuntariness do not exhaust the possibilities.

In 1110b1 ('What sorts of things, then . . . ?'), Aristotle shows that he is answering (1). He does not deal so directly with (2), but he answers it by explaining how mixed actions can be voluntary.

The case of the tyrant's threat is meant to appear an involuntary action. To show that the appearance is misleading, Aristotle counters with the case of the cargo, which he takes to be a clear case of voluntary action. Mixed actions are a mixture of voluntary and involuntary, but the voluntary element predominates. They reflect NECESSITY (compulsion; see note to 1110a25), but do not make the agent's choice irrelevant to the action—hence praise and blame may still be appropriate.

1110a9 'UNCONDITIONALLY'   (*haplōs*) Here and in a18 ('with the [appropriate] conditions') and b1 ('forced unconditionally'), Aristotle has in mind the contrast between simply doing F and doing F when . . . , where the 'when . . .' mentions the conditions in which it is reasonable to do F. He marks the same contrast when he speaks of choosing to do F 'in itself', *kath'hauto* (a19, b3). Cf. note to 1151b2.

1110a25 'overstrain'   Cf. 1115b8, 1116b16, 1121b26. 'Compel' here translates *anankazein* (necessitate), distinguished from 'force', *biazein*. Cf. note to 1180a5. I am not forced to do these actions, because it is my choice that makes me do them; if I say 'I had no choice', I mean

316

that there was no reasonable alternative, not that my choice made no difference.

1110b18 The distinction between the non-voluntary and the involuntary is irrelevant to the agent's relation to his action; either way he is not responsible for it. But it is relevant to his character. If he is pleased at something he has done because of ignorance, he shows what sorts of actions he is willing and prepared to do, and is rightly blamed or praised for his attitude to these actions. This passage is one that shows that Aristotle is concerned with more than responsibility for actions; cf. note to 1110a2.

1110b30 'But talk of involuntary . . .' The translation and supplements assume: (1) 'ignorance of what is beneficial', 'ignorance in the decision' and 'ignorance of the universal' all refer to the same thing; (2) this is the type of ignorance ascribed to the drunken and angry people described here. Aristotle is thinking of someone whose anger makes him think it is all right to shoot the offender (cf. 1149a25), not of someone whose anger blinds him to the fact that he is shooting, or that he is shooting this person.

In these cases it is the fault in the agent's character, not ignorance, that causes the action. Hence it is not action because of ignorance, of the sort that removes us from blame (see further 1113b30 on ignorance of fact).

1111a1 'consists in' Lit. 'in which the action is'. Perhaps 'which the action depends on'; for 'in' cf. notes to 1097b26, 1109b22.

1111a30 'ought (*dei*; see RIGHT) **to desire'** Aristotle endorses the principle 'ought implies can'.

1111b5 'most proper' (See 1107a1) Why should voluntary choice falling short of decision not be enough for virtue? Why would a non-rational desire to be virtuous for its own sake not be enough? Rational wish and deliberation are needed for someone to have a correct conception of what makes virtuous action FINE and good in itself. Probably this is why Aristotle thinks virtue requires decision.

1111b9 'on the spur of the moment' Cf. note to 1117a22.

1111b17 'concern of decision' The point is not that we do not consider pleasure and pain when we make a decision, but that we are concerned with them only in so far as they contribute to good and bad.

1111b20 In each occurrence of 'decide to do' 'to do' is supplied.

'what is impossible' As 'anyone claiming . . .' shows, the point is that we do not decide to do what we *think* is impossible; cf. 'what is up to us', b30.

1111b23 'through our own agency' Lit. just 'through us', but agency is clearly intended. If you force me to stand between you and someone firing shots at you, you are not protected 'through me' in the sense that concerns Aristotle here.

1111b24 'actor or athlete' Prizes were awarded to the best actors in the Athenian dramatic festivals. Cf. 1166b35.

1111b27 'what promotes the end' Lit. 'things towards the end', *ta pros to telos*. 'Means to the end', a frequent rendering, is liable to mislead, since Aristotle is not concerned only with instrumental means; I can also decide on something as a good in itself that promotes a further good in itself by being a part of the further good. See DECISION #2, note to 1140a28.

1112a5 On correctness of belief and desire, see 1142b11.

1112a7 '[even] when . . .' Alternatively, and less probably, Aristotle might mean that knowing is a necessary condition for deciding.

1112b11 'not about ends' See note to 1111b27, *Rhet.* 1355b10. To deliberate about action we must begin with some conception of an end; but finding things that promote it may show us ACTIONS that are FINE and good in themselves. This is how the INTELLIGENT person deliberates.

1112b15 'ways and means' Lit. 'how and through what things it will be'. 'Means' is a convenient translation here, but may mislead us in the way noted in note to 1111b27.

1112b21 'analysing a diagram' The geometer considers how to construct a complex figure by analysing it into simpler figures, until he finds the first one that he should draw.

1112b26 'undertake' Lit. 'put our hand to'. The decision is the last mental event preceding the action; hence the process described in 1147a25-31 should be part of the deliberation.

1113a12 'expresses our wish' Reading *boulēsin* rather than *bouleusin*, 'deliberation'. This passage and 1113b3-5 make it fairly clear that DECISION requires wish, not just any sort of DESIRE.

1113a15 The exact point is obscured by the ambiguity of 'wished' (*boulēton*, cf. CHOICEWORTHY) between (a) what is wished and (b) what deserves to be wished. Two points might be relevant here. (1) When I wish e.g. for health I wish for it 'as good', i.e. I want it because I believe it is good, not because I believe it appears good. (2) The proper object of wish—i.e. the suitable object for the well-informed person—is the good, but each person thinks that what appears good to him is the proper object of wish. Similarly what is known by nature (1095b3) is what the fully informed person thinks he knows. Probably Aristotle's main point here is (2). See also note to 1155b21.

318

1113a27 'healthy to sickly people' The 'to' translates the Greek dative case, which might also be translated 'for'. However, 'to' seems better here; Aristotle's argument requires him to say that things appear healthy to sickly people when in fact they are not healthy. Cf. notes to 1173b20, 1176a10.

1113a29 The excellent person as standard; 1166a12, 1170a21, 1176a16. Aristotle replies here to Protagoras' principle, Plato, *Tht.* 152a (cf. note to 1094b15).

1113a34 'In the many' See PLEASURE #4.

1113b3 Here Aristotle turns to one major task of his discussion of voluntary action (see note to 1109b30) — to show that being virtuous is up to us, something that we can determine by our own voluntary action and decision. He argues first that since 'the activities of the virtues' are up to us, being virtuous is also up to us. These activities might be (a) those that cause and develop the virtue; or (b) those that are produced by it (see note to 1103b22). Here (a) is more suitable to Aristotle's argument (see 1114a7).

1113b13 'and if . . . person' Lit. 'and being good and bad people was this'. If Aristotle is right, then 'this' must refer to more than simply doing the right actions, since being virtuous requires the further conditions described in ii 4. But probably he has these conditions in mind when he mentions 'the activities of the virtues' in b5. The relevant activities are the actions based on wish and decision that produce and develop states of character (hence not the actions we do as children in the early stages of development, 1111b8). To agree with Aristotle's claim that these actions are up to us, we must also agree that the relevant mental states — wish and decision — are up to us. This claim is defended in 1113b21-1114a3.

1113b25 'responsible' See CAUSE. In 1114a1 'caused by' translates *dia*. No sharp difference should be assumed.

1113b30 'for ignorance itself' Aristotle supplements, but does not reject, the treatment of ignorance of fact at 1110b18-1111a2. He does not claim that we are responsible for the action caused by ignorance, but only that we are responsible for the ignorance that caused the action.

1114a3-11 'But presumably . . .' Aristotle has argued that legal practices show we are held responsible for our mental states. An opponent now argues that these legal practices are unjustified: (a) our mental states are simply the effects of the characters we have, and hence (b) we are not responsible for them. Aristotle accepts (a), but denies that (b) follows from (a). He argues:

(1) We were in control of forming our characters.

(2) Hence we are responsible for the characters we have.

(3) Hence we are responsible for the mental states formed by these characters.

In claiming (1) Aristotle must assume that childhood training does not form our character to an extent that puts it beyond our control.

1114a11-21   Aristotle replies to an apparent objection to (1), above. Someone might remark

(4) We cannot now change our characters.

Aristotle is ready to concede that (4) is at least sometimes true; but he argues that it is consistent with (1), and that (1) is sufficient for (2).

1114a31 'But someone . . .'   Aristotle considers this argument:

(i) The character we form depends on our appearance of the good.

(ii) But our appearance of the good depends on the character we already have.

(iii) Hence we are not in control of the appearance.

(iv) Hence we are not in control of the character we form.

(v) Hence we are not responsible for the formation of our characters.

Aristotle denies that (iii) follows from (ii). In the first reply he insists that the character forming our appearance is itself malleable and hence the appearance is in our control.

1114b1 'If each person . . .'   Aristotle clearly accepts the antecedent of this conditional.

1114b3-16 'If, on the other . . .'   Aristotle explains that if we deny responsibility for states of character, we must treat both virtue and vice as entirely non-voluntary.

1114b16-21 'Suppose then . . .'   Aristotle first repeats his first reply. In 'or, alternatively . . .' he argues that we can reject the first reply and still ('In either case', b19) make virtue voluntary. Even if we are not responsible for the appearance of the end (i.e. if Aristotle's first reply is rejected), we still need not embrace the position whose consequences are expounded in b3-16. For we can allow that the virtuous and the vicious person share the same conception of the end, for which neither is responsible, and differ in their conception of 'the other things', i.e., presumably, the things promoting the end. Given the wide scope of 'things promoting the end' (see DECISION #2), differences about these may make the difference between virtue and vice. In offering this reply Aristotle assumes that the 'fixed' conception of the end will be rather schematic (with its specific content to be filled in by deliberation), and not as determinate as it is taken to be in b3-16.

1114b20-1 'for the bad . . .'   Lit. 'for similarly to the bad person also belongs the because of (*dia*) himself in the actions, even if not in the end'.

320

1114b21-4 'Now the virtues . . . end we do' Lit. 'If, then, the virtues . . .' But Aristotle clearly endorses it; he is reasserting his first reply (in b1-3).

Does Aristotle mean to claim that everyone, no matter what his nature or upbringing may be, is fairly held responsible for his character? Cf. vii 5, 1149b27-1150a8.

1114b23 'jointly responsible' We are not the sole causes of our states, since nature and upbringing contribute also.

1114b25-1115a3 This passage summarizes the whole of ii-iii 5, showing again that iii 1-5 is part of the discussion of virtue of character in general.

1115a4 Bravery (*andreia*; see HUMAN BEING #2) and temperance are the first two virtues to be discussed because they are the two primary virtues concerned with FEELINGS (1117a24). See Plato, *La.*, *Charm.*, *Rep.* iv, *St.* 306e-end.

1115a7 'fear and confidence' The structure of bravery is more complex than that of some virtues (for generosity cf. 1121a16, b17). It involves the correct training of two feelings, not (as with temperance) of just one. Someone could train himself not to be excessively afraid, and still have no positive confidence or enthusiasm for facing dangers in a good cause. Since confidence also affects someone's readiness to face danger, it must also be trained if someone is to acquire the right attitude towards danger.

1115a8 'frightening' (Or 'fearful', *phoberon*) This term covers actual, possible and appropriate objects of fear; see CHOICEWORTHY.

1115a9 'People define' See Plato, *Prot.* 358d.

1115a13 'disgraceful' *Aischron*, usually rendered 'shameful'. See iv 9 and SHAME.

1115a20 In saying that cowards can be generous Aristotle seems to challenge his belief in the inseparability of the virtues; see 1144b32, VIRTUE.

1115a30 'the finest conditions' In his historical circumstances Aristotle regards death in war as the FINEST way to die. The reason he gives is that here (as opposed to death in a shipwreck) someone has a chance to display his abilities in action; he does not just keep a stiff upper lip. But, probably, Aristotle also assumes that the conditions are fine in so far as it is fine to defend one's city and its common good (contrast the attitude of mercenaries, 1116b5).

1115b8 'too frightening for a human being to resist' Lit. 'beyond a human being'. They involve 'overstraining'; see 1116b16, note to 1110a25.

321

1115b12 'will stand firm'   The brave person is not supposed to be fearless, and will not fear the danger less than it warrants. Nor does he force himself to act despite a strong desire to run away (this would make him analogous to the CONTINENT person). When he has the right degree of fear it does not overcome or paralyse him.

1115b21 'to the brave person . . .'   His judgment is correct, given the principle in 1113a29, 1166a12, 1176a15. The argument here assumes also that if a virtue is FINE, the end that defines it (actions expressing its state of character) is also fine.

1115b25 'has no name'   See note to 1107a34, VIRTUE.

1115b29 'boaster'   See 1127a20.

1116a14 'softness'   See 1145a35, 1150b1.

1116a15   Aristotle has explained that bravery demands the proper training of the feelings, and demands the right motive; action must be for the sake of the fine. He now considers the APPEARANCES (see ETHICS #7). He explains why commonly accepted types of bravery are not genuine bravery, and why they can easily seem to be.

1116a28 'shame'   (*aidōs*) See iv 9, SHAME. 'Disgraceful', *aischron*, usually 'shameful'.

On the inadequacy of HONOUR see 1095b23, 1159a22.

1116b16 'professional soldiers'   ('Professional' supplied.) Aristotle refers especially to mercenaries. These are not simply paid volunteers defending their own city for pay, but foreigners hired by a city, and with no further attachment or loyalty to it.

1116b16 'overstrains'   Cf. 1115b8, 1110a25.

1116b23 'emotion'   (*thumos*) See DESIRE. This passage (cf. 1111b18, 1149a25) makes clear the association of *thumos* with spirited, self-assertive and impulsive feelings and actions; hence 'spirit' or 'temper' might be an appropriate translation here.

1117a4 'most natural'   Cf. note to 1144b4.

1117a20 'when we have no warning'   Lit. 'sudden things', or 'things done on the spur of the moment' (cf. 1111b9). Here Aristotle assumes that these can be matters for decision. Someone's decision to meet danger forms his STATE of character; and when a danger arises suddenly he does not need *further* deliberation to cause him to act. The virtuous person's action can express his decision even if deliberation and decision do not immediately precede it; see DECISION #4, notes to 1142b2, 1144b26, 1150b19.

1117b7 'if this is also true . . .'   Aristotle does not mean that the end pursued in bravery really is small, or that the brave person does not take pleasure in it, but that it is surrounded by evils which he regrets and which might lead someone else to overlook the pleasure to be found in brave actions.

1117b17 'best soldiers' Cf. note to 1116b6. Here Aristotle stresses again that the brave person is not unafraid. He is free from paralysing fear in cases where he sees that it is fine to face dangers, and he sees this only when he thinks some worthwhile cause is at stake. Cf. 1124b6.

1118a10 'coincidentally' See *EE* 1231a6.

1118a15 'if they are hungry' The intemperate person enjoys these things even if he is not hungry.

1118a23 Why does Aristotle limit temperance to this narrow range of desires? Probably he thinks that this range indicates desires that develop in relative independence of those he excludes from temperance. We have them as part of the nature we share with other animals (1118b1), apart from our particular social environment or our individual choices and rational preferences. Aristotle rejects the view that there is some common explanation of over-indulgence in desires as a whole, and hence he refuses to treat over-indulgence as a single vice. Different forms of over-indulgence associated with different desires need separate training; a reduction in someone's desire to listen to music will not necessarily reduce his excessive liking for whiskey. Aristotle's view of the scope of a virtue partly rests on such psychological assumptions as these. For similar arguments about incontinence see vii 4, note to 1151a29.

1118b19 'gluttons' Lit. 'ravenous about their bellies'.

1119a11 In 'For he finds no . . . ' Aristotle stresses a point he stressed about bravery; see note to 1115b12. The temperate person does not have to restrain or overcome intense, wayward appetites; that is what the CONTINENT person does. His appetites agree with his rational decision about the right extent of indulgence; see 1102b27, 1152a1.

1119a21 The different degrees of resemblance to involuntary actions and conditions depend on the extent of pleasure and pain (cf. 1110b11, 1111a32). Cowardice seems more voluntary than cowardly actions because it is less painful; cowardice is a source of pain in particular circumstances. Intemperance, however, is a source of pleasure in particular circumstances, so that particular intemperate actions seem more voluntary than the state of being intemperate.

1119b3 Aristotle appeals to the relation between 'intemperate' (or 'unrestrained', *akolastos*) and 'temper' (or 'check', *kolazein*; see CORRECTIVE TREATMENT and TEMPERANCE) to make his point about children.

1119b14 'guide' (*paidagōgos*) This is the slave who took a child to school and elsewhere, mentioned by St. Paul in *Galatians* 3:24. Cf. 1121b11.

Book IV

1119b25 'Take' and 'acquire' both translate *lambanein* and cognates.

1119b33 'not properly . . . ' As often (cf. note to 1118a23), Aristotle wants to distinguish virtues and vices more sharply than they are commonly distinguished; see GENEROSITY.

1120a4 'Whatever has a use . . .' We now turn to virtues concerned with external GOODS, those that have to be used well if they are to benefit the person who has them. The generous person is the one who takes and gives money correctly. Aristotle does not say much about where he takes it from and to whom he gives it; but cf. 1120a5, b3; 1121b5; 1122a10. The answer will partly come from the requirements of justice (1120a20), but even more from the requirements of friendship (cf. ix 2). The FINE goal pursued by the generous person will reflect his desire to benefit friends and fellow-citizens. He is not indiscriminately open-handed or charitable.

1120b13 'his own products' Cf. Plato, *Rep.* 330bc; 1161b18, 1167b34.

1121a20 Aristotle supports his general view that often one extreme is 'more contrary' to the mean than the other, for the two reasons given in ii 8 (see note to 1109a5). This wasteful person has the desirable trait and motive, which needs to be cultivated further to produce generosity, while the ungenerous person does not have it at all. Hence (a25) Aristotle notes that this wasteful person does not even seem to be base. This view rests on the degree of benefit or harm done to other people by the vices; see 1121a29, 1123a32. The tendency of a virtue to benefit others is not often stressed by Aristotle, but here he plainly takes it for granted (see FINE # 4).

1121b3-12 Someone who is prone to intemperance is also prone to wastefulness and susceptible to flatterers (1127a7). Though Aristotle wanted to distinguish wastefulness from intemperance and from vice in general (note to 1119b31), he is equally concerned to show the connections between different vices; see note to 1159a13.

1121b11 'without a guide' See note to 1119b14.

1121b13 'old age' See HUMAN BEING # 10.

1121b26 'compelled' See note to 1110a25.

1121b28 'afraid' Cf. 1115a20. Virtue requires some confidence in one's own ability and in FORTUNE (1178a28), the sort of confidence that is naturally associated with magnanimity.

1121b33 'degrading' *Aneleutheron*, also translated by 'ungenerous'; see GENEROUS.

1122a24 'warship captain . . . leader of a delegation' I.e. someone providing the expenses of the warship or delegation. These are two *leitourgiai*, 'public services' (1163a29, 1167b12). In Athens these services were imposed on wealthy citizens at their own expense (cf. 1122b22, three services). A public-spirited citizen would be keen to over-fulfil his task in a way that would benefit the community (e.g. he might fit out a warship to sail and fight better than the average), and this would be a legitimate source of honour. For someone else, over-fulfilment in a pointlessly extravagant way would be an opportunity to display his wealth; he might decorate his ship expensively without making it a better warship (1123a19-27). The opportunities for virtue and temptations to vice offered by *leitourgiai*, and even more generally by benefactions to the public, are Aristotle's concern in the discussion of magnificence (*megaloprepeia*, from 'great' and 'fitting, appropriate').

1122a29 Why is generosity a virtue distinct from magnificence? Is it simply because not all generous people are wealthy enough for large benefactions? This would not be a very good reason for distinguishing two STATES. Probably Aristotle means that if a generous person came into money, his generous desires would not be enough to make him magnificent; for without further practice and habituation he would lack the judgement and tact that are needed for suitable large benefactions.

1122b2 'achievements' Lit. 'things of which it is'. In b3-6 'achievement' translates *ergon*; see FUNCTION.

1122b15 'achievement' Or 'product', *ergon*.

'excellence' (*aretē*) Usually translated 'virtue'. The point of this paragraph is that the magnificent person has the judgement that produces FINE results on the grand scale.

'provoke . . . honour' (*euphilotimēta*) On *philotimia*, love of honour, see iv 4. Aristotle recognizes that this is a reasonable motive when it has the right objects; cf. 1169a8, note to 1168b26.

1123a5 'to the benefit of the community' Lit. 'towards the COMMON'. So also in 'common good', 1123a5, 'good ' is supplied, being taken for granted by Aristotle.

1123a7 'adornment' Cf. note to 1100b26, 1124a1.

1123a16 'paltry' *Aneleutheron*, usually rendered 'ungenerous'.

1123a22 'club' A private dining club in which each member takes turns in providing dinner for the club. 'Purple': an expensive dye in the ancient world. It is like bringing them on in mink coats.

1123a26 'And so where . . .' (lit. 'and where') Sometimes a large expense may be appropriate but inconspicuous, and here the niggardly person will stint. A warship, e.g., might look seaworthy, but be unsafe if it meets bad weather; and a niggardly person might gamble on the chance of good weather, whereas the magnificent person would equip the ship for bad weather.

1123a34 'Magnanimity' is the traditional Latinized form of *megalopsuchia* (lit. 'having a great soul'), and captures some aspects of it fairly well. The *megalopsuchos* will not be calculating, suspicious, ungenerous or prone to nurse petty grievances, 1125a3. *Megalopsuchia* is concerned with HONOUR in its different aspects:

(a) how and for what a person honours and esteems himself;

(b) what he expects others to honour him for;

(c) which other people he honours, and for what;

(d) which other people he wants to honour him.

The magnanimous person takes the right attitude to honour. Aristotle rejects the view of life that aims exclusively and indiscriminately at honour from other people's good opinion (cf. 1095b23, 1159a22-5). But he does not want the virtuous person to ignore honour altogether. It is a genuine good, 1123b20; the virtuous person demands it for himself for his virtue, accords it to others for their virtue, and listens to others when they are qualified to honour him. He does not isolate himself from other people's opinions; nor does he try to make himself agreeable by taking their opinions of him more seriously than they deserve, or by honouring them more than they deserve. Here magnanimity is closely associated with truthfulness; cf. 1124b30 with iv 7.

Aristotle's virtue of magnanimity is often contrasted with the Christian or quasi-Christian virtue of humility. The justice of the contrast is unclear. Aristotle certainly opposes lying about one's own merits or other people's from a desire to ingratiate oneself with others; but does a genuine virtue of humility require the actions and attitudes that Aristotle condemns?

1123b2 'worthy' *(axios)* Sometimes 'deserve' and 'desert' are appropriate. But here 'worth' is better, since Aristotle is concerned with an objectively valuable quality rather than with the basis of an entitlement. I may deserve and be entitled to unemployment pay because I am out of work, but being out of work is hardly part of my WORTH.

1123b8 'not beautiful' Cf. *Poet.* 1450b35.

1123b24 'and honour . . . ' I.e., honour is what they deserve. A less probable translation: 'and of honour that will befit their worth' (i.e., they demand what they regard as worthy honour).

1123b29 'must be good' He demands honour for himself for the right reasons; but what is most worthy of honour is virtue; hence the magnanimous person must be virtuous. Magnanimity will make the virtues greater (1124a2) because his self-esteem and true perception of its proper basis will make him want to deserve it. Since the magnanimous person values virtue above all, he will not be attracted by the rewards of cowardice or injustice, 1123b31; nor will he be shattered by strokes of adverse FORTUNE, 1100b32, 1124a12-20.

1124a1 'adornment' Cf. 1123a7, note to 1100b26.

1124a24 'more magnanimous' In giving an account of common beliefs Aristotle is careful not to endorse the common view that wealth by itself is appropriately honoured. But he agrees that when it is honoured, the honour makes (the right sort of) people more magnanimous, since it stimulates them to do more to deserve honour and to show that they deserve it; see note to 1123b29.

1124b6 This attitude to danger is evidence of bravery. The magnanimous person would not be braver if he faced any danger indiscriminately; see 1117b17, 1169a22.

1124b9 The magnanimous person will be the benefactor in unequal FRIENDSHIPS. On the proper conduct of these cf. note to 1163b3. For the explanation of his attitude see 1168a10.

1124b19 'displays his greatness' Lit. 'is great'.

1124b20 'ordinary people' Lit. 'intermediate'.

1124b23 The magnanimous person's attitude is to some extent competitive; see note to 1168b26.

1124b27 'concealment is proper . . .' The magnanimous person is not ready to sacrifice virtue to curry favour with others for his security or profit; nor does he think so much of the penalties of honesty that he is afraid of them.

1124b30 'except . . . self-deprecating' The magnanimous person avoids displaying his own greatness in a way that humiliates inferior people, b19. His reason is contrasted with the self-deprecating person's reason, though their behaviour may be similar; see 1127b22. A less probable translation would be: 'except for the things he says because of self-deprecation to the many'. This would imply that the magnanimous person sometimes does speak in a self-deprecating way.

1124b31 'He cannot let . . .' Lit. 'he cannot live in relation to another'; cf. note to 1177a8, *EE* 1233b36, *Pol.* 1254a8-17, b21, *Met.* 982b25. Having our own ends determined not by our own choices and values, but by the use someone else can make of us, is repugnant to the magnanimous person; it is an aspect of slavery (see HUMAN BEING # 8) that Aristotle also sees in flattery (see iv 6). The magnanimous person makes an exception for his friend because the best kind of friendship allows virtuous people to share their ends; see 1156b7-24.

1125a8 'except . . . aggression' Lit. 'except because of wanton aggression'. The Greek allows 'except to commit wanton aggression on others' (presumably by insulting them). But though a magnanimous person will respond to WANTON AGGRESSION (cf. 1126a7), there is no reason to think he will commit it himself; it is for those who counterfeit magnanimity, 1124a29.

1125a13 'slow movements' Some have supposed that Aristotle is satirizing the magnanimous person here. But the whole account does not suggest this. 'Seems' (see APPEARANCE) suggests a popular stereotype. Aristotle is not necessarily fully endorsing it, or insisting that you cannot be magnanimous unless you have a deep voice. He suggests that his account explains why this stereotype is reasonably associated with magnanimity.

1125a33 'more, opposed' See note to 1109a5.

1125b1 'first discussion' See 1107b25.

1125b8 Here Aristotle argues for recognition of a nameless virtue (see note to 1107a34) that confirms the doctrine of the mean. If we see only a choice between love of honour and indifference to honour, we find ourselves praising both on different occasions. Hence the state that we ought to cultivate cannot be either of them; the reasonable state must be intermediate between them.

1125b14 'since . . . loving something' Cf. 1118b22.

1125b26 Mildness is another virtue concerned with FEELINGS, as bravery and temperance were, and, like bravery (1116b23), it is concerned with emotion (see DESIRE), especially as displayed in ANGER. But it is discussed at this stage, with the next three virtues, because they all concern ways of getting on with other people. Aristotle is concerned with anger especially in so far as it tends to offend and antagonize others, and with lack of anger in so far as it reflects an unreasonable (and, in a wider sense than Aristotle allows, cowardly) fear of offending others.

1126a7 'accept insults' Cf. note to 1125a8. **'Slavish'** See HUMAN BEING #9, note to 1133a1.

1126a30 'comes more . . .' Lit. 'it is more human'.

1126b1 'manly' See HUMAN BEING #2. We incline to think that someone who complains about ill treatment is a properly self-respecting and self-assertive person who will be able to dominate others.

1126b11 The sources of the vices opposed to friendliness are very similar to the sources of the vices opposed to mildness — excessive concern for, or excessive indifference to, other people's opinions. These attitudes in turn may result from the wrong attitude to honour — the attitude that the magnanimous person avoids. The attitude expressed in the irascible and ill-tempered people is a source of indifference to honour that is not considered in iv 3-4.

1126b11 'ingratiating' Lit. 'pleaser'.

1126b22 'in not . . . feeling' Lit. 'because it is without feeling'. See FRIENDSHIP # 6.

1126b27 'for the proper . . . strangers' We do not owe to strangers either the degree of delicacy in sparing feelings, or the degree of frankness in pointing out defects, that would be appropriate between friends. A less probable translation: 'For it is not equally proper to spare the feelings of familiar companions and of strangers, nor equally proper to cause them pain' (i.e. it is more proper to spare the feelings of friends, and less proper to cause pain to friends).

1126b29 Consideration of what is fine and what is expedient is prior to consideration of pleasure, even of future against present pleasure, 1127a5. For the three aims of action see *Top.* 104b30; 1155b18.

1127a4 'consequences' Here we are given some idea of how the virtuous person will consider particular cases (see note to 1165a3). He will not be guided by rules requiring or forbidding actions of certain types without regard to consequences. If he considers the fine and the expedient in general, he will have to consider the action from the point of view of each virtue, supporting the claim in 1144b32. This general method does not prevent Aristotle from being confident in some particular cases; cf. 1107a11.

1127a8 'with no ulterior purpose' Lit. 'not because of something else'. Cf. 1127a26 (lit. 'not for the sake of something'). It does not follow that the ingratiating person is unselfish. He may still be currying favour with you, but he is not out for your money or political influence, as the flatterer is, but only for your favour. Cf. note to 1171a17.

1127a20 'boaster' Cf. 1115b29.

1127a25 'acknowledges that . . .' The truth-telling that concerns Aristotle here is not honesty in general, but honesty about oneself. The motives for deviating from it are similar to the motives that cause the extremes about honour, and are related to the sources of the vices in iv 5-6. Hence truthfulness is characteristic of the magnanimous person, 1124b27.

1127b11 'pointlessly foolish' Lit. 'vain' (*mataios*, also 'futile' in 1094a21).

1127b14 'capacity . . . decision' These different people have the same capacity for exaggeration, but different states of character because they decide to use their capacity in different ways. Cf. 1106a2-10, 1117a4, 1152a13-14, *Met.* 1004b24, *Top.* 165a30, *Rhet.* 1355b17.

1127b25   Aristotle refers to Socrates' frequent disavowal of knowledge about the virtues, which was often regarded as self-deprecation (*eirōneia*; hence 'Socratic irony', Plato, *Rep.* 337a). He does not say that Socrates had the vice of self-deprecation; if Socrates' disavowals of knowledge were sincere and truthful, no self-deprecation was expressed.

1127b28   The Spartans were ostentatiously austere in their dress, to display their indifference to comfort.

1128a4 'buffoons'   *(bōmolochoi)* A *bōmolochos* 'hangs around altars *(bōmoi)*' to steal bits of sacrificial meat. Hence the term applies to someone who plays tricks and tells jokes to ingratiate himself with another. Hence his motives are very similar to those of the flatterer or ingratiating person. Similarly, the 'boorish' (lit. 'rustic', as opposed to urbane) people (cf. 1156b13) show the crusty indifference of the ill-tempered people in iv 6. The proper sort of wit is an Aristotelian virtue because it reflects the right attitude to pleasing others; this in turn reflects the right valuation of other people's good opinion of us. See 1156a13, 1158a31, 1176b14.

1128a17 'dexterous'   This trait has a wider scope than wit; cf. note to 1171b3.

1128a23 'shameful abuse'   This probably includes both obscene language and personal insults, a combination easily illustrated in the plays of Aristophanes. The New Comedy of Menander reflects the difference Aristotle describes (though here he is probably not using 'new comedy' in any technical sense).

1128a25-8 'Then should . . . hateful or pleasant.'   The second definition at first sight seems more precise than the first. But Aristotle raises a doubt about it in 'Perhaps . . .'. The witty person's jokes may displease some people, e.g. boors or those who prefer buffoons. Hence the first definition is more suitable.

1128b10   In this chapter 'shame' translates *aidōs*, and 'disgrace' indicates *aischunē* or a cognate; Aristotle's argument, however, seems to depend on the identification of *aidōs* with *aischunē*. See SHAME.

1128b30 'irrelevant to the virtues'   The assumed situation that would warrant shame is so far from anything that the virtuous person would do that it is pointless for him to acquire a tendency to be ashamed in that situation. 1124b10 is not an exception to Aristotle's claim here, since it is not concerned with base actions.

Aristotle is concerned here with retrospective shame at actions we have done, and, reasonably enough, denies it to the virtuous person. He does not consider the anticipatory shame of 1115a16, where I am properly ashamed when I even think of the possibility of doing a wrong action. He need not be rejecting that type of shame here, since it will apparently be a motive for the virtuous person (though not one of his virtues).

Book V

1129a3   The three books *EN* v-vii are also, according to manuscripts of *EN* and *EE*, the three books *EE* iv-vi. The manuscripts do not say which treatise the three books originally belonged to, or how they came to belong to both treatises. Stylistic and doctrinal evidence links these books with the rest of the *EE*; but it does not follow that Aristotle did not also intend them to be part of the *EN*. If the *EE* is earlier than the *EN*, Aristotle may have used these books, perhaps revised, in his new course of lectures. A decision on this issue is related to a decision on the relative date of the two treatises. See further the notes to 1152b4, 1176a30.

1129a6 'We see . . .'   We begin with some standard dialectical forms of argument. See *Top.* 106a9, 145b34, 147a17.

1129a8   In 'doers (*praktikoi*) of just actions' Aristotle probably includes the two components distinguished as DOING JUSTICE and wishing what is just.

1129a27 'homonymy'   Though the two types of justice are HOMONYMOUS, they do not have only the name in common (as in the example of 'key'—probably this is referred to as 'homonymous by mere chance' in 1096b27). They also have connected definitions.

1129a32 'greedy'   (*pleonektēs*) Or 'grasping', 'overreaching' (see JUST, EQUAL). *Pleonexia* involves a desire to have more than I am entitled to, so as to get the better of someone else. See Hobbes' description of the law of nature: 'that . . . no man require to reserve to himself any right, which he is not content should be reserved to any one of the rest. . . . The Greeks call the violation of this law *pleonexia*; that is, a desire of more than their share' (*Leviathan* 15). See note to 1136b22.

On **'fair'** (*ison*) see EQUAL.

1129b2 'goods'   On these goods related to FORTUNE see 1098b12, 1099a31, note to 1153b24; *EE* 1248b28. In 'UNCONDITIONALLY' (*haplōs*) Aristotle means that it is true to say e.g. 'wealth is good for a human being', without any condition, qualification or reservation. But this is true only in the sense that a human being can use wealth well, and if he uses it well, it will promote his happiness. Even though wealth is good for a human being, speaking unconditionally, it may still be bad for this or that particular vicious human being (we now no longer speak unconditionally) who uses his wealth to make himself more intemperate and less happy. Only the good person will use these goods of fortune so that they are reliably good for him. (Hence these are sorts of *haplōs agatha* different from those mentioned in 1113a23, 1155b24, 1157b27.)

Aristotle should have mentioned an important point about these goods of fortune. They are in limited supply, and therefore matters of competition (*EE* 1248b28; note to 1168b19). No one can get more of them without depriving someone else of them; if I get more wealth or honour than you have, there is less of it left for you. Hence the greedy person is unfair because he profits by another's inappropriate and undeserved loss. See note to 1167b4-16.

1129b12 'whatever is lawful . . .'   Aristotle does not say here that every system of positive law is just. *Nomimon* is ambiguous between 'legal' and 'lawful' (see CHOICEWORTHY for this sort of ambiguity); but the reference to 'legislative science' ('science' supplied) shows that Aristotle is thinking of the correct laws, not of every sort of positive law, as defining general justice. See note to 1130b22.

1129b14 'Now in every matter . . .'   Or: 'Now the laws deal with every matter, aiming either. . . .'

1129b15 'either at . . . such basis'   This refers to the distinction between correct and deviant political systems, described further in viii 10.

1129b18 Parts of happiness   Cf. *EE* 1214b27, *Rhet.* 1360b19, *MM* 1184a26. For the account of justice see *Pol.* 1283a38.

1130a9 'another person's good'   Aristotle alludes to Thrasymachus' claim in Plato, *Rep.* 343c, that justice is good for other people, but harmful to the just person himself (cf. 1134b5). Aristotle accepts the first part of Thrasymachus' claim, but not the second part (though he does not argue against it here).

1130a5 'The worst'   Cf. 1160a5.

1130a8 'difficult'   Cf. 1106b32.

1130a12 'what it is to be virtue'   (Lit. 'the to be it') This is a standard way (cf. 1141b24, *DA*427a2; cf. 'two in account', 1102a30) of indicating that two distinct DEFINITIONS are satisfied by one thing because of its different properties. Because virtue as a whole benefits others in the ways described it can properly be called justice.

1130a14   The argument in ch. 1-2 is as follows:
> (1) 1129a26-b11: Aristotle claims that justice and injustice are homonymous because one type of each is associated with lawfulness, and the other type with fairness.
> (2) 1129b11-1130a13: The type associated with lawfulness is the whole of virtue.

(3) 1130a14-32: The type of injustice associated with greed is a part of vice.

(4) 1130a32-b7: Hence the partial justice that avoids greed is a part of virtue.

(5) 1130b7-18: It is the part concerned with fairness, which is a part of lawfulness.

In (5) Aristotle reintroduces the distinction between lawfulness and fairness, first introduced in (1), to explain the facts about injustice mentioned in (3) and (4); he is arguing from contraries, in the way described in 1129a17.

1130a16   If I avoid military service because I am willing to take advantage unfairly of others who accept military service and defend me, I need not be moved by cowardice. I am moved by a motive that seems close to 'greed' (since that includes unfair avoidance of harm, 1129b7). Should we not count this as injustice in a more specific sense than Aristotle's general sense? If so, then Aristotle is restricting partial injustice too narrowly when he refers it to the desire for gain (unless our case could be covered by a wide use of 'gain'; cf. 1130b1). Nor is 'gain' sufficient for injustice. Aristotle wants to say that the unjust person wants gain that is unfair, at the expense of what is justly due to another; but his definition does not fully capture that aspect of partial injustice.

1130b2 'single name'   Cf. note to 1132a7.

1130b20 'set to one side'   We need not here take on the task of subdividing general justice, since its subdivisions will simply be those of virtue as a whole, i.e. the particular virtues that have been described in Books iii-iv.

1130b22 'for practically the majority . . . every sort of good citizen'   On 'lawful' see note to 1129b12. Since Aristotle thinks positive law is fallible in its moral prescriptions, he emphasizes that not every good citizen (i.e. a citizen matching the ideal of a given system of positive law) is a genuinely good man.

1130b23 'expresses (*kata*) each virtue . . .'   The broad scope of *kata* (see EXPRESS) makes it hard to say whether, in Aristotle's view, laws prescribe being virtuous or simply action in conformity to virtue.

1130b29 'being a good man . . .'   On the distinction between the virtues of a man and of a citizen see *Pol.* iii 4. The question about EDUCATION is considered again in x 9 (but not in the surviving *EE* — see note to 1129a3) and in *Pol.* vii.

1131a10-15 'fair . . . equal'   Aristotle of course uses 'equal' throughout. But the translation tries to suggest how he moves here from the fairness which is a general feature of partial justice to the different types of equality that embody that fairness in different types of partial justice.

1131a24 Different political systems agree on the importance of distributive justice and equality, and all insist that distribution should be equal to worth, *axia* (see note to 1123b2). But they differ on what counts as the sort of worth relevant in just distributions of powers and offices. (Greek cities normally regard public offices as rewards and advantages; they are sources of honour, and usually also of profit without any necessary dishonesty.) Cf. *Pol.* iii 9.

1131a30 'special to . . . units' Aristotle contrasts (a) 'The number 3 is the successor of 2' with (b) 'There is a large number of people in the room'. In (b) the number consists of people, not of abstract units as in (a). Cf. *Phys.* 219b5, 224a2.

1131b1 'When e.g. . . .' E.g. if line A is 3 inches, line B 6 inches and line C 12 inches, then the proportion of A to B is the same as that of B to C.

1132a6 'judge' In Athens the judges are usually the members of large popular juries, whose president is not a trained or authoritative legal official. Here Aristotle is not discussing their punitive function, but only one sort of injustice that they have to correct.

1132a7 'For [not only . . .]' In this section Aristotle explains that rectification and adjustment is appropriate even in cases where no definite sum of profit and loss can be identified, as it can be in financial transactions. 'Profit has to be taken in the wide sense that was suggested in 1130b2; it is used as the single name that Aristotle suggests would be useful.

1132a22 'living embodiment' Lit. 'a just ensouled'.

1132a25-b2 Aristotle is thinking of a single line like this:

A	E	D	C	B

On this line AD = DB and ED = DC. In a32, 'For when . . . to the other', Aristotle assumes that the offender begins with AD, the victim with BD, and the offender takes DC off the victim, adding DC to AD (AD = BD); then 'the one part (AC) exceeds the other (CB) by the two parts (ED and DC)'. Restoration of equality requires us not only to take DC from the offender (who then still exceeds the victim by ED; 'for if a part . . . by just one part'), but also to restore DC to the victim, (who would otherwise fall short of BD by DC; 'Hence the larger . . . one part').

1132b6 Here the illustration involves lines:

334

```
        A         E         A'

        B                   B'

  D     C         F         C'
```

Here CF = AE. This differs from the previous illustration in that we need not assume that DC = CF (and hence DC = AE), i.e. we need not assume that the offender gains exactly what the victim loses.

1133a1 'slavery' Failure to retaliate shows lack of concern for one's own status and worth; cf. 1126a7.

1133a3 'Graces' *Charis* includes grace, gratitude, thanks and favour; see CULTIVATED.

1132b35 Rhadamanthys In mythology a judge in the underworld. See Plato, *Gorg.* 523e.

1133a17 An association (see COMMON) requires members who are dissimilar enough to gain from it; see *Pol.* 1261b22-34.

1133a27 'need' Cf. Plato, *Rep.* 369b-d. Currency (see LAW) is a 'pledge' of need to the extent that my need for a bed is a reason to pay you money for it. Aristotle does not go into much detail about the correlation between need and the monetary price. But the sort of proportion described in 1133a32 suggests that A and C achieve equality when the price that A pays for the shoes corresponds to his need for them. Need should not be identified with demand; A's need for C's shoes does not change even though C may increase demand for his shoes by restricting production or buying out his competitors. On exchange cf. 1163b32.

1133b1 fixing the price See 1164b20.

1134a23 'We have previously . . .' This rearrangement of the ms. text offers a more consecutive order of exposition, with 1133a29-b16 as a summary of the discussion and 1133b16-23 as an introduction to the topics of ch. 7. Hence the translation assumes the transposition of these two passages to precede 1135a5.

1134a26 At the beginning of his general remarks on justice in political society (in a *polis;* see POLITICAL) Aristotle distinguishes this type of justice from the types found in other associations (see COMMON); cf. viii 9-11. For the account of the *polis* see *Pol.* 1252b27, 1278b15, 1280b40.

1134a32 'doing injustice . . . injustice' (i.e. being unjust) This distinction has been drawn in ii 4, and is to be explained more fully in v 8.

1134a34 'UNCONDITIONALLY' See note to 1129b2.

1134a35 'reason . . . human being' Aristotle associates the rule of LAW with the impersonal and impartial rule of reason (which will be correct reason when the law is correct); cf. *Pol.* 1287a18-32.

1134b5 'another person's good' See note to 1130a3.

1134b8 On tyrants see *Pol.* 1266b38-1267a17.

1134b10 'no UNCONDITIONAL injustice' I.e. there is only a derivative sort of injustice, partially resembling the injustice that is properly so called.

1134b11 On parts of oneself, see 1161b18.

1134b15 'equality in ruling and being ruled' 'Equality' here must include an equal right to rule and be ruled. Aristotle takes this to be characteristic of free citizens; *Pol.* 1283b14.

1134b16 'wife' Cf. 1162a16, HUMAN BEING #3-4.

1134b23 Brasidas was a Spartan general who after his death received sacrifices in Amphipolis as a liberator; his cult is introduced as an example of a strictly local observance initiated by decree (see note to 1137b29).

1134b28 'with the gods' What is natural for them is also invariable.

1134b30 Aristotle returns to the question about LAW and NATURE that was raised at 1094b16 (cf. *Top.* 173a7), and answers it more confidently than clearly by the comparison with the right hand; cf. *PA* 666b35, 671b28, 672a24, 684a25; *MM* 1194b30. Natural facts about a human being make it easier and more beneficial, Aristotle thinks, to use the right hand more than the left, though it is possible to disregard this natural advantage and to use both hands equally. Analogously, human communities can survive under many sorts of laws and conceptions of justice, but it remains true that human nature and the human good make one conception of justice the correct one.

1135a4 'since political . . .' The 'since' reflects Aristotle's view that the content of law both should and characteristically does reflect the character of the political system; *Pol.* 1289a11-25. He describes the best political system in *Pol.* vii. In saying that it is the best everywhere, he does not mean that every city should try to achieve it.

1133b29 For the order of the text see note to 1134a23, above. Here Aristotle summarizes his account of justice, and connects it with the doctrine of the mean.

1133b33 'concerns (lit. 'is of') an intermediate' The way in which justice is a mean is determined by the way in which just actions and states of affairs are intermediate and EQUAL—between suffering undue harm for another's benefit and gaining undue benefit by another's harm. With

336

the other virtues the property of being intermediate belongs to the state of the virtuous person, not to the corresponding ACTIVITIES. With justice it belongs to the activities. In pointing out this difference Aristotle does not deny that the state of character which is justice is a mean in the ordinary sense, between grabbing benefits at other people's expense (DOING INJUSTICE) and acquiescence in suffering harm from reluctance to assert one's claim against another (suffering injustice); cf. 1138a28.

1134a17 'Since it is possible . . .' If this is the right place for this passage, it introduces the question about unjust actions and being unjust that is discussed more fully in ch. 8 (see also note to 1134a23 above). See note to 1136a2.

1135a10 'when this has been done' Cf. 1110a14. Aristotle seems to be contrasting action types ('universals', e.g. killing an innocent victim) and determinate action tokens ('particulars', e.g. Smith's killing the innocent victim Jones yesterday). He insists, as he insisted in iii 1, that what is voluntary or involuntary is a determinate action-token.

1135a15 This chapter repeats some of the distinctions drawn in iii 1, now in a specifically juridical context (cf. 1109b34). Cf. also *EE* ii 6-10, esp. 9.

1135a23 'And as I . . .' Lit. 'I call voluntary, as has also been said before, whatever among the things up to him someone does knowing and not being ignorant either of whom or by what or for the sake of what (e.g. . . .) and each of these not coincidentally nor by force . . .'. Clause (1) seems to be an addition to the account in iii 1 (cf. *EE* 1225b7-11). The syntax makes it unclear whether 'and each of these not coincidentally' should be attached to 'knowing' or (more probably) to 'does'. If 'knowing coincidentally' is intended, it is presumably explained in b28-31. Doing something coincidentally is explained in 1135b2-8.

1135a28 'However . . .' (*de*, answering *men* in a23) Aristotle points out that the list in a25 is not discriminating enough. For I could know one thing about my victim and be ignorant of something else; what I have done voluntarily to him depends on what I knew about him.

1135b2-8 I do an unjust action coincidentally if the action is in fact unjust, but its being unjust does not explain my doing it – it is no part of my reason (cf. 1138b3, *Met.* 1025a25, 1027a1). If I do an unjust action because of ignorance (I break my promise without realizing I am doing it), it is easy to see why Aristotle thinks this is only doing injustice coincidentally. But suppose I know it is unjust and either (a) I don't care but I do it for some other reason, or (b) I do care but still do it because I am threatened with death if I don't do it. Aristotle seems to think that

(b) counts as doing injustice coincidentally; but what about (a)? And is the account of (b) consistent with 1110a4-b9? Cf. *EE* 1225a3-33. For coincidences cf. 1154b17, 1157a35.

1135b17-18   Misfortunes and errors are two subclasses of the class of errors introduced in b12.

1135b25 'But when his . . . '   This is the third of the three types of harm mentioned in b11. Aristotle contrasts disputes involving acts of injustice and anger with disputes involving unjust DECISION and character. To illustrate the second kind of case he mentions deliberate and premeditated fraudulent transactions.

1136a2 *'this* sort'   This is the answer to the question raised in 1134a17.

1136a7   For 'in ignorance' and 'caused by ignorance' cf. 1110b24-1111a2. Here Aristotle distinguishes actions done in ignorance and caused by a vice or a human feeling from those caused by a feeling that is neither natural nor human; cf. 1148b15-1149a10, 1149b27-1150a1 and note to 1149b4. We can see why people are not blamed for such states (cf. 1113b21-1114a3), but why should they not be pardoned for acting on them? Perhaps Aristotle means that an agent moved by these states will not respond suitably to pardon as an ordinary rational agent would.

1136b6 'but no one suffers . . .'   The argument is odd. For it seems that on Aristotle's own account the incontinent suffers harm (e.g. if he ruins his health by over-indulgence, knowing he should not) against his wish (his rational DESIRE); hence he seems to satisfy the conditions for suffering injustice. Aristotle replies that the incontinent person does not wish to suffer injustice; but wishing is not normally a necessary condition for voluntariness (though cf. 1169a1).

1136b22 'greedy'   Cf. note to 1129a32. Speaking of greed for what is UNCONDITIONALLY fine is an oxymoron, since such a desire does not match Aristotle's account of greed, and is not vicious at all; cf. note to 1168b26. 'Greedy' (*pleonektein*) is closely related to 'having more' (*pleon echein*); cf. Plato, *Rep.* 349b.

1137a9 'and not up to us'   Cf. 1114a3-21. Aristotle does not mean that it is not up to us to take steps to make ourselves just, but only that it is not up to us in the way it is up to us to do particular actions, 1114b30.

Here two features of the virtuous person are combined: (1) He responds flexibly to particular situations, more accurately than someone who just has true beliefs about actions that are virtuous. (2) He does the right actions from the right STATE and motive. Aristotle thinks (2) explains (1) because the right state includes INTELLIGENCE, which responds flexibly and correctly to particular situations; cf. 1114b14, note to 1180b20.

1137a19 'even more . . .' See note to 1140b21-5.

1137a30 'something human' I.e., suitable for normal human beings.

1137a31 The discussion of DECENCY may be out of place, since v 11 resumes the topic of v 9. However it is relevant to 1137a4-26; decency about particular cases will be part of the just person's character.

1137b1 'transfer' See HOMONYMY. As the *EN* itself often makes clear, it is common to use 'decent' to refer, by meiosis, to goodness in general.

1137b19 'subject-matter' See 1094b12, 1098a28.

1137b24 In his usual way Aristotle tries to remove the puzzles about common views of decency, and to show why the beliefs causing the puzzles are true up to a point (see ETHICS #7). If we confine justice too strictly to law-observance (cf. 1129b11) then it will seem as though justice and decency conflict, to the disadvantage of justice. Aristotle's own view of justice, however (1129b17), shows that it is what the law aims at, not necessarily what it achieves; hence justice and decency need not conflict.

1137b29 'decree' Cf. note to 1134b23; 1141b27, 1151b16, 1152a20. A decree is made for a specific occasion, not framed as a LAW is, in general terms. Cf. *Pol.* 1292a6, 32.

1138a13 'dishonour' In particular the loss of the status of a free citizen (see Aeschines, *Ctes.* 244).

1138a28 The account of doing and suffering injustice reflects Aristotle's application of the doctrine of the mean. See note to 1133b33.

1138a33 'combined with [the state of] injustice' Aristotle reverts to the distinction drawn in ch. 8.

1138b5 See 1166b19, Plato. *Rep.* 442d-444e.

Book VI

1138b18-20 The general formula in the account of the virtues needs to be made more precise; cf. 1103b21, *EE* 1220a13-29, 1222b5-9, 1249a22-b7. In 1107a1 Aristotle has already suggested that some reference to INTELLIGENCE will be needed to explain what correct reason is and what it aims at. Here the search for an account of correct reason leads naturally into a discussion of the virtues of thought (1103a3), which include intelligence. This discussion is begun in 1138b35.

1138b26 'not at all clear' See *EE* 1216b32, 1220a16.

1138b34 'i.e.' Lit. 'and'.

1138b35-1139a17 Aristotle distinguishes the part of the soul concerned with SCIENCE from the part concerned with non-scientific rational calculation about non-NECESSARY states of affairs. In fact not all of these states of affairs are matters of rational calculation and deliberation, as 1112a26-b9 makes clear.

1139a16 'best state' See *EE* 1218b38. On function, 1106a15.

1139a17 In this chapter Aristotle seems not to distinguish UNDERSTANDING (*nous*) from THOUGHT (*dianoia*) and REASON (*logos*).

1139a20 'no share in action' Here 'action' is used in a restricted sense, confined to rational action on a DECISION. See ACTION #2.

1139a21-b5 The search for correct reason leads appropriately to a discussion of the right decision. We need virtue of thought to find the true reasoning, and we need the right sort of character if we are to follow true reasoning in our actions. Aristotle does not say that a virtue of character is separable from true reasoning. His point is that the character must agree with true reasoning if we are to have a genuine virtue of character. The rest of Book vi looks for the true reasoning that is needed.

1139a29 'For truth . . .' Explains why the practical thought must be concerned with truth.

1139a31 'the source . . .' Lit. 'that from which the movement [is] but not that for the sake of which (*hou heneka*) [the movement is]'. Aristotle refers to the efficient and final CAUSES. 'Goal' translates both *telos* and *hou heneka*.

1139a35 Thought moves us to action only when it is for the sake of some end, something that we already desire. However, our DESIRE may be a rational wish, the product of further thought, not an irrational desire. Aristotle does not say that thought moves us to action only if it depends on a desire that is independent of thought. Hence he falls short of a Humean view of the relation between reason and desire (see Hume, *Treatise* ii 3.3).

1139a36 'concerned with action' Or 'practical', i.e. concerned with *praxis*. Here *praxis* is used in its narrowest sense, referring to action done for its own sake, as explained in vi 4. See ACTION #3.

1139b2 'unconditional' The 'conditional' end of a production is an end only relative to that production; it is a means to some further end for which we want the product. For the unconditional end see note to 1142b30.

1139b3 'achieve in action' Or 'do in action', *prakton*.

1139b4 'the goal. Now desire . . .' A different punctuation would yield 'the goal, and desire is for the goal. Hence . . .'.

1139b12 'Hence the function . . .' Since practical thought is concerned with action and decision, it must be concerned with deliberation, and hence must belong to the rationally calculating part. Aristotle returns here to the division into two rational parts at 1139a6-16.

1139b18 'if we must . . .' Aristotle indicates that he is speaking in the strictest sense, so that practical 'sciences' do not count. See SCIENCE #2.

1139b26 'all teaching . . .' See *An. Post.* i 1. **'already known'** *progignōskomenon*. The verb used here, *gignōskein*, has a wider scope than *epistasthai*, the verb corresponding to *epistēmē*, scientific knowledge. We can *gignōskein* (i.e. grasp, be acquainted with) something without scientific knowledge of it.

1139b28 On induction, see INFERENCE.

1139b32 'Analytics' See *An. Post.* i 3.

1140a1 Aristotle begins to draw the important distinction between ACTION and PRODUCTION by describing production and the CRAFT that is concerned with it. For the distinction see *MM* 1197a3; Plato, *Charm.* 163b. Much of Aristotle's discussion here is an implicit reply to SOCRATES' identification of virtue with craft-knowledge. See note to 1140b21-5.

1140a9 'popular works' See 1096a3.

1140a15 'by nature' See CRAFT.

1140a28 'promotes living well as a whole' For 'promotes' (*pros*) see note to 1111b27, DECISION #2. 'Living well' is equivalent to 'happiness'; see 1095a19. On the general scope of intelligence see 1094b6 (for the connection with POLITICAL SCIENCE see 1141b23), 1160a21, Plato, *Prot.* 318e. The intelligent person does not simply find means to ends that are taken for granted. He begins with the very indefinite conception of the end as 'living well', and his deliberation shows him the sorts of actions and states that living well consists in.

'restricted' Or 'partial' (*kata meros*).

1140a30 'no craft' See 1112a34, *Rhet.* 1357a1. The common use of 'intelligent' for deliberation outside the area of a craft is justified; for since intelligence is concerned with living well in general, it must be concerned with ACTION (#3), not with production; hence it cannot be a craft.

1140b6 'For production . . .' The 'for' explains why intelligence is concerned with action (in the narrow sense) and not with production. If it is concerned with living well in general, it must also be concerned with the unconditional end, which is action, the end of production (1139b1-4).

What does Aristotle mean by distinguishing action from production? He will face serious difficulties if he does not allow the same event to be both an action (in so far as it is done for its own sake) and a production (in so far as it is done for the sake of some end external to it). Many events that are virtuous actions, and as such decided on for themselves, are also productions; consider, e.g., a magnificent person's efforts to have a suitable warship equipped. Similar questions arise about the relation between MOVEMENTS and ACTIVITIES. Cf. note to 1177b18.

1140b7 'Hence Pericles . . .' Aristotle appeals to the APPEARANCES (see ETHICS #7) to confirm his account. The account in turn vindicates the appearances, showing that they are reasonable if they rest on something like Aristotle's conception of intelligence. Aristotle is not committed to endorsing all the appearances. He rejects some appearances about intelligence at 1141b28.

1140b11 Aristotle's fanciful etymology (cf. Plato, *Cra.* 411e) indicates the special relation of intelligence, as opposed to some other virtues of thought, to character. Since it knows about human good, its knowledge is liable to compete with conceptions of good that we can form from our uneducated desire for pleasure; cf. 1113a33.

Here Aristotle suggests that repeated mistaken indulgence in the wrong pleasures will result in our losing our belief in their wrongness; cf. note to 1144a31. Repeated INCONTINENCE degenerates into intemperance; cf. 1114a15.

1140b21-5 Aristotle rejects SOCRATES' attempts to identify intelligence with a craft. See 1137a19, *MM* 1197a18, *Rhet.* 1355b2, *Met.* 1025a6; Plato, *Hipp. Mi.* 375d-376c, *Rep.* 333e. The disagreement with Socrates is implied in Aristotle's distinction between CAPACITIES and STATES.

1140b29 'forgotten' See note to 1100b11. Since intelligence is about human goods, we do not find ourselves with no occasion to use it, so that we might come to forget it. Aristotle probably also refers to the close connection of intelligence with character and habit, and hence with the virtuous person's immediate response to situations; I do not have to remember that I ought to be angry about injustice.

1141a2 The supplement '[exclusively]' seems to be required by 1141a18, showing that wisdom includes understanding.

1141a7 Here 'UNDERSTANDING' has its strictest use (#3a). When SCIENTIFIC KNOWLEDGE is also spoken of in the strictest way, so that it requires demonstration, understanding a truth excludes having scientific knowledge of it, since no further account or REASON (1140b33) can be given of the ORIGINS or principles of which we have understanding. See also 1142a25, 1143a35.

1141a9 'EXACT' I.e. complete and finished in detail.

1141a12 'excellence' *Aretē* (see VIRTUE) used with its most general scope.

1141a18-20 Aristotle justifies his restriction of 'wisdom' from its ordinary use, so that it is confined to scientific knowledge and understanding, and thereby to necessary truths. These are also the subject-matter of theoretical STUDY. The common view that wisdom requires exact knowledge is taken to justify Aristotle's restriction.

1141a20 'Science' is supplied here and until 1141b33. (But in 1141b3 'scientific knowledge' = *epistēmē*..) Though it is hard to avoid speaking, as Aristotle himself speaks, of political science and medical science, these disciplines do not meet Aristotle's strictest criteria for a SCIENCE.

1141a20-b8 Unlike Plato, Aristotle sharply distinguishes the subject-matter of wisdom and of intelligence. Wisdom not only has no immediate practical end; it does not even study the same things, because the things studied by intelligence are not necessary states of affairs. The objects of demonstrative science are the most honourable (or 'valuable', *timion*). They deserve most HONOUR because (a) they are the necessary and unchanging principles of the universe, and necessity and unchangingness are the marks of divine realities (see GOD #6); and (b) they are thoroughly intelligible to reason because the truths about them are necessary and exceptionless, not exposing reason to ignorance or mistake (cf. 1139b21 on the non-necessary). Hence demonstrative scientific knowledge of necessary truths is the fullest expression of a human being's capacity for rational thought, hence the best ACTIVITY, and hence the highest VIRTUE of thought; in demonstration rational inference by itself can reach justified true conclusions starting from necessary premises, with no exceptions or qualifications.

1141a23 'the content of . . .' Lit. 'the wise', 'the intelligent' (and 'what is white' = lit. 'the white').

1141b3 'Anaxagoras or Thales' See 1179a15; *EE* 1216a11, *Pol.* 1259a6; Plato, *Tht.* 174a.

1141b15 Here 'PARTICULARS' (#2) refers to more determinate types (e.g. 'bird meat' as opposed to 'light meat') – though no doubt Aristotle also means that the intelligent person needs familiarity with particular instances too. Such information will be a source of useful specific descriptions; see note to 1143b4.

1141b22 'Here too . . .' Cf. 1180b11-28. Aristotle wants to correct a false impression that might be created by his previous remarks; he does not mean that general principles are unimportant for the intelligent person. Intelligence must include a ruling science (cf. 1094a27, 1152b2); and at once he proceeds to explain this.

1141b24 'their being . . .' See note to 1130a12. Aristotle qualifies the previous section, which insisted on the application of intelligence to particulars, and now insists on its universal, comprehensive scope —the scope he claimed for POLITICAL SCIENCE in 1094a26 (cf. *EE* 1218b12). Here he rejects the common, restricted conception of intelligence and political science which (a) confines intelligence to concern for my own good and no one else's, and (b) confines political science to the political and legislative process. In (a) we neglect the connection between the agent's good and other people's (1097b9) that makes ethics inseparable from political science. In (b) we neglect the principles that should guide political action.

1141b27 'decree' See note to 1137b29.

1142a2 'too active' Or 'busibodies' (*polupragmones*), a standard pejorative term for over-involvement in politics (especially on the side disapproved of by the speaker). Cf. Plato, *Gorg.* 485e-486d. Aristotle neither endorses the ordinary political life (cf. 1095b22, 1179a1; *Pol.* vii 3-4) nor recommends withdrawal from political concerns.

1142a8 'Hence this belief' The common view about intelligent people is understandable once we see that it rests on a false belief about the human good. See ETHICS #7.

1142a11 'A sign . . .' The reference of 'what has been said' is not clear. Probably it refers to a10, 'Moreover . . .'. In explaining the different views about intelligence Aristotle mentions the difficulty of its subject-matter, and this leads him back to the topic of 1141b18-22.

1142a18 'abstraction . . . experience' ('reached' supplied; it is not certain that Aristotle refers to the process of discovery.) Abstraction (*aphairesis,* removal) involves the removal in thought, i.e. ignoring, of all the features of an object except those relevant to the particular question—e.g. the non-geometrical properties of physical objects are abstracted when we study them geometrically (i.e. in so far as they are geometrical objects); see *Phys.* 193b31-4, *Met.* 1077b17-1078a31. Since these disciplines attend to fewer properties of physical objects, they demand less detailed empirical familiarity with the objects, and especially demand less than is demanded by natural science.

1142a20 'young people' See 1147a21.

1142a22 'particular' Probably here the particular instances (e.g. this water here), rather than the determinate type, are intended (cf. note to 1141b15), because of the reference to action (cf. 1110b6) and perception in 1142a24-7.

1142a24 'last thing' I.e., last as you proceed from more general to more particular, and hence in this case the particular (cf. note to 1143a35; 1146a9). Understanding is concerned with the terms (*horoi*; or DEFINITIONS—in 'All A is B' either A alone or the whole statement might be called a *horos*) that come first in a demonstrative science (not in a practical science) because they are the most universal. Intelligence is concerned with terms that come last in a practical science (not in a demonstrative science) because they are the most particular. For the sake of a neat contrast here Aristotle does not assert, though he also does not deny, his normal claim that intelligence also grasps the first principles in practical affairs; for this claim cf. 1140b18, 1142b33.

1142a27 'special objects' ('Objects' supplied in this paragraph.) I.e., colour, sound, etc., the objects proprietary to sight, hearing, etc. See *De An.* ii 6.

1142a28 'the sort by which . . .' We have to recognize, without being given any further reason, that the triangle is the last, i.e. the simplest, mathematical figure. The sort of perception required here is somewhat analogous to the perception that is required by intelligence (though 'However . . .' in a30 indicates that the analogy is not complete).

1142b2 'good guessing' Aristotle makes it clear that he thinks deliberation, and hence DECISION, requires a process that takes time and precedes the action. Cf. 1117a20.

1142b10 'no correctness in scientific knowledge' I.e. there is no proper subset of scientific knowledge that is correct, since it is all correct.

1142b11 '[but correctness . . .]' For the supplement see 1112a5.

1142b17 Since there are different types of CORRECTNESS, the correctness of the intelligent person's deliberation must be distinguished from the other types. Here Aristotle shows that good deliberation is not simply the discovery of the most effective means to ends that are taken for granted; for, as he says, on that standard the incontinent and the base person deliberate just as well as the good person (see DECISION #1). Good deliberation 'reaches good', a22, by finding what the good consists in (DECISION #2). In a22, 'However, it is possible . . .'. Aristotle insists that the good deliberator, and therefore the intelligent and virtuous person, must reach the correct conclusion by the right method. This is part of having the right state; he must make valid inferences from true premises.

1142b29 'Further . . .' Lit. 'Further, it is possible to have deliberated well both UNCONDITIONALLY and towards some end.'

1142b30   The 'unconditional end' is unconditional because it is the end for a human being, not just in relation to some limited aim or imperfection of a particular human being; cf. 1139b2.

1142b32 'promoting the end'   We should not suppose that the true supposition about the end only precedes deliberation, Intelligence is deliberative, 1140a26; and though deliberation requires some initial, schematic conception of the end, a more determinate true supposition about a more fully specified end will be the result of good deliberation. See notes to 1144a8, 1144a31.

1143a8 'prescriptive'   See *EE* 1220a9, b6. Comprehension says, 'If you apologize to him, he will be less resentful'. Intelligence says, 'Since you must remove his resentment, you must apologize to him'. Aristotle does not mean that intelligence produces imperatives rather than statements; the distinction between intelligence and comprehension does not rest on a grammatical distinction.

1143a17 'found in learning'   The Greek *manthanein* used here is applied both to the process of learning and to the grasping of the subject that we have learnt; it is this grasping that is identified with comprehension.

1143a19   Aristotle describes the connections between 'consideration' (*gnōmē*; or 'good judgment') and 'considerateness' (*sungnōmē*; see PARDON) and their relation to the decency that is described in v 10.

1143a35 'last things'   See note to 1142a24.

1143a35-b1 'with the last things'   'In both directions' indicates that here 'last' indicates both the last things as you go towards the more universal (hence in a36 they are the 'first terms') and the last things as you go from universal to particular (hence 'last' in a36). As in 1142a25, Aristotle contrasts (a) understanding in demonstrative science with (b) the way in which intelligence is aware of particulars. In 1142a25 he called (b) a type of perception that he opposed to understanding. Here he calls (b) a type of understanding. He calls it understanding because it is analogous to (a), in so far as no further account or reason can be given for our grasp of the particular, just as none can be given for our grasp of a first principle of demonstration. Despite this analogy the basic contrast between intelligence and understanding remains. Though the terms used here are different from those in 1142a25, the same basic contrast is drawn.

1143b2-5 'about the last . . . particulars'   Lit. 'of the last and the admitting and of the other premise (*protasis*); for these are the origins of that for the sake of which; for universals are from (or 'out of', *ek*) particulars; we must, then, have perception of these . . .'.

1143b3 'the minor premise'   Aristotle presupposes the account of practical INFERENCE at 1147a25-31; cf. 1144a31. Understanding is needed to find the relevant features of particular situations, so that general principles can be applied to them (e.g. if a general principle says 'Excessive display in equipping warships should be avoided', some grasp of what would be excessive in this particular case, in fitting out this warship, is needed).

1143b4 'the origins of the end' Seeing the right features in particular situations will allow us to form more useful and determinate rules; see note to 1141b15. This will be a process of induction; see INFERENCE.

1143b6 'seem to grow naturally' Aristotle does not think that they really do come by nature, or that age implies intelligence. But the fact that EXPERIENCE is important for intelligence explains the mistaken view that intelligence grows naturally.

'No one seems to have natural wisdom' because wisdom requires demonstration, which requires teaching (1139b25).

1143b9 'nature were the cause.' After this the mss. add: 'Hence understanding is both origin and end. For demonstrations are from these things, and about them.' This does not seem to fit into the context and is probably spurious.

1143b21-8 'For knowledge . . . in actions.' Lit:'What do we need it for, if intelligence is that about the just things and fine things and good things for a human being, and these are the things it belongs to the good man to do, but we are no more prone to act by knowing them, if the virtues are states, just as neither the healthy things nor the fit things (as many as are spoken of not by producing but by being from the state) – for we are no more prone to act by having the medical and gymnastic?'

This second puzzle rests on the assumption that just as (1): (a) I can do what is healthy and hence (b) be healthy, without (c) knowing medicine, so also (2): (a) I can do what is virtuous and hence (b) be virtuous, without (c) having intelligence. Aristotle challenges the alleged parallel between (1) and (2). He denies that (2b) follows from (2a), if (2a) is understood so as not to require intelligence; see 1144a11.

1143b30 'those who are not' The third puzzle assumes that intelligence is analogous to a specialized CRAFT whose products are useful to me, but whose practice I can leave to someone else; though I value the product of medicine, I needn't be a doctor myself. This objection reflects failure to distinguish intelligence and virtue from craft (cf. 1105a26-b5).

1143b33-5 'Besides, it would . . .' The fourth puzzle relies on the assumption, accepted by Aristotle, that intelligence produces wisdom; see note to 1145a6.

1143b35-1144a11 Aristotle's first replies insist on the intrinsic value of wisdom and intelligence. These are part of the formal CAUSE of happiness. We say 'He is healthy because his body is in a healthy condition which is . . . ʻgiving details ', and thereby say what health consists in. Similarly we say 'He is happy because he is wise and . . . (adding the other components)', saying what happiness consists in.

1144a4 '. . . health produces [health]' Less probably: 'health produces [happiness]'.

1144a8 'makes the goal . . .' Cf. 1144a20, 1145a4. Aristotle speaks of virtue and intelligence as though they made quite distinct contributions to the correct decision. But this cannot be right. For, as vi 13 argues, virtue itself requires intelligence. We should not suppose the virtue has the correct goal before intelligence finds what promotes it. On the contrary, virtue has the correct goal only because intelligence has found what promotes it; see note to 1142b32. On this question about virtue cf. *EE* ii 11.

1144a15 'unwillingly or . . .' Presumably 'unwillingly' here refers to force, or perhaps to the conditions mentioned in 1135b4-8. Ignorance is, of course, in Aristotle's view, another source of unwilling and involuntary action.

1144a19 'because of decision and . . .' See 1105a32 (cf. 1134a20, 1135b35).

1144a22 'another capacity' Cf. *EE* 1227b40. We should not suppose that this capacity is entirely separate from virtue; since intelligence requires cleverness, and virtue requires intelligence, it follows that virtue requires cleverness. See notes to 1144a8, 1171b3.

1144a30 'Intelligence . . . virtue.' Lit. 'The state comes to be for this eye of the soul not without virtue.' Until someone is virtuous he has only an aptitude for intelligence, not intelligence itself. Cleverness at finding means to ends is not sufficient for intelligence, which also requires the right ends that belong to virtue, and hence requires the correct decision (1152a10). Aristotle does not mean, however, that the intelligent person is simply a clever person who has also been well brought up. He has the right end because he has deliberated 'well' in the way explained in vi 9.

1144a31 'For INFERENCES . . .' Cf. note to 1143b3. Here Aristotle considers the major premise. Only the good person has the correct conception of what the highest good consists in; he reaches this conception by good deliberation; cf. note to 1142b32. For the bad effects of vice cf. note to 1140b11.

1144b3 'natural virtue' Cf. 1117a4, 1127b14, 1151a18, 1179b21-6;

NATURE #1. Aristotle refers to natural aptitudes, not to genuine virtues (cf. 1103a23). Without intelligence someone will lack full (see CONTROLLING) virtue, because he will lack the appropriate discernment and flexibility in less familiar situations (cf. notes to 1137a9, 1180b20).

Aristotle does not consider here the results of good upbringing without intelligence (cf. 1095b4-9). He does not recognize this as virtue of character (or 'habituated virtue,' 1151a18-19). Virtue of character includes intelligence, and hence Aristotle cannot regard the process of habituation as complete until the person being habituated has acquired intelligence.

1144b19 '[instances of] intelligence' Lit. 'intelligences'; perhaps '[forms of] intelligence'.

1144b21 'Whenever people . . .' Aristotle now answers the question about correct reason raised in ch. 1 (cf. 1103b32). Correct reason is specified by intelligence (1107a1); and the description of intelligence has explained more fully what the content of correct reason will be. Aristotle still has not explained as fully as some might wish what correct reason will prescribe. The reader needs to be convinced that someone who deliberates in the way prescribed in Book vi and who accepts the conception of happiness in Book i will decide on the virtues described in Books iii-iv.

1144b26 'expressing . . . involving . . .' Probably Aristotle means to contrast (a) the actions that express the virtuous person's decision with (b) those (instinctive reactions and feelings) that do not express his decision, but still would not be what they are without his rational reflection and decision (cf. note to 1117a22). The same distinction is drawn in 'reason . . . involve reason' (b29-30) and 'intelligence . . . require intelligence' (b20). Cf. 1098a7, 1102b28-1103a3. Intelligence is a necessary part, not the whole, of virtue.

1145a1 Though Aristotle rejects the Socratic belief in the unity and identity of all the virtues, he thinks (a) each virtue is inseparable from intelligence (1107a1, 1138b18-34, 1178a16-19), and since (b) intelligence is inseparable from all the virtues, it follows that (c) each virtue is inseparable from all the other virtues. We have seen why he believes (a); but (b) and (c) seem to neglect the role of external conditions in making some of the virtues possible; cf. 1122a28, 1123b5, 1125b4 (and for a different sort of exception see 1115a20). To cope with these cases (b) and (c) seem to need revision. Cf. *MM* 1199b35-1200a11.

1145a2 'And clearly . . .' We return to the first puzzle. Though Aristotle has officially been answering the second and third puzzles until now, he has also made his answer to the first more convincing by suggesting how intelligence is the virtue of a rational part of the soul.

1145a4 'and because . . .' Or 'and also, clearly, the decision . . .'

1145a5-6 'For virtue . . . end.' Lit. 'for the one makes us do the end, the other the things towards the end.' Cf. note to 1144a8. Intelligence is deliberative, and hence concerned with what promotes the end. Virtue makes us do the actions achieving the end because it determines our actions; but we have now seen that virtue and intelligence require each other. Cf. 1178a16.

1145a6 Wisdom has its place in a life organized and planned by intelligence, but it is not thereby of less value than intelligence. The place of wisdom in happiness is explained in x 6-8.

Book VII

1145a26 On the gods cf. 1178b10; becoming gods, 1159a5, 1166a19.

1145b1-7 See ETHICS #4. Incontinence is one case in which Aristotle does not think all the common beliefs can be defended.

1145b21 'the sort of . . .' 'SUPPOSITION' is the generic term for a cognitive state, and Aristotle thinks it is important to decide exactly what sort of cognitive state, and about what, the incontinent is in. 'Knowledge' in this discussion renders *epistēmē*.

1145b27 'This argument . . .' Aristotle rejects the Socratic claim that the presence of knowledge ensures I will not act against what I know to be best. Knowledge is relevant because it is firm and not liable to change. If at time t_1 I have true belief that x is better than y, and at a later time t_2 I do y rather than x, then, in SOCRATES' view, I must have changed my mind between t_1 and t_2 so that at t_2 I believe that y is better than x. Aristotle rejects this Socratic claim, but not entirely; as 'If ignorance . . .' shows, he thinks ignorance of a certain type may be relevant.

1145b29 'to be affected' (*pathos*) See FEELING.

1146a4 Intelligence requires right action and virtue, and so is incompatible with incontinence; 1144a29, 1152a6.

1146a24 On puzzles as binding, see *Met.* 995a28.

1146a31 'decides' This is the intemperate person. The restricted scope of DECISION (#1) is important; cf. 1146b22.

1146b3 'simple' (*haplōs*; see UNCONDITIONAL) I.e. said simply to be incontinent, without mention of any specific area of incontinence (in American idiom 'incontinent, period').

1146b7 'solution' Lit. 'loosing'. The metaphor of binding is continued from 1146a24. Cf. *EE* 1215a7.

1146b31-1147a10 The first three ways of knowing and not knowing are not directly relevant to the incontinent person. They all explain why someone does not draw the right conclusion about a particular case. The incontinent, by contrast, does draw the right conclusion, since he makes the right DECISION (1148a9, 1150b30, 1151a25, 1152a17). But parts of these cases are also relevant to the incontinent.

1146b33 'attend' See STUDY.

1147a3 'particular premise' Lit. 'partial' (*kata meros*), mentioning particulars (*kath'hekasta*).

1147a4 'types of universal' Not universal premises, but universal terms or concepts (e.g. 'healthy' or 'dry').

1147a12 'both have . . . ' Someone may know French but have no access to his knowledge because of his condition; he does not apply the knowledge in the normal way.

1147a14 'those affected by strong feelings' Lit. 'those in affections' (*pathē*); see FEELING.

1147a18-24 'Saying the words . . . ' Aristotle is trying to associate incontinents with the people he has just mentioned. An objector says: 'But you can't associate them. If I'm asleep, my knowledge is unavailable to me because I don't draw any conclusions at all. But the incontinent draws the right conclusions.' Aristotle replies that simply saying the right words is not proof of really *drawing* the right conclusion.

Here Aristotle is describing the state of the incontinent, while, not before, he is overcome by his incontinent desire. In a24 he reverts to the time before the incontinent is overcome. The account of the incontinent's knowledge applies to stage (4) (see note to 1147a31-b5).

1147a24-31 Aristotle discusses the question from a natural (i.e. psychological; see NATURE) point of view, referring to the structure of practical INFERENCE; cf. *De An.* 431a15, *Mot. Anim.* 7, *Rhet.* 1392b19. Step (c) is the formation of the conclusion, which at once leads to action. If the incontinent forms the conclusion and the conclusion leads to action, how can it fail to have its usual effect on action? This is the question Aristotle tries to answer in his account of how incontinence happens.

1147a26 'And in the cases . . . ' Lit. (following the Greek word-order) 'Whenever one comes to be from them, it is necessary that the thing concluded, in the one case the soul affirms, and in productive [beliefs] does at once.' 'The thing concluded' is the object both of 'affirms' and 'does'.

1147a30 'unhindered' Probably Aristotle has in mind external hindrances as in *Met.* 1048a10-24, *De An.* 417a27. An incontinent desire does not count as a hindrance; hence the incontinent acts on the conclusion of correct practical inference (see next note).

1147a31-b5 The account of incontinence is brief and obscure. The reference letters in the translation are supplied. They suggest one possible, but disputed interpretation, as follows:

(1) By 'the belief tells him . . . ' Aristotle shows that the incontinent has reached stage (c), drawn the right conclusion, and hence formed the right decision (cf. note to 1112b26). In 'this belief is active' (b32) Aristotle makes it clear that the first three cases of actual and potential knowledge (1146b31-1147a10) do not apply to the incontinent at this stage.

(2) Hence (see 1147a24-31) he must immediately act. And so he does; he tries to avoid tasting this sweet thing.

(3) But he also 'has appetite'; and so belief (b) excites his appetite for what is pleasant, focusing the belief on this situation. When this happens, belief (b) is attached to the appetite, and no longer attached to belief (a). When (b) is detached from (a), he can no longer infer (c) from (a); hence this is no longer (though it previously was) one of 'the cases where these two beliefs result in one belief', 1147a26 (cf. *An. Pr.* 67a37). The incontinent is no longer genuinely inferring (c) from (a). He still repeats the words of the inference, but the conclusion is now unavailable to him, as Aristotle said in 1147a18-24.

(4) Hence, when he is being incontinent, the incontinent (i) has belief (b), since he needs it to focus his appetite in this situation; (ii) does not have (b) as a premise of an inference whose first premise is (a), since appetite has detached (b) from (a) and attached (b) to appetite. Cf. note to 1152a15.

1147a32 'he has (b) . . . is sweet' Alternatively (i) 'everything sweet is pleasant' and (ii) 'this is sweet' might be taken as two distinct beliefs, in which case 'this [belief] is active' (i.e. not merely potential) will refer to (ii).

Grammatically, 'Hence this belief . . . ' might refer to (a) rather than (c); but (a) hardly tells him to avoid this particular thing.

1147b9 'premise' (*protasis*) 'Proposition' is a less likely rendering; in that case (c) would be intended. If 'premise' is correct, it refers either to the whole of (b) or to (ii); see note to 1147a32, 'Last term' (for 'term' cf. note to 1142a21) also refers to this 'last premise'.

1147b11 'Or rather . . . ' 'Rather' is supplied, but seems necessary; Aristotle is agreeing that in every case the incontinent person has the second premise. When he is being incontinent, he is in the condition described in 1147a18-24, since he is not performing an inference from his correct universal belief (a) to the conclusion (c), but merely saying the words.

1147b16 'dragged about' I.e. detached from the correct principle (a), and attached to appetite. Socrates is correct in thinking that some type of ignorance is needed to explain incontinence; but, contrary to Socrates, incontinence does not require a change of mind about such general principles as (a).

1147b24 'choiceworthy in themselves' Cf. 1110b3, 1129b1; see UNCONDITIONAL. Continence and incontinence have a limited range for the same reason that temperance has; see note to 1118a23.

1147b35 The winning boxer in the Olympics of 456 was called Anthropos (see HUMAN BEING).

1148a3 'Either unconditional (haplōs) **or partial'** might less plausibly be attached to 'incontinence' rather than to 'vice'. In that case it will presumably refer to two types of simple incontinence.

1148a17 'decides on them' Cf. 1119a1; 1146b22; 1150a19-23, b29; 1151a7, 22; 1152a4, 15-24. The intemperate person has a settled decision and policy of pursuing the bodily pleasures before him; this is what he mistakenly regards as the good to be pursued, 1113a28. Hence he does not suffer the conflicts of the incontinent; but cf. 1166b5-29.

1148b2 'vice' (mochthēria) See VICE. In 1148a3, b10, 'vice' = kakia.

1148b32 'women' Aristotle relies on the association between 'incontinence' (akrasia) and being overcome or failure to control (kratein). He means that women are by nature the passive partners in sexual intercourse.

1149a10 'only by perception' I.e. like beasts. See 1147b5, ANIMAL #1.

1149a33 'it is right' When we act on emotion (thumos; evidently Aristotle has ANGER especially in mind here) we have some beliefs about the RIGHTNESS of what we are doing—we are not simply moved by pleasure or pain. For this contrast cf. 1146b23, 1151a23, 1152a6. 'As though' indicates that we are not acting on a genuine DECISION here; see 1111b18. Pleasure, however, provides a reason for action by itself.

1149b4 The actions considered here are pardonable not because they are involuntary, but because they reflect pardonable lapses in human nature (1110a23), expressing tendencies that we recognize as appropriate for a human being (1115b8), though they have misled someone on this occasion. No such excuse can be given for the excessive appetites of the incontinent person. (The point here is different from the point at 1136a5, where Aristotle refers to involuntary but unpardoned actions.)

1150a1 'madmen' Having decision and RATIONAL CALCULATION is necessary for the possibility of virtue, vice or incontinence. The comment on madmen suggests that someone incapable of being moved by decision is also incapable of any of these states.

'less grave' Cf. *Pol.* 1253a31.

1150a4 'For in each . . . ' Lit. 'for always the badness of what lacks an origin is less destructive, and understanding is an origin'. Even soulless things, if they are natural, have an internal origin of some of their movements (see NATURE); and so do beasts. But only rational agents have an internal origin that explains their goodness and badness; it is subject to their choice and DECISION.

1150a13 'most people' See ETHICS #4, 1118b23, 1125b14, 1150b12, 1151a5, 1152a7. Deviations from the average or USUAL are what we remark most easily in calling someone incontinent, just as when we call someone tall. However, Aristotle recognizes that the average is not the proper norm for complete virtue.

1150a21 'for he is . . . ' The 'for' explains why 'intemperate', *akolastos*, is the right name for him. Aristotle relies on the association of *akolastos* with *kolazein* and CORRECTIVE TREATMENT (see also TEMPERANCE). He means, 'He is *akolastos*, incorrigible, because he is incurable and hence incorrigible'. He has 'no regrets', because he acts on his firm and settled DECISION. See 1105a33, 1110b19, note to 1148a17; but cf. 1166a29, notes to 1166b6-25.

1150a31 'softness' See 1116a14, 1145a35, 1148a11, 1179b33; *Rhet.* 1384a2. It implies inability, reluctance or refusal to undertake necessary pains and burdens; it often includes a suggestion of effeminacy (cf. 1150b15).

1150b2 'self-indulgent' The term used, *trupheros*, is cognate with *truphē*, 'luxury'; cf. 1145a35; *Pol.* 1295b17, 1310a23.

1150b19-28 Cf. 1151a1-3, 1152a17. It is easy to see how the weak incontinent conforms to the account given in 1147a31-5. But how does the impetuous incontinent conform to it? If he does not deliberate, how can he make the correct decision? See note to 1117a20, DECISION #4. He can make the right decision because of his previous deliberation even if he does not deliberate afresh on this occasion.

1150b22 'tickle someone else first' If A tickles B, he will expect B to tickle him back, and if A expects this, he will not find it so ticklish.

Cf. [*Probl.*] 965a11. 'Notice something in advance' marks the point of comparison with impetuous people.

1150b25 'ardent' (*melancholikos*) Cf. 1154b11. In Aristotle's physiological theory (see [*Probl.*] 30; *Parva Nat.* 453a19) excessively hot black bile (*melaina cholē*) makes someone easily excitable and prone to strong feelings when he is excited. Hence an ardent person is prone to incontinence.

1150b32 'incurable' See 1114a16, 1121a20, 1121b33, 1165b18, 1180a9. Why is the incontinent person curable? Aristotle seems to think that if he deliberates better (or, in the case of the impetuous person, if he deliberates at all on these occasions, 1152a27), he will see that it is not worthwhile to abandon his decision for the pleasure offered by incontinent action; and this conclusion is supposed to cure the incontinence.

1151a17 'assumptions' These are the basic principles and ORIGINS grasped by UNDERSTANDING, with no more basic principles (see *An. Post.* 72a14-24, *EE* 1227a5-13). Is Aristotle's claim here consistent with the role assigned to intelligence? See notes to 1144a8, 1144b3, 1145a4.

In stressing the limits of reason in ethical first principles Aristotle insists that more than purely cognitive training is needed. But habituated virtue itself requires intelligence (see note to 1144b3). Aristotle allows reason a role in forming the grasp of origins.

1151a26 'the origin' Cf. 1140b12, 1144a34. He has the right origin because he has the right wish and DECISION, though habitual incontinence would expose him to the corrupting effects of pleasure.

1151a29-b4 Why does Aristotle not say that the person who abides by the right principles and the person who abides by the wrong principles are continent in just the same way? For his justification see the note to 1118a23. The claims about pleasure and good, and about the corrupting effects of pleasure, will not apply in the same way to a 'continent' or 'incontinent' about bad principles. If I don't always follow my intemperate desire, it will not be because the pleasure at hand is too attractive (for the pleasure is what the intemperate decision decides on); nor will repeated failure to follow the intemperate decision make me more prone to intemperance. Since different psychological explanations and treatments are required, these are different conditions.

1151b2 For 'unconditionally' and 'in itself' see note to 1110a9; a19. If I do not choose F in itself, then I do not choose F unconditionally, but only with the added condition that F is a means to G. Here what the continent person abides by in itself and for its own sake is his true decision; it is because it is true that he abides by it. Since his true decision is his decision, he abides coincidentally by his decision, but he does not abide by it because it is his decision.

1151b4 'Now these are . . . ' Aristotle wants to distinguish continent people from those whose behaviour displays some similarity to continent behavior; as usual, he wants to identify the underlying state, not simply to classify types of behavior.

1152a1 'lacks them' On this difference between temperance and continence see the note to 1119a11.

1152a7 'for we have shown' 1144a23-b1 distinguishes intelligence from mere CLEVERNESS.

1152a13-14 'though they . . . decision.' Lit. 'and according to the account (or 'reason', *logos*) they are near, but differ according to the decision.' On difference in decision, see note to 1127b14.

1152a15 'willingly' See 1135b19-1136a5. 'In a way' perhaps indicates both the incontinent person's knowledge or belief (b) and his failure to connect it with his good principle (a) when he acts. See note to 1147a31.

1152b4 On the virtues see 1104b3, 1172a21; *EE* 1220a37, 1221b32. On happiness see 1098b25.

The discussion of pleasure follows naturally on the account of the virtues, to which the account of incontinence was an appropriate supplement. However, Aristotle discusses pleasure again in x 1-5 with no reference to the treatment in vii. This is one reason for thinking that the three books including the first treatment of pleasure were originally written for the *EE*; see note to 1129a3. But Aristotle may have meant them to be part of the *EN* too. Though the two discussions overlap in places, vii discusses and rebuts anti-hedonist arguments in some detail, and Aristotle may have thought this discussion worth keeping. See notes to 1153b10, 1175b34, 1176a30.

1152b8-24 On pleasure, the common beliefs, including those of the WISE, seem to be in sharp conflict. In this book Aristotle attacks the arguments against pleasure. In x he accepts some objections to the claims of pleasure.

1152b13 'nature' I.e. its natural, and therefore perfect and complete, state. See NATURE #2.

1152b25 'These arguments . . . ' Aristotle does not agree that pleasure is the final good; he only claims these objections do not, by themselves, show it is not. For an objection Aristotle accepts see 1172b26-35.

1152b26 Aristotle applies his distinction between types of goods to types of pleasures; see UNCONDITIONAL. On (iii) cf. 1113a31, 1173b20, 1176a22.

1152b28 'processes and becomings' See MOVEMENT. The difference between them is not exploited in vii; see note to 1173a31.

1152b33 In (ii) Aristotle rejects the identification of the pleasure with the process of recovery or the replenishment of an appetite or a lack. In recovery it is not the process, but the ACTIVITY of the healthy part, that is the source of pleasure; the pleasure itself neither is nor requires any process of recovery.

1153a6 'for as . . .' Here Aristotle seems to distinguish the activity in which pleasure is taken from the pleasure that is taken in it. Hence when he says in a14 that pleasure is *an* unimpeded activity, he probably does not mean that the pleasure taken in running is the unimpeded activity of running, but that the pleasure is an unimpeded activity additional to the running. If this is the view, it is not very different from the view in Book x; see note to 1174b31.

1153a10 'activities, and an end' Here Aristotle presents his own alternative to his opponents' view of pleasure as a becoming or process (cf. note to 1173a31). His view is fully developed in x 4.

1153a31 'painlessness' Aristotle rejects the exaggerated view (perhaps held by SPEUSIPPUS) previously rejected in 1104b24.

1153a35 'since there are . . .' Cf. 1104b24, note to 1118a23.

1153b1-12 'Moreover . . . activity.' Lit. 'Presumably it is also necessary, if there are unimpeded activities of each state, whether the activity of all of them is happiness, or of some one of them, if it is unimpeded, for it to be most choiceworthy; and pleasure is this.' Some resolutions of the ambiguities in the Greek would require us to ascribe a hedonist argument to Aristotle here. But probably the argument is meant to show not that pleasure is the highest good, but that for all the objections it still might be; cf. notes to 1152b35, 1173b31. Pleasure meets one necessary condition for happiness, since it is an unimpeded activity; and so the right sort of pleasure might, as far as this goes, be the activity that is happiness. Aristotle's own view on this question is explained only when he explains more fully the relation between the activity that is pleasure and the activity in which the pleasure is taken; see 1175a19. Nothing in Book vii requires him to deny that these two activities are different; cf. note to 1153a6.

1153b14-25 Aristotle rejects the identification of happiness with virtue; cf. 1095b31. The virtuous person who is tortured can be brave, but he is hindered from activating his other capacities; hence his activity cannot be complete. On FORTUNE see 1099a31; *EE* viii 2; *Phys.* 197b25.

1153b24 'no longer . . . ' Good fortune is subject to the limits that apply to the goods described in 1129b2 (see note).

1153b32 'divine' See GOD #4.

1154a1 Aristotle assumes that happiness is the highest good including all goods (HAPPINESS #2). Hence if pleasure is not a good, there is no reason to expect happiness to include pleasure; but then we will be in conflict with the common belief that happiness must include pleasure and exclude pain.

1154a22 For this procedure see ETHICS #7.

1154b9-13 'However . . . intense desires' Aristotle contrasts (a) normal people who are used to the pains involved in natural processes and exertions, (b) young people for whom natural processes are actually pleasant, and (c) ardent people, for whom the natural processes are abnormally painful.

1154b26 The GOD is better than we are because he can attain all at once what we can obtain only to some degree over time. Complete human happiness must be complex, and must include various activities if we are to approximate to the happiness that is complete all at once Cf. *Met.* 1072b14-20.

Book VIII

1155a4 'most necessary' We might expect examples of the instrumental value of friendship, but not all the examples are easily understood that way. Aristotle seems to mean more generally that friendship is a necessary part of any tolerable human life.

1155a22 Friendship and justice; viii 9-11. Concord; ix 6.

1155a29 'also fine' 'Fine' repeats the claim in 'a virtue or involves virtue' in 1155a4. Friendship might be necessary for a good life, as FORTUNE and pleasure are, without being admirable and praiseworthy (cf. 1101b11, 1109b31), as a person's own achievement; hence Aristotle is careful to insist that friendship is also praiseworthy. See note to 1159a23; 1169a8, 35.

1155b1 In his ethical argument Aristotle likes to avoid digressions into cosmology or other non-ethical areas, thinking them inappropriate; cf. 1096b31, 1159b23; *GC* 316a11-14; *EE* 1217a3, 1218b33. For the disputes referred to here see 1159b12-24; Plato, *Lys.* 214a.

1155b15 'more and less' The mss. add: 'We have spoken about them previously.' These words are probably spurious; they may refer to *Catg.* 6b20-7.

1155b18 'lovable' See CHOICEWORTHY. For the three objects of love see 1104b30.

1155b21-7 Here Aristotle distinguishes (a) what is lovable unconditionally, (b) what is lovable for (or to; cf. note to 1113a27) each person, and (c) what appears lovable to each person. This division needs to be compared with iii 4. See also UNCONDITIONAL, 1156b13.

1155b31 'for his own sake' Apparently this does not apply to wine because it has no choices, desires or aims of its own. We regard a friend's having certain aims and desires as a good reason (under certain conditions) for us to satisfy them. This is the same attitude that we take to our own aims and desires.

1156a4 'must have goodwill' The definition of goodwill implies that in all friendships A must wish good to B for B's sake. But see note to 1156a10.

1156a5 'from one . . .' Lit. 'because of (*dia*) one of the three things mentioned above'. The different types of friendship are 'for' (*dia*) character, utility and pleasure. Here '*dia*' might refer either to the final or to the efficient CAUSE of the friendship. (Cf. 'They're hanging men and women for the wearing of the green', clearly with an efficient-causal rather than a final-causal sense.) Most probably it refers to both; 1156a31, 1172b21 associate '*dia*' clearly with the final cause.

1156a10 'in so far as . . .' Probably Aristotle means to restrict the extent of goodwill in the incomplete friendships (those for utility and pleasure). In these A wishes good to B only in so far as B is useful or pleasant to A, not for B's own sake. 1167a10-21 seems to exclude unconditional goodwill from the incomplete friendships; cf. 1156b8; 1157a15, 18; 1164a10.

The three types of love are literally 'because of (*dia*; see note to 1156a5) the pleasant', 'because of the useful' and 'because of being such' (*poios*, i.e. a certain sort of person).

1156a24 On age and youth see HUMAN BEING #10.

1156a31 'hosts and guests' (*xenikē*) If A is an Athenian and B is a Spartan, each is the *xenos* of the other if A provides B with hospitality in Athens and B does the same for A in Sparta, and they provide each other with other sorts of reciprocal mutual aid.

1156b7-10 Aristotle implies that in the best kind of friendship three conditions coincide:

(1) A loves B for B's own sake.

(2) A loves B for what B really is.

(3) A loves B because B has a virtuous character.

He suggests that each of these conditions implies the other two. He defends the connection between (2) and (3) in 'they are good in themselves' (i.e. their good character is an essential property of them). To connect (1) and (2) he seems to assume that A would not find B worth loving for B's own sake if he did not love B for himself, for what B essentially is, and A would not love B for what B essentially is if B were not essentially good (cf. 1157a18).

1156b12 'enduring' See note to 1100b11. Complete stability is not guaranteed; see 1165b23.

1156b13 'Each of them . . .' Cf. note to 1155b21-7.

1156b15 On pleasure see 1099a7, 1176a10.

1156b26 'Moreover they need . . .' Lit. 'time and accustoming are needed'; cf. 1157a11, 1158a15, 1167a11.

1156b33 'This sort . . .' Aristotle now exploits the comparison of the three types of friendship to explain the ways in which the inferior types do and do not count as friendship.

1157a18 'Clearly, however . . .' Cf. 1156b7-10. Bad people can find some pleasure in features of each other (cf. 1159b10, 1166b13), but a bad person, Aristotle assumes, cannot find pleasure in the other person himself—only in some non-essential property of him.

1157a25-32 Aristotle does not say that the friendships are HOMONYMOUS. But his reasons for recognizing different species of friendship are similar to his reasons for recognizing homonymy; he wants to explain the common beliefs and to justify them as far as possible. His view here seems to be that there is one DEFINITION of friendship, which is fully satisfied only by complete friendship, and is only partly satisfied by friendships for pleasure and utility; see 1158b1-11. Cf. the relation suggested in *EE* 1236a7-32, b17-27.

1157b4 'friends coincidentally' In this case A is not a friend of B himself, but of the pleasant or useful features that coincidentally (non-essentially) belong to B.

1157b18 'live together' See note to 1097b9. Aristotle is not thinking of people living in the same house (which was not a very important centre of a Greek man's life), but of shared activities; hence they 'spend their days' in the ways described in ix 12.

1157b31 'and what makes . . .' The argument implies that a good person wishes good because of his DECISION (#5). Like the virtues, friendship is associated with the appropriate state and decision.

1158a2 On youth and old age see HUMAN BEING #10.

1158a10 On number of friends see 1171a6.

1158a22 A BLESSEDLY HAPPY person requires friendship as part of his life, as Aristotle argues more fully in ix 9.

1158a24 'The Good Itself' This is probably a joke about the Platonic Idea discussed in i 6.

1158a31 'witty' See notes to 1128a4, 1176b14. These favourites of tyrants cannot be expected to have the virtue of wit; if their main object is to please the tyrant, they will tend to be buffoons – not the sort of condition a virtuous person would tolerate.

1158b11-28 The threefold division of friendships between equals is meant to apply to unequals too. Aristotle does not say so here, but see 1162a34-b4.

1158b29-1159a3 The type of EQUALITY relevant in friendship is not the proportional equality of 1131a11, but numerical equality; the friendship is in danger if this is violated too seriously. Cf. note to 1163b11.

1159a3-12 The puzzle is this:

(1) The greatest good is to be a god.

(2) If you are a god you have no friends.

(3) If I am your friend, I don't wish you to have no friends.

(4) Hence I do not wish you to be a god.

(5) Hence I do not wish the greatest good to you.

Though (2) and (3) are not explicit in the text, they seem to be needed.

Aristotle's reply assumes a distinction between (1) and the claim:

(1a) The greatest good for you is to become a god.

Though (1) is true, (1a) is false, because you cannot both remain in existence and become a god. Becoming a god is the replacement of you by a god, not a further state of you. Since the only way for you to be a god would be to remain in existence and to become a god, and this is impossible, being a god is not a possible good for you; it could only be a good for the god who replaces you. Hence (5) does not follow from (4). See also 1166a20.]

1159a7 'For [if . . .]' This might less plausibly be translated 'For he will no longer be our friend, and hence will not be a good for us . . .'.

1159a12 'to himself' On self-love see ix 4, 8.

1159a12-28 The connection between this section and a28 ff. is not clear. All Aristotle shows here is that the many value being loved for itself, not merely as a means to being honoured. How is this connected with the point of a28 ff., that friendship consists more in loving than in being loved? Perhaps Aristotle means that if we see we value the passive aspect of friendship for itself, we will also more easily see reason to value the active aspect; see note to 1167b17.

1159a13 Love of HONOUR (see iv 4) makes someone susceptible to the attention of flatterers (see iv 6). In the right conditions one person's vices encourage further vices in others. This point might be usefully considered for the other Aristotelian virtues and vices too (cf. 1121b3-12).

1159a23-33   On love by mothers cf. 1161b26, 1166a5, 1168a25.

1159a33-b2   See 1155a29. We now explain why friendship is a virtue and praiseworthy; its active aspect is a praiseworthy ACTIVITY.

1159b2-10   On the virtuous see notes to 1156b12, 1157a18. On the vicious see 1166b6-29, 1172a9; *EE* 1239b11. For the vicious person's stability cf. notes to 1148a17, 1150a21, 1150b29. The vicious person has no reason to value his vicious friend's vice for its own sake as a good. He may find it pleasant because of the similarity to his own character. But this will be only one of the many pleasures the vicious person pursues because of his decision; his friend cannot rely on him when something pleasanter comes along. The virtuous person, by contrast, values virtuous action as good in themselves.

1159b10 'useful or [lit. 'and'] **pleasant . . .'**   These should be either (a) useful friends and pleasant friends who are not vicious, or less probably (b) vicious people who are both useful and pleasant, not just one of the two.

1159b12-24   The common beliefs in 1155b1-6 reflect over-emphasis on friendship for utility.

1159b25 'at the beginning'   See 1155a22. Cf. 1162a29.

1159b32   Aristotle's claim shows that 'companion' indicates a relatively close and long-term relationship of habitual companions rather than, e.g., people making just one journey together.

1160a4 'becomes more unjust'   See 1130a5. Justice is concerned with the COMMON good of a community (1129b17), and the growth of friendship will increase the desire to treat other people justly. We might be inclined to see possible conflicts between the demands of friendship and the good of a community (suppose the good of the community requires the sacrifice of my friend's interests). Here Aristotle will see conflicts between two types of friendships. It is only in the best community that such conflicts will not happen—elsewhere the states of character required by the community will not be the same as those of the virtuous person (cf. 1130b29; *Pol.* iii 4).

1160a5 'more shocking'   Cf. 1130a5.

1160a8-30   The other communities are parts of the political community because each is affected by its relation to other social institutions and the political community regulates them for the common good —Aristotle mentions religious festivals as an example. The comprehensive character of POLITICAL SCIENCE corresponds to the comprehensive character of the political community; cf. *Pol.* 1252b27-31, 1278b15-30, 1280b23-1281a4. Partly, Aristotle is describing the activities of states he knows. But he also thinks these activities are essential for happiness, and hence wants them extended beyond their present scope; cf. 1180a24-9.

1160a11 'common advantage' Cf. 1129b14-19. Aristotle does not say here that the city aims only at advantage. He leaves room for the important further aims mentioned in *Pol.* 1280a25-1281a4.

1160a19 'Religious societies' are associated with dining clubs because the religious sacrifice of animals would be an occasion for a common meal.

1160a23 'life . . .' Something seems to have been lost from the text here.

1160a31 For detailed discussion of these political systems and their changes see *Pol.* iii 7-8, 14-17; iv-vi.

1160a34 'polity' Aristotle uses *politeia* both for a political system or constitution in general and for what he calls the timocracy; see *Pol.* 1279a37.

1160a28 On rule over slaves see 1161b3; *Pol.* i 4, 1254b2-24, 1255b16-22.

1161a9 'free' See FREEDOM. For this feature (in Aristotle's view, a regrettable feature) of democracy see *Pol.* 1310a31 (associated with *eleutheria*; see GENEROUS). It is not a vice confined to democracy; cf. 1180a26.

1161a35 The SOUL uses the body as its instrument. See *De An.* 412b10-413a3; *Part. An.* 642a12; *Pol.* 1254a34, b4.

1161b2 'soulless things' See note to 1155b31; 1157b29. We can benefit these, since things are good and bad for them. But they have no aims and desires for us to consider and to share; hence we cannot respect or advance their aims by justice or friendship.

1161b2-8 The force of 'in so far as he is a human being' is not clear; cf. *Pol.* 1255b12. Aristotle admits that the natural slave is not just like an animal, but insists that he lacks a proper human soul, *Pol.* 1254b20-4, 1260a10. If he is a human being to any extent, must it not be to that extent unjust to treat him as a tool? Cf. note to 1177a8.

1161b14 'more like . . .' This suggests that it is more natural to speak of a *koinōnia* when some voluntary agreement is required than in e.g. families. Aristotle discusses the sort of agreement and association that is needed for a political community at *Pol.* 1280a25-1281a4.

1161b16-1162a4 On family friendships cf. 1134b11, 1167b33; *MM* 1211b18-39. The father identifies the child's interest with his own because he regards the child as his own in something like the way his tooth or foot is his own. The natural and social relation of father to child causes the father to extend his self-concern in these ways, and (to a lesser degree) causes the child to extend his self-concern to his parents. How is this kind of friendship related to the three species described in viii 1-6?

1161b19 The love of children for parents is important in education. See 1180b6.

1161b21 'Regards as his own' translates *sunoikeiousthai*, cognate with *oikeion* (see PROPER). 'Is attached' or 'becomes close' might also be adequate. Some reference to beliefs and attitudes seems implied by the remarks about knowledge and perception. These remarks also justify 'because he regards (they regard)' in 18, 19, 29, where the Greek is simply *hōs* ('as').

1161b26 'why mothers' If this is so, why are all these friendships said to depend on paternal friendship in particular?

1161b28 'other himself' 'Separate' explains what makes the child other. 'Himself' insists that the child is still the father himself – i.e. John Smith's son is another John Smith. Cf. 1170b6; *EE* 1245a29-35; *MM* 1213a12.

1161b31 'the same thing for both of them' Lit. 'the same for each other', i.e. the same blood, etc. An alternative translation, 'the same as each other', is less probable, since this claim seems to be *inferred* in 'Hence they are . . .'.

1162a9-16 Here (cf. note to 1161b16) Aristotle seems to connect fraternal friendship with his original three species. Because of their similarity and early associations brothers will find it easy to take the sort of interest in each other that complete friends take in each other; the sources of the friendship are different, but the sorts of attitudes and actions expected seem to be similar.

1162a16 'natural' Cf. *Pol.* 1252a26.

1162a21 'in their life' Cf. *Pol.* 1278b17-30, 1280a13. Aristotle is thinking of living well, not merely of staying alive and satisfying natural desires.

1162a25 'for virtue' Here again (see note to 1162a9) Aristotle refers to his threefold division. On women's virtue, cf. *Pol.* 1260a13.

1162a29 On justice and friendship see 1155a22, 1159b25.

1162a34-b4 The threefold division is applied to unequal friendships, though its application to family friendships is not explained. Here Aristotle considers specific conflicts and difficulties arising in friendships, following the principle of 1104a10, 1165a34.

1162b6 The discussion of conflicts is a further defence of the claim of complete friendship to be complete. It avoids the conflicts and quarrels that make the others fall short of complete friendship; cf. 1156b17, 1157a20, 1159b4. This is partly because virtuous friends have more

364

reasonable expectations of each other, partly because they are more reasonable in judging each other's success or failure in fulfilling these expectations; see 1163a21-9, 1164b1.

1162b36 DECISIONS are concerned with what promotes ends. Ordinary people may wish for FINE things, but when they have to act on some wish, the wish that forms their decision is not their wish for the fine, but their wish for some other pleasure or good to themselves. The virtuous person is different because his wishes for what is fine are not ineffective; they are focused by deliberation on decisions to do fine actions.

1163a21 A virtuous person in a friendship for utility will not be a dupe (1165a31); but he will still consider what is fine.

1163b3 HONOUR is the reward that the magnanimous person expects for his benefits to others; see 1124b9 (though he does not benefit others only for the sake of honour, he will form friendships for honour with some people). Honour as a reward for service: 1134b6.

1163b11 'corresponds to worth' Cf. 1158b27, 1159a35, 1162b2. The point here is consistent with 1158b29. The friend's worth determines what sort of good he should get, and friends of different worth will be due different goods. But the quantity of one good should be equal to the quantity of the other, as far as this is determinable and possible; that is what prevents friendship from collapsing into entirely one-sided 'public service' (1163a29).

Book IX

1163b32 There is no break between Books viii and ix. Aristotle continues the discussion begun in viii 13. On proportion in exchange see 1132b31, 1133a31, note to 1163b11.

1164a10 'not fond of the other himself' See note to 1156a10.

1164a12 'in itself' Probably this abbreviates 'in which each loves the other in himself, not coincidentally, i.e. for what he is'; cf. note to 1156b7-12.

1164a17 'pleasure for pleasure' One had the pleasure of listening to the music, and the other the pleasure of anticipating payment.

1164b1 'decision' See note to 1162b6; 1163a31-3. Sophists like Protagoras (see Plato, *Prot.* 318d-e) offered general moral, political and rhetorical instruction, claiming to equip a pupil for success in public life, but without any systematic inquiry into the justification of the assumptions they relied on. This feature of sophists aroused the hostility of both Plato and Aristotle. Aristotle's claims about philosophy contrast sharply with his attack on sophistry: see 1180b35, 1181a13; *Top.* 165a19-31; *Met.* 1004b22-6. The philosopher has a decision different from the sophist's, and so deserves a different response. Aristotle speaks of his philosphical colleagues in the Academy as friends (1096a13); cf. 1172a5, 1177a34.

1164b20 On when the price should be fixed, cf. 1133b1. These transactions between friends are intended to follow the principles of justice in exchange.

1164b23 'Or must . . .' I.e. instead of obeying his father's instructions. It is assumed that someone has a general obligation to obey his father's orders, an obligation that creates conflicts (cf. 1149b8).

1165a3 'being finer or more necessary' Cf. note to 1127a4, on the virtue similar to friendship. Aristotle's examples here show why he thinks EXACT and useful ethical rules cannot be found. The USUAL rules we can find are liable to exceptions reflecting the fine or expedient consequences of violating the rules. Cf. note to 1109a30.

1165b8 Here we face the difficulties in the best type of friendship. Since this is concerned with the friend's character, the friendship is threatened when the character changes. Aristotle urges that only deterioration to incurable vice (cf. note to 1150b32) should break the friendship. The importance of shared activities and characters in the best friendship makes it unreasonable to continue a friendship with someone who has become vicious beyond recovery.

1165b16 'What is bad (*ponēros*) is not lovable . . . neither to love what is bad (*philoponēros*), nor . . . bad (*phaulos*).' 'Vicious' renders *mochtheros*. No clear distinction between the three terms appears here (see VICIOUS).

1165b23 Probably Aristotle does not mean here that the inferior person is really virtuous; if he were, then could the superior person not still admire his character and share his activities? Probably we are to suppose two developing characters (as suggested in 1157a10, 1162a9-15), one of which develops into a virtuous character while the other does not.

1165b31 Even here the friend's present character is not all that matters; we should still be concerned about him because of the past association. Why should we still be concerned, in Aristotle's view? And how are his reasons related to his general views on friendship?

1166a1 In ch. 4-9 Aristotle describes the different attitudes that belong to friendship, and argues that they are both psychologically intelligible and rationally defensible in a virtuous person. First he derives the features of friendship from features of the good person's attitude to himself. This is important because it shows:

1. Self-love is sometimes good, since the virtuous person has it (ix 8).

2. The friend is another self (1166a31, note to 1161b28), in so far as we treat him as we treat ourselves.

3. We can justify friendship if we can justify treating other people as other selves (ix 7,9).

1166a12 'As we have said' See 1113a29, 1176a15.

1166a13-22 The good person has a coherent and steady outlook on his life that gives precedence to his reason and understanding; see note to 1097b22; 1168b30, 1178a2. Here Aristotle does not mean that all the good person wants to do is think, but that he wants to actualize his reason in directing his desires and actions; hence he wants to act on his virtuous decision.

1166a20 'become another' The example about god makes the point suggested in the note to 1159a3-12. Concern for myself requires concern for me as the sort of being that I essentially am.

1166a29 'never regrets' The good person will surely be sorry if things have gone wrong, e.g. if his children have all died, or his friend was crippled in an accident. However, he will not decide he should change his principles, or that he could reasonably have made past decisions different from those he made. Hence he will have nothing to blame or reproach himself for. The major component of happiness is acting virtuously; and this does not require success in the results it aims at. See note to 1100b32.

1166a33 'Is there . . .' Even if we cannot properly speak of Smith's friendship to Smith, we can speak of friendship between different parts of Smith's SOUL (cf. 1138b15), corresponding to his different DESIRES.

1166b6-25 Aristotle argues that vicious people fail to meet the various conditions for friendship to themselves. But does he ascribe to the vicious the sort of psychic conflict that in fact belongs only to the incontinent? See notes to 1149a17, 1150a21; 1150b32. If the vicious person has the wrong first principles, how can he regret his pursuit of pleasure? He is simply following his principles. In 1166b7-10, 18-22 Aristotle perhaps suggests the answer. An intemperate person (a) has a conception of his good that requires him to satisfy his strongest appetites for pleasure; to do this he will plan prudently, e.g., to make money, form friendships etc. But (b) he also has strong appetites for immediate pleasures that will disrupt his more prudent plans — hence his appetite and his wish will conflict. Now in these cases, if the appetite is strong enough the intemperate person's initial wish gives way, and he forms a new rational plan. Since he has strong appetites and aversions, it becomes rational for him to act on them (e.g. on his intemperate appetites or his cowardly fears) if the pain resulting from their frustration will be greater than the pain resulting from their satisfaction. Hence he will act on his rational wish and decision; but since the rational choice he acts on is different from the one he would have acted on if he had not had such strong particular appetites, he will regret the necessity for acting on the choice he does act upon. He will suffer conflict no less than the incontinent person suffers it, but a different conflict with different results.

1166b20-2 'Part' supplied.

1166b24 'regret' Unlike the virtuous person, the vicious person does not value acting on the right decision for its own sake; he values it only as a means to the satisfaction of appetite. Hence he will be disturbed by failures that will not disturb the virtuous person; and these failures will multiply if his decision is liable to change in the way suggested above.

1166b30 'goodwill' See 1155b32, 1157b18, 1158a7.

1166a35 'contestants' This is the wish without decision mentioned in 1111b24.

1167a10 'go to any trouble' Concern for someone's good for his own sake is not enough for regarding him as a friend or other self. This requires time and familiarity (1157a10, 1162a12), which will also produce the FONDNESS that is found in friendship (1126b21).

1167a11 'grow accustomed' See note to 1156b26.

1167a12 'It does not . . .' See note to 1156a10.

1167a14 'For a recipient . . .' Probably Aristotle is contrasting goodwill, as the just and proper reaction to being benefited, with the calculating expectation of future benefits that belongs to friendship for utility. Why, however, does friendship for pleasure not produce goodwill? Probably Aristotle means that such friendship implies no desire for the benefit of the other, whereas friendship for utility at least implies a desire for his benefit as a means to one's own benefit.

1167a33 'wants the same thing' Or 'wishes' (*boulesthai*, see DESIRE). Cf. Kant *KpV* Ak. p. 28. Euripides' *Phoenissae* is about the bitter and unscrupulous struggle between Eteocles and Polyneices for absolute power in Thebes.

1167b2 'political friendship' Cf. 1160a8-14.

1167b4-16 Concord, resulting from community and association for a common good, is a foundation of justice and of a stable friendship. This is easier for virtuous people (see note to 1162b6; 1164b1); for they are not concerned with getting some good at the other's expense, but with virtuous action, which benefits all of them. Contrast the greedy (cf. notes to 1129a32, 1130a16) attitude of the vicious friend with the sort of competition between virtuous people described in 1169a6-11, 28.

1167b17-33 The active aspect of friendship was mentioned in 1159a27. Aristotle now seeks to prove what he earlier assumed, that the active aspect is valuable for its own sake. He presents and rejects the common view that assumes a person values for its own sake nothing but states of himself alone that do not essentially involve the states of another (cf. note to 1169b22). On this view the benefactor cares only about the return he hopes for. Aristotle argues that active friendship is a NATURAL tendency of human beings even apart from any hope of reward.

1167b32-1168a5 Cf. 1120b13, 1134b10, 1161b18. Though he does not say so, Aristotle here applies the explanation of parents' love for their children to active friendship in general.

1167b34 'his own product (*ergon*)' See FUNCTION. The connection between *ergon* as product and *ergon* as function is important in the argument.

1168a6 'actualization' (*energeia*) See ACTIVITY. 'Activity' is not a suitable translation here, since the product is treated as an *energeia* of the producer (contrast 1094a4-5). Both the exercise of skill in the productive activity and the product resulting from this exercise actualize the agent's capacities, and so express his being. See also 1176a3.

1168a7 'The product . . .' Or 'the producer in his actualization is, in a way, the product.' The product is only the actualization in a way, not unconditionally, *haplōs* (see UNCONDITIONAL). It is the exercise of productive skill that is the primary actualization of the producer; that is the actualization 'indicated' by the product. Since the agent values the exercise of his capacities, he values the product (or, in the case of friendship, the beneficiary) that expresses the actualization. This is a source of pleasure to him, for the reasons explained in 1174b11.

This account of love for a beneficiary of one's benevolence does not explain all the special features of friendship for a person—those that reflect his being another self valued for his own sake (see note 1161b2). These features are relevant in ix 9.

1168a10 'fine' This explains the attitudes of the magnamimous person (1124b9).

1168a25 On mothers, see notes to 1159a28, 1161b26.

1168a29 The second puzzle (the first is discussed in ix 7) results from (a) the common belief that self-love is bad (*Rhet.* 1389b35, cf. 1168b25; *Pol.* 1263b1; Plato, *Laws* 731e), and (b) Aristotle's claim in ix 4 that the virtuous person's self-love is good. In his defence of (b) Aristotle argues that (a) is too sweeping, because it overlooks some relevant examples, though it is right for the examples it considers (see ETHICS #7).

1168a31 'of his own accord' Lit. 'from himself'. The vicious person (cf. 1167b15) does nothing willingly and spontaneously, without calculating his own selfish interest. Less probably the phrase means 'away from himself', i.e. separated from his selfish interest.

1168b19 'contested' Or 'fought over', i.e. the objects pursued in competition. See 1169a21, note to 1129a32; *Pol.* 1271b8; Plato, *Rep.* 586b-c. It is because these are contested goods (cf. note to 1167b4), where my gain is your loss, that self-love about these is bad for other people, and hence (cf. 1121a29, 1123a32; FINE #4) regarded as vicious (cf. 1169a6-11).

1168b26 'excel' Here and in the rest of the chapter Aristole describes the virtuous self-lover in competitive terms, to distinguish his sort of competitiveness from the bad kind expressing GREED and excessive love of HONOUR. This is the only sort of competitiveness appropriate to the magnanimous person; cf. 1124b23, note to 1136b22.

1168b31 'a city and . . .' cf. 1166a17, note to 1178a2. A complex system is most of all its most CONTROLLING (or important) part because this part represents the interests of the whole; the direction and fortunes of the whole depend on this part. The rational part controls a human being in so far as its condition and outlook both reflects and determines the state of the whole person by the way it controls or fails to control his actions.

1168b34 Aristotle refers to the association of continence, *enkrateia*, with mastery, *kratein*. I have mastery over my appetites when my understanding has mastery over them, since my understanding is to be identified with myself.

1169a1 'voluntary' Though Aristotle allows VOLUNTARY action on non-rational DESIRES, he thinks it is most voluntary when it results from rational desire and DECISION. For this is most of all *my* own voluntary action, in which the origin is most of all in *me*.

1169a6 'fine . . .' See note to 1162b35, FINE #1. The vicious person cares about something's being good in itself, as certain pleasures are, in his view. But he does not care about its being FINE and praiseworthy (see note to 1155a29).

1169a8 'contends' Perhaps 'competes'. See notes to 1168b26, 1122b22.

1169a18-25 This is the attitude of the magnanimous person

(1124b6-9, 23-6) displaying bravery (1116a10-15, 1117b9-20). The virtuous person's self-love will make him want to do virtuous and fine actions; these are the actions required by the best sort of friendship and by the COMMUNITY that the virtuous person belongs to. Hence self-love is not only the paradigm of friendship (as ix 4 has argued); it is also the basis for friendship, since the virtuous person's self-love will move him to the fine actions that are expected of friends.

1169a32-4 'It is also . . .'   This principle is followed in 1171b19.

1169a35-b1   Clearly the virtuous person's attitude to his friend's good is not entirely selfless and self-forgetful. But Aristotle takes it to be consistent with concern for the friend's good for his own sake. It is because this sort of concern is fine that the virtuous person thinks it is part of his good. Hence the virtuous friend never 'sacrifices himself', if that implies sacrifice of his own interests to another's; but he is no less concerned for the friend's good for the friend's own sake than a 'self-sacrificing' person would be. That is why, in Aristotle's view, the virtuous person is a self-lover without being selfish.

1169b3   The third puzzle (cf. note to 1168a23) arises from Aristotle's answer to the second. He has argued that the virtuous self-lover will be concerned with his friends because he is concerned with the fine. But what is fine about concern for friends? Are they not just an instrumental good, and hence not fine, but dispensable for a happy person? Aristotle answers this question here.

1169b4-8   Aristotle is not claiming that if someone is HAPPY and BLESSED without friends, he needs friends as well. He is claiming that someone cannot be happy without friends, so that friends are necessary for happiness, and that some of the happy person's activities are essentially shared with friends.

1169b10-16   The importance of active beneficence has been discussed in ix 7. The role of friends in good and bad FORTUNE is discussed in ix 11.

1169b16 'solitary'   See note to 1097b9.

1169b22-8   The false belief underlying one side of the puzzle is exposed. As in ix 7 (cf. note to 1167b17) the objection assumes friendship is only an instrumental good because it recognizes only friendship for advantage or pleasure. When we recognize the best sort of friendship, we can also see why this kind of friendship can be an intrinsic good.

1169b26 'imported'   Cf. 1099a16.

1169b28-1170a4   This argument rests on some assumptions that are explained in 1170a13 ff. Here it is assumed the good person enjoys his own virtuous activities, and hence enjoys his friend's too. The different uses of 'his own' (see PROPER) are important here. In b35 our friends' actions are not our own, since we do not do them ourselves. But in 1170a3-4 our friends' actions are our own, for reasons explained in 1170b5.

1170a7 'More continuous' indicates (cf. note to 1100b11; 1175a3) the importance of cooperation in shared activities.

1170a13 'nature' Cf. 1167b29. Aristotle explains how the preferences of the virtuous person in 1169b28 ff. are not his arbitrary inclinations, but the expression and realization of natural tendencies.

1170a16 On life, see 1097b33, and SOUL. Here as in 1168a5 the natural preference for life makes intelligible the preference for ACTIVITY over mere CAPACITY.

1170a20 'has definite order' Lit. 'is defined'. See note to 1173a16. Life by itself has a definite order in so far as human capacities fit each other in a mutually supporting and fulfilling way. The virtuous person does not invent an order, but develops the order that is already present in the natural capacities (as complete virtue does in vi 13), whereas the vicious person perverts and destroys the natural order by misusing his natural capacities; cf. note to 1166b6.

1170a23-5 Pain prevents the full actualization of our capacities; cf. 1153b16, 1175b17.

1170a29-b5 Steps (8)-(13) introduce self-awareness (see *De An.* iii 2) as a further good depending on the goodness of the activity we are aware of.

1170b5-7 Here (14) is the crucial premise. See 1156b17, note to 1161b28. The best kind of friend is referred to here, since he is the one whom the virtuous person regards as he regards himself. Since he regards his friend as he regards himself, he will want to be aware of his friend's activities as he is aware of his own.

Aristotle has argued that if I have a friend, then the friendship with him is a part of my good. But how does this show I have reason to acquire friends, or that I can't be happy without them? Aristotle needs to make it clear that I am better off if I have a friend to whom I take this attitude (cf. 1169b33, 1170a5). I extend my concerns and interests more widely, in a wider range of fine and virtuous activities, if I share them with a friend; hence I am better off if I have a friend than if I never have one; hence having friends is a part of my happiness.

1170b11 'live together' See 1095b30; notes to 1097b9, 1157b18.

1170b17 'whatever is . . .' Aristotle appeals to the COMPLETE and SELF-SUFFICIENT character of happiness, taking it to include everything good and choiceworthy; cf. notes to 1097b6, 1097b16-20.

1170b20 In ch. 10-12 Aristotle discusses some of the details of the friendship he has defended in ch. 9. In particular 1170b10-19 raise the questions: How many friends are needed for 'living together'? What sorts of obligations and activities should be involved in living together? **1170b31** On cities see *Pol.* 1326a5-b25. The use of 'HUMAN BEINGS' suggests that Aristotle means the total population of a city; in that case he is ruling out classical Athens as a city. A more moderate view results from taking 'human beings' to refer to the number of citizens (the only ones who are really parts, as opposed to necessary conditions, of a city); this number will exclude resident aliens, women, children and slaves. **1171a6** On the difficulty of having many friends see 1158a10. **1171a17 'ingratiating'** See note to 1127a8. Ingratiating people show to many people the attentions that are appropriate only to close (*oikeios; see* PROPER) friends, and so try to secure the favour due to close friends. They do not know what is required for the right sort of close friendship, and in fact all they have is the friendship of fellow citizens, despite their efforts to make it look like something more. **1171a21** This question was raised in 1169b13. **1171b3 'dexterous'** See 1128a17. Here as before dexterity requires someone to say the appropriate things, knowing the circumstances and feelings of the people involved. Here would be one occasion for the intelligent person to display CLEVERNESS. **1171b6 'manly'** This will also be a sign of magnanimity, 1124b9, 1125a9. **1171b19 'whenever they will . . .'** Here the friend inviting help follows the principle of 1169a32-4. Presumably, however, the friend who gives the help will do something finer if his help is more difficult for him to give. Aristotle does not seem to pursue the full implications of his own views here. **1171b29-1172a2** The argument of 1170a13-b12 is summarized here. **1172a8** Virtuous people's stability is contrasted with vicious people's instability. See notes to 1156b12, 1166b6, 1167b4. When virtuous people practise their virtues and express their characters towards each other, they benefit each other and so strengthen the friendship, while the opposite is true for vicious people.

Could someone take the virtuous person's attitude to his friend, and yet be intemperate and unjust in his attitude to everyone else? And could two people be friends on this basis, each admiring the virtue of the other as far as it goes? Aristotle might answer:

(1) Vice involves perverted affections and appetites, which are not easy to restrain at will; can such friends trust each other to restrain

the vice from its natural development (cf. 1140b12)?
(2) If someone really understands the value of virtuous friendship,
will he not also see the value of justice and temperance?

Book X

1172a16-27   On the importance of pleasure cf. ii 3, 1152b4.

1172a27-1172b7   Aristotle objects to a misinterpretation of his advice in 1103b26, 1109b1-12. The practical aim of ethics does not justify
pious frauds. These are self-defeating, since the facts (*erga*; see FUNC-
TION) make the extreme theories incredible. Someone who says pleasure
is base will not be able to avoid pursuing it himself on some occasions;
since he cannot live by the implications of his theory, the many will
neither believe in his sincerity nor take his theory seriously. Cf. note
to 1179a19.

1172b9   The argument of EUDOXUS looks more plausible when the
ambiguity in CHOICEWORTHY is remembered.

1172b26-35   Aristotle replies briefly, using Plato's *Philebus* 20d-22b,
to the hedonist arguments. His assumption – that if x is the good (i.e.
the highest good) nothing can be added to x to make the result a better
good than x – underlies the argument in 1097b16-20.

1173a1 'seem [good] to all'   Aristotle endorses common beliefs about
something's being a good, though he does not necessarily endorse all
universally agreed common beliefs; see ETHICS #4.

A less likely translation: 'Things that seem [true] to everyone we say
are [true].'

1173a5   As in vii, Aristotle answers some of the anti-hedonist objections. Here they are the preparation for his positive account in x 4.

'superior to themselves'   Cf. 1153b11.

1173a13 'quality'   The opponents assume that a good must be in the
category of quality (cf. 1096a19). Aristotle agrees with this for 'good'
as in 'good person', but not for 'good' as in 'good for a person'.

1173a16 'definite'   Cf. note to 1170a20. The first argument relies
on features of the experience of pleasure (i.e. we can be more or less
pleased). The second argument ('If, on the other . . .') relies on the claim
that some pleasures are more pleasant than others.

1173a31 'not even a process'   Aristotle replies to a criticism of
pleasure in Plato, *Phil.* 53c-54c. In 1153a7 he only discussed the view
that pleasure is a becoming. Here he seems to distinguish the generic
notion of process (or change; see MOVEMENT) from the specific process that is a becoming (*genesis;* see *Phys.* 225a12: something comes

374

into being when there is a becoming, and passes out of being when it undergoes destruction).

1173b1 'not possible to be pleased quickly' Even if I am enjoying watching a game that happens quickly, my enjoyment itself is not quick or slow.

1173b9 'They do indeed say . . .' The view is probably derived from Plato, *Phil.* 31e (though it is not necessarily the same view; see next note).

1173b11 'This does not . . .' Aristotle assumes that pleasure is a condition of the SOUL, not a purely bodily condition, since it requires awareness (and Plato recognizes this, *Phil.* 34a).

1173b20-5 In solution (1) does 'pleasant to x' mean 'it seems pleasant to x (though perhaps it is really not pleasant)', or 'it is really pleasant for x (though perhaps it would not be pleasant for someone else)'? See note to 1113a27. Aristotle eventually adopts solution (3) at 1175a21; but he still appeals to (1); see note to 1176a10.

1173b25 'choiceworthy, but not . . .' Solution (2) relies on the distinction between 'choiceworthy UNCONDITIONALLY' and 'choiceworthy in these conditions'.

1173b29 'the just person's pleasures' Cf. 1099a7-21.

1173b31-1174a8 Here as in 1172b26-35 Aristotle agrees that, despite his defence of pleasure as *a* good, it is not the only good or the highest good. He rejects the Eudoxan position that he left unrefuted, without endorsing it, in 1153b9-14.

1173b32 On flatterers see 1127a8.

1174a1 'Besides . . .' Cf. 1176b22, 1177a6; *EE* 1215b22. Aristotle appeals to the general principle stated in 1095b20.

1174a4 For a similarly counterfactual test (introduced by 'Moreover . . .') cf. 1097b3. Aristotle warns that his own account of pleasure as 'necessarily following' on activity does not imply that pleasure is the highest good.

1174a13 Here the positive account of pleasure begins; it was already anticipated at 1173a29, 1153a7-17. It relies on the distinction between processes which are incomplete ACTIVITIES, and complete activities; see also ACTION and PRODUCTION. Pleasure is not a process that has only an external goal; hence the arguments that rest on treating it as a process are irrelevant.

1174a19 'its form' See CAUSE. Here the form is closely associated with essence and DEFINITION; something achieves its form to the extent that it acquires the character that makes it the kind of thing that it is. The building of a temple takes time to acquire all that makes it a complete building of a temple; hence it takes time to achieve its form. An enjoyment does not take time to acquire all that makes it a complete enjoyment. Though certainly I might prefer my enjoyment to be prolonged, it is no more an enjoyment by being prolonged.

1174a21-3 'Moreover . . . each other.'   Lit. 'And in the parts and in the time they are all incomplete, and they differ in form from the whole and from each other.' The words 'they are all' must apparently refer to (a) processes such as temple-building, and 'they differ in form' must refer to (b) the parts of (a). The next sentence relies on the distinction between (a) and (b).

1174a26 'incomplete'   Even when any one of (b) is finished, it looks forward to a further production. This explains why the whole production (a) is incomplete at any time when it is still going on.

1174a27 'Hence . . .'   'Differ in form' refers to (b), and 'a process' to (a).

1174a30 'For if . . .'   First Aristotle considers locomotion as an example of (a), and then various possible examples of (b). Then ('And besides . . .') he takes walking, e.g. from London to Glasgow, as an example of (a), and its parts (e.g. walking from London to Birmingham, from Birmingham to Preston etc.) as examples of (b).

1174b2 'elsewhere'   E.g. *Phys.* v 1-4.

1174b9 'instant'   Lit. 'now'; cf. *Phys.* 218a6, 220a18. An instant is unextended; it is not a duration or an interval, and hence is not a part of time. There is no coming into being of pleasure because coming into being requires the parts to come into being one after the other, and pleasure is present as a whole all at once.

1174b14   'Faculty of perception' translates *aisthēsis*, lit. 'PERCEPTION' or 'sense', exercised in the ACTIVITY of perceiving. The 'object' (lit. 'perceptible' or 'thing perceived', *aisthēton*) is the special sensible (sight, sound etc; b27; note to 1142a27) or common or coincidental sensibles.

1174b17 'the subject that has it'   Lit. 'that in which it is'.

1174b25   The doctor is the efficient CAUSE, and health the formal cause, of being healthy. This does not mean that Aristotle intends the different ways of completing an activity (or 'bringing it to its goal', *teleioun*; see COMPLETE, note to 1097a28) to be the efficient and formal causes. On the contrary, they seem to be different final causes.

1174b31 'Pleasure completes . . .'   Probably Aristotle here distinguishes two types of final CAUSE—two ways in which an activity can achieve its END: (1) Perceiving is good as an end in itself, as the activity of a desirable capacity or state—the action has the state 'present' in it in so far as that is the state it actualizes. (2) The pleasure is a further end, another good in itself, which is consequent on our choosing the action as a good in itself. It is an extra good added to the good of the action as the 'bloom' of youth – the attractiveness of a youth which made him an object of desire and pleasure to an older man (1157a6-10) – is added to his youth. See also 1153a6.

1174b33 'consequent end' (Or 'supervenient end'; cf. 1104b4.) This is contrasted with the inherent or intrinsic end of the activity – i.e. the realization of the desirable state, which is an end in itself.

1175a5 'continuously' See note to 1170a6; 1154b20.

1175a18 'Do we choose . . .' Though Aristotle sets aside the question, his answer to it emerges from 1174a4 and from what he has just said. We do not choose life and its activities purely for the sake of pleasures; we choose for their own sakes the activities that constitute our living (cf. 1168a5). Nor do we choose pleasure purely for the sake of living; it is one of the desirable activities that constitute our living. See note to 1175b34.

1175a21-b1 Here Aristotle accepts solution (3) proposed in 1173b20-5. Just action and sunbathing are not two sources of a qualitatively uniform sensation in the way that two cows are sources of the same milk; we cannot ask how much sunbathing we would need to replace the pleasure lost by failing to do just actions. Since pleasures differ in species, Aristotle insists that the virtuous person must get the specific pleasure of virtuous action. He must enjoy it because it is virtuous; and that enjoyment will require him to value it as virtuous for its own sake. Cf. 1099a17, 1104b3.

1175a22 'species' (*eidos*)   Also translated 'form'. See note to 1174a19; DEFINITION.

1175b34 Aristotle makes it clearer here than in vii that the pleasure of e.g. fishing is not simply the unhindered activity of fishing itself, but a further activity (cf. 1153a12-15, note to 1153b10; but this is not clearly inconsistent with Book x). Though Aristotle does not say exactly what the extra end is, it is natural to think of the feeling of pleasure that is taken in a valued activity. Once we distinguish the activity and the pleasure, we can see that we do not choose life and its activities purely for the sake of pleasure; see note to 1175a18.

1176a10-24 The good person is the standard not only of what is a good pleasure but of what is really a pleasure. Here Aristotle seems to accept solution (1); see note to 1173b20. Vicious people are mistaken in their views about what is pleasant; they mistake what appears pleasant to them for what is really pleasant (really pleasant for them too, though not pleasant for them in their depraved condition). Cf. note to 1113a27.

1176a30 This summary places the discussion of pleasure after friend-ship, omitting the discussion of pleasure in Book vii. However, the sum-mary is too compressed to allow a firm inference about the question raised in the note to 1129a3.

1176a33 'not a state' See 1095b31, 1153b19.

1176b2 On types of activities see 1097a30-b11; HAPPINESS #2-3.

1176b5 'self-sufficient' A self-sufficient end

(a) is pursued for its own sake;

(b) is not pursued for the sake of anything else.

Here Aristotle says correctly that self-sufficiency implies (a), and that virtuous actions satisfy (a). Virtuous actions do not satisfy (b); see note to 1177b1.

1176b9 Aristotle deals with the claim of pleasure to be the highest good more fully than when he briefly dismissed it in 1095b19. He has now discussed the nature and varieties of pleasure, and can explain what error someone makes if that person identifies pleasure with happiness and does not (a) specify the type of pleasure, and (b) see that the value of the pleasure depends on the value of the associated activity.

1176b12 On powerful people cf. 1095b11.

1176b14 'witty' See notes to 1158a31, 1128a4. Here again these people do not have the virtue described in iv 8, but are more like the ingratiating people and flatterers of iv 6. Powerful people admired for their happiness have no more understanding of it than their imitators have; cf. 1159a12-17.

1176b20 'civilized' As opposed to slavish. Cf. 1177a7; HUMAN BE-ING #9.

1176b22 'boys' See 1174a1.

1176b24-35 To rule out amusement Aristotle appeals to the excellent person as the standard for selecting the worthwhile activities and plea-sures; see 1176a15.

1177a5 On 'serious' see EXCELLENT.

1177a8 On slaves see HUMAN BEING #9; notes to 1124b31, 1161b2. They lack the capacity for life according to reason, and so are incapable of happiness; see note on 1099b32; cf. 1178b27.

1177a14 'ruler and leader' This seems to refer to the practical func-tions of understanding. But Aristotle's next remarks refer to STUDY, not practical thought, as the activity of reason that is to be identified with its proper virtue. Perhaps he has two points in mind: (1) The ruling func-tions of reason show it is our best capacity. (2) Hence the best activity of all is the best activity of the best capacity – i.e. the activity of study. See also note to 1178a2.

1177a16 'Hence complete . . .' This need not mean that complete happiness is exclusively this activity. It may mean that for happiness to be complete it must include this activity. The same applies to 'express the supreme virtue' in a13. Cf. note to 1178b32.

1177a18 'We have said' Where? Not explicitly; but cf. 1139a6-17, 1141a18-22, 1143b33-1144a6, 1145a6-11. Aristotle does not say here that the activity of understanding that constitutes happiness is exclusively concerned with study.

1177a19 Aristotle argues by appeal to his previous criteria for happiness that

(a) study is the single activity that best fits the criteria for happiness; so that

(b) if happiness must be some single activity, study is the best candidate, and

(c) if happiness includes more than one activity, study will be the most important.

These do not imply that

(d) study is the whole of happiness.

But does Aristotle accept (d)?

1177a21 'most continuous' See notes to 1100b11, 1175a5.

1177a27 'found in study above all' The 'above all' allows us to say the life of study fails the conditions for self-sufficiency in 1097b6-21. A life consisting of study alone contains the most valuable single good; but it does not contain all the goods needed to make the life lack nothing; cf. note to 1169b4-8.

1177b1 'because of itself alone' Cf. note to 1176b2. Study is not chosen for any end wholly external to it. Aristotle's remarks here do not show that it cannot also be chosen for the sake of happiness (i.e. as a part of happiness). Cf. 1097b2. (An alternative translation, 'it is the only virtue chosen because of itself', is less well supported by the next clause.)

1177b18 'and are choiceworthy . . .' Lit. (1) 'and are choiceworthy not because of themselves' or (2) 'and are not choiceworthy because of themselves'. Whereas (2) appears to conflict with Aristotle's frequent claim (e.g. at 1176b8), (1) does not, and is preferable. Aristotle points out that virtuous action has two aspects. Campaigning against racism, e.g., is (a) a just action, and hence fine and choiceworthy in itself, and (b) aimed at a result wholly external to it, the passage of a law and its success in eliminating some racism. It is (b) which distinguishes these virtuous actions from pure theoretical study, and hence makes the morally virtuous person dependent on external circumstances. Cf. note to 1140b6.

1177b25 'complete span' See note to 1098a18; 1101a16.

1177b26-31 Study is the activity of the most divine part of a human being, and hence offers him a life that is more than merely human; cf. *Met.* 982b28-983a11.

1177b28 'Element' is supplied in the next two paragraphs.

'compound' Probably this is the compound of the understanding and the other parts of the SOUL. But perhaps it is the compound of soul and body. Cf. 1178a20.

1177b33 'pro-immortal' *(athanatizein)* Perhaps it means 'make oneself immortal'. But probably it is modelled on *mēdizein, lakōnizein,* used for pro-Medes (Persians) and pro-Laconians (Spartans).

'go to all lengths' Lit. 'do all things'.

1178a2 'if he is . . .' Or 'if it (i.e. understanding) is the controlling and better element in him'. See note to 1168b31. Some qualification is suggested by 'if understanding above all' in a7. Previously Aristotle has identified a person with his understanding because of its practical role; cf. note to 1177a14. If that is the understanding referred to again here, can Aristotle be supporting an exclusive concentration on study? In so far as we are understandings, study is our happiness; but since we are more than that, our happiness must include more than study; see note to 1178b5.

1178a9-1178b7 Aristotle supports his defence of the superiority of study as part of happiness. The activities of the other virtues depend on the human and non-divine parts of the compound (see note to 1177b28), and hence are subject to some of the limitations of human beings and their external circumstances. In particular, the virtues of character need external goods more than study needs them, and hence are more vulnerable to FORTUNE.

1178a16 Intelligence and virtue of character: see note to 1145a4.

1178a24 'external supplies' See GOOD.

1178a32 'power . . . freedom *(exousia)*' Bravery requires me to stand firm, but if I am so feeble that I am immediately overpowered, I will never manage to stand firm. If I never find anything that would appeal to my appetites, I lack the freedom or opportunity to be intemperate, and so cannot do what temperance requires. Aristotle does not say that I cannot be brave or temperate in these cases, but only that I cannot achieve the results aimed at by the virtues.

1178a34 'disputed' Aristotle usually takes decision to be the crucial aspect; see 1111b5, 1163a21, 1164b1.

1178b5 'In so far . . .' In referring to the political nature of human beings (see note to 1097b9) Aristotle seems to concede that a human

being's happiness includes the activity of other virtues besides understanding devoted to study.

1178b7-23 On the gods see 1101b18, 1145a26; *Pol.* 1253a26. The
gods do not suffer from the human limitations that make virtues of
character necessary and praiseworthy for human beings. There is no point
in praising them for not having base appetites, as we would praise the
temperate person (1119a11-20); for the gods were never in danger of
having them, and did not need to train themselves.

1178b24-32 On the capacity for happiness see note to 1099b32.
Aristotle may be making the same point here, if understanding in study
and in practical thought are the same capacity; cf. notes to 1177a14,
1178a2.

1178b32 'will be some kind of study' Here and in 'more than any
others' (b23) Aristotle may, but need not, be identifying happiness with
study alone; cf note to 1177a16.

1179a1-9 Here again (note to 1178b5) Aristotle seems to think the
happy person is concerned with fine actions that express virtues of
character. See *Pol.* vii 2-3.

1179a6 On beliefs of the WISE see ETHICS #4.

1179a19 'from what we do and how we live' Lit. 'from actions (or
'facts', *erga;* see FUNCTION) and lives'. We must pass the test stated in
1172a35, showing that we can apply our principles in practice. Aristotle thinks that some consistent ideals of life are so hard for a normal
person to act on that they cannot be taken seriously.

1179a33-b4 Aristotle reasserts the practical aim of ETHICS
(1103b26) and returns to the beginning of the *EN*. Having found what
happiness is, and especially that it requires virtue of character to be acquired by moral EDUCATION (1104b11), we must now turn our attention to that. At the same time we return to explicit concern with the
political community; see 1094b7, 1102a7, 1103b2, 1113b21, 1141b23,
1152b1. A design for happiness must extend beyond the person to the
city he belongs to, and in particular the city must direct moral education.

1179b16 'For it is . . .' This explanation suggests that it is the bad
habits of the many that make them unreceptive to moral reasoning, as
though good upbringing would have made them receptive. But in b11,
'naturally obey . . .', Aristotle suggests that their nature was defective
from the start; even with the right habituation they apparently could not
reach complete virtue.

1179b19 'what we seem . . .' Lit. 'through which we seem to become decent'.

1179b21 On nature see note to 1144b3.

1179b25 'but the soul . . .' Cf. 1095a2, b4. The three passages provide different, though related, reasons for requiring a good upbringing.

1179b33 'resistant' I.e., to pain. Cf. note to 1150a31.

1180a5 Compulsion is distinguished from force (1179b29); see note to 1110a25. The role of punishment explains the relevance of iii 1, 5 and v 8. The distinctions drawn there will presumably be used in determining the proper treatment of different offenders.

1180a21 On LAW as rational see *Pol.* 1287a28-32.

1180a26 Neglect of moral education; cf. note to 1161a9. Aristotle's approval of Spartan concern for moral education does not imply approval of Spartan moral education. See *Pol.* 1333b5-35.

1180a30 'If, however . . .' Aristotle offers second-best advice (characteristic of parts of the *Pol.*, e.g. iv 1) for someone who is not living in the right community; he advises systematic education by individuals, if the community will not do its part.

1180a33 'legislative science' 'Science' is supplied in this phrase from here on.

1180b6 'fond of him' An expression of friendship in families; see 1161b19.

1180b8 'Generally' translates *katholou*, translated by 'universally' in b14, 21. The patient who does not benefit is not exactly an exception to the general rule. In so far as he is feverish he may benefit from the normal treatment; but since he has other conditions too, the normal treatment may not, everything considered, be best for him, even though it is always best for fever, considered by itself.

1180b20 'Nonetheless . . .' Though experience may make someone competent in a restricted range of cases, general competence and understanding require the grasp of the universal. The two features of the virtuous person mentioned in notes to 1137a9 and 1144b3 are relevant here in distinguishing the expert craftsman from the merely experienced practitioner.

1180b28-1181a9 Like Plato (e.g. *Meno* 99-100), Aristotle is dissatisfied with politicians and with those who profess to offer instruction in POLITICAL SCIENCE. The practical politicians simply rely on experience, while the instructors overlook its importance.

1180b35 On sophists see note to 1164b1.

1181a1 'political activists' Or 'professional politicians', those regarded as over-active in 1142a2.

1181a19-b12 Practical EXPERIENCE is no less necessary in political science than in intelligence as a whole; cf. 1143b7.

1181b12 On predecessors cf. *Top.* 183b14. Aristotle does not deny that his predecessors have made particular suggestions about legislation (some are discussed in *Pol.* ii). He claims they have left the general area 'uncharted' (or 'unexamined'), with no systematic survey of the data, and no account of the proper method.

1181b12-23   Aristotle announces the programme of the *Pol.*, as the natural completion of the *EN*. He relies on the 'collected constitutions' (158 of them, only one of which, the *Constitution of Athens*, largely survives). At the same time decisions about the best political system and laws require use of the ethical principles defended in the *EN*.

Glossary

account   See REASON #4

achievement   See FUNCTION

action, *praxis*   There are three main uses: (1) Aristotle uses '*praxis*' and the cognate verb' *prattein*' broadly for all intentional actions (translated 'do' or 'do in action' or 'achieve in action'). What we can achieve by *praxis* is what we can achieve by our own efforts (1096b34, 1147a3). Probably a *praxis* must be VOLUNTARY. In this sense children and non-human ANIMALS are capable of action (1111a26). Such action has a DESIRE for some END as its efficient CAUSE; the desire is focused on a PARTICULAR situation by further beliefs, and it is a particular action that is done (1147a25, 1110b6) and that we are responsible for. (2) More strictly, *praxis* is confined to rational action on a DECISION. This is what non-human animals cannot do. See 1094a5,7; 1139a20; *EE* 1222b20, 1224a29 (cf. 1111b8). (3) Most strictly of all, *praxis* is confined to rational action which is its own END, and is not done exclusively for the sake of some end beyond it. (This is not to say it has no end beyond it. HAPPINESS is an end beyond virtuous action, which nonetheless is chosen for its own sake: 1097b1-5, 1174a7-8.) In this sense action is contrasted with PRODUCTION, 1139a35-b4, vi 4-5, note to 1105a26. It is a complete ACTIVITY, and not just a MOVEMENT.

It is not always clear (e.g. at 1094a1) how strictly Aristotle uses '*praxis*'. The three uses above perhaps do not mark three different senses of the word. They may be (cf. Aristotle's view of the three types of FRIENDSHIP in viii 3-6) more and less complete specimens of action; the first two types share some of the features of the third — the first is voluntary and goal-directed, the second is also rational, and the third is complete.

activity, actualization, *energeia*   A subject's *energeia* realizes its CAPACITY; hence the *energeia* of a CRAFT, e.g. shoemaking, and the craftsman can include both the activities involved in the exercise of the

385

craft and the product, the shoes, that is aimed at in the exercise (cf. notes to 1094a3, 1168a6; FUNCTION).

The scope of *energeia* is narrowed in two ways in some contexts, by contrast with *hexis* and by contrast with *kinēsis:* (1) In *De An.* 412a22-8 Aristotle contrasts 'first' activity with 'second'. Someone is in first activity in relation to his knowledge of French if he has learnt French and can speak it on the right occasions, but at the moment is asleep or thinking about something else. He is in second activity when he is actually speaking French (1146a31). To have a SOUL is to have a first activity. In the *EN* a first activity is called a STATE. When Aristotle defines HAPPINESS as an activity of the soul, he is requiring it to include second activities, not merely states (1095b32, 1178b18-20). (2) In 1174a14 ff., *Phys.* 201a9, *Met.* 1048b18 Aristotle draws a further contrast: (a) A MOVEMENT is an incomplete activity, the degree of activity consistent with the retention of the capacity realized in the activity, where the complete activity implies the loss of the capacity. E.g. the movement of housebuilding is going on when the bricks and stones have incompletely actualized their capacity to become a house; when they completely actualize that capacity and the house exists, they no longer possess that capacity, since a house is not still capable of becoming a house. (b) A complete activity does not imply the loss of the capacity that is actualized in the activity — e.g. seeing or living does not imply the loss of the capacity to see or live. A movement is incomplete because it aims at some end beyond itself (e.g. the building process aims at the house being built) whose achievement makes that movement impossible to continue (we cannot keep building the house when it is already built), whereas a complete activity is its own end. Hence complete activity is identical to ACTION in Aristotle's narrowest sense. This is the type of activity that PLEASURE is (1153a10, 1174a14). **Activities of virtue,** see VIRTUE. **Activity and FRIENDSHIP,** 1168a5, 1170a18.

agapān   LIKE
agathos   GOOD
aidōs   SHAME
aischros   shameful; see FINE.
aisthēsis   PERCEPTION
aitia, aition   CAUSE
akolasia   intemperance; see TEMPERANCE.
akrasia   INCONTINENCE
akribēs   EXACT
anankē   NECESSITY
anger, *orgē*   Anger is a FEELING (1105b22) especially associated with

emotion (see DESIRE). Its treatment is discussed in iv 5 (note to 1125b26). See also 1103b19, 1110b26, 1111a26, 1117a6, 1130a31, 1135b29, 1138a9, 1149a24-b33, 150a29; *Rhet.* 1378a30.

animal, *zōon* Aristotle normally uses *zōon* for the genus to which insects, dogs and human beings belong (*Pol.* 1253a3, 8). Sometimes he uses it for what he also calls 'the other animals' (1111b9), excluding HUMAN BEINGS (1099b33); these animals are also called 'beasts' (*thēria*, e.g. 1139a20, 1147b4). Some of the differences between human beings and other animals are these:

(1) Other animals have a SOUL defined by PERCEPTION. They live by perception and APPEARANCE without REASON (1098a2, 1139a20, 1147b4, 1149a10, 1170a16).

(2) They share with human beings non-rational DESIRE (1111b12, 1118b1) but not rational desire. Hence they act VOLUNTARILY, but not on a DECISION (1111a25, b8).

(3) They are not capable of HAPPINESS (1098b32, 1178b27) or of the VIRTUES of character (1149b31, cf. 1141a26; *EE* 1240b32), since these require decision.

aporia puzzle; see ETHICS.

appear, appearance, evident, apparent The verb '*phainesthai*', 'appear', has two constructions in Greek:

(a) with the participle ('being wise, he appears so', i.e. 'he is evidently wise'), endorsing what appears (this is also the sense of the adjective '*phaneron*', 'evident'); (b) with the infinitive ('he appears to be wise'), neither endorsing nor denying what appears. Sometimes the verb is used without either participle or infinitive, and hence is indeterminate between (a) and (b). These cases are translated by 'is apparently'. This translation may mislead if it suggests that Aristotle is necessarily being tentative or non-committal in his assertion; this may, but need not, be true (just as what is apparent may, but need not, be misleading or dubious).

'Would seem' normally translates *eoike* (lit. 'it looks like', or 'is like', a translation also sometimes used), which may, but need not, be less committal than *dokein*.

Hence, when Aristotle reports what appears, or sets out the appearances (1096a9, 1145b3) only by context can one decide whether he endorses or rejects (e.g. 1113b1) or neither. The same applies to his use of 'seem' ('*dokein*' cognate with '*doxa*', 'belief'), which is equivalent to 'appear' in the *EN* (e.g. 1095a30, 1113a21). The appearances include all the commonly accepted beliefs which Aristotle takes as the material for arguments in ETHICS.

The condition I am in when something appears to me is *phantasia*, 'appearance' (1113b32, 1141a32). The appearance can result from PERCEPTION or from REASON (*DA* 434a5-10), and ANIMALS who have perception without reasoning are directed by perceptual appearance (1147b5); a HUMAN BEING may act on this contrary to reason (1149a32, 1150b28).

appetite, *epithumia* See DESIRE.

archē ORIGIN

ardent, *melancholikos* See note to 1150b25.

aretē VIRTUE

argument See REASON #3.

associate, association See COMMON.

athlios MISERABLE

attend, attention Usually the Greek is *epimeleisthai* and cognates (e.g. 1099b20, 1114a3, 1180a25), indicating systematic practice and training. When attending is contrasted with CAPACITY or potentiality, in 1147a33, the Greek is *thēorein*; see STUDY.

autarkēs SELF-SUFFICIENT

avoid See CHOICEWORTHY.

axia WORTH

bad See VICIOUS.

base See VICIOUS.

beautiful See FINE.

becoming, *genesis* See note to 1173a31.

bia FORCE

blessed, blessedly happy, *makarios* We might expect this to be especially closely associated with the life of the GODS (cf. *EE* 1215a10; 1178b9), in which happiness is entirely stable and immune to the limitations of the human condition. In fact, however, the *EN* seems to use the term interchangeably with 'HAPPY'. Unless the terms are interchangeable the argument at 1100b33-1101a21 becomes unintelligible. The reader need not look for any difference between 'blessed' and 'happy' in the *EN*.

boulēsis, **wish** See DESIRE.

bouleusis, **deliberation** See DECISION.

bravery, *andreia,* **cowardice** These are discussed in full in iii 6-9. See also 1102b28, 1103b17, 1104b8, 1119a21, 1123b31, 1129b19, 1130a18, 1137a20, 1144b5, 1166b10, 1167a20, 1169a18, 1177a32, 1178a32.

capacity, capable, power, powerful, *dunamis, dunatos* If x has the capacity to F, it is capable of F and will F in the right conditions. If fire, e.g., has a capacity to burn, it will burn unprotected flesh close to it; this is a non-rational capacity. If Smith has a capacity to build, he will build when he chooses to build in the right conditions for building; this is a rational capacity. See *Met.* ix 1-7, esp. 5. Hence a capacity is what is realized in an ACTIVITY.

Capacities include CRAFTS and branches of STUDY (1094a10, 26) and also the natural capacities from which the VIRTUES are developed (1103a25, 1106a6, 1144a23, b1). *Dunamis* is also applied to power over things and people (1099b2, 1161a3; see also FREEDOM) 1178a32. HAPPINESS is not a capacity; see 1101b12. Virtue requires not only capacity, but also DECISION (1127b14).

cause, reason, responsible, *aitios, aitia* In *Phys.* ii 3 Aristotle explains the doctrine of the four causes. Reference to an *aition* (neuter of adjective *aitios*) or *aitia* answers the question 'Why?'. Different 'why' questions about an object (e.g. a statue) can be answered by reference to (a) its MATTER ('because it is made of bronze'); (b) its form, *eidos*, stating its DEFINITION and essence, and hence the species (also *eidos*) it belongs to ('because it is a bust of Pericles'), see note to 1174a19; (c) its efficient cause, the ORIGIN of MOVEMENT ('because the sculptor made it'), see 1110a15, note to 1139a31; (d) its final cause or END (*telos, hou heneka*, 'that for the sake of which') e.g. 'to represent Pericles'.

Aristotle's four types of explanation include more than those we commonly call causal explanations, and so sometimes (e.g. 1100a2, 1137b27) 'reason' is an appropriate translation. 'Cause' also renders the preposition *dia* ('because of'; *dia ti* = 'why?'; cf. note to 1095b7); see note to 1156a5.

In legal contexts the adjective *aitios* often indicates not only causation but also blameworthiness (correspondingly the abstract noun *aitia* indicates both the cause and also the ground of accusation). Hence 'responsible' is sometimes apt, e.g. 1110b13, iii 5 (see note to 1113b25). See also CONTROLLING, VOLUNTARY.

change See MOVEMENT.

character, *ēthos, ēthikos* The *EN* is about the formation of VIRTUES of character. These are the STATES resulting from (a) early habituation, to acquire the right DESIRES, FEELINGS, PLEASURES and PAINS, 1104b11, 1179b24 (hence Aristotle connects character closely with habit, 1103a14-26); (b) the correct use of rational deliberation that makes an INTELLIGENT person who makes the correct DECISION, a necessary condition for virtue.

The formation of the right character requires the EDUCATION of the nonrational parts of the SOUL (1103a3). But since they are to be trained to act according to correct REASON, training in reasoning and deliberation is required too. It is someone's character that makes him the 'sort of' (*poios*) person he is. Hence 'character' often translates *poios*.

The actions appropriate to a person's character are those said to be 'proper to him' or those he 'is the sort' to do (e.g. 1120a31, 1146a6, 12, and 'not for him', a32). All these phrases translate the Greek genitive case, i.e. 'is not of the generous (etc.) person'.

charieis CULTIVATED

child See HUMAN BEING #6.

choiceworthy, *hairetos* This includes the GOOD, the FINE, the PLEASANT and the expedient (see 1104b30, 1155b18; *Top.* 118b27). The term is an adjective formed from the verb '*hairein*', 'choose' (a part of *prohaireisthai*, 'DECIDE') plus a verbal adjective ending, which is ambiguous between (a) actually chosen, (b) capable of being chosen, (c) deserving to be chosen. Which Aristotle means in a particular context is not always clear. Similar questions arise about the opposite of *hairetos*, 'to be avoided' (*pheuktos*; e.g. x 2); about *bouletos*, 'wished' in iii 4; about *philetos*, 'lovable' in viii 2; about *gnorimos*, 'known' in i 4; and about *phoberos*, 'frightening' (note to 1115a8). See esp. 1172b9-28, where (c) is required at some stage, but we might suppose that (a) is assumed at the beginning. Our view about this ambiguity will affect our view on the relation of GOOD (#1) to choice; cf. 1097a18-b6.

city See POLITICAL SCIENCE.

civilized See GENEROUS.

clever *deinos* *Deinos* is also rendered 'terrifying', e.g. 1103b15, 1115a26, 1116b35. It is used for anything remarkable or formidable, and hence is used, as Aristotle uses it, for cleverness (1144a23, 1152a10, 158a32). Cleverness is not said to be a deliberative capacity, but a capacity for finding what is needed to fulfil an end—which need not always require deliberation (a clever debater will be able to find the telling reply on the spur of the moment).

coincidence See note to 1135b2-8, IN ITSELF.

common, shared, *koinos*; association, community, *koinōnia*; associate, *koinōnos*; share, *koinōnein* The general sense of *koinon* is the basis of some more specialized uses: (1) A UNIVERSAL is common because it is shared by the instances that it belongs to (1096a28, 1107a30, 1141b26, 1180b15). (2) 'Common good' renders *koinon* at e.g. 1122b21, 1123a5, 1162a23. (3) People who share some common pursuits and goals are associates or members, *koinōnoi*, in an association or community. A *koinōnia* can be a loose or a close connection; hence 'association' and 'community' seem necessary on different occasions; see v 5, viii 9, 1170b11; *Pol.* 1252b12-34. The common pursuit of a common good in a *koinōnia* is the foundation of FRIENDSHIP and of JUSTICE (1129b17, 1155a22).

compel   See NECESSARY.

complete   See END #4, HAPPINESS #2.

condition   See STATE.

consideration   See PARDON.

content   See FOND.

continent   See INCONTINENT.

controlling, in control, important, full *kurios*   (1) If someone is *kurios* over me he controls me and my actions (1110a3, 6) hence the *kurios* is often the ruler (1116a30, 33). To be *kurios* over an event is to be in control of whether it happens or not. In so far as I am *kurios* I am the ORIGIN and CAUSE of an ACTION, the action is up to me and VOLUNTARY, and I am responsible for it (1113b32, 1114a32; *EE* 1222b21). (2) Since what controls and rules a process is the most important thing about the process, determining whether it happens or not, *kurios* is also used more generally to mean 'important'. Often both control and importance are suggested (1143b34, 1145a6, 1168b30, 1178a3). (3) If a property is found in degrees, the application of the term to the complete instance controls its application in partial instances. Hence the *kurios* F is F most completely, and 'F' applies to it better than to things that are partially F or less F. Here *kurios* is rendered 'full', e.g. 1098a6, b14; 1103a2, 1115a32.

convention, conventional   See LAW.

conversation   See REASON #6.

correct, *orthos*   The verb *katorthoun*, translated, 'be correct', (1098b29; 1104b33; 1106b26, 31; 1107a14, 1142b30) might also be translated 'succeed'. '*Orthos*' indicates success in pursuing an END or correctness in picking it (1144a20), as opposed to error (*hamartia*, 1135b18; sometimes 'fail' would also be suitable). Like 'right' *orthos* is applied to right angles and to straight lines. It is not confined to moral rightness: nor is any special moral sense of the term required. The virtuous person is guided by correct REASON in so far as he has the true conception of the end and its constituent ACTIONS (1142b32, see DECISION); then he does what is FINE and RIGHT.

corrective treatment, *kolazein*   Aristotle uses two terms for punishment, *kolazein* and *timōrein* ('exact a penalty'). Though they are sometimes used together (1126a28, 1180a9), Aristotle conforms to the distinction drawn at *Rhet.* 1369b12. *Timōria* is concerned with satisfaction for the harm done—hence often associated with revenge. 1126a21,

28; 1149a31. *Kolazein*, however, is forward-looking, concerned with restraining (or 'tempering'; see 1119a33, note to 1150a21, and TEMPERANCE) and improving the offender. See 1104b16, 1109b35, 1113b35, 1113b33, 1132b30, 1180a11; *EE* 1214b33, 1230a39; *Rhet.* 1374b30.

craft, *technē* See vi 4. A craft is a rational discipline concerned with PRODUCTION. Hence Aristotle sometimes associates craft with SCIENCE (1094al, 7), though it does not meet the strictest conditions for a science (1140b2, 34). Craft involves inquiry and deliberation, and so Aristotle often uses its methods to illustrate the procedures of VIRTUE and INTELLIGENCE. Still, there is a basic difference. Intelligence is concerned, unlike craft, with ACTION (1140b3, 1153a25), and involves more than the CAPACITY which is a craft, 1140b28. Hence the virtuous person is not practising a craft, and the *EN* itself is not the exposition of craft-knowledge. See 1104a5-11, 1106b5-16, 1112a34-b31, 1120b13, 1122a34, 1133a14-16, 1141b14-22, 1146b31-1147a10, 1152b2, 1167b28-1169a19, 1174a19-21, 1180b7-23. **Craft and nature**: 1099b20-3, 1106b14, 1140a15, *Phys.* 192b8-33.

cultivated, gracious, *charieis* The cultivated (or 'sophisticated') person may be the one who has gone more deeply into his particular craft or discipline (1102a21), or, more generally, the one who has a more discriminating view of life than the MANY have (1095a18, b22, 1127b23). In this sense being cultivated is an aspect of being civilized (see GENEROUS); 1128a15, 31; notes to 1133a3, 1162b10.

currency See LAW.

death See 1100a10, 1115a26, 1117b9, 1124b8, 1138a9, 1169a18.

decent, *epieikēs* This is cognate with *eikos*, 'likely', and means 'plausible, reasonable, respectable' (as we say 'a likely lad' or 'a reasonable candidate for the job'). Hence it is used more generally for a decent person, and hence interchangeably with 'GOOD' in the right contexts, as Aristotle remarks at 1137a35. (Cf. 1102b10, 1168a33; and for the political use which is a feature of most of Aristotle's moral terms cf. *Pol.* 1308b27.) In some contexts the term suggests someone who will do the decent thing even when the law does not require him to. This is the sort of decency (some translators use 'equity') discussed in v 10. See also 1143a20 (for its relevance to PARDON); *Rhet.* 1374a18-b22; *Top.* 141a15.

decision, *prohairesis* A decision is the result of (a) a wish, a rational DESIRE for some GOOD as an END in itself (1111b26, note to 1113a2; 1113a15); (b) deliberation, systematic RATIONAL CALCULATION about how to achieve the end (1112b15, vi 9). These result in (c) the decision, which is a desire to do something here and now, the action that deliberation has shown to be the action required to achieve the end (1112b26, 1139a21-b5).

Some results and difficulties of this account: (1) Not any desire followed by deliberation results in a decision—emotion and appetite do not (1142b18). Hence the INCONTINENT's incontinent action is not the result of his decision; his decision is correct, because his rational wishes are correct (1150b30, 1152a17). (2) Deliberation, and hence decision, are not about ends, but about 'things towards' or 'promoting' them, 1112b1; see notes to 1111b27, 1140a28; 1162b36. These things towards ends need not only be instrumental means—efficient causes of the end, neither wholly nor partly coinciding with it. (Shopping for food is an instrumental means to eating dinner.) They may also show us what counts as achieving the end, so that we find its components (eating the main course is 'towards' eating the meal because it is part of eating the meal). See INTELLIGENCE. (3) Hence Aristotle is justified in saying that the virtuous person decides on virtuous action for its own sake (1105a32, 1144a19). (4) A virtuous person, however, can show his virtuous decision especially clearly in emergencies that allow him no time to deliberate afresh, 1117a17-22 (cf. note to 1142b2, 1150b25). The deliberation about this type of situation must have been done earlier, and its result is available without further lengthy deliberation. (5) The correct decision is necessary for virtue of character, and expresses a person's virtue. See 1106a36, 1110b31, note to 1111b5; 1117a5, 1127b14, 1134a17, 1135b25, 1139a22-6, 1144a13-22, 1145a2-6, 1157b30, 1163a22, 1178a34.

Etymologically *prohairesis* suggests 'choosing (*hairesis*) before'. For Aristotle the 'before' has a temporal sense (1113a2-9) though no doubt also a preferential sense. Many translators use 'choice' to translate it; but Aristotle allows choice without deliberation or decision, and such choice will not count as *prohairesis*; hence the rendering 'choice' is better avoided.

decree See note to 1137b29.

define, *horizein*, **define, distinguish,** *dihorizein* (1) These terms are derived from *horos*, 'limit, boundary' (see note to 1142a24; cf. 'definition' derived from *finis*), and often *dihorizein* is translated 'distinguish' (e.g. 1099a25). Similarly *horizein* is associated with limiting, bounding and determining (1170a22). (2) Often, however, the terms indicate definition, also expressed in the account of something (see REASON #4), telling us what the essence of something is (*to ti ēn einai*, or *ousia*, 'SUBSTANCE', 1107a6; *Top.* vi 4, *Met.* 1029b13-22). When we define functionally organized things, either artifacts or natural organisms, the definition will tell us their FUNCTION and END (e.g. 1107a6). Aristotle seeks a definition for happiness, the virtues, friendship etc. He is not looking simply for a verbal equivalence, a phrase that can replace the word being defined while preserving truth. Such a formula for defining happiness does not satisfy him (1095b18). He wants an account that will explain and justify the common beliefs (1098a20, b9). (3) The canonical form of definition places something in its species, *eidos* (see CAUSE), by stating its genus and the differentia of the genus that isolates the species (e.g. 'Man is a biped (differentia) animal (genus)'). Aristotle does this with virtue of character (1105b20, 1106a15; cf. *Top.* vi 5-6). Often the genus is associated with the question 'What?' (e.g. 'What is a man?'—'An animal'), and the differentia with 'What sort of?' (e.g 'What sort of animal is a man?'—'A biped animal'). See 1098a31, 1105b19, 1106a14, 1174a13; *Top.* 128a20-9, 144a15-22.

dein   RIGHT

deinos   CLEVER

deliberate   See DECISION.

demonstration   See SCIENCE.

desire, *orexis*   Aristotle normally recognizes three types of desire, corresponding to Plato's tripartition of the soul in *Rep.* 435 ff. (See 1138a5-13.) The three types are these: (1) Rational desire, wish, *boulēsis* (see DECISION) is for an object believed to be good. See 1111b26; note to 1113a12; 1113a15, 1114a14, 1136b5, 1155b29, 1156a31, 1162b35, 1178a30. (2) Appetite, *epithumia*, is nonrational desire for an object believed to be pleasant. (See 1103b18, 1111a31, 1117a1, 1118b8, 1119a14, 1136b5, 1155b29, 1156a31, 1162b35, 1178a30.) The most striking examples of appetites are desires associated with basic biological needs, but appetite is not confined to these (e.g. 1111a31). And while the virtuous person has to have his appetites trained, he does not lose them, but transforms them into good appetites. (3) Emotion, *thumos*, is non-rational desire for objects that appear good, not merely pleasant, because of the agent's emotions; see 1149a25 on the relation of emotion to reason. Aristotle regularly associates with *thumos* the self-assertive feelings involved with pride and (when frustrated) with ANGER. Hence 'spirit' or 'temper' might be a suitable rendering in 1105a8, 1111b18, 1116b23, 1135b26.

The different forms of appetite and emotion are FEELINGS, whereas rational desires are not. For this division elsewhere see *De An.* 414b2, 432b4-7; *EE* 1223a27; *Rhet.* 1368b37-1369a7; *Top.* 126a3-13. While it is not so explicit in the *EN*, it is often assumed. See 1095a2-11, 1098a3-5, 1102b13-1103a3, 1111a27, 1111b10-30, 1116b23-1117a9,

1119b3-18, 1135b19-1136a5, 1136b6, 1147a31-b5, 1149a24-b3, 1166a33-b25, 1168b28-1169a6.

dianoia   THOUGHT

differentia   See DEFINE.

dikaiopragein   DO JUSTICE

dikaios   JUST

discussion   See REASON #6.

disgraceful   See FINE, SHAME.

distinguish   See DEFINE.

distress   See PLEASURE.

divine   See GOD.

do   See ACTION, PRODUCTION.

doing justice, *dikaiopragein*, **doing injustice,** *adikein*   Aristotle defines these terms narrowly to mark the distinctions he thinks significant, 1135a8-23. They are confined (with the cognate abstract nouns 'act of injustice' and 'just act') to voluntary actions, which need not be the expression of a just or unjust DECISION, and hence of a just or unjust CHARACTER. The passive forms 'suffer injustice' and 'receive justice' indicate voluntary action by the agent from whom we suffer or receive it. Sometimes Aristotle coins or uses terms to mark the same distinction with other virtues, indicated by, e.g., 'unjust or intemperate action' (1114a12, 1172b25).

dokein   Seem; see APPEAR.

dunamis   CAPACITY

education, *paideia*   *Paideia* is cognate with *pais*, 'child' (1161a17). But, for Aristotle, it is not confined to children. The types of education relevant in the *EN* are these: (1) Moral education assumes that someone has the right sort of NATURE, and it trains him by habituation, *ethismos* (1098b4, 1099b9; 1103a20, b16; 1119a27, 1121a23, 1151a19, 1152a29; 1180a3, 15) until he acquires the right habits (*ethos*; 1095a4, 1103a17, note to 1103b22; 1148b17, 34; 1154a33, 1179b21, 1180b5, 1181b22). These habits are patterns of action, acquired by training that uses pleasure and pain as incentives. But, equally important, they include tendencies to feel pleasure and pain, and to have other FEELINGS, in the right way, which is a precondition for genuine virtue. See PLEASURE #4, 1103a33, 1152b4, 1172a20, 1179b25. (2) However, childhood instruction is not enough. Training must continue with adults, to make them as virtuous as possible, 1130b25, 1180a1. This is why moral education concerns POLITICAL SCIENCE. (3) The educated person will be cultivated, so that he acquires the tastes and outlook of the civilized (see GENEROUS) rather

than the slavish person (see HUMAN BEING #9). (4) In the most specialized sense the educated person is the one who has learnt enough about
different branches of knowledge and methods of inquiry to understand
the right demands to make of ETHICS, 1094b23; *PA* 639a5; *Met*. 1006a5.
(5) Aristotle does not say how INTELLIGENCE is related to education.
But since education aims at producing virtue of character in those capable
of it (1099b19, 1180a5-15), and virtue requires intelligence, intelligence
must be the result of moral education. It follows that this education must
include the sort of intellectual training that produces the correct deliberation (vi 10) and DECISION required for intelligence.

eidos   species, form; see CAUSE.

eleutherios   GENEROUS

emotion   See DESIRE.

empeiria   EXPERIENCE

end, goal, aim, *telos*   The *telos* of a process is its final CAUSE, a state
which (a) benefits some being with a SOUL; (b) is caused by the process as efficient cause; and (c) whose occurrence, in particular the benefit
it causes, explains the occurrence of the process. In this sense, cutting
steak is the end of a steak knife, pumping blood is the end of a mam-
mal's heart, and winning the game is the end of playing chess. The FUNC-
TION of an artifact or organism is also its end, 1097b24. See *Phys*. ii 8;
1097a18, 1110a13, 1111b16; 1113a15, b5; 1115b20, 1139a36; 1140b6,
16; 1144a32, 1151a16, 1174b33.

Some particular comments: (1) Every ACTION in the broad sense has
something good or pleasant for its end (i.e. its intended goal). Every
rational action based on rational DESIRE and DECISION has some good
for its end, iii 4. (2) Though every action in the narrowest sense has
an end, it does not have only an end outside itself (1094a3); an external
end makes an event or sequence of events a PRODUCTION. Internal and
external ends distinguish MOVEMENTS from ACTIVITIES (in the narrow
sense), and CRAFT from INTELLIGENCE. (3) Deliberation and decision
are concerned with what promotes ends, not with ends themselves. Intelligence is deliberative, but is a true supposition about the end (see
DECISION #2). (4) Though several things (virtue, pleasure etc.) are ends,
only one thing, HAPPINESS (#2), is a complete (*teleion*) end. (5) Sometimes *skopos*, 'target, goal', is used, sometimes in a consciously meta-
phorical way (1094a24, 1138b22, 1144a25), with no obvious distinction
in sense from *telos*.

energeia   ACTIVITY

enjoy   See PLEASURE.

enkratēs   continent; see INCONTINENT.

eoike would seem; see APPEAR.

epieikēs decent

epistēmē SCIENCE

epithumia appetite; see DESIRE.

equal, *isos* What is *isos* is neither more nor less—either (a) neither more nor less than a given amount, e.g. an inch, or (b) neither more nor less than the RIGHT amount. *Isos* shares the ambiguity that Aristotle points out in 'intermediate' and 'MEAN' (1106a26). Hence when the *isos* is associated with JUSTICE, Aristotle means not that justice always requires numerical equality, but that it forbids having more or less than is right. Hence it forbids grasping greed—*pleonexia*, lit. 'trying to have more', i.e. 'more than is right' (note to 1129a32). Hence, when Aristotle associates justice and 'equality', it is sometimes appropriate to think of fairness rather than what we would naturally call equality. On different types of equality cf. 1131b31, 1157b36, 1158b29, 1162a35, 1168b8.

ergon FUNCTION

erotic passion, erotic love, *erōs, erōtikos* *Erōs* is one of the terms that might be translated by 'love'; see FRIENDSHIP. Sexual desire is a component of, but not sufficient for, *erōs*. The mere appetite (see DESIRE) for sexual gratification, *ta aphrodisia*, cognate with Aphrodite (see 1149b15), need not include *erōs* (see 1117a1, 1118a31, 1130a25, 1147a15, b27, 1148b29, 1149b15, 1152b17, 1154a18). *Erōs* reflects the condition of those who might be said to be 'in love', though Aristotle in fact seems to restrict it in the *EN* to the paederastic desire of an older male for a younger. Unlike simple sexual appetite, *erōs* includes intense interest in the beloved himself, desire for his presence and company (1158a11, 1167a4, 1171a11), and friendly feelings towards him; this is why it is a source of friendship. See 1116a13, 1156b1, 1157a6-13, 1158a11, 1159b16, 1164a3, 1167a15; 1171a11, b9, 31. The verb *eran* is rendered by 'long passionately' (1155b3) and 'heart's desire' (1098a28).

error See CORRECT.

essence See DEFINE.

ethics 'Ethical' is derived from *ēthikos*, the adjective cognate with *ēthos*, 'character'. Hence ethics is the part of POLITICAL SCIENCE that studies HAPPINESS; since virtue of character is a major component of happiness, this part of political science studies character; hence the traditional name of the *EN*. In the work itself Aristotle calls his inquiry 'political science', not 'ethics' (see also *Rhet.* 1356a26-7); but for use of the term cf. *Met.* 987b1, *An. Pos.* 89b9, *Pol.* 1261a31.

The methods and aims of ethics:

(1) It is concerned with ACTION, not only with knowing and STUDY-

ING the truth, 1095a5, 1103b27 (cf. *EE* 1216b11-25, *MM* 1182a1-7), 1179a35. Knowledge of the truth is not the end, but the means (though cf. *Pol.* 1279b11-15). This does not make the knowledge unimportant.

(2) Because ethics is concerned with action, INTELLIGENCE and DECISION are important parts of it.

(3) For the same reason, ethical truths are only USUAL (1094b21) and hence lack the EXACTNESS that would be needed for a SCIENCE in the strict sense.

(4) The method of ethical inquiry is dialectical, described in *Top.* i 1-4, 10-12. Hence it begins from common beliefs, what seems or APPEARS to the MANY or the WISE (i 4, *EE* i 6). Aristotle takes commonly held beliefs very seriously (1098b27, 1153b31, 1173a1-4, 1179a16). But he does not regard them as unrevisable; often he criticizes the many (1095a22, b16, b19; 1113a33, 1153b35, 1159a19, 1163b26, 1167b27, 1172b3, note to 1150a13). He begins with these ORIGINS because they are 'known (or 'familiar') to us'. See 1095b3; *Phys.* 184a16; *An. Post.* 71b33; *Met.* 1029b3; *Top.* 141b8 (and see CHOICEWORTHY). They are what we think we know, and argument requires some accepted beliefs to begin with. See "Aristotle's Literary References".

(5) Discussion of these common beliefs shows that they raise puzzles, *aporiai*, when we find apparently convincing arguments from common beliefs for inconsistent conclusions (*Top.* 145b16, 162a17). Aristotle stresses the importance of a full survey of the puzzles (*Met.* 995a27) and follows his advice in i 10-11, ii 4, iii 4, v 9-11, vi 12-13, vii 2; 1155a32; ix 8-9, x 2-3. (Some of these are surveys of the common beliefs that include reference to the puzzles too.)

(6) To solve (or 'loose', 1146b7) the puzzles Aristotle looks for an account which will show the truth of the most and the most important of the common beliefs, 1145b5. This account will provide us with a first principle or origin that is 'known by nature' or 'known UNCONDITIONALLY', not merely to us (see #4 above). It is a principle that really justifies claims to knowledge.

(7) A defence of a theoretical principle shows how it vindicates many of the common beliefs (1098b9). But it does not vindicate them all. Hence a proper defence should also show why false common beliefs appear attractive and rest on explicable misunderstandings; see notes to 1116a15, 1137b24, 1140b7; see 1154a22, 1169b22.

(8) Since practically useful exact rules about particular cases are impossible (see #3 above), Aristotle offers his general principles and his account of the virtues; see 1094a25, b20; 1098a20, 1101a27, 1104a1, 1129a11, 1179a34. For PARTICULAR circumstances PERCEPTION and EX-

PERIENCE are needed, though some general rules will help; 1109a30, 1126b2, 1164b27, 1165a34.

(9) Since ethics is to guide action (1105b12-18), it should be addressed to those who are capable of guiding their action by it, and hence to those whose upbringing has not made them incapable of acting on ethical instructions (1095a2, b4; 1104b11, 1179b4-31).

These different features of ethics might be regarded as aspects of (a) the moral principles and moral deliberation of the virtuous and intelligent moral agent; (b) the theories and arguments of the moral philosopher. It is doubtful if Aristotle recognizes any sharp distinction between (a) and (b). The *EN* is a part of political science, and hence of intelligence, using dialectical method. It is both a contribution to moral theory and the account of a process of practical deliberation (see e.g. 1168b26).

ethos HABIT

ēthos CHARACTER

eudaimonia HAPPINESS

Eudoxus Eudoxus (c.390-c.340) was a leading mathematician and astronomer as well as philosopher. His hedonist views may underlie some of the argument in Plato's *Philebus*. He is cited or alluded to at 1094a2, 1101b17, 1172b9.

exact, *akribēs* A CRAFT and its products (1094b14, 1112b1) are called exact when they are finished and complete in details (cf. 1141a9); the most exact craft gives accurate detailed instructions, leaving nothing to chance or guesswork, and so produces a product that has every detail right. Hence an exact statement is correct and accurate in detail, and as applied to particular cases, without any further restriction or reservation (see UNCONDITIONAL). It may be exact in either of two ways: (1) It is a general statement which applies to every case without the need of any qualification, e.g. 'The angles of a triangle add up to 180 degrees'. (2) It is a suitably specific statement in which all the necessary qualifications have been made, e.g. 'In Europe the rule of the road is to drive on the right, except that in the British Isles they drive on the left'.

When Aristotle compares one discipline with another for exactness, he sometimes has just one of these aspects in mind, sometimes both. When he denies exactness to ETHICS he intends both points (1094b13, 1098a27, 1103b34-1104a7, 1112b1; 1141a9, 16; 1164b27). The generalizations are not exceptionlessly, but only USUALLY, true, and the exceptions cannot usefully be listed in an exhaustive and helpful qualified generalization. This lack of exactness means that ethics cannot meet Aristotle's strictest criteria for a SCIENCE.

excellent, *spoudaios* A *spoudaios* matter is a serious matter deserving to be taken seriously (*spoudazein*). Aristotle regularly uses the term as the adjective corresponding to 'virtue', and hence as equivalent to 'good'. The association with taking seriously is exploited at 1177a1-6, where 'serious' renders *spoudaios*; cf. 1125a10.

exousia FREEDOM

expect, reasonable to   See REASONABLE.

experience, *empeiria*   Aristotle sharply distinguishes experience from CRAFT and SCIENCE (1180b20, *Met.* i 1, cf. Plato, *Gorg.* 465a). Experience of PARTICULAR cases may allow us to form rules of thumb (e.g. in medical treatment) that yield some practical success. But science and craft know why something works, and do not merely believe that it works (cf. 1095b6). They can provide a general explanation and justification, and deal successfully with unfamiliar types of cases.

At the same time Aristotle insists that experience is important. Varied PERCEPTIONS and experience are the material for reasonable induction (see INFERENCE, *An. Post.* 100a3). We need experience to make reasonable decisions in cases requiring perception (1109b20). Hence experience is an important aid to INTELLIGENCE; 1141b18, 1142a15, 1143b11, 1147a21. Cf. 1103a16, 1154b4, 1116b3, 1158a14, 1181a19.

express, *kata*   The Greek preposition '*kata*' means 'according to', and includes both (a) actual guidance (e.g. I build a shed *kata* the design if I consult the design as I work); (b) mere conformity (e.g. bodies fall *kata* the laws of nature without consulting these laws).

When Aristotle speaks of action *kata* virtue (decision, etc.) it is often both important and difficult to decide if he means (a) or (b) or something intermediate between them. 'Express' is used for the cases that seem close to (a). Cf. 1098a7, 1105a25, 1111b10, 1144b26, 1151a7, 1178b7. For other cases 'fit', 'befit', 'guided by', 'conform to' are used; cf. 1120b7, 1123b24, 1131b24, 1134b13, 1162b27, 1169a5. For a difficult case see note to 1130b23.

Sometimes 'by' is appropriate (at 1100b22, e.g, 'are matters of fortune' = 'happen by [*kata*] fortune').

facts   See FUNCTION.

feeling, *pathos*   '*Pathos*' is cognate with '*paschein*' ('undergo, be affected, suffer'), and indicates a mode of passivity rather than activity (e.g. 1132a9, 'suffering'). Hence 'be affected' is sometimes (e.g. 1147a14) the appropriate rendering. Usually 'feeling' is fairly close; for Aristotle regularly restricts *pathos* to conditions of the SOUL that involve PLEASURE or pain (1105b21; *EE* 1220b12; *Pol.* 1342a4; *Rhet.* 1378a19). These include the DESIRES and feelings belonging to the non-rational part of the soul (1111b1, 1126b33, 1135b21, 1136a8, 1168b20, 1178a15) presumably because these appear to be passive in certain ways, as reactions to external stimuli. 'Passion' might also be a suitable translation, except that not every *pathos* is passionate; '*pathos*' corresponds to the older use of 'passion' found in Descartes and Hume 'on the passions'.

A virtuous person will not be without feelings altogether (1104b24) and some feelings are both natural and necessary for a human being (1115b7, 1135b21, 1136a8, 1149b14). But he will not be controlled by his feelings; control by feelings is characteristic of the young (see HUMAN BEING #6-7) and the incontinent; 1095a4, 1128b17, 1144b9, 1150a30, b21-4; 1151a20, 1156a32, 1179b13, 27; *Pol.* 1312b25-34.

fine, beautiful, *kalos* What is *kalos* is what deserves admiration; the term is applied to aesthetic beauty (e.g. 1099b3), and its opposite '*aischros*' ('shameful') to ugliness (e.g. 1099b3). '*Aischros*' is usually translated 'shameful', but by 'disgraceful' in contexts where its cognate *aischunē* ('disgrace') and *aidōs* ('shame') are being used; see note to 1115a13, iv 9. Often, especially in such phrases as 'said finely' and 'spoken finely' (e.g. 1094a2), 'finely' means nothing very different from 'well'. But in 'judging finely' and 'deliberating finely' the term has its narrower force (e.g. 1099a23, 1112b17, 1114b8, 1140a26, 1143a15, 1169a23, 1170b27). Doing something finely is associated with doing it RIGHTLY (1116b2, 1119b16, 1121a1) and CORRECTLY (1119a29).

The narrower force of *kalos* associates it especially with the virtuous person. He is the one who DECIDES on actions that are fine and 'for the sake of the fine'—it is their fineness that causes him to decide on them (1115b12; 1116a28, b2-3; 1117b9, 14; 1119a18, b16; 1120a12, 23; 1122b6, 1123a24, 1136b22).

(1) Acting for the sake of the fine is contrasted with acting under compulsion (1116b2), and with acting only for some further end to which the fine action is merely instrumental (see DECISION #2, 1123a25); hence the fine is contrasted with the pleasant and the expedient (1104b31, 1162b35, 1169a6; cf. 1155b19), and associated with LEISURE (*Pol.* 1333b1).

(2) Hence it seems that doing x because x is fine is not to be opposed to doing x for its own sake. Hence the virtuous person's concern with the fine does not conflict with his deciding on virtuous actions for their own sake (1105a32, 1144a19). He decides on them for their own sake in so far as he decides on them for the sake of the fine.

(3) Then is the fine identical to the intrinsically good (cf. *Rhet.* 1364b27, 1385b36)? The *EN* is not clear on this; but it does not call an intrinsic good such as health *kalos*, and does not suggest that if I enjoy sitting in the sun as a good in itself, it must be *kalos* to sit in the

sun. Probably Aristotle accepts the extra condition imposed in *EE* 1249b19 and *Rhet*. 1366a33 (cf. note to 1155a29) that the fine is the intrinsic good which is praiseworthy (cf. i 12, 1109b31). Hence the fine must be something that the agent can be praised for, as a result of his own VOLUNTARY action expressing his CHARACTER and DECISION.

(4) But will an action be praised as fine with reference to the agent's own interests alone? Actions are normally praised for being virtuous in ways that benefit others (cf. 1155a29), and this partly explains why sacrificing one's life is fine (1169a18-b2). Here 'fine' indicates something very close to the moral value of the action.

(5) How then can Aristotle suppose that the virtuous person concerned with his own HAPPINESS will choose virtuous actions for the sake of the fine? This depends on what motive a virtuous person will have for being concerned with others for their own sakes. Aristotle considers this question in his account of FRIENDSHIP, esp. ix 9.

fond of, *stergein* Sometimes (cf. LIKE) '*stergein*' has a fairly weak sense ('be content', 1162b30). Usually, however, it indicates the FEELING associated with FRIENDSHIP and love (1126b22, 1156a15, 1157a11, 28; 1161b18, 1162a12, 1164a10, 1167a3, 1168a2, 22; 1179b30, 1180b6). Aristotle seems to think *stergein* is necessary for friendship (1126b22) but it is not clear if all the types of friendship he recognizes include *stergein*—perhaps they include it to different degrees.

force See notes to 1110a2, a25.

form See CAUSE.

fortune, *tuchē* *Tuchē* (cognate with *tunchanein*, 'happen'; hence 'chance', 'luck') and *automaton*, 'spontaneous', events are discussed in *Phys*. ii 4-6. In the *EN tuchē* is used more broadly than in the *Phys*.; x is a matter of furtune for S if and only if (a) x benefits or harms S; (b) S's DESIRE or DECISION does not CONTROL x. Fortune is involved not only in events entirely uncontrolled by S (e.g. if S's uncle leaves him a legacy) but also in processes initiated by S in which something outside S's control is needed for success (e.g. S's building a house is the result of his decision, but it is vulnerable to ill-fortune, since a storm might blow down the half-built house). Aristotle's main remarks on fortune:

(1) GOODS of fortune affect HAPPINESS (1096a1, 1099a31-b8, 1100a5, b22; 1101a28, 1129b3, 1140a18, 1153b17). Hence they contribute to the exercise of some virtues (1124a20).

(2) However, happiness should not be identified with good fortune. Goods of fortune are actually bad for a VICIOUS person; and a virtuous person's happiness depends primarily (though not exclusively) on his vir-

tuous character, which is not subject to fortune. Hence the virtuous person's primary aim will be to act virtuously, not to achieve the goods of fortune (1099b9-25, 1100b7-1101a21, 1120b17, 1124a12; *EE* viii 2).

freedom, *exousia* '*Exousia*' is not the legal status of a free citizen as opposed to a slave; see GENEROSITY. It is derived from '*exeinai*', 'to be open, possible', and indicates the condition of someone with options open to him. Hence 'free to' (1114a16, 1163b19), 'freedom' (1161a9, 1178a33), 'could have' (1163a13) all render '*exeinai*' and cognates.

Since power over others leaves the ruler with more options about how to treat others, '*exousia*' often indicates the position of a ruler—hence 'power' (1095b21, 1158a28, 1159a19).

friendship, *philia;* **love,** *philein;* **beloved, friend,** *philos* *Philia* is discussed at length in viii-ix. While 'friendship' is the best English rendering, it lacks a cognate verb, and 'love' has to be used.

Philia is different from what we might expect friendship to be: (1) It includes the love of members of families for each other. (2) It includes the favourable attitudes of business partners and associates and of fellow-citizens for each other. (3) The attitude of some *philoi* towards each other is different from what we might expect. In the best kind of friendship one virtuous person admires the other's objective merits, his virtuous CHARACTER (cf. esp. 1165b13). (4) In general, these differences reflect the smaller role of purely idiosyncratic preferences, inclinations and choices in *philia* than in friendships we might be used to. Some *philiai* are made appropriate by my family circumstances, some by the usefulness of the other, some by his objective merits—not by my whims and inclinations. Aristotle's *philia* for pleasure is probably the nearest to modern ways of thinking about friendship. However, *philia* has aspects that make it recognizably friendship: (5) It requires some degree of goodwill and mutual recognition (1155b32-1156a10, 1158a7, ix 5) and shared activities (1157b19). (6) It also requires some FEELING, actual FONDNESS for the other, not mere goodwill and benevolence (1126b20-8, 1166b32).

Aristotle classifies different types of relations that meet the conditions for *philia* to different degrees (1158b5). He distinguishes:

(1) the three species with three objects (a) the good, (b) the useful, and (c) the pleasant;
(2) friendships between (a) equals and (b) unequals;
(3) friendships in different types of COMMUNITIES, 1161b11, e.g. families, clubs, cities.

The relations between these different divisions is not always clear. For instance, how many in (3) conform to (1a)? Sometimes Aristotle suggests only virtuous people are capable of (1a), 1156b7; how does this affect *philia* in families?

More of the *EN* is devoted to friendship than to any of the virtues. It is a necessary component of HAPPINESS, not merely instrumental to it (see DECISION # 2; 1097b10; 1155a3, 29; 1157b20, 1162a17, 1169b3, 1170b14, 1177a34, 1178b5; *Rhet.* ii 3). The study of friendship is equally important to POLITICAL SCIENCE (1155a22, viii 9-11).

full, fully See CONTROLLING.

function, product, achievement, *ergon* The best single translation for '*ergon*' would be 'work'. These different uses (sometimes closely related; see notes to 1106b8, 1167b34) can be distinguished:

(1) Process of PRODUCTION or task (1109a25, 1124b25).

(2) Product, outcome of the process (1094a5-6, 1106b10, 1133a9, 1167b34).

(3) Achievement, when no product need be involved (1100b13, 1101b16, 1120b13; note to 1122b3).

(4) Action, more or less equivalent to ACTIVITY, (e.g. 1104b5).

(5) Contrasted with *logos* (see REASON #6); hence 'facts' (1168a35, 1172a35), 'what we do' (note to 1179a19).

(6) Function, characteristic task, ACTIVITY and END (1097b25, 1106a16, 1139a17, 1144a6, 1162a22, 1176a3; see PLEASURE). This is the use that connects something's *ergon* with its ESSENCE and its VIRTUE; in animate beings the *ergon* defines the type of SOUL.

generous, civilized, *eleutherios* '*Eleutherios*' is cognate with '*eleutheros*' ('free'), indicating the status of a free person rather than a slave (1131a28, 1134a27; see also FREEDOM). The *eleutherios* has the outlook appropriate to a free citizen (hence 'liberal' might be a suitable translation). But Aristotle understands this in a wider and a narrower sense.

(1) The wider sense of '*eleutherios*' is rendered by 'civilized', to indicate the contrast with boorishness and slavishness (see HUMAN BEING #9). The civilized person has the right sort of EDUCATION, and hence is concerned with the virtues and with the sorts of PLEASURE that are appreciated only after training and cultivation (see also CULTIVATED). The civilized person avoids the narrow-minded, calculating attention to bodily needs and the satisfaction of non-rational desires; this attitude is characteristic of the slavish person, who cannot use LEISURE correctly, but goes in for 'degrading' ('*aneleutheros*', lit. 'unfree') activities (1121b33; at 1123a16 'paltry' renders '*aneleutheros*'). See 1118b4, 1125a9; 1128a25, 31; 1176b20, 1179b8. (The wide and the narrow senses of '*eleutherios*' are perhaps associated in 1158a21, 1168b27.)

(2) In its narrow sense '*eleutherios*' indicates the particular virtue described in iv 1 (cf. 1115a20, 1130a19; 1178a28, b14), the appropriate generosity in giving money and the appropriate restraint in taking it. Here 'generous' is the appropriate translation.

Though Aristotle does not say so, he might have regarded these two types of *eleutherios* as HOMONYMOUS. But they are clearly connected. The virtue of generosity that he describes is so called because it is a particular manifestation of the more generally civilized character. Aristotle says less about the broader type of *eleutherios* because it is really virtue as a whole (i.e. the appropriate non-slavish attitude to happiness) viewed in a particular way (here it is similar to general JUSTICE, 1130a10); it is especially clearly displayed in magnanimity.

genesis   becoming; see note to 1173a31.

genus   See DEFINE.

goal   See END.

god, divine, *theos, theios*   In the *EN* Aristotle does not try to describe the nature of the divine, as he does in, e.g., *Met.* xii 7-10. But he speaks of it in these ways:

(1) He notices the ordinary use of 'divine', to indicate something marvelous, beyond normal human capacities, 1145a21.

(2) He refers to traditional views of the gods as objects of worship, prayer and sacrifice (1122b20, 1160a24) without himself endorsing these views.

(3) He refers to common views of the gods influencing the FORTUNES of human beings. '*Eudaimonia*', rendered 'HAPPINESS', by its etymology suggests 'having a good *daimōn*' (divine spirit, translated 'god', 1169b8), and so suggests some belief in the role of gods (cf. 1099b9). Aristotle is willing to concede that there is something plausible in these views, (1179a24).

(4) Something divine, not very clearly articulated, can be seen in nature and in the natural desires and tendencies of natural organisms, (1153b32, 1173a4; cf. *DA* 415a29; *Phys.* 192a16; *DC* 271a33; *PA* 658a9).

(5) Aristotle wants to correct some common anthropomorphic views of the gods. They cannot have anything like human personalities or characters, (1101b18, 1178b8). When a human being becomes a god, the change is so radical that he ceases to exist (1145a23, 1159a5, 1166a19).

(6) However, Aristotle is not agnostic about the divine. He recognizes a divine being that has a rational SOUL, but no FEELINGS or non-rational DESIRES; it is self-sufficient (see HAPPINESS #3), and needs nothing, and hence has no need of virtues of character. The divine is unchanging,

a permanent and essential feature of the universe (see 1134b28; note to 1141a20-b8; 1154b26). Hence a god never passes from CAPACITY to AC-TIVITY, but is always in activity. The god's activity is STUDY, and this is the object of divine PLEASURE (1154b26; cf. 1175a3).

(7) These features of the god make it an ideal for our own pursuit of happiness. In so far as each of us has the capacity for rational study, and in so far as the activity of this capacity is the single activity that best fulfils the criteria for happiness (x 7) we have reason to imitate the god as far as possible, and pursue study (1177b26). See HAPPINESS # 5.

good, *agathos*   The main uses:

(1) A good aimed at (1094a1, 1097a16). The good aimed at by x is the result that x rationally aims at. What I regard as a good is what I regard as achieving my aim. In this sense there will be many goods corresponding to my many rational aims (1097a15-22). But I will have a further rational aim: to satisfy each of these aims to the right extent and in the right relation to each other. When I have a conception of the right extent and relation I will have a conception of my complete good, which is my HAPPINESS (1097a22-b21) discovered by REASON (#1). See also CHOICEWORTHY.

(2) 'Good for'—things are good for a result in so far as someone aiming at the result has reason to aim at them. They are good for a person (e.g. exercise, knowledge of arithmetic) in so far as they contribute to aims it is rational for him to have (exercise would still be good for me even if I were irrational enough not to aim at health). Hence Aristotle contrasts UNCONDITIONAL goods, good for anyone òr for people with the right aims, with goods 'for someone', good only for those in special conditions with particular aims (1113a22, 1129b2, 1152b26, 1155b24, 1157b26).

(3) 'A good F' (1098a8, 1106a15). A good horse is a good specimen of horses—its goodness is determined by what horses characteristically do and can be expected to do—what Aristotle calls the FUNCTION of horses. Hence a good person does well (1098a12) what persons can be expected to do, and has the VIRTUE appropriate to persons.

These three uses are related: what makes a knife a good knife (3), depends on what good (1) we want the knife to achieve, and that will depend on what the knife is good (2) for. Similarly a good (3) person will be able to achieve goods (1) that depend on what is good (2) for a person—his final good or HAPPINESS.

Here, however, there may be some dispute. We might say that what makes a person good depends on what (if anything) a person is used for, just as what makes a knife good depends on what a knife is used for; hence if a person is not used for anything, Aristotle's account of good (3) will imply that there are no good persons. Aristotle disagrees. A person is not an artefact or an organ, and his goodness, VIRTUE, is not to be measured by his use, but by his own intrinsic good—his HAPPINESS.

Goods of body and soul and external goods 1098b12, 1099a31, 1129b2, 1153b21, 1178b33. See FORTUNE. On good and PLEASANT see 1111b17, 1113a34, 1140b13, 1153b7, 1155b19, 1156b15, 1157a1; 1172b9, 28; 1173b20-1174a12, 1176a15-29.

gracious See CULTIVATED.

greedy See EQUAL, note to 1129a32.

habit, *ethos* See EDUCATION #1.

hairetos CHOICEWORTHY

hamartanein be in error; see CORRECT.

haplōs UNCONDITIONAL

happiness, *eudaimonia* Aristotle follows common beliefs in identifying the highest human GOOD with happiness, also identified with 'living well' or 'doing well' (1095a18; cf. 1139b3, 1140a28, 1140b7). He argues for the identification in 1097a15-b21, appealing to common beliefs about happiness in support of his account (1096a1; i 8; 1153b14; x 7; see also GOD #3).

(1) 'Happiness' is a misleading rendering of '*eudaimonia*' if we identify happiness with pleasure. (a) If Aristotle understood it this way, the question about what happiness is (1095a18) would hardly be puzzling. (b) A hedonist account would make it hard to see any real question about the identity of pleasure and *eudaimonia*. But Aristotle not only thinks there is a question; he denies the identity of the two (1175b34). (c) A hedonist account should make the agent's feelings and opinions decisive about whether he is *eudaimōn* or not. But such a view makes nonsense of the puzzles in i 10-11, and, more generally, of Aristotle's account of the VIRTUES. He thinks the virtues he describes are necessary for *eudaimonia*; he does not mean that they are necessary to make someone pleased or contented.

(2) Happiness is the complete (*teleios*) END, the only one that does not promote any other end. It is complete because it is the most comprehensive; there is no more comprehensive end for it to promote. On completeness see 1094b8, 1095b32, 1097a25-b21; note to 1097a28; 1098a18, 1099a15, 1100a4, 1101a14, 1102a1, 1103a25, 1129b26, 1153b16, 1154a1; note to 1154b26; 1156a7, 1174b15-33, 1177a17, 1178b7; *Met.* v 16.

(3) Aristotle makes the same point in calling happiness self-sufficient, *autarkēs*, lacking nothing—i.e. lacking no reasonable object of desire (1097b6, 1134a27, 1160b4, 1169b3-8, 1170b17, 1177a27; *Pol.* 1252b29,

1253a26, 1256b4, 1275b21, 1280b34, 1326b3, 1328b17). A person is self-sufficient (1125a12) to the extent that his complete happiness depends on himself, and not on external conditions (cf. 1177a27-b1). The virtuous person wants to make himself as self-sufficient as is compatible with the self-sufficiency of happiness.

(4) Since it is complete and comprehensive, happiness includes other ends pursued for themselves. To find what happiness is is also to find what these ends are (1097b2, 1174a4). The task of finding them belongs to INTELLIGENCE, which deliberates about them (1140a28) and finds what it is RIGHT to do. The result is the virtuous person's DECISION to pursue virtuous action for its own sake (1105a31, 1144a19; see FINE, LEISURE).

(5) In x 6-8 Aristotle argues that STUDY has some special place in happiness. Does he mean (a) that it is the whole of happiness, contrary to (2) - (4) above, or (b) that it is the single most important component? See 1145a6, 1177a12-18, 1178a2-9; 1178b5, 28.

(6) Because happiness must be complete, including all types of goods, and some goods depend on FORTUNE, happiness must partly depend on fortune. But its major components—the virtues—do not depend on fortune. See BLESSED.

hēdonē PLEASURE

hekousios VOLUNTARY

hexis STATE

homonymous, *homōnumos* Two things are homonymously F if and only if they share the name 'F', but the account (see REASON) of F is different for each. If the account is the same, then they are synonymously F. Hence we might say that the chest of an animal and a tea chest are homonymously chests. See 1096b27, 1129a27, 1130a33; *Catg.* 1a1-12; *Top.* i 15. Aristotle also refers to homonymy when he says that Fs are spoken of or so called in many ways (1096a23; 1125b14, cf. 1118b22; 1129a25, 1136b29, 1142b17, 1146b31, 1152b27), and when he says that some Fs are so called by metaphor (1115a15; 1119b3, 'transferred', *metapherein*; 1137b1, 1138b5, 1149a23, b32; 1167a10). He is concerned to preserve the common beliefs (see ETHICS) and the common use of names, as far as is reasonable (cf. *Top.* 110a14-22, 148b16-22). Hence he wants to avoid the assumption that one name corresponds to one nature (so that everything to which the name is truly applied is synonymous). When several natures of F correspond to the name 'F' the assumption that there is only one nature will lead us to dismiss as non-Fs all those Fs that fail to fit one account, so that we will have to dismiss many of the common beliefs (*EE* 1236a25-32; cf. 1157a25-33, 1158b5).

honour, price, *Timē* *Timē* reflects other people's judgement of some-

408

one's WORTH—of his useful or FINE or GOOD qualities (1095a22-30, 1159a12-27). 'Honour' suggests primarily the attitude of esteem and admiration. *Timē* includes this, but also includes the expression of this attitude in 'honours', the awards given to recognize worth (1123b1-24, 1124a4-25, 1134b6, 1163b5). We can show how highly we estimate something's worth and how highly we honour it by how much we will pay for it. Hence 'price' or 'value' and the cognate adjectives are suitable at e.g. 1123a15, 1133b15, 1164b17, 1165b12 (see also note to 1141a20). A *timokratia* is a political system requiring a property qualification for active citizenship, based on the value of a citizen's property (1160a34).

Aristotle advocates neither the single-minded pursuit of honour nor its rejection as irrelevant to happiness. He devotes iv 3-4 to the virtues concerned with the proper attitude to honour.

horismos, horos DEFINITION

hubris WANTON AGGRESSION

hulē MATTER

human being (1) 'Human being' translates '*anthrōpos*', indicating the human species (Latin *homo*, as opposed to *vir*). Sometimes Aristotle may use the plural just to mean 'people'. But usually it indicates some characteristically human features (a) of human beings as opposed to other ANIMALS (1097b25, 1148b20, 1150a2, 1170b13); (b) of human beings and their circumstances, as opposed to GODS (1100b9, 1101a21, 1141a34, 1178b33); (c) of human nature in general (1110a25, 1113b18, 1115b8, 1121b14, 1178b7). Some examples can be understood in more than one of these ways. (See also POLITICAL).

(2) 'Man' translates '*anēr*', the adult male human being (1149b10, 1165b27, 1171b10, 1176b23). Often this is associated with the CHARACTER expected of a 'manly' (*andrōdēs*) person; the term is cognate with '*andreios*', 'brave' (1109b18, 1125b12, 1126b1, 1171b6). More generally Aristotle speaks of an EXCELLENT man, where we might expect 'person' (1098a14, b28; 1101b24; 1130a2, b27; 1143b23, 1145a28, 1176a27). He evidently assumes that being a man is a necessary condition of fully manifesting the VIRTUES of a human being.

(3) 'Woman', *gunē*, refers to the adult female. Her natural differences, leading to a FUNCTION different from a man's, are assumed in the *EN*. (1162a19-27; cf. *Pol.* 1259b28-1260a24, 1277b20. See also note to 1148b32.)

(4) Greek uses the same words for 'man' and 'husband' and for 'woman' and 'wife'. In viii 10-12 Aristotle is plainly concerned with relations between husband and wife. But 'man' and 'woman' are usually the preferable translations; the roles of husband and wife are taken to be explained by

the different natural capacities of men and women. ('Wife', however, is found at 1097b10, 1115a22, 1134b16, 1162a30.)

(5) 'Person' is used on the many occasions when Aristotle uses the masculine definite article with an adjective or participle to refer to an agent or a possessor of a virtue or affection or state. 'Man' would be misleading here, since it would suggest the special force of *anēr*. But no doubt the people Aristotle has in mind are primarily men.

(6) In the *EN* children are regularly associated with non-human animals because they still lack REASON and rational DESIRE (1100a1; *Rhet.* 1384b23). They need primary moral EDUCATION (1104b11; 1119a33-b15.

(7) The relation between the children and the 'youths' or 'young people' who are excluded from study of ETHICS (1095a2) because they follow their FEELINGS, is not clear; Aristotle does not say when, for these purposes, someone stops being a child or a youth.

(8) Adult human beings are capable of virtue and vice because their desires are capable of being directed by DECISION; hence their VOLUNTARY actions are responsible, properly open to praise and blame. The exceptions are bestial people and those overcome by madness (vii 5; 1149b27-1150a8).

(9) Slaves are in an ambiguous relation to other adult human beings. Though Aristotle can hardly deny they are human, he has to say that natural slaves have souls different enough to justify treatment of them as tools or instruments (1161a32-b8; *Pol.* i 4-7, 13). Hence the slavish, *andrapodōdēs* person is the one who cares about nothing beyond the satisfaction of his nonrational desires; he does not deliberate about changing them, but simply plans for their satisfaction. That is all a slave can do, and all a slavish person wants to do. His narrow range of desires and concerns makes him lack self-esteem, so that he will accept any humiliation to avoid pain. See 1095b19; 1118a25, b26; 1126a8, 1128a21, 1177a8, 1179b10. The opposite of him is the civilized person (see GENEROUS). See note to 1124b31.

(10) Aristotle associates the different periods of a person's life with different tendencies to virtue and vice (*Rhet.* ii 12-14). This division is not so prominent in the *EN* (but see 1119a33-b18; 1121a16-30, b13; iv 9; 1154b9, 1156a24-b6, 1158a1-10; cf. 1126b16).

hupolēpsis SUPPOSITION

important See CONTROLLING.

incontinent, *akratēs* The incontinent—as opposed to the continent, *enkratēs*—lacks 'control' or 'mastery' (*kratein*) over himself, and specifically over his nonrational DESIRES (1168b34; cf. 1138b5-14, 1148b32; Plato, *Gorg.* 491d, *Prot.* 352bc, 355b, *Rep.*430e-431d). The inconti-

410

nent has the correct DECISION (1152a17), but acts on appetite instead.

Incontinence is fully discussed in vii 1-10; see esp. the notes to 1147a31-b5. See also 1095a9, 1102b14-28; note to 1104b6; 1111b13-15, 1114a13-16, 1119b31, 1136a31-b9, 1142b18-20, 1166b6-11, 1168b34, 1179b26-9.

individual The Greek (e.g. at 1094b7) just means 'one'.

induction See INFERENCE.

inference, *sullogismos* Inference is the exercise of REASON and of RATIONAL CALCULATION (in a wide sense) in combining propositions or beliefs to reach others. More narrowly, a *sullogismos* is the deductive form of inference commonly called 'syllogism' and described in *An. Pr.* 24b18. *Sullogismos*, translated 'deductive inference' in vi 3, is required for demonstrative SCIENCE. In this sense it is contrasted with induction, *epagōgē* ('leading on', i.e. from particulars to universals), which proceeds from PARTICULAR facts, observations or examples to a UNIVERSAL conclusion (1098b3, 1139b27, 1143b4; *An. Post.* 84b23, *Top.* i 12).

When Aristotle mentions *sullogismos* about action (1144a31) he cannot have in mind a syllogism in the full technical sense (since *sullogismos* about action, unlike a strict syllogism, has a particular premise); the translation 'inference' (cf. 1149a33) avoids assuming too much. 'Practical syllogism' is a term often used by critics, but not by Aristotle, for the type of inference described in 1147a25. Aristotle does indeed speak of the conclusion (1147a27) and of a premise (1147b9; cf. 1143b3).

in itself, *kath'hauto* If x is F in itself, it is F in its own right, because of what x is and not coincidentally (*kata sumbebēkos*; note to 1135b2-8). Hence, e.g., virtuous friends are good in themselves (1156b19). Something that is good in itself is not good just as a means to something else (1096b10) and hence choosing something in itself is choosing it without regard to conditions that make it a means to some other end (1110a19, 1151b2). Something that exists in itself is something in its own right, not dependent on its relation to something else (1095a27, 1096a20; and hence 'by himself', 1177a33).

intelligence, *phronēsis* The verb *phronein* indicates intelligent awareness in general (1096b17, 1152b16; *DA* 417b8, Plato, *Gorg.* 449e6), and the noun *phronēsis* is used in this general sense in both Plato and Aristotle. In the *EN,* however (unless 1096b24, 1172b30 are exceptions, when Aristotle refers to Plato), *phronēsis* is applied to the practical intelligence described in vi 5, 1141b8-1142a30. Intelligence is good deliberation about things towards one's own HAPPINESS in general (1140a25-8), resulting in a correct supposition about the END (1142b33) which in turn will be the ORIGIN of further correct deliberation (1140b11-20, 1144a31-6).

411

A good translation for *phronēsis* would be 'wisdom' if that were not already needed for *sophia*. 'Intelligence' is misleading to the extent that we associate it with an intellectual ability that someone might have without any wisdom in planning his life (this mere ability would be somewhat like Aristotle's 'comprehension', vi 10). 'Prudence' might be preferable in so far as it suggests good sense about one's own welfare; but we tend to associate prudence with a rather narrow-minded caution, and we do not assume that a prudent person is necessarily reflective or deliberative at all. (The 'prudence' in 'jurisprudence' comes closer to Aristotle's use of *phronēsis*.) 'Intelligence' at least suggests the essentially intellectual component of *phronēsis*. Some of Aristotle's claims:

(1) Since it is deliberative, intelligence is about things towards ends (1144a20-9, 1145a5-6). How then can it also be correct supposition about the end? The explanation of Aristotle's similar claims about DECISION (#2) answers this question too.

(2) Intelligence finds the right actions to be done, and hence requires a grasp of PARTICULARS, since this is needed for the deliberation to conclude successfully (1141a8-23, 1142a23-30, 1145a35). This is why intelligence needs CLEVERNESS (1144a28-9, 1152a10-14), PERCEPTION and UNDERSTANDING.

(3) Since intelligence is concerned (a) with action, and hence with USUAL truths, and (b) with particulars, it cannot be SCIENCE.

(4) Intelligence is both a necessary and a sufficient condition for complete VIRTUE of character (1107a1, 1138b18-34, 1144b14-1145a2, 1178a16-19).

(5) Because intelligence is practical, someone cannot both have it and fail to act correctly. Hence an intelligent person cannot be incontinent (1145a4-9, 1152a6-14).

intemperate See TEMPERATE.

intermediate See MEAN.

involuntary See VOLUNTARY.

isos EQUAL

justice, *dikaiosunē* Aristotle treats justice as he treats some other virtues (see TEMPERANCE, GENEROSITY) that in ordinary beliefs have a wide scope; he narrows them so that each virtue is concerned with a distinctive range of feelings and actions. In v 1 he narrows the scope of justice by claiming that it is HOMONYMOUS; the name is applied to general and to partial justice. In v 3-5 the types of partial justice are described; but v 6 ff. seems equally relevant to both types of justice.

Aristotle thinks two types of justice must be recognized because general justice is not a distinct virtue. General justice is what is pre-

scribed by correct LAWS of a city for the COMMON good: correct laws
are concerned with all the virtues; hence it looks as though justice will
be the whole of virtue in relation to others (1129b25). Aristotle sees that
some unjust actions are the result of greed, *pleonexia* (note to 1129a32),
for more than is fair and EQUAL. Since not all vicious actions are caused
by this desire, the injustice associated with greed cannot be the whole
of vice; hence there must be another type of justice and injustice besides
the general types. Aristotle associates this partial injustice with love of
gain (1130a24).

We can see why Aristotle thinks 'general justice' is too wide for a
specific virtue; it is also wider than what we would call justice. But his
partial justice seems rather narrower than we would expect. If I act
viciously to avoid my share of a fairly distributed burden, I am acting
unjustly and unfairly in a way recognizable to Greeks and to us, but not
clearly included in Aristotle's partial injustice.

kakos   VICIOUS
kalos   FINE
kata   EXPRESS
kath'hauto   IN ITSELF
kath'hekaston   PARTICULAR
katholou   UNIVERSAL
kinēsis   MOVEMENT
know   See SCIENCE.
koinos, koinōnia   COMMON
kolazein   CORRECTIVE TREATMENT
kurios   CONTROLLING
lack   See RIGHT #2.

law, convention, *nomos*   '*Nomos*' is cognate with '*nomizein*' ('think,
believe, recognize', as we speak of recognizing a government) and
'*nomisma*' ('currency'; the connection with *nomos* is exploited in 1133a30).
Nomos includes laws enacted by some legislator, but also includes less
formally enacted rules, habits, conventions and practices. The wide scope
of *nomos* should be remembered at 1129b11, note to 1094b15, 1134b18;
Rhet. 1373b1-18.

Aristotle regards legislation as part of the general task of POLITICAL
SCIENCE (1141b25). The happiness of the citizens requires virtue; and
virtue requires moral education, which is best managed by legislation
(1179b34). Hence moral training is the proper concern of the legislator,
and a city that neglects this will undermine its political system and harm
its citizens (1102a7, 1103b3, 1129b19, 1180a24; *Pol.* 1289a11, 1310a12,
1337a11). Though Aristotle insists that virtue includes more than mere

413

conformity to law (1144a13), he thinks it will develop and flourish only in a city where it is supported by legal enforcement. He regards the view that law should allow the maximum individual freedom as a reflection of serious errors about happiness (*Pol.* 1310a28).

Aristotle refers to an old debate in Greek ethics about whether principles of JUSTICE are the product of NATURE or of *nomos* (1094b16, 1129b11). The defenders of *nomos*, e.g. Protagoras, maintain not merely that different laws affect beliefs about justice, but that there are no facts about justice apart from the beliefs of different societies about it. In 1129b11 Aristotle rejects this denial of objectivity for justice (see also v 7). He rejects it for other virtues also (FINE things are mentioned at 1094b14).

On **laws and decrees** see note to 1137b29; on **law and DECENCY, v 10; on law and general justice** see notes to 1129b12, 1130b22-9.
leisure, *scholē* The correct use of leisure is the mark of the civilized (see GENEROUS) person as opposed to the slavish (HUMAN BEING #9) person, and of the well EDUCATED person. Someone is at leisure when he is free of NECESSITY in some significant area of his life; he need not devote all or most of his time and energy to securing the means for staying alive and satisfying his most immediate and basic desires (1177b4; *Pol.* 1333a30-b5, 1334a11-40).

Though leisure is mentioned only briefly in the *EN*, it is assumed as the background. For Aristotle is addressing someone who lives in a city, a political COMMUNITY aiming at the good and not only at the necessary (*Pol.* 1252b29, 1279a20, 1280b33), someone who has the necessities he needs. He can choose to accumulate superfluous stocks of necessities (pursuing food and drink, e.g., both necessities up to a point, beyond the point where they are necessary), as the slavish person does (1118a25, 1147b23), or he can choose to pursue new goals that he regards as FINE. Aristotle urges someone to choose the second option, and tells him what to regard as fine. The virtuous person is not restricted to the exclusively utilitarian calculation of expediency and instrumental value that restricts the unleisured and slavish person. This freedom is shown in bravery, GENEROSITY and magnanimity.
like, *agapān* Sometimes its sense is fairly weak, and 'be satisfied' is the right rendering, e.g. 1094b19, 1171a20. Often, however, the sense is stronger, and it is closely associated with FRIENDSHIP (1156a13, 1165b5, 1167b32). It lacks the special associations of other terms of endearment (cf. FOND, EROTIC), and is readily used for non-personal objects (1096a9, b11; 1118b4).
logos REASON

lovable See CHOICEWORTHY, FRIENDSHIP.

love See FRIENDSHIP.

magnanimity See note to 1123a34.

makarios BLESSED

man, manly See HUMAN BEING #2.

the many, most people, *hoi polloi* The opinions of the many are accepted as the starting-point, though not the unrevisable basis, of ethical argument (see ETHICS #4). '*Polloi*' is sometimes used in a statistical sense, for which 'most people' is a suitable rendering (e.g. 1150a12, 1151a5, 1152a26). But sometimes it has a rather more pejorative association (e.g. 1095b16). Since Aristotle thinks that the majority of people have the defects that he ascribes to 'the many', we should not think of two sharply distinct senses of *polloi*; but the pejorative association is clearer in some contexts than in others.

matter, *hulē* See CAUSE. By a natural extension it is also applied to the subject-matter of a discipline, the sorts of actions or events or states of affairs that the discipline must study (1094b12, 1098a28, 1104a3, 1137b19).

mean, *mesotēs* '*Mesotēs*' is the abstract noun cognate with '*mesos*', 'intermediate'. Aristotle explains in ii 6 the sense in which he thinks VIRTUE of character is a mean, and the limits of the quantitative analogy (cf. EQUAL). The point of the doctrine of the mean is indicated in 1107a1. Each virtue is a STATE, not merely a CAPACITY or FEELING, since it requires training and rational control of the affections and capacities by INTELLIGENCE. The mean Aristotle has in mind is the state in which affections are neither indulged without restraint nor suppressed entirely, and in which external goods are neither pursued without limit nor totally rejected; in each case the right extent must be determined by reason and INTELLIGENCE (1138b18-34, 1144b21).

This doctrine is applied to the individual virtues of character in ii 7 and iii-v, to show that the same principles apply to each genuine virtue, even when this does not look obvious. To show that the doctrine applies, Aristotle isolates and names means and extremes which are overlooked (1107b2, 30; 1108a4, 1115b24, 1119a5, 1121a16, 1125b1-29, 1126b11-20, 1133b29-1134a16).

mesotēs MEAN

metaphor See HOMONYMY.

miserable, *athlios* A miserable person or condition is contrary to a HAPPY one (1100a9, 29, b5, 34; 1101a6, 1102b7, 1150b5, 1166b27). It appears from 1100b34 and 1101a6 that being miserable is not simply failing to be happy; for Aristotle describes people who lose happiness without becoming miserable. A miserable person is to be pitied for his bad circumstances, but also to be despised for having managed his life badly, contrary to his interests, when it was up to him to manage it well; this is the result that the virtuous but unfortunate person avoids. Someone can be in a miserable condition without being miserable (1100a9, b34). Hence, Aristotle believes, a miserable person will also be VICIOUS –though this does not seem to be part of the meaning of the term, (cf. esp. 1166b27).

mochthēros VICIOUS

movement, change, process, fluctuation, *kinēsis, metabolē* In the broadest use of the term, a *kinēsis* is any difference in something's condition between two different times. Only something absolutely stable and invariant is exempt from *kinēsis* (1154b26). More specifically, Aristotle uses the term for the varieties of change distinguished in *Phys.* v 1. In the discussion of PLEASURE (see notes to 1173a31, 1174a19) Aristotle contrasts *kinēsis* (here translated 'process') with ACTIVITY (#2).

Change and variation are necessary features of human life (1134b28). But the virtuous person achieves the desirable degree of stability that is compatible with these human limitations; (1100b15, 1101a8, 1140b29; notes to 1156b12, 1166a29).

must See RIGHT.

natural virtue See note to 1144b3.

nature, *phusis* Things that have a nature have an internal ORIGIN of change (or MOVEMENT) and stability. They include all living organisms (1140a15; *Physics* 192b8-33; *DA* 412a11, b15; *Met.* v 4). Nature in general is discussed in the *Physics*, i.e. 'On Nature'. Both the material and the formal CAUSE can be ascribed to something's nature (*Phys.* 193a9-b21). Two important aspects in the *EN*:

(1) Something's nature is its original constitution or tendency apart from human intervention; hence it is contrasted with LAW and EDUCATION (1094b16, 1103a19, 1106a9; 1134b18, 33; 1144b3, 1149b4, 1151a18, 1179b20).

(2) Something's nature indicates its FUNCTION and the final cause or END to which it tends. In ETHICS our task is to develop the natural tendencies so that they achieve the appropriate natural end, (1097b11, 1103a25, 1152b13; 1153a12, 14, b32; 1162a16, 1170a14, 1173a4; *Pol.* i 1-2). The nature that is to be developed and realized will include some original tendencies, but not all (1109b1-7).

When Aristotle discusses something 'from nature' or 'from the natural point of view' (*phusikōs*) he refers either to (a) appeals to general theories of nature (1155b2) or to (b) appeals to human nature, especially to human psychology (1147a24, 1167b29, 1170a13). While he avoids (a) in the *EN*, he regularly relies on (b).

necessity, *anankē* Sometimes rendered by 'compulsion'. See *Met.* v 5. Main uses:

(1) The objects of demonstrative SCIENCE are necessary truths, about necessary, not merely USUAL, states of affairs. Since these are always the same way, no matter what we do about them, we do not deliberate and DECIDE about these (1112a1, 1139b20).

(2) The necessity involved in the 'mixed' actions described in iii 1 is hypothetical (*Met.* 1015a20). If I am to stay alive or to avoid some catastrophic evil, I must do this (1110a26, 1115b8, 1116b16; 1121a34, b26). Similarly, pleasant things that are necessary are those that are necessary for life or for a reasonably healthy life (1147b23). Freedom from exclusive concern with these sorts of necessities is LEISURE.

(3) Necessity is also found in psychological states and in actions. Aristotle claims there is a set of beliefs, desires and inferences that necessitates action once they occur, the action is necessary because nothing but the action can happen (1147a27). This is distinct from the necessity in (1), since it depends on previous particular conditions (the state corresponding to the minor premise of the inference).

need See RIGHT.

nomos LAW

nous UNDERSTANDING

observe See STUDY.

oikeios PROPER

open to See FREEDOM.

opportunity See FREEDOM.

orexis DESIRE

orgē ANGER

origin, *archē* '*Archē*' is cognate with '*archein*', meaning both 'begin' and 'rule' (cf. the use of 'lead' and 'first'). Often an *archē* is just a beginning or starting point. But the term has more specialized, connected uses (see *Met.* v 1):

(1) Each of the four CAUSES can be called an origin, and especially the efficient cause (1110a15, 1113b20, 1114a19, 1139a31).

(2) In the growth of knowledge there are two types of origin – those known to us and those known by nature (see ETHICS #4). The origins we begin with are common beliefs (1095b6, 1143b4). The origins we seek to discover are the first principles of a theory explaining the com-

mon beliefs (1098b2, 1140b34). In ethics our knowledge of these principles provides us with an origin—a conception of the END, the good
to be pursued—for deliberation and DECISION, (1140b16, 1144a32).

orthos CORRECT

ought See RIGHT.

ousia SUBSTANCE

paideia EDUCATION

pain See PLEASURE.

pardon, *sungnōmē* '*Sungnōmē*' is derived from '*gnōmē*', 'mind' or
'judgement'. It is the exercise of judgement and consideration that finds
circumstances (as we say, 'special considerations') in an action which
exempt the agent from the blame that would ordinarily and USUALLY
be attached to that type of action. Hence in the discussion of voluntary
action, in iii 1, *sungnōmē* is suitably translated 'pardon' (1109b32,
1110a24, 1111a2, 1126a3, 1136a5, 1146a2, 1149b4, 1150b8). In
1143a19-24, however, Aristotle plays on the etymological connection
with '*gnōmē*', and 'consideration' is needed. The connection is not merely
etymological; for the DECENT person's judgement will often find something pardonable in cases where the inflexible application of a rule that
is only USUALLY true would result in mistaken blame.

particular, *kath'hekaston, kath'hekasta* (1) Particulars include individual objects—this man or this tree—but also particular actions
(1110b6, 1135a7, 1141b16, 1143a32) or situations (1109b22, 1126b3).
What I actually do when I act is not just e.g. killing, but a particular
token of that type—killing in a definite way at some definite place and
time (cf. 1110b32-1111a21). Particulars are the objects of PERCEPTION,
not of SCIENCE.

(2) When we describe a particular we form a more specific and determinate description adding to our description of the universal. Hence
Aristotle also speaks of particulars when he refers to more specific and
determinate descriptions (1107a29 [the particulars here are not particular
action-tokens at definite times and places, but the specific virtues]
1141b14-22). Here, we might say, the particulars are not genuine spatio-
temporally located individuals, but simply more determinate types or
general properties.

In vi-vii (e.g. 1143a32; 1147a3, 26) it is not always clear which conception of particularity Aristotle has in mind.

Aristotle often stresses the importance of studying particular cases
or subdivisions that fall under a general account or definition. They allow
us (1) to understand the general account, by seeing what it implies, (2)
to apply it more successfully in practice, and (3) to test and confirm it,

418

by showing that it fits the cases it is supposed to fit. See 1107a28, 1141b14 (INTELLIGENCE #2), 1180b7; *Pol.* 1260a25; *Rhet.* 1393a16.

penalty See CORRECTIVE TREATMENT.

perception, *aisthēsis* The verb *aisthanesthai*, translated 'perceive', refers both (1) to the exercise of any of the five senses, each with its special object (colour, sound etc.; see note to 1142a27), or of the common sense (see *DA* ii 5–iii 2); 1103a29, 1118a1-26, 1149a35, 1174b14; and (2) to noticing or being aware of something (as in English 'I see') without any very specific reference to the five senses, and with no suggestion that everything noticed is a feature that is noticed by the senses. Both aspects of 'perceive' affect Aristotle's use:

(1) Perception is characteristic of the animal SOUL. Hence perception and non-rational DESIRE are contrasted with rational desire and DECISION (1098a2, 1139a20, 1147b5, 1149a9-10, 1170a16, cf. 1095a4, 1111b18, and see FEELING).

(2) Perception is important in applying ethical principles that are USUAL and may have exceptions in PARTICULAR cases. Actions are concerned with particulars (1107a31, 1110b6, 1135a7, 1147a3) and perception is what makes us aware of these (1109b20-3, 1113a1, 1126b2-4, 1147a26). We need perception to notice the facts of the situation.

(3) We also need it to notice the moral features of a situation (e.g. 'This isn't harmless teasing, but wanton cruelty', or 'Giving him the book would be a kind thing to do'). Aristotle distinguishes this awareness of particulars needed by INTELLIGENCE (1141b14-22) from ordinary perception (1142a20-30) and calls it a type of UNDERSTANDING, though also (because of its reference to particulars), a type of perception (1143b5).

'Moral' perception is probably not sharply distinct from 'ordinary' perception, and probably does not involve a specific 'moral sense' beyond the normal five. Aristotle means that the trained judgement of an intelligent person will be able to identify the perceptual features that are morally relevant, and will realize that they are. (It takes trained judgement to see the features of a work that show it to be Titian's, but there is no special 'Titian-perception' needed.)

person See HUMAN BEING #5.

phainesthai, phaneros APPEAR

phaulos VICIOUS

philia FRIENDSHIP

phronēsis INTELLIGENCE

phusis NATURE

Plato (427-347) Aristotle was a member of Plato's Academy for nearly twenty years, and the *EN* reflects both what he learned from Plato and what he found to criticize in him. *EN* i 6 on the Form of the Good (cf. note to 1158a24) expresses Aristotle's criticism of Platonic metaphysics. Some of the discussion of pleasure as a process or becoming may reflect Aristotle's objections to arguments in Plato's *Philebus* (see note to 1173a31-b11). At the same time Aristotle agrees with Plato on some important principles (see 1095a32, 1104b12; note to 1138b5; 1172b28). Moreover, the general aim and conclusion of the discussion of virtue and happiness in the *EN* follows Plato's *Republic* quite closely. Like Plato, Aristotle wants to show that the virtuous person is happier than anyone else even if he does not achieve complete happiness. See also SOCRATES.

pleasure, *hēdonē* '*Hēdonē*' is the abstract noun corresponding to the verb '*hēdesthai*' ('take pleasure, be pleased') and to the verb '*chairein*' ('enjoy, find enjoyment'). Its opposite is '*lupē*' or '*algos*' (these show no difference in use, and are both rendered by 'pain' or 'distress').

(1) Aristotle is neither a hedonist about good, identifying it with pleasure, nor an extreme anti-hedonist, denying that pleasure is any sort of good at all (vii 13; 1172b26, 1173b31-1174a8).

(2) The extent to which pleasure is good is explained by Aristotle's account of pleasure. It is an ACTIVITY, not a MOVEMENT or process; and it is consequent on some other activity. The pleasure is good if and only if, and because, it is consequent on a good activity (1153a9, x 4-5).

(3) Pleasure is the object of appetite (see DESIRE, 1111b17). Hence non-human ANIMALS have an APPEARANCE of the pleasant, though not of the GOOD (see REASON #1), and human beings are guided by pleasure in so far as they follow the FEELINGS.

(4) Hence pleasure is important in moral EDUCATION. Pleasure can mislead us about the good (1104b30, 1109b7, 1113a33) and destroy our conception of the good (1140b13, 1144a34). Even if we have the right conception of the good, conflicting desires for pleasure may cause us to be INCONTINENT. Hence moral education requires the right pleasures and pains (ii 3).

(5) The virtuous person must take pleasure in being virtuous and in the actions prescribed by the virtues (1099a7-21, 1104b3, 1117a35-b16, 1119a11-20, 1120a23-31, 1166a23-9, 1170a19-b8, 1175a29). This is the natural result of his DECIDING on these actions for their own sake and because they are FINE.

(6) Aristotle's way of distinguishing among pleasures shows that he does not think pleasure is some introspectively uniform state, or that its different sources ('pleasant things') are merely different and interchangeable instrumental means to the same end. The pleasures of dice

playing, sunbathing and music are different in kind, not merely in origin (iii 10; 1147b24-31, 1154a7-b5; x 5; see also FUNCTION).

(7) Pleasure is not identical to HAPPINESS, but an important part of it (1095b16, 1096a1, 1098b25, 1099a7, 1153b14, 1172b26-1173a5, 1176a26, 1177a2).

pleonexia GREED

poiein PRODUCE

poios CHARACTER

political science, politician, *politikē, politikos* Political science is concerned with political questions about the good of a 'city' (*polis*) a political COMMUNITY or association consisting of free citizens (*politai*) governed by a political system, *politeia* (or constitution); see *Pol.* i 1-2; iii 1-3, 8-9. A *polis* differs from a monarchy (1115a32) in having a political system and LAWS that assign some rights and functions to the citizens even if, as under a tyranny (1160b10), these rights and functions are temporarily ineffective. When Aristotle speaks of a *polis* he has in mind something much smaller than most modern states; see 1170a31, and the contrast between a *polis* and a people (or race, *ethnos*) in 1094b10. But the *polis* is a sovereign political unit making alliances on its own initiative (1157a26), and with the functions of a modern state.

Aristotle argues that the proper concern of the state and of political science is to achieve HAPPINESS for all the citizens of the city (1094a26-b6, 1152b1-3; note to 1160a8-30). To discover this we must know what happiness for a human being is. That is the task of the *EN*. A human being is political by nature (note to 1097b9) because his nature is not fully developed so as to achieve his complete happiness, except in a political community; hence the inquiry in the *EN* is part of the same inquiry continued in the *Politics* (see ETHICS). Since happiness requires virtue, the intelligent politician will want the citizens to be virtuous (1102a7-10, 1103b2, 1180a5-12). He will be concerned with moral EDUCATION, and with the motives and rewards that are part of it (1152b1-8, 1172a19-26). He will seek to punish vicious actions and to reform those who commit them, by CORRECTIVE TREATMENTS and penalties (1104b16, 1109b30-5, 1113b21-1114a3, 1180a12). See LAW.

Since political science is concerned with ACTION, and hence with the USUAL, it is not strictly a SCIENCE. ('Political science' translates the adjective *'politikē'*; the noun understood with it is usually not expressed.) Since it deliberates and DECIDES about happiness, it is the same STATE as INTELLIGENCE (1141b23-1142a10).

The politician is an active participant in political affairs (1142a2, 1181a1), not a 'professor of politics' or 'political scientist'. But Aristotle thinks the 'true politician' (1102a8) will have intelligence, and hence will be guided by his knowledge of political science and the human good. That will make him superior to contemporary politicians (1180b13-28). See also ETHICS.

polloi   MANY
ponēros   VICIOUS
praxis   ACTION
price   See HONOUR.
process   See MOVEMENT.

produce, production, do, *poiēsis*   Sometimes the verb '*poiein*' is used broadly for doing something or acting in general (sometimes where we would expect 'ACTION', e.g. 1147a28; cf. 1136b29). But its restricted use is explained in vi 4, 1140b6. It belongs especially to CRAFT, aiming at some end separate from the sequence of production itself. In so far as a sequence of events is a production, it aims at an end outside itself, and hence satisfies the conditions for a process or MOVEMENT (1174a19-b5). This is why virtuous activity cannot be merely production, but must be ACTION. For 'product' see FUNCTION #2.

prohairesis   DECISION
promote   See note to 1111b27

proper, own, close, akin, suitable, *oikeios*   '*Oikeios*' is cognate with '*oikos*' ('household') and indicates the sort of closeness expected in one's relations with oneself and one's own family. Sometimes it indicates nothing more than 'one's own'. But often (esp. in viii-ix) it indicates the recognition of closeness resulting from shared concerns and interests; hence kinship and closeness help to explain FRIENDSHIP, 1155a21, note to 1161b21; 1165a30, 1169b33. On 'proper' or 'appropriate' arguments see note to 1155b1. On actions 'proper to' the virtuous person, see CHARACTER.

pros to telos   See DECISION.
psuchē   See SOUL.
public service   See note to 1122a24.
puzzle   See ETHICS #5.
ratio   See REASON #5.

rational calculation, *logismos*   *Logismos* is the exercise of reason in rational INFERENCE and thought, often in Greek associated especially with arithmetical calculation or reckoning. Aristotle narrows the use of the term to exclude the sort of inference required in SCIENCE, involving NECESSARY truths, and confines it to the area of deliberation (see DECISION), concerned with what is only USUAL (1139a11).

reason, reasoning, account, argument, discussion, conversation, speech, words, ratio, *logos*   '*Logos*' is cognate with '*legein*' ('say'). A

422

logos is what is said, or the thought expressed in what is said. The main relevant uses are these:

(1) *Logos* as reason belongs to HUMAN BEINGS as opposed to other ANIMALS, and to the rational part of the SOUL as opposed to the non-rational DESIRES; hence an adult human being can be guided by reason rather than by FEELING. See 1095a10, 1098a3, 1102b15, 1111b12, 1119b11, 1147b1, 1150b28; 1169a1,5; 1172b10. Reason makes human beings aware of the GOOD, not merely of the PLEASANT (*Pol.* 1253a7-18; cf. 1170b12). Awareness of the overall good requires comparison of present and future (*DA* 433b5-10, 434a5-10) in a single APPEARANCE, and the estimate of one desire and possible aim against another to find the complete good; and this sort of deliberation is characteristic of reason.

(2) Virtue is often said to express CORRECT reason. See 1103b31; *EE* 1220b19, 1222a8, b5; 1107a1, 1115b12, 19; 1117a8, 1119a20, b18; 1125b35; 1138a10, b20-34; 1144b23-8; 1147b3, 31; 1151a12, 22. Here *logos* might refer to the activity of reasoning or to its product, the rule or principle discovered by the activity of reasoning, or to both the activity and the product.

(3) When reasoning, premises and conclusions are implied, '*logos*' is translated 'argument' (1094b13, 1095a30, 1104a1, 1144b32 etc.).

(4) Sometimes rational understanding of something is expressed in a DEFINITION of what it is; here 'account' translates '*logos*' (e.g. 1096b1, 1103b21).

(5) In geometrical contexts the *logos* is the 'ratio' between quantities (e.g. 1131a31).

(6) In its broadest use '*logos*' refers to more or less organized speaking —hence 'discussion', 'conversation', 'speech' (e.g. 1126b11, 1170b12, 1181a4). In this use *logos* can be contrasted, as mere words, with actions. See FUNCTION; 1105b13, 1168a35, 1172a35, 1179a22.

reasonable to expect, *eulogos* A *eulogos* state of affairs is one that we have some good reason or argument (*logos*) for expecting, without having a conclusive reason. Similarly a *eulogos* claim is plausible without being conclusively supported. Since ETHICS is not a SCIENCE and relies on USUAL truths, many of its arguments have to be plausible and reasonable without being certain (*GA* 763a4; 1097a8, 1098b28, 1120b18).

require See RIGHT.

responsible See CAUSE.

right, must, require, need, *dein* The best single translation of '*dein*' would probably be 'must'. The difference between '*dein*' and '*chrēnai*' (translated 'ought') and the gerundive form of a verb (translated 'should') is not clear in the *EN*. The main uses are these:

(1) What the GOOD person must do is what is NECESSARY to achieve his happiness; hence it is what is CORRECT (1122b29) and what is FINE or expedient (*Top.* 110b10; *Rhet.* 1360b12). 'Right' is suitable for the use of '*dein*' in the rules that expound the doctrine of the MEAN, e.g. at 1106b21 (notice the connection with 'well'). Aristotle assumes that what is right and required of us is up to us to do, and that we can justly be praised for doing it and blamed for not doing it (1111a29, 1113b34). '*Dein*' does not have a purely moral sense, if such a sense requires duties imposed on the agent without reference to his ends and his good. But it can prescribe actions as valuable for their own sake, when it is associated with the FINE. Hence in the right contexts it may convey awareness of an unconditional duty; see also note to 1149a33 (*dei* = 'ought', note to 1111a30).

(2) What I must have for my survival or other ends is what I need. The verb 'need' translates '*dein*', but the noun, in e.g. 1133a27, translates '*chreia*'. (This seems more suitable than 'demand', since need may not be expressed in any actual demands.) When I don't have what I need I am *endeēs*, 'lacking'.

(3) Sometimes it is not clear if '*dein*' refers to an actual need or to a claim that I need something and hence to a demand, request or appeal for it (e.g. 1125a10, 1162b17). To reflect the ambiguity, 'require' is used for '*dein*' here.

science, knowledge, scientific knowledge, *epistēmē* *Epistēmē* is a cognitive STATE of the soul, contrasted with mere *doxa*, belief. When this is the primary contrast 'knowledge' is the translation (as e.g. in vii 2-3). But, unlike 'knowledge', '*epistēmē*' is found in the plural. The different *epistēmai* are the different sciences with their different subject-matters, and the state we are in when we grasp one of these sciences in the right way is *epistēmē*, here rendered (e.g. in vi 3) 'scientific knowledge'. Two uses need to be distinguished in the *EN*:

(1) An *epistēmē* is any systematically organized, rationally justifiable and teachable body of doctrine or instructions. *Epistēmai* include CRAFTS (1094a28) such as medicine or gymnastics (1180b16; cf. 1106b5, 1112b1), and exclude pursuits that proceed by mere EXPERIENCE, rules of thumb, maxims and hunches that cannot be rationally explained and justified (1180b17; *Met.* 981a1-20; Plato, *Gorg.* 465a). For this reason 'political science' and 'legislative science' are used in the translation where the Greek has only the adjectives 'political' and 'legislative'.

(2) In *EN* vi *epistēmē* is confined to knowledge of scientific laws, to necessary and invariant truths about necessary and invariant states of affairs (vi 3, 5; cf. *An. Post.* 71b9-72a14). The knowledge must be

the conclusion of a demonstration, a syllogistic INFERENCE in which the premises are necessary truths explaining the conclusion, and themselves reached either by UNDERSTANDING or by further demonstration ultimately derived from understanding.

In this second sense the sciences will include mathematics and some studies of the natural universe. They will not include productive crafts or political or legislative science (which lack the EXACTNESS needed for necessary truths). Hence INTELLIGENCE cannot be a science.

seem See APPEAR.

self-sufficient See HAPPINESS.

sense See PERCEPTION, UNDERSTANDING.

serious See EXCELLENT.

sex See EROTIC.

shame, *aidōs* See iv 9. '*Aidōs*' indicates modesty and restraint in behaviour; someone who has it is scrupulous in observing his standards and ideals, and prone to shame if he violates them. Aristotle associates shame closely with the sense of disgrace (*aischunē*; see note to 1115a13). Though he sometimes commends shame (1115a14, 1179b11), he denies it is a virtue, and thereby rejects a long Greek tradition (see also *EE* 1233b27).

shameful See FINE.

share See COMMON.

should See RIGHT.

sign, *sēmeion* We call x a sign of y when x is easier to notice than y (or the occurrence of x is less controversial than the occurrence of y), and noticing x makes it REASONABLE to expect y, without necessarily giving a certain proof of y. (See *An.Pr.* ii 27; *Rhet.* 1357a34-b21; 1104a13, b3; 1159a21.)

simple See UNCONDITIONAL.

slave, slavish See HUMAN BEING #9.

Socrates Aristotle's remarks about Socrates (469-399) in the *EN* could all be explained from PLATO's dialogues. But he is careful to distinguish Socrates from Plato (cf. *Met.* 987b1, 1086b3; *Top.* 183b7; *EN* 1127b25). The ethical doctrines ascribed to Socrates in the *EN* are familiar from Plato's *Laches* and *Protagoras*; see 1116b4, 1144b18, 1145b23, 1147b15. For other probable allusions, see notes to 1096a2, 1140b21-5.

softness, *malakia* See note to 1150a31.

sophia WISDOM

sophist See note to 1164b1.

sōphrosunē TEMPERANCE

soul, *psuchē* In *DA* ii 1 Aristotle defines *psuchē* as the first ACTIVITY of a living body. If an axe were alive, then cutting (i.e. its characteristic activity or FUNCTION) would be its soul. For a living organism the soul is also related to its work: the soul is the characteristic functions and activities that are essential to the organism and explain (as formal and final CAUSE) the other features it has. Compare 'the axe has a sharp edge for cutting' with 'animals have hearts for pumping blood' and 'human beings have senses and limbs for rational activity'. Aristotle thinks the three explanations are analogous. This conception of the soul underlies the important arguments in 1097b34-1098a5, 1170a16, and 1178a9-22. (Cf note to 1161a35.)

The soul is divided into rational and non-rational parts (i 13, vi 1-2, 1144a2, 1145a3, 1166a16, 1168b30, 1178a2). See DESIRE, PERCEPTION.

Aristotle does not regard soul and body, as Plato does, as two separable SUBSTANCES; the soul is no more separable from the body than the axe's cutting FUNCTION is separable from its MATTER (*DA* 412b6). In the *EN* Aristotle is careful to avoid any commitment to separable parts of the soul in which he disbelieves (1102a28 is consistent with *DA* 433a11 ff.). Still, one part of the soul, the UNDERSTANDING capable of theoretical STUDY, has a special status, giving it the special place in HAPPINESS described in x 6-8 (where it is contrasted with the 'compound'; see note to 1177b28).

species See DEFINE.

speech See REASON #6.

Speusippus Speusippus (?407-339) was Plato's successor as head of the Academy. Aristotle refers to his metaphysical doctrine (1096b7) and to his views on pleasure (1153b5). His views may be Aristotle's targets elsewhere in the discussion of pleasure. See note to 1104b24.

spoudaios EXCELLENT

state, *hexis* (Lit. 'having, possession', see note to 1105b25.) A *hexis* is a first actualization or ACTIVITY, and hence, in relation to complete activity, a type of CAPACITY (*DA* 417a21-b16). In the *EN* Aristotle is especially concerned with a state that includes a tendency to do F on the right occasions because the state has been formed by repeated activities, i.e. by habituation in the regular practice of F actions (1103a26-b25, 1104a11-b3, ii 4). Because it has been formed by training, VIRTUE is a state rather than a mere capacity or FEELING (ii 5) and it is firmer and more stable than a mere condition (*diathesis*; cf. *Catg.* 8b26-9a13).

A state is not merely a tendency to behave. If it were only that, two people who displayed the same behaviour on the same occasions would have the same state. Aristotle, however, denies the same behaviour implies the same state. Someone's state also includes his desires, feelings and DECISION. That is why 'habit' and 'disposition', sometimes favoured by translators, are best avoided as renderings of *'hexis'*. The literal sense of *'hexis'* is exploited at 1146b31.

study, observe, attend, *theōrein, theōria* *'Theōrein'* is cognate with *'theasthai'* ('gaze on') and indicates having something in clear view and attending to it. The main uses:

(1) *Theōria* of a question or subject is looking at it, examining it carefully and seeing the answer (1098a31, 33; 1100b19, 1104a11).

(2) *Theōrein* is the ACTIVITY of the CAPACITY of knowledge. I may know Pythagoras' theorem even if I am not thinking of it; Aristotle regards that as knowing in capacity. The capacity is actualized when I consciously observe or attend to (*theōrein*) the theorem (1146b33).

(3) In Aristotle's most specialized use *'theōrein'* refers to the contemplative study that he identifies with the whole or an important part of HAPPINESS (#5). This is study in the sense in which I study a face or a scene that I already have in full view; that is why the visual associations of *theōrein* are appropriate. Aristotle is not thinking of the inquiry needed to find answers I do not already have; he probably thinks of surveying the deductive structure of a demonstrative SCIENCE, seeing how each proposition is justified by its place in the whole structure (1177a26). In x 7 Aristotle explains why he thinks study is the ACTIVITY that comes closest to meeting the conditions for complete happiness.

'Theōria' does not actually mean 'theory' as opposed to 'practice'; but the origins of this contrast are clear in 1103b26, 1177b2. In the *EN*, *theōria* is contrasted with ACTION (1177b2; but cf. *Pol.* 1325b16-30).

substance, *ousia* *Ousia* is the first category (also called 'what-it-is', 1096a20), including subjects (e.g. men, horses) as opposed to their qualities and other non-essential properties (see *Catg.* 2a10-19; *Met.* v 8; 1096a21). *Ousia* is also used as equivalent to 'essence' (1107a6; see DEFINE).

suffering See FEELING.

sumbebēkos COINCIDENCE

sungnōmē PARDON

supposition, *hupolēpsis* 'Supposition' is the generic term for cognitive states, including both knowledge (see SCIENCE) and belief. It does not always indicate something tentative or conjectural. See 1095a16, 31; 1140b13, 31; 1145b21, 26; 1147b4.

syllogism See INFERENCE.

synonymous See HOMONYMOUS.

target See END #5.

techne CRAFT

teleios Complete; see END #4, HAPPINESS #2.

telos END

temperance, sōphrosunē This conventional rendering of '*sōphrosunē*' indicates correctly that the concern of the virtue is moderation in the satisfaction of bodily desires. But it may mislead:

(1) Aristotle's restricted conception of *sōphrosunē* (iii 10-11) tends to conceal the cognitive aspect of the Greek term, which sometimes indicates good sense, prudence and the moderation resulting from them. Aristotle is aware of this (cf. 1140b11) though his etymology is wrong; '*sōphrusunē*' probably means 'sound (*sōs*) mind (*phronein*, as in *phronēsis*, 'INTELLIGENCE').

(2) Temperance does not require total abstinence from bodily pleasures, but the right extent of indulgence.

(3) Temperance requires not merely partial abstention, but abstinence without severe pain (1119a1-20). Here the temperate person must be distinguished from the continent (see INCONTINENT; 1104b5, 1120b35).

'*Akolasia*', Aristotle's term for the vice of excess opposed to temperance, is derived from '*kolazein*' ('punish, correct') and so indicates someone whose desires lack the CORRECTIVE TREATMENT they need to make them subject to correct REASON (1119a33-b19, 1150a21, 1180a11).

term See note to 1142a24.

thought See UNDERSTANDING #1.

timē HONOUR

transfer (name) See HOMONYMY.

tuchē FORTUNE

ugly See FINE.

unconditional, without qualification, simple, haplōs The adjective '*haplous*' means 'simple, uniform' (i.e. not compound or complex, e.g. 1154b21). The adverb '*haplōs*' indicates a statement made without qualification or reservation, or a property that belongs to a subject without restriction or qualification. Hence doing F *haplōs* is simply doing it, not doing it only in certain circumstances or with certain conditions (1106a8; note to 1110a9). The 'simple incontinent' is the one who is just incontinent, not incontinent in a particular, limited way (1146b3).

Sometimes when we speak *haplōs* we speak inexactly, and conditions or qualifications must be added to produce an EXACT statement; it is the task of dialectic (see ETHICS #4) to find these appropriate additions (*Top.* 115b3-35, 166b22, 166b37-167a20). If I say water is good to drink, that is true *haplōs*, but to be more exact I should mention the conditions in which it is and is not good to drink. See 1095a1, 1097a33, 1098a10,

1104b25, 1105b33, 1110a9, b1; note to 1129b2; 1129b26, 1130a19, 1147b20, 32; 1148b8, 1151b2, 1156b13.

Sometimes, however, the *haplōs* statement is true and exact without qualification, even though it is true in some definite circumstances. Virtues, e.g., are good *haplōs* because they are good for the good person in the condition of a human being (1115b21, 1176a15). See 1095b3 (for 'known unconditionally' see ETHICS #4,6), 1113a24; notes to 1139b2, 1142b30; 1147b24, 1152b27, 1155b24, 1157b27; *EE* 1227a18, 1234b31, 1236a9, b27; 1237a27, 1238a3, b5; 1248b26, 1249a17.

understanding, sense, *nous* The term is used in both a loose and a strict sense (cf. SCIENCE):

(1) It is applied generally to rational thought and understanding, not distinguished from '*dianoia*' ('thought'; 1139a26, 32, 35, b4-5; 1144b9, 12; 1168b35, 1170a19, 1178a7, 1180a20).

(2) In one idiomatic use it is fairly represented by the English 'sense'. Someone with *nous* has common sense; he understands what is going on and reacts sensibly (1110a11, 1112a21, 1115b9).

(3) In its most restrictive use '*nous*' is confined to true rational thought and understanding not resting on further justification.

At 1143a35 Aristotle distinguishes (a) theoretical *nous*, applied to the first principles of demonstrative SCIENCE: this is of necessary truths and admits of no further justification (*An. Post.* 100b5-17); (b) practical *nous*, that grasps the relevant features of particular cases (*nous* shows that what is happening is a theft, and so I can apply some general principle about trying to stop thefts to this occasion); this is not of necessary truths. See PERCEPTION.

Probably the idiomatic use (cf. the archaic use in 1116a34, where 'notice' translates '*noein*') in (2) encourages Aristotle to use '*nous*' in his technical use (3).

universal, *katholou* A universal (or 'common' property; 1096a23, 1180b15) corresponds to every natural kind (e.g. dog, human being) and to every science (*Met.* 980a21-981b13; 1180b15). Hence SCIENCE studies universals (1139b29, 1140b31). ETHICS studies them too so far as it can within its confinement to USUAL truths.

Universals must be grasped by REASON (1147b4; see ANIMAL), and grasp of them is an important part of deliberation leading to DECISION, since that applies universal principles to PARTICULAR situations (1141b14, 1142a20, 1144a32; 1147a2, 25).

Aristotle criticizes the Platonic Form of the Good in i 6 because he thinks it rests on the mistaken belief that a single universal corresponds to 'good' (1096a23). He is careful to insist on the recognition of HOMO-

NYMY, to discover more than one universal corresponding to one term (1129a26).

unwilling See VOLUNTARY.

up to us See VOLUNTARY.

usual, *hōs epi to polu* A usual truth is a universal judgement that is true for most of the cases it applies to, but not for all (e.g. 'Men go gray in old age', *An Pr.* 32b5). The state of affairs corresponding to this judgement is also called usual. ETHICS is concerned with the usual, not with the exceptionless UNIVERSAL and the NECESSARY (1094b21: cf. 1110a31, 1129a24, 1161a27). That is why deliberation (see DECISION) is important in ethics (1112b8) and why PARTICULAR cases must be judged by PERCEPTION (1109b20-3, 1126b2-4). Since principles of JUSTICE are only usual, they must be adjusted by DECENCY (1137b14). Aristotle's casuistry reflects reluctance to offer exceptionless rules (ix 2, esp. 1164b31). Concern with the usual deprives ethics of EXACTNESS, and prevents it from being SCIENCE.

Ethics has to offer usual truths if it is to guide action, as a practical discipline should (1103b26-1104a11). Aristotle does not say that all ethical truths (e.g. 'Bravery is finer than cowardice') are only usual. He means that those giving relatively specific practical advice (e.g. 'Stand firm in the battle line' or 'Keep promises') will be only usually true. Aristotle does not try to add the exceptions to make a more complex, exceptionless rule (e.g. 'Keep your promises except in conditions A,B,C'). He might argue that such rules will be so complex as to be unlearnable and useless; he prefers the agent to use deliberation, perception and UNDERSTANDING to see what different moral principles apply to a situation, and how they affect each other. This is what the INTELLIGENT person can see because of EXPERIENCE and familiarity with particular cases.

vicious, bad, base, *kakos, phaulos, ponēros, mochthēros* It is hard to see any clear distinction in Aristotle's uses of these terms, which are all used for the contrary of GOOD and EXCELLENT. (Cf. 1148b2-4, where 'vice' = '*mochthēria*' and 'bad' = '*phaulos*' might suggest that *phaulos* is sometimes weaker than *mochthēros*; but this is not true as a general rule.) Like many Greek moral terms (see DECENT) these terms also have a social and political use; they are applied especially to the lower classes, the MANY, in contrast to the decent and respectable upper classes.

virtue, *aretē* If x is an F (e.g. a knife), then the virtue of x as an F is that STATE of x that makes x a GOOD F (e.g. in a knife its virtue will be cutting well, durability, etc., that make it a good knife). Hence x's virtue will reflect its good performance of the FUNCTION of Fs (see Plato, *Rep.* 352d-353e).

430

Aristotle's conception of virtue is wider than moral virtue. In some cases 'excellence' is the best rendering of *aretē* (e.g. 1122b15, 1141a12), and Aristotle develops his conception of a good person from excellence in a CRAFT (see notes to 1098a12, 1106b8). This does not mean he has no conception of a moral virtue, or that he thinks virtues of character are just craft-knowledge. He distinguishes being good at something from being a good person (1148b7); and the good person is the person who has the virtues aiming at FINE and RIGHT action.

Virtues are divided into virtues of thought (see UNDERSTANDING) and virtues of CHARACTER. In his account of the individual virtues Aristotle relies on common beliefs about their scope. But he often reforms common usage: he is concerned to associate each virtue with its own distinctive range of actions, motives and CAPACITIES (see GENEROSITY, JUSTICE, TEMPERANCE, INTELLIGENCE, WISDOM; notes to 1118a23, 1151a29). To articulate the virtues clearly he is also ready to give names to states of character that have not been recognized explicitly as virtues but are shown to be virtues with the help of the doctrine of the MEAN (1107b2, 1108a16, 1125b23-8, 1126b19, 1127a13).

See also DECISION, DESIRE, EDUCATION, HAPPINESS, INCONTINENCE, REASON #2, SOUL, VOLUNTARY. On **virtuous ACTIVITIES** see 1100b12, 1103a27; note to 1113b3; 1115b20; 1177a10, b6. On **natural virtue** see note to 1144b3. On the **unity of virtue** see note to 1145a1.

voluntary, willing, *hekousios, hekōn* Aristotle seems to treat these two terms as synonymous. In ordinary Greek they both suggest absence of compulsion and of reluctance, as we speak of willing helpers, volunteers and voluntary (as opposed to compulsory) service. Aristotle, however, regards unwilling, reluctant, and non-volunteered actions as *hekousia*—that is the point of 1110a4-b17. For this reason 'intentional' has sometimes been suggested instead of 'voluntary'. But 'voluntary' is still preferable in suggesting a reference to the agent's desires and preferences. See 1110b12, 1111a32, 1169a1; notes to 1110a2, 1110b18.

'Voluntary' and 'willing' are too narrow for Aristotle's terms if they suggest reference to the agent's will. For Aristotle ascribes *hekousia* actions to ANIMALS and children that have no will—if will requires rational DESIRE and DECISION (1111a25, b8). The *hekousia* actions belong only to agents with desire, and are those caused by desires (notice 1110b18-24).

Aristotle defines *hekousia* actions so that he can say when praise and blame are appropriate for an agent (1109b30); hence we may say he is defining conditions for holding an agent responsible. Voluntary action justifies holding someone responsible in agents capable of DECISION (cf.

431

1149b30-1150a1). In Aristotle's strict use of ACTION (#2), not every-thing done voluntarily counts as an action (1139a19).

Aristotle assumes that if an action is voluntary and expresses deci-sion it is 'up to us', *eph'hēmin* (1113b6) and seems to assume that if it is up to us it is voluntary. It is up to us if the ORIGIN of the movement (i.e. the efficient CAUSE) is in us (1110a15) or (in other words) we are the cause and CONTROL what happens (1113b21-1114a7, 1114a21-31). To avoid odd results, 'in us' must be taken to mean 'in our beliefs and desires'. For a perhaps different view of 'up to us' see 1135a23-b2, *EE* 1225b8.

Apart from the main discussion of voluntary action in iii 1,5 and v 8, see also 1119a24-33, 1128b28, 1131a34, 1132b13, 1136b5; 1138a12, 28; 1140b23, 1152a15, 1153b21, 1163a2, 1164b13, 1169a1, 1180a16.

wanton aggression, *hubris* An act of *hubris* involves attacking or in-sulting another, but in a special way: so as to cause dishonour and shame to the victim (*Rhet.* 1378b23) for the agent's pleasure (1149b20). See 1115a20, 1124a29, 1125a9, 1129b32, 1148b30 (for sexual assault), 1149a32.

what, what sort See DEFINITION #3.

wife See HUMAN BEING #3.

willing See VOLUNTARY.

wisdom, *sophia* 'Sophia' has a fairly broad use, as *'phronēsis'* ('IN-TELLIGENCE') has, in ordinary Greek, and Aristotle restricts its use for his purposes:

(1) Any sort of expert could be called wise, in a CRAFT (1127b20, 1141a9-16) or in giving practical advice (e.g. Solon and the Seven Wise Men, 1095a21, 1098b28, 1130a1, 1179a20). See the section "Aristotle's Literary References" (below) for questions Aristotle assigns to intelligence.

(2) In Aristotle's narrower use wisdom excludes both craft and in-telligence, and is confined to the best kind of knowledge (vi 7). Since neither craft nor intelligence can achieve the degree of exactness needed for demonstration, neither can be SCIENCE, which alone can constitute wisdom. Hence wisdom must be concerned purely with STUDY, not with ACTION.

wish See DECISION, DESIRE.

woman See HUMAN BEING #3.

words See REASON #6.

worth, *axia* Sometimes 'value' and 'desert' might also be suitable. See 1119b26; note to 1123b2; 1131a26, 1133b24, 1158b27, 1159a35, 1160b33.

youth See HUMAN BEING #7.

Aristotle's Literary References

In the *EN* Aristotle cites illustrations of the views of the many and the wise, to show how his argument conforms to, or explains, or modifies the common beliefs — and sometimes just for decoration (1098b27, 1179a16, ETHICS #4). He quotes and refers to poets, 'wise men' and philosophers. A list will show something about Aristotle's reading and about what he assumes his audience will know (some of the quotations or allusions are very short, and assume some knowledge of their original context).

Aristotle's use of these references can be classified as follows: (a) opinions that confirm his view; (b) views he rejects; (c) opinions for discussion and criticism; (d) ornamental references, simply making Aristotle's point in a literary or proverbial phrase; (e) illustrations, adding examples of views he discusses.

The prominence of Homer is obvious — and Aristotle's inaccuracies suggest quotation from memory of familiar phrases. Hesiod and the Seven Wise Men (Solon, Bias, Anacharsis are cited), Theognis and Simonides are cited for proverbial expressions of old saws and conventional wisdom. Solon is taken more seriously than the others. Euripides — as opposed to Aeschylus and Sophocles — is the dramatist often quoted and discussed, probably because he presents controversial or puzzling questions in a pointed way.

A list of these references follows, giving type, location, and a brief description.

a	1094a3	Probably Eudoxus.
a	1095b9	Hesiod, *Works and Days*, 293, 295-7, poet (8th cent.).
b	1095b22	Sardanapallus, Assyrian king (669-626); cf. Aristotle, *Protrepticus*, f 16 (Ross).
c	1096a11	Plato.

433

a	1096b5	Pythagoreans; see *Met.* 987a13-27, 989b29.
a	1096b7	Speusippus.
b	1099a27	Inscription, temple of Leto, Delos; cf. *EE* 1214al, Theognis 255.
c	1100a11	Solon (first half, 6th cent.), Athenian politician and 'wise man'; cf. Herodotus i 32.
a	1100b21	Simonides (?556-468), poet; cf. Plato, *Prot.* 339b.
a	1104b11	Plato, *Rep.* 401e; *Laws* 653e.
e	1105a8	Heracleitus (c. 500), philosopher; DK 22 B 85.
a	1106b29	Pythagoreans; cf. *Met.* 986a22.
a	1106b35	Author unknown.
a	1109a33	Homer, *Odyssey* xii 219 (inaccurately quoted).
a	1109b9	Homer, *Iliad* iii 156.
e	1110a28	Euripides (?485-?406), dramatist.
e	111a12	Euripides, *Merope*; cf. *Poet.* 1454a5.
b	1113b14	Epicharmus (c. 500-475), dramatist; DK 23 B 7.
b	1115a9	Plato, *Prot.* 358d.
a	1116a23	Homer, *Iliad* xxii 100.
a	1116a25	Homer, *Iliad* viii 148-9.
a	1116a34	Homer, *Iliad* xv 348-51 (inaccurately quoted; cf. ii 391-3).
b	1116b4	Socrates; Plato, *Prot.* 360d.
a	1116b27-8	Homer, *Iliad* xi 11, xiv 151, xvi 529, v 470, xv 232, 594, *Odyssey* xxiv 318-9.
a	1116b29	Lost epic? Cf. Theocritus, xx 15.
d	1116b36	Homer, *Iliad* xi 558-62.
d	1118a22	Homer, *Iliad* iii 24.
e	1118a32	The glutton Philoxenus; see *EE* 1231a17, [*Probl.*] 950a3.
a	1118b11	Homer, *Iliad* xxiv 130-1.
b	1121a7	Simonides; cf. *Rhet.* 1391a8.
d	1122a27	Homer, *Odyssey* xvii 420.
e	1124b15	Homer, *Iliad* i 504-10 (inaccurately remembered?).
a	1129b28	Euripides, *Melanippe*, *TGF* fr. 486.
a	1129b29	Theognis, 147, poet (7th cent.).
a	1130a1	Bias, one of the Seven Wise Men (6th cent.).
b	1130a3	Plato, *Rep.* 343c.

b	1132b22	Pythagoreans; cf. DK 58 B 4.
b	1132b27	Hesiod, fr. 174.
e	1136a13	Euripides, *Alcmaeon*, *TGF* fr. 68.
e	1136b9	Homer, *Iliad* vi 236.
a	1139b9	Agathon, *TGF* fr. 5 (late 5th cent.), dramatist.
a	1140a19	Agathon, *TGF* fr. 6.
a	1141a15	Homer (??) *Margites*, fr. 2.
b	1142a3	Euripides, *Philoctetes*, *TGF* fr. 787, 782.
a	1145a20	Homer, *Iliad* xxiv 258-9.
e	1146a9	Sophocles, *Philoctetes* 895-916, (?496-406), dramatist.
a	1149b19	Homer, *Iliad* xiv 214, 217.
e	1150b9	Theodectes (375-334), dramatist; *TGF* p. 803.
e	1150b10	Carcinus (4th cent.), dramatist; *TGF* p. 797.
e	1151a9	Demodocus (6th cent.), poet; fr. 1 Diehl.
e	1152a22	Anaxandridas (c. 382-349), comic dramatist; fr. 67 Kock.
a	1152a32	Euenus (5th cent.), sophist; fr. 9 Diehl.
a	1153b27	Hesiod, *Works and Days* 763.
e	1154b23	Euripides, *Orestes* 234.
a	1155a15	Homer, *Iliad* x 224.
b	1155a34	Homer, *Odyssey* xii 218.
b	1155a35	Hesiod, *Works and Days* 25.
b	1155b2	Euripides, *TGF* fr. 898.
b	1155b4	Heracleitus, DK 22 B 8, 80.
b	1155b17	Empedocles (?493-?433), philosopher; DK 31 B 22, 62, 90.
a	1160b26	Homer, *Iliad* i 503.
a	1161a14	Homer, *Iliad* ii 243.
e	1164a27	Hesiod, *Works and Days* 370.
e	1167a33	Euripides, *Phoenissae* 588.
a	1167b25	Epicharmus, fr. 146 Kaibel.
a	1168b7	Euripides, *Orestes* 1046.
b	1169b7	Euripides, *Orestes* 667.
a	1170a12	Theognis 35; Plato, *Meno* 95d.
a	1170b21	Hesiod, *Works and Days* 715.
a	1172b28	Plato, *Phil.* 60b.
a	1176b9	Heracleitus, DK 22 B 9.
a	1176b33	Anacharsis (early 6th cent.) one of the Seven Wise Men? DK 10 A 1.
b	1177b32	Euripides, *TGF* fr. 1040; Pindar (518-438),

435

		Isth. 5.16; and others.
a	1179a9	Solon; Herod. i 30.
a	1179a13	Anaxagoras (?500-?428), philosopher; DK 59 A 30.
a	1179b6	Theognis 432.
d	1180a28	Homer, *Odyssey* ix 114.

Further Reading

This list contains only a few of the main items likely to be useful to those beginning detailed study of the *EN*. Fuller bibliographies will be found in W.F.R. Hardie's *Aristotle's Ethical Theory*, 2nd ed. (Oxford, 1980) and in *Articles on Aristotle*, vol. 2, ed. J. Barnes, M. Schofield, and R. Sorabji (London 1977).

The most convenient work of reference for historical events, dates, details of authors' lives and works, and conventions of reference to Greek texts is the *Oxford Classical Dictionary* (2nd ed., Oxford, 1970). For a general history of Greece see J. B. Bury and R. Meiggs, *History of Greece* (4th ed., London, 1975).

The Aristotelian Approach to Ethics

Some idea of the influence of Aristotelian ideas in modern moral theory can be gained from:

Prichard, H.A., 'Does Moral Philosophy Rest On a Mistake?', 'Duty and Interest', and 'Moral Obligation', in *Moral Obligation* (reissue, Oxford, 1968).

Green, T.H., *Prolegomena to Ethics* (Oxford, 1883), Book 3, ch. 5.

Falk, W.D., 'Morality, Self and Others', in *Morality and the Language of Conduct*, ed. H.N. Castañeda and G. Nakhnikian (Detroit, 1963)

Anscombe, G.E.M., 'Modern Moral Philosophy', *Philosophy* 33 (1958), 1-19.

Foot, P. R., 'Moral Beliefs', in *Virtues and Vices* (Oxford, 1978).

Geach, P.T., *The Virtues* (Cambridge, 1977).

Wallace, J.D., *Virtues and Vices* (Ithaca, 1978).

Von Wright, G.H., *The Varieties of Goodness* (London, 1963).

Hampshire, S.N., *Two Theories of Morality* (Oxford, 1977).

437

Further Reading

Historical Background
On the history of Greek ethics before Aristotle:

Adkins, A.W.H., *Merit and Responsibility* (Oxford, 1960).

Dover, K.J., *Greek Popular Morality in the Time of Plato and Aristotle* (Oxford, 1974).

Irwin, T.H., *Plato's Moral Theory* (Oxford, 1977), ch.2.

It is especially useful to read some of Plato's dialogues, in particular the *Laches, Charmides, Protagoras, Gorgias, Republic* i-ii, iv, viii-ix and the *Philebus*.

It is sometimes interesting and amusing to compare and contrast the *EN* with the approach and outlook of Theophrastus' *Characters*, ed. and trans. by R.C. Jebb (2nd ed., London, 1907).

Aristotle: General
A clear, stimulating, short account of Aristotle is:

Ackrill, J.L. *Aristotle the Philosopher* (Oxford, 1981).

A fuller summary of the contents of Aristotle's works is:

Ross, W.D., *Aristotle* (London, 1923).

The standard English translation of Aristotle (the 'Oxford Translation') has been revised by J.Barnes and published in two convenient volumes with a helpful index (Princeton, 1984).

Nicomachean Ethics: General
The best commentary on the Greek text:

Gauthier, R.A. and Jolif, J.Y., *Aristote: L'Éthique à Nicomaque* (2nd ed., 4 vols., Paris and Louvain, 1970).

The main English commentaries:

Stewart, J.A. *Notes on the Nicomachean Ethics* (2 vols., Oxford, 1892).

Burnet, J., *The Ethics of Aristotle* (London, 1900).

Joachim, H.H., *Aristotle: Nicomachean Ethics* (Oxford, 1951).

The classic English translation of the *EN* is by W.D. Ross (revised by J.L. Ackrill and J.O. Urmson, Oxford, 1980).

The most helpful general guide to the *EN* is: Hardie, W.F.R., *Aristotle's Ethical Theory* (2nd ed., Oxford, 1980). It contains chapters on all the topics listed below, and is always worth consulting.

Useful collections of essays:

Barnes, J., Schofield, M., Sorabji, R., eds., *Articles on Aristotle*, vol. 2, (London, 1977); cited below as '*Articles*'.

438

Rorty, A.O., ed., *Essays on Aristotle's Ethics* (Berkeley, 1980), cited
below as *'Essays'*.
On the relation of the *EN* to Aristotle's other ethical works:
Kenny, A.J.P., *The Aristotelian Ethics* (Oxford, 1978).
It is often instructive to compare the *EN* with the other ethical works.
A good translation and edition of part of the *Eudemian Ethics* is:
Woods, M.J., *Eudemian Ethics I, II, VIII* (Oxford, 1982).

Method
Owen, G.E.L., *'Tithenai ta phainomena'*, in J. Barnes et al., *Articles
on Aristotle*, vol. 1 (London, 1975), 113-126.
_____, 'Aristotle; method, physics, cosmology', in *Dictionary of Scien-
tific Biography*, ed. C.C. Gillespie (New York, 1970).
Barnes, J., 'Aristotle and the Methods of Ethics', *Revue Internationale
de Philosophie* 34 (1980), 490-511.
Irwin, T.H., 'Aristotle's Methods of Ethics', in *Studies in Aristotle*, ed.
D.J. O'Meara (Washington, 1981).

Happiness
Cooper, J.M., *Reason and Human Good in Aristotle,* (Cambridge, Mass.,
1975), chs. 2-3.
Ackrill, J.L., 'Aristotle on *Eudaimonia*', in *Essays.*
Hardie, W.F.R., 'Aristotle on the Best Life for a Man', *Philosophy* 54
(1979), 35-50.
McDowell, J.H., 'The role of *Eudaimonia* in Aristotle's Ethics', in *Essays.*
On the relation between Aristotelian *eudaimonia* and happiness:
Kraut, R., 'Two Conceptions of Happiness', *Philosophical Review* 88
(1979), 167-97.
On the relation between conceptions of happiness in *EN* Book i and
Book x see Cooper (above) and:
Keyt, D., 'Intellectualism in Aristotle', in *Essays in Ancient Greek Phil-
osophy*, vol. 2., ed. J. P. Anton and A. Preus (Albany, 1983).

Virtue
Many of the items under 'The Aristotelian Approach to Ethics' (above)
are relevant.
Engberg-Pederson, T., *Aristotle's Theory of Moral Insight* (Oxford,
1983).

Further Reading

Dent, N.J.H., *The Moral Psychology of the Virtues* (Cambridge, 1984).
Foot, P.R., 'Virtues and Vices', in *Virtues and Vices* (Oxford, 1978).
Frankena, W.K., 'Prichard and the Ethics of Virtue', in *Perspectives on Morality*, ed. K.E. Goodpaster (Notre Dame, 1976).
Burnyeat, M.F., 'Aristotle on Learning to be Good', in *Essays.*
Urmson, J.O., 'Aristotle's Doctrine of the Mean', in *Essays.*

Voluntary Action and Responsibility

Furley, D.J., *Two Studies in the Greek Atomists* (Princeton, 1967). Partly reprinted in *Articles* 47-60.
Kenny, A.J.P., *Aristotle's Theory of the Will* (London, 1979).
Sorabji, R.R.K., *Necessity, Cause and Blame* (London, 1979).
Irwin, T.H., 'Reason and Responsibility in Aristotle', in *Essays.*

Justice

Allan, D.J., 'Individual and State in the Ethics and Politics', in *La Politique d'Aristote* (*Fondation Hardt, Entretiens* 11, Geneva, 1964).
Williams, B.A.O., 'Justice as a Virtue', in *Essays.*
Feinberg, J., 'Justice and Personal Desert', in *Doing and Deserving* (Princeton, 1970).

Aristotle's views on justice are closely related to the political theory expounded in the *Politics*. The most useful English translations of this work are by E. Barker (Oxford, 1948) and by T.A. Sinclair, revised by T.J. Saunders (Harmondsworth, 1981).

Practical Reason, Deliberation and Intelligence

Cooper, J., *Reason and Human Good in Aristotle* (Cambridge, Mass., 1975), ch. 1.
Dahl, N.O., *Practical Reason, Aristotle, and Weakness of the Will* (Minneapolis, 1984).
Anscombe G.E.M., 'Thought and Action in Aristotle', in *Articles on Aristotle*, 61-71.
Wiggins, D., 'Deliberation and Practical Reason', in *Essays.*
Sorabji, R.R.K., 'Aristotle on the Role of Intellect in Virtue', in *Essays.*
Irwin, T.H., 'Aristotle on Reason, Desire and Virtue', *Journal of Philosophy* 72 (1975), 567-78.

Practical Reason and Incontinence
The items under the previous heading are relevant here also.

Raz, J., ed., *Practical Reasoning* (Oxford, 1978). See especially the contributions by Anscombe, Von Wright, Kenny, Harman.

Charles, D., *Aristotle's Philosophy of Action* (London, 1984).

Davidson, D., 'How is Weakness of Will Possible?', in *Essays on Actions and Events* (Oxford, 1980).

Watson, G., 'Scepticism about Weakness of Will', *Philosophical Review* 86 (1977), 316-39.

Wiggins, D., 'Weakness of Will, Commensurability, and the Objects of Deliberation and Desire', in *Essays*.

Friendship
Vlastos, G., 'The Individual as Object of Love in Plato', in *Platonic Studies* (2nd ed., Princeton, 1981).

Nygren, A., *Agape and Eros*, trans. P.S. Watson (London, 1953).

Cooper, J.M., 'Aristotle on Friendship', in *Essays*.

Annas, J., 'Plato and Aristotle on Friendship and Altruism', *Mind* 86 (1977), 532-54.

Bradley, F.H., 'Selfishness and Self-sacrifice', in *Ethical Studies* (2nd ed., Oxford, 1927).

Pleasure
Ackrill, J.L., 'Aristotle's Distinction Between *Energeia* and *Kinesis*', in *New Essays on Plato and Aristotle*, ed. R.Bambrough (London, 1965).

Penner, T., 'Verbs and the Identity of Actions', in *Ryle: A Collection of Critical Essays*, ed O.P. Wood and G.W. Pitcher (London, 1970).

Owen, G.E.L., 'Aristotelian Pleasures', in *Articles*.

Gosling, J.C.B., and Taylor, C.C.W., *The Greeks on Pleasure* (Oxford, 1982), ch. 11-17.

Gosling, J.C.B., *Pleasure and Desire* (Oxford, 1969).

TERENCE IRWIN is Professor of Philosophy, Cornell University. Born in Enniskillen, Northern Ireland, he received a B.A. from the University of Oxford in 1969 and a Ph.D. from Princeton in 1973. He taught at Harvard University from 1972 to 1975 and has taught at Cornell since 1975. He is author of *Plato's Moral Theory* (1977), *Plato's Gorgias* (translation with notes, 1979), *Aristotle's First Principles* (1988), and *Classical Thought* (1988), all published by Oxford University Press. Hackett published *Selections* in 1995, a translation of selections from Aristotle done by Irwin and Gail Fine.